P9-ECR-562

*Alternative Social Services for Women*

# Alternative Social Services for Women

NAOMI GOTTLIEB, EDITOR

1980
Columbia University Press
New York

Library of Congress Cataloging in Publication Data
Main entry under title:

Alternative social services for women.

   Bibliography: p.
   Includes index.
   1. Women—Services for—United States—Addresses,
essays, lectures.   2. Sexism—United States—Addresses,
essays, lectures.   3. Social service—United States—
Addresses, essays, lectures.   I. Gottlieb, Naomi,
1925–
HV1445.A45     362.8'38'0973     80-164
ISBN 0-231-04212-4
ISBN 0-231-04213-2 pbk.

Columbia University Press
New York   Guildford, Surrey

## Acknowledgments

The main intent of this book has been to describe new, alternative services for women. Because these services are usually struggling, nontraditional operations, my appreciation is especially extended to all of the individuals associated with these services who spent the time gathering and submitting material for use here. Because of space limitations, not all the submitted material could be used, but I want to thank all those who took the time to send descriptions of their services.

I want to acknowledge Trova Hutchins' contribution. We worked together on the original conceptualization and organization of the book, on the problems of locating and compiling resource material, and on the difficult decisions about what could be included within the constraints of a book of reasonable length. The introduction was also a collaborative project. These efforts were both fun and hard work, and I appreciate Trova's clear thinking on a number of issues.

My thanks go to the other contributors as well. Their separate areas of expertise have added in important ways to the objective of presentations of sound empirical knowledge as background to the descriptions of services.

A group of enthusiastic and able graduate students helped in the early efforts to look at research about women's concerns. My thanks to that group—Sandi Armstrong, Dianne Burden, Alison Clarke, Nancy Contro, Miriam Myerson, Julee Rosanoff, Priscilla Solarz, and Catherine Unseth.

Typing the different drafts of the manuscript was a long and tedious task. I appreciate the fine work of both Mitsi Vondrachek and, for the major sections, Sandy Brown.

I am grateful for permission to quote from the following copyright materials: Morton Bard and Joseph Zacker, "The Prevention of Family Violence: Dilemmas of Community Intervention," *Journal of Marriage and the Family* 33 (1977), © 1977 the National Council on Family Relations; Diana E. H. Russell, *The Politics of Rape* (New York: Stein and Day, 1975) © 1975 Diana E. H. Russell; Anne Seiden, "Overview: Research on the Psychology of Women. II. Women in Families, Work, and Psychotherapy," *American Journal of Psychiatry* 133 (1976), © 1976 the American Psychiatric Association.

This book is the result of the efforts of many individuals. Each of them has been a proponent of effective, nonsexist services for women. I hope that this book will further that goal.

# Contents

# Contributors

**Vee Baxter** is a volunteer counsellor at the Open Door Clinic, Seattle, Washington.

**Dona Lansing Bracht** is Project Coordinator, Changing Times For Families Program, St. Paul, Minnesota.

**Annette N. Brodsky** is Associate Professor of Psychology, University of Alabama, Tuscaloosa, Alabama.

**Dianne Burden** is the Coordinator of the Project on Women and Mental Health, School of Social Work, University of Washington, Seattle, Washington.

**Julie Campbell** is a student of law, Seattle, Washington.

**Rita Cepeda** is a Doctoral Fellow in Education at the University of California, Los Angeles, California.

**Naomi Gottlieb** is Associate Professor and Associate Dean, School of Social Work, University of Washington, Seattle, Washington.

**Barbara B. Hauser** is Clinical Director, Family Service Clinic, Middlesex Probate Court, Cambridge, Massachusetts.

**Trova Hutchins** is Assistant Professor, School of Social Work, University of Washington, Seattle, Washington.

**Irma Levine** is Coordinator of Women's Programs, North Seattle Community College, Seattle, Washington.

**Darla Martin-Shelton** is a Researcher Program Developer, and Direct Service Worker, at Women, Inc., Dorchester, Massachusetts.

**Barbara R. Masnick** is Program Director, Therapeutic Foster Care Program, Tufts-New England Medical Center, Boston, Massachusetts.

**Jane Page** is a free-lance writer dividing her time between Washington and California.

**Carol G. Radov** is Chairperson, Department of Social Services, Salem State College, Salem, Massachusetts.

**Mindy Resnik** is Director, Assault Crisis Center, Ann Arbor, Michigan.

**Cheryl A. Richey** is Associate Professor, School of Social Work, University of Washington, Seattle, Washington.

**Pamela J. Schwingl** is a financial and evaluation consultant, and instructor in the state college system of Vermont.

**Barbara Solomon** is Professor, School of Social Work, University of Southern California, Los Angeles, California.

**Laura Sperazi** is a researcher at Women, Inc. Dorchester, Massachusetts, and a doctoral student in sociology at Brandeis University, Waltham, Massachusetts.

**Doris Stevens** is Chief Social Worker, Sexual Assault Center, Harborview Medical Center, Seattle, Washington, and Clinical Assistant Professor, School of Social Work, University of Washington, Seattle, Washington.

**Brenda Weathers** is Director, Whitman-Radcliffe Foundation, San Francisco, California.

# Introduction

## NAOMI GOTTLIEB AND TROVA HUTCHINS

The women who are consumers of social servies in America present a considerable range of circumstances, needs, and problems. Some have been defined by society as deviant because of their criminal behavior, sexual preferences, or abuse of drugs or alcohol. Many face double discrimination because they are women with other ascribed statuses related to age, race, or physical characteristics. Others are confronting interpersonal problems and role conflicts. Women also seek assistance when they have encountered indifferent or inadequate institutions, and when they have been victims of personal abuse.

Women are concerned about their health, their roles, their creativity, their sanity. They have problems that are physiological, psychological, interpersonal, economic, social—or some combination of these—and they turn daily to social service practitioners or other helping professionals for assistance in solving their problems, changing their situation, and improving their lives.

Whatever the situation, and whether the service is sought voluntarily or not, these clients have one fact in common: They are women who live in a society that imposes myriad sexual distinctions that are not inherently defined by gender. These societally defined distinctions have tended, by and large, to discriminate against and devalue women. The devaluation and discrimination have, in turn, contributed to the personal and social problems of women to such an extent that their pain and distress can never be wholly separated from their gender and their special experience as women in a sexist society.

This book recognizes at least three major dimensions to which social workers and other helping personnel need to be attuned whenever they face a woman client.

First, social service workers need to be aware of the pervasiveness of sexism and of how sexual stereotyping, conditioning, and discrimination can affect the individual woman. The degree to which the experience of being a woman in a sexist society is salient—to the woman and to the circumstances that bring her to seek help—will vary. It may be the central issue, as in the case of women who want to join a feminist consciousness-raising group or who seek counsel because they have been discriminated against owing to their sex. It may be (or appear to be) a relatively peripheral issue, as with a woman who wants advice on placement for her mentally retarded child, or one who wants to pursue an interest or develop a skill.

Frequently, the fact of being a women in a sexist society is a contributing and complicating element. Being female may interact with other imposed conditions, such as being old, nonwhite, or physically disabled and being poor, sick, or institutionalized. Some problems (such as rape, an abusive husband, certain health care needs) are exclusive to women; others (alcoholism, depression, the need for self-fulfillment) are not. But all are affected and complicated by the woman's sexual status, and no matter how directly or indirectly this may relate to the immediate reason that brings the woman for service, it is a dimension that must be assumed and explored with each client.

A second, related dimension concerns the specific ways in which sexism has been manifested in the helping professions. Practitioners need to be cognizant of their own personal attitudes and biases about women, and to deal with them accordingly. But beyond personal feelings, social service workers need to know about the institutionalized sexism that may be operative in agencies and programs (in health and welfare systems, for example) as well as the sexism inherent in traditional practice theories and techniques. These manifestations can be comprehensive and blatant, as with the concepts that are basic to psychoanalytic theory, or more subtle and insidious, as with family therapy techniques or rehabilitation methods that encourage adjustment to narrowly defined roles. They are reflected, too, in the many gaps and inadequacies in social service provisioning—that women who are raped, for instance, may have nowhere to turn, that the resources allocated to training programs for women offenders are insufficient, or that counseling about sexual alternatives is not offered to disabled women in rehabilitation centers.

Historically, the overall result for women clients has been the provision of services that are too often ineffective. Such services are not merely insufficient or inappropriate. Sometimes they are harmful, actually worsening the woman's situation.

There is a continuous and complex interaction between these first two dimensions. Helping professions and personnel reflect the societal conditions that cause or complicate the struggles of women. They also help perpetuate and exacerbate those conditions. Then, within this context, they attempt to offer service, and often they fail because they lack appreciation and awareness of the dilemma as well as the means or inclination to deal with it effectively. Helping personnel must be informed about and sensitive to this ubiquitous context in order to work effectively with women clients.

Certainly, helping personnel also can work, as citizens and as professionals, for the eradication of sexism in society, in the helping fields, and in their own thinking and practice, because it is through large-scale reform, if not revolution, that the lot of women as a group can be significantly and permanently improved. There is ample disagreement as to whether reformist or revolutionary approaches will best effect such improvements. However, most would agree that in the meantime there are individual women clients who need help.

This book contends that the people rendering such help need more than sensitivity to the dilemmas and more than commitment to broad-based change. There is a third dimension to which social workers and other helping personnel need to be attuned, and it is this dimension that is the primary concern of this book.

Helping personnel need specific, practical ideas and information on ways to serve particular women—ways that can be used, right now, to solve problems, change situations, and improve lives. Accordingly, the purpose of the book is not to document the complexities of sexism in society and the helping professions, nor is it especially to promote nonsexist consciousness, sensitivity, or values. That problems indeed exist, and that helpers need to be aware of them, is assumed. Little space is devoted here to arguing the validity of such assumptions. Rather, they constitute the common starting point from which the ideas presented in the book have been launched and developed.

The ideas are presented here as approaches to types of situations and problems that typically bring women to seek help. The ideas are theoretical, technical, programmatic, and institutional. They may represent old ideas put together in different ways, reflect substantial modification or adaptation of existing ideas, or offer entirely new thinking. However, they are all innovative in the sense that they address the special circumstances of women; accept (and abhor) these circumstances as reality based; and assert that knowledge and action, applied in a context of specific values, are powerful tools for change.

The approaches described in the book have other features in common: (1) They are addressed to the kinds of problems and clients encountered daily by those in social work and other helping professions; (2) they are currently being used in an effort to serve contemporary women, and some have been tested systematically to determine their effects and their effectiveness; (3) they are sufficiently generalizable to be of use to others and, in some cases, presented specifically enough to be replicable by others.

The book is organized around designated issues and population groups. The major intent in each instance is to present specific descriptions of innovative services that have been developed to address the issue or group. In each section the descriptions of services are preceded by a definition of the presenting problem or client population; a critical review of the relevant research and literature documenting the substance, etiology, and ramifications of the identified problem; and a brief overview of the approaches discussed in the sections that follow. Though the emphasis is on the services, the format reflects the belief that as new services are initiated, there should be a continual interplay between those services and the development of empirical knowledge—each making a contribution to the other and to the needs of women. The extent of research-based knowledge varies considerably depending on the subject and is sparse in such new areas as the displaced homemaker.

## Focus and Scope

A number of crucial limitations in the focus and scope of this book will be evident to the reader. Some of these limitations were intentionally imposed from the outset, while others were unanticipated and are due either to the lack of sufficient material on a subject or to failure to locate such material. An intentional limitation is seen in the literature reviews and problem discussions that introduce each section. None of these reviews is exhaustive or definitive. The selections from the literature are purposeful and exemplary, and are used to provide a background to the descriptions of services that follow, rather than a comprehensive analysis of the problem area. Particularly with well-researched subjects, it was necessary to be highly selective in the literature chosen for review. There was an attempt to include material with a perspective on the distinctive needs of women that is illustrative, provocative, or both, and, within that context, to be as accurate as possible. Experts on particular subjects will readily observe the limitations in the reviews, and it is hoped that they will understand the modest nature of the contributors' intentions with regard to this aspect of the book.

There are also notable limitations in the types of services and programs described. The fundamental guideline used was that the service or program must fall within the purview of direct social services, broadly defined. This meant that certain innovative developments in other fields (for example, new educational programs and opportunities for nontraditional employment) had to be excluded. Deciding on these exclusions was difficult and painful because many of these programs reflect the basic philosophy espoused in the book and, moreover, are having a profound and positive impact on the lives of women.

Other exclusions were even more painful. A number of subject areas were abandoned, albeit reluctantly, simply because of time and space limitations or because of the inability to locate examples of services that are clearly nonsexist or alternative. Two large populations that appear to be neglected, for instance, are welfare recipients and adolescent girls. The needs of both populations are great, but according to the best of the knowledge obtained, they are not being addressed by the social services network in an innovative way. In the conclusion of the book these and other neglected populations are noted and recommendations are made about future service and research priorities.

In other instances knowledge of the existence of innovative developments came too late for inclusion, or, owing to lack of resources, they could not be tracked down. Services for rural women, for physically disabled women, and for certain racial–ethnic minority groups are examples.

Even with those services which are included, an unevenness in coverage will be apparent. In some sections a variety of programs are described, while in others only one or two are included. Again, it was not always possible to determine whether this imbalance is an accurate reflection of the reality of social services for women or a result of failure to pursue fruitful avenues in obtaining information.

Other factors of importance were the extent to which a service could be construed as operating from a nonsexist or feminist perspective; whether, where services are provided for women, the woman is the victim of the primary problem; and whether the services address a single problem or population rather than multiple ones. The first criterion was used primarily when there were a number of possible services to choose from; although there are some clear exceptions, the general rule was to include services with the most explicit nonsexist or feminist orientation. As to the second criterion, some services were excluded that, though offered to women, appeared to define the woman's problems relative to others in her life. Thus, for example, there are services for wives of alcoholics and wives of men in prison. Without in any way depreciating the need for or value of such services, the focus remained instead on programs addressed to those women directly experiencing the problems at issue (e.g., the alcoholic woman). Other examples of services that were omitted because the woman is not the sole or primary client are day care services, marital and relationship therapy, and family counseling.

It was heartening and surprising to discover the large number of multiservice programs for women as well as services geared toward women who represent more than one problem or more than one population. Multiservice feminist agencies and organizations are rapidly emerging throughout the country. So, too, are highly specialized programs for women from particular population groups who are experiencing common problems. For the most part, the selections are restricted to single-service programs or techniques addressed to one particular population or problem. Again, however, there are some exceptions. The sections on treatment for lesbian alcoholics and programs for lesbian single parents are examples.

Geographic location was a final consideration. The initial intent was to have wide representation of cities, states, and regions of the United States. It will be evident that this objective was met only moderately. Though services in a number of different states are included, the Pacific Northwest is overrepresented, particularly in the state of Washington and the city of Seattle. Because innovative services for women are nontraditional and are often developed by community members who are deeply concerned about women but have few resources, the programs are small, bootstrap operations, usually in need of funds, perhaps harassed by their communities, and sorely understaffed. As a result, there are few resources for anything other than survival efforts. Though many of the programs were appreciative of our interest and supportive of the project, it was understandably difficult to mobilize them to respond to requests for materials appropriate for publication. The resolution of this problem was to focus the data gathering, in some instances, within the state of Washington. The possibility of local, personal contact eased the difficulties for individual programs in submitting the needed reports. From data received from other programs in a wider geographic range, however, it is assumed that the nearby programs represent similar services elsewhere. In all instances the time and efforts of program personnel in offering the material for the core of this book are deeply appreciated.

Thus, the process of locating, selecting, and rejecting material for this book was an ongoing one, filled with satisfactions and frustrations, and guided by practical matters as well as substantive and philosophical considerations. Individuals who are involved in creative social service programs for women may feel fully justified in complaining that their program is not included or represented. It is hoped that such omissions as do exist are not too glaring or extensive.

## *Data-Gathering Procedure*

Information about alternative social services for women was obtained in three basic ways: by consulting directories listing services and programs for women [e.g., the *New Woman's Survival Sourcebook* (1975)]; by regularly pursuing relevant publications, including feminist literature as well as academic and professional journals; and through the assistance of individuals in educational and community centers. In these ways names were obtained of individuals (invariably women) involved in creative services for women. These individuals were contacted by letter or phone with an explanation of the purpose of the book and the need for information. Word of mouth was by far the most productive procedure. Even when a contact could not herself be of direct help, she would often have names and addresses of others who could. In virtually all instances the response to inquiries was one of warmth, interest, and support. Getting to know and talk to many of the women who are helping other women was a delightful and exciting by-product to the writing of this book.

The information obtained was dealt with in several ways, depending on such factors as the amount of material, its quality and completeness, and the willingness and ability of the source to prepare actual copy for the book.

In some chapters, specific programs are presented, either in their entirety or by focusing on one or more aspects of their services. In other discussions, several similar programs are summarized in order to present an overview of the services available. Specific service methodologies, rather than individual programs, are used to illustrate a feminist approach to some problems. In a few instances there are discussions of how a program was established or a report on the outcome of services.

Sometimes the people directly concerned with the program have written the description; this contribution is acknowledged in the chapter. Elsewhere the program descriptions are adaptations and summarizations of various materials submitted. The final presentations have received the approval of the individuals concerned.

In a few cases the program described no longer exists, either in the form described or at all. These are included nonetheless because they represent a type of recently developed innovative service and because the change accurately represents the reality of fluctuating services.

## The Anticipated Audience

It is expected that the people most interested in this book will be social workers and similar helping professionals, including the professional and paraprofessional staffs of a wide range of service facilities—mental health services, hospitals and clinics, senior centers, prisons, drug abuse and alcoholism centers, counseling agencies, and so forth—as well as community members who are concerned about the needs of women. The terms *social worker, social service practitioner, helping professional,* and the like are used more or less interchangeably throughout the book unless otherwise indicated. Some of the personnel staffing the new services described are nonprofessionals and paraprofessionals. Many are nonestablishment feminists who started services because they saw an unmet need. Many of the tasks inherent in those programs are not traditionally associated with the helping professions, but it is contended that professionals should know about the issues for women that those services highlight. For example, women trained in feminist health care serve women in new health centers. It would be useful for professionals who work in traditional medical settings to know the rationale and details of those health services.

In addition, the book is addressed to educators and students in social work and other helping professions. Its content calls into question the rationale for many established services and suggests that women have been deeply affected by the institutionalized sexism found in traditional social service practices and theories.

The book's content can be utilized in several ways. Individuals who have recognized the need for distinctive services for women may find both the impetus and the information to motivate concrete action toward initiation of new programs. Feminists already working in one area may be encouraged by the extent to which feminist services for women have been established for a range of problems and issues. Finally, individuals in traditional service programs as well as educators may be moved to incorporate both the perspective and the services presented here.

## Socialization of Women as Context

The existence of sexism and the deleterious effect of the socialization of women within a sexist social context is the basic stance of this book. Woman are raised to fulfill certain circumscribed roles and, as a direct consequence, are restricted in their capacities to face particular social circumstances. There is an extensive literature documenting the impact of stereotyped socialization (Maccoby and Jacklin 1974; Rossi 1964; Rossi 1972; Angrist 1969; Bernard 1972; Hoffman 1972; Hochschild 1973a). The theme of women's conditioning will be developed to a varying extent within each chapter in relation to the particular problem at issue, and in fact will become redundant. That redundancy reflects the problem precisely. The impressive characteristic of sexism is its pervasiveness. Repeatedly, as women confront such situations as widowhood, poor health, sexual dysfunction, or single parenthood, another version of the limitations derived from their socialization comes into play. The same socialization process that leads adolescent girls away from school subjects that will prepare them for well-paying careers and inhibits their potentialities are in operation as women struggle with the economics of single parenthood. The same socializing forces that lead women to passively accept inappropriate medical care affect their inability to protest against physical battering. The socializing theme and the sexism issue will be repeated because they are the essence of the problem.

Another theme that recurs throughout the book is that problems related to sexism are heavily compounded by racism. Although there is a separate chapter on issues that are relevant to racial–ethnic minority groups, the concerns of ethnic women are addressed, if only briefly, in each chapter; in a few instances services geared primarily toward women of racial–ethnic minority status are highlighted.

It was emphasized earlier that the validity and worth of the focus in this book will not be argued. Space does not permit such debate. However, there is one question that inevitably will be raised by those who have doubts about the need for a book—any book—devoted to women clients in the social services. This oft-repeated question is, "Why women, when the real need in the social services is for better knowledge *per se*—knowledge that can be effectively applied toward all individuals?"

Such questions can be answered in various ways, and most of the answers would emphasize the differences between men and women clients—differences that must be taken into consideration because they bear on both the causes and the solutions for specific problems. That the concern in this book is limited to the special circumstances of women does not necessarily mean that the needs and problems of men are any less important. But they are different. This line of reasoning could also be applied to rationalize a book about social services for men or, for that matter, to populations defined in countless other ways. There is a need for more knowledge, and here the focus is on new knowledge about effective service approaches for women.

The preparation of this book took two years. A dilemma regularly faced was that information gathered would so quickly become outdated, sometimes in a matter of months. Although this is frustrating to authors concerned with accuracy, the fact that it happened so often is, in a more important sense, vastly encouraging. The social changes occurring in behalf of women have achieved a decided and it is hoped, irreversible momentum. The facts presented in the book represent the situation "as of this writing"—a phrase used throughout to emphasize that time, and the efforts of those working for the eradication of sexism, will render much of its content obsolete. Perhaps the ideal goal will be reached when a book like this is not only dated but unnecessary.

# Part One

*Women and Health*

# 1. Women and Mental Health: The Problem of Depression

NAOMI GOTTLIEB

THOUGH THE mental health problems of women encompass a range of conditions, this chapter focuses on the issue of depression. This emphasis was selected for several reasons. To begin with, depression is a serious and prevalent incapacity in women. Depression is the most frequent psychological disorder experienced by women as outpatients and is exceeded only by schizophrenia among women who are hospitalized for mental problems. Second, the problem can illustrate the connection between stereotypic role expectations for women and their mental health problems, for there appears to be a significant relationship between some of the more important consequences of women's socialization and the etiology of depression. Further, the descriptions of and rationale for new approaches for this difficulty can serve as models for analogous developments of alternative therapies for other psychological problems that women experience. Depression is not the only mental health proolem from which women suffer, but it is a prominent one, and the pathways to understanding its etiology and treatment can be utilized for other conditions.

Depression is fast becoming one of the most prevalent and serious conditions for which individuals use mental health services. As the country's second most important mental health problem (again, exceeded only by schizophrenia), depression in a significant form is estimated to affect about 15 percent of American adults. It is a condition of special significance for women. Recent findings indicate that, in each type of mental helath facility reviewed in a national survey, women clearly exceeded men in diagnosed depression. This was true in every age group, calling into question the assumption that depression in women is predominantly a phenomenon of middle age (Guttentag and Salasin 1978). The same predominance of depression among women is found among untreated populations (Goldman and Ravid 1978). Klerman and Weissman (1978) considered several explanations that might indicate that the higher rate of depression in women is an artifact of such factors as help-seeking behavior or perception of stress and concluded that in fact the differences are real.

## Description of Depression

Though there is no single generally accepted definition of depression, certain commonalities appear in most discussions. The typology of Lewinsohn and his colleagues (1976) comprises a range of factors reflective of most descriptions. Their list includes dysphoria (e.g., sadness, apathy); constant fatigue; behavioral deficits (e.g., staying alone, neglect of personal appearance); decreased sexual activity; behavioral excesses (e.g., complaints about lack of affection and about the demands of others); expression of guilt about suffering caused others; indecisiveness; crying; suicidal behavior; somatic symptoms (e.g., headaches, sleep disturbances, dizzy spells, fatigue); and cognitive manifestations (e.g., low self-evaluation, self-blame, and self-criticism (p. 94). Lewinsohn cautions that "depressed patients manifest *different combinations* of the problematic behaviors shown" (p. 93, italics in original). Common to most definitions is a variety of behaviors and types of affect, each of them having a negative or depressive quality—hopelessness, criticism, directed at both self and others, and a general slowing down and retreat from life—at times literally, through suicidal behavior.

Though depression has long been described in the psychiatric and psychological literature, only in recent years has study of the condition been advanced through a range of perspectives. Before then, "the study of depression was dominated by psychoanalytic formulations . . . which emphasized the internalization of hostility and other intra-psychic processes as the critical etiological mechanisms" (Lewinsohn 1975a:58). Now, a diversity of approaches has developed, and in a recent overview of research in depression Akiskal and McKinney (1975:286) could report on ten etiological models ranging from the psychoanalytic, cognitive, and behavioral to the sociological, existential, and biological. Each frame of reference suggests major causative agents and the mechanisms by which depressive symptoms are triggered. They vary from the aggression-turned-inward process and the effect of object loss (in the view of the psychoanalytic school) to the loss of the meaning of existence (in the existential view). However, the very recent developments in the cognitive and behavioral fields appear to have potential for proposing tenable hypotheses, for spawning specific treatment interventions, and for relating specifically to depression in women.

## Cognitive and Behavioral Perspectives on Depression

These recent views are represented in the work of Beck (1974) on negative cognitions and depression, of Seligman (1975) on the learned-helplessness model, and of Lewinsohn (1974) on response-contingent positive reinforcement.

Beck's formulation (1974), developed specifically to address the problem of depression, relates negative self-evaluation and excessive and distorted self-criticism to depressive symptomatology (Beck 1974). Beck's work centers on the negative cognitive set that influences how a person reacts to external events. These events may appear to precipitate the depressive state, but Beck's focus is the person's own cognitive evaluation of these events as the determinant of the affective impact.

The interventions proposed by Beck derive directly from the theoretical formulation linking negative cognition to depressive symptoms (i.e., the patient learns a set of skills intended to identify and alter the dysfunctional beliefs that predispose her to distort and negatively evaluate her experiences). The individual may also learn to prevent an incipient depression by using these techniques whenever dysphoric and negative cognition become apparent.

Seligman's learned-helplessness model shares with Beck's formulations the emphasis on a psychological set that influences behavior. The learned-helplessness construct is derived from animal experiments in which dogs, previously subject to inescapable shock, passively accepted subsequent shocks even when there was an opportunity to escape. A behavioral pattern becomes established in which "negative expectations about the effectiveness of one's efforts in changing the environment under control (hopelessness, helplessness and powerlessness) lead to passivity and diminished initiation of responses" (Akiskal and McKinney 1973:24).

Seligman observed that as traumatized dogs could not experience the connection between their own behavior and relief from shock— that is, as they learned that response and outcome were independent of each other—they exhibited many of the same symptoms that depressed people manifest.

Hooker (1976) argues for the utility of the learned-helplessness model in the treatment of depression by stressing the characteristic of lack of control over events.

At the core of reactive depression is the real or imagined loss of control over life events and the belief in one's helplessness that results. . . . It is this learned cognitive distortion—the belief that action is futile—that results in both the behavioral and affective symptoms of depression. (pp. 195–196)

Though there are only limited studies that attempt to demonstrate a closer analogy between the animal experience and that of humans (Miller and Seligman 1975; Klein *et al.* 1976) and, as McLean suggests, the development of depression in individuals may not be through single episodes of shock or trauma, still the learned-helplessness model does present a "plausible paradigm for how aversive events can result in depression" (Lewinsohn 1975a:34). The model also leads logically to a treatment approach: Encourage the person to learn that his or her behavior can control the outcome of events. In one study, changing perceptions in individuals of the connection between their actions and later consequences caused "escape performance" to improve (Klein and Seligman 1976). In another (and here the overlap of the model with Beck's formulations is evident), the investigators noted that depressed individuals could increase their abilities to solve problems "by instruction to blame failure not on incompetency, but on the harshness of the environment" (Klein *et al.* 1976:514), that is, by altered cognition about the source of the difficulty.

The third approach, that of Lewinsohn, is more clearly behavioral and considers depression to be the consequence of a sustained decrease in the level of personal reinforcement an individual receives. This low rate occurs because few events are reinforcing, only limited reinforcing events are accessible in the individual's social activities, and/or the person, perhaps lacking social skills, seldom engages in behavior that would be reinforced. The low rate of reinforcement is also conceived of as a stimulus for depressive behavior such as dysphoria, fatigue, and other bodily symptoms.

Some of the empirical findings derived from this model have been summarized by McLean (1976):

Depressed individuals elicit fewer behaviors than other people relative to normal controls. . . . There is a relationship between mood and both the number and kind of pleasant activities in which an individual is engaged. . . . Depressed individuals show a greater sensitivity to aversive stimuli than do non-depressive subjects . . . , and depressed individuals exercise fewer social skills than do non-depressed individuals. (p. 56)

Empirical studies based on each of the three models just described are in their relatively early stages, though the literature reflects increased activity each year. It is likely, as knowledge accumulates, that these and probably other models will be found useful to an understanding of depression through functional interdependence, rather than through the discovery that one paradigm alone holds the etiological answer. Berlin (1977) suggests that possibly some of the elements may play a stronger role in initiating depression and others in maintaining it. The models represent a healthy extension of the range of possible explanatory paradigms from the very few perspectives, mainly psychodynamic, of the recent past. Most important for our purposes here, these models suggest reasons for the greater incidence of depression among women and, as Richey discusses fully in the next section, suggest specific interventions for the alleviation of depression.

## Women's Socialization and the Etiology
## of Depression

One avenue of inquiry that has received only limited attention is based in the observation that depression is far more prevalent among women than among men (Beck and Greenberg 1974). The issue of whether this prevalence has a spurious quality will be considered later, but to the extent that there is validity in the proposition, it is assumed that the greater vulnerability would derive from the socialization of women and not from any inherent female characteristics. On this basis, some aspects of the socialization of women will be pursued here in order to make two points. The first is to understand the relevance to women of the newly developing theories about depression and related therapies reviewed earlier. The second is to suggest that the question of etiology might be turned around. Instead of assuming that depression is unaffected by sex-typed social roles, one might take the view that if the ratio of women depressives of 2:1 or 3:1, as has been reported (Seiden 1976:1115), is a true ratio, the condition of women as a source of understanding depression might be worth some intellectual pursuit. If there is a basis to the stand that women do in fact experience depression to a greater degree than men, what can be learned from the socialization of women that can throw light on the condition of depression found in all individuals? Selected factors relevant to female socialization are presented now in large part to see the applicability of the cognitive, behavioral, and other theories of depression and also to suggest possibilities for future research into the depressive syndrome.

As discussed at the outset of this book, women (and men) are affected profoundly by their gender role and by the socialization process that is meant to ensure that each sex learns the appropriate behaviors and attitudes of the role. "Though sex role, or gender role, is the first and most pervasive role an individual acquires in the socialization process" (Kirsch 1974:327), sociological and psychological research, for the most part, has not reflected the implications of this most important aspect of socialization. Hochschild (1973a) notes that "most research in the social sciences is on male subjects, yet there are significantly different findings on males and females which are often ignored" (p. 249). For example, Goldberg and Lewis (1972:33) caution that research on infant development must take account of sex differences before data are pooled to form generalization about children's behavior. As a correction, most of the recent sex role research has focused on women, and as a result distinctive aspects of gender roles have become clearer.

This recent research has indicated that the socialization process begins in the first weeks and months of life. Studies that have investigated sex differences in infancy indicate that mothers interact differently with their babies depending on the child's sex (Moss 1972) and that there are marked differences in boys' and girls' behavior at the age of one year (Goldberg and Lewis 1972). At those early ages boys are encouraged to be more active and independent, and girls to be more verbal with and imitative of the mother. Girl infants (from 3 weeks to 3 months) were found to be more uniformly responsive to maternal behavior and, as a result, exhibited a greater degree of attachment behavior (Moss 1972:28). Moss (1972), who looked carefully at the infant's behavior as a trigger to the mother's activities, conjectured that the explanation for differential maternal handling may not lie only in the infant's innate characteristics.

An alternative explanation is that mothers respond contingently to the girls and not to the boys as a form of differential reinforcement, whereby, in keeping with cultural expectations, the mother is initiating a pattern that contributes to males being more aggressive or assertive and less responsive to socialization. (p. 28)

By the age of one year there are important differences in the behaviors of boys and girls, particularly to their mothers, to frustration, and in play behavior (Goldberg and Lewis 1972:32). As an example, girls were more reluctant to leave their mothers, cried and motioned for help more than boys, and took less initiative in overcoming obstacles. These traits—greater dependence and attachment behaviors, quiet style and less autonomy—approximate later characteristics in adult women and, as illustrative of the socialization process, indicate how "parents can be active promulgators of sex-role behavior through reinforcement of sex-role appropriate responses within the first year of life" (Goldberg and Lewis 1972:33).

The process continues, not only in the family but through other socializing agents (e.g., school and media). Sex differences in intellectual development are observed throughout the school years. Though girls consistently excel at verbal ability, boys exhibit better developed spatial and analytic competencies. Though girls receive higher grades than boys, they do not compare favorably in intellectual achievement in adulthood. Even gifted girls do not realize their potential to the same extent as gifted boys (Maccoby 1972:34–35). There are mixed findings when certain personality characteristics, such as impulse control, fearfulness, and anxiety, are linked with intellectual achievement, but there appear to be important age-related differentials in the connection of achievement and motivation. In the early school years girls, more than boys, appear motivated to achieve well at school, but with the onset of puberty girls begin to exhibit an achievement dropoff. "The social pressures to do well or poorly in school may have a reverse time sequence for the two sexes" (p. 37). There is also a relationship between extent of dependency and intellectual achievement. The greater the degree of independence, the better the performance on a range of intellectual tests. This is an important difference in view of the sex-related contrasts in independent behaviors noted from children's early models.

Another well-recognized sex difference needs to be considered here as well. Physiologically, girls mature more quickly than boys, and there are some intellectual developments that parallel the physiological progress. However, there does not appear to be a consistent tie between the rates of physical and mental growth. Further, as Maccoby (1972) observes,

> Even if some of these differences could be accounted for in terms of different developmental timetables, it is doubtful whether some of the differences we have noted could be so explained. It is difficult to see, for example, why maturational factors should produce greater differences between the sexes in spatial than verbal performance. Nor why a fast-developing organism should show different kinds of relationships between intellectual functions and personality traits than a slow-developing organism. (p. 39)

The explanation, as Maccoby goes on to suggest, may very well be in the different sex-related adult expectations. Boys excel in math because they, their parents, and their teachers expect that this skill will be needed in such occupations as engineering or science. Girls do not do well in math because they, their parents, and their teachers do not visualize the adult female role—primarily family related—as needing such intellectual skills. Analogies could be made to other intellectual areas in which boys show greater achievement, especially in the later school years. Further, girls respond to the dilemma between achieving to their potential and risking popularity with boys by opting for the latter's social reward. For socialization toward accepted sex role behavior is pervasive and strong.

Keller (1974) outlines the core aspects of the female role in our society as follows:

1. A concentration on marriage, home and children as the primary focus of feminine concern.
2. A reliance on a male provider for sustenance and status. This important component of the wife role is symbolized by the woman taking her husband's name and sharing her husband's income.
3. An expectation that a woman will emphasize nurturance and life-preserving activities, both literally, as in the creation of life, and symbolically, in taking care of, healing and ministering to the helpless, the unfortunate, the ill. Preeminent qualities of character stressed for women include sympathy, care, love and compassion, seemingly best realized in the roles of mother, teacher and nurse.
4. An injunction that women live through and for others rather than for the self. Ideally, a woman is enjoined to lead a vicarious existence—feeling pride or dismay about her husband's achievements or failures or about her children's competitive standing.
5. A stress on beauty, personal adornment and eroticism which, though a general feature of the female role, is most marked for the glamour girl.
6. A ban on the expression of direct assertion, aggression and power strivings except in areas clearly marked women's domain—as in the defense of hearth and home. There is a similar ban on women taking the direct (but not the indirect) sexual initiative. (pp. 417–418)

The roles of wife and mother carry far greater importance for a woman's self-concept than the roles of husband and father do for the man. The man has the more important role of provider and worker in the world of business, from which he obtains his status and major role fulfillment. The man achieves by his own work efforts, the woman by her affiliations and by proxy. Even when the woman works, she most frequently chooses an occupation that is an extension of the nurturing role (e.g., nurse, teacher, secretary, social worker), and when married women work, home responsibilities tend to remain theirs and to take precedence over other activities. This pattern is not restricted to the United States but holds for other countries as well.

The effects of these role expectations are profound. Socialization for the female role and the contemporary set of behaviors and activities necessitated by it results in distinctive psychological characteristics and behavioral responses. Because the wifely and maternal roles require the merger of the wife's aspirations with those of her husband and children, activities limited primarily to the demands of the home, and power restricted to the domestic domain, the outcomes of this traditional model for the woman are dependence and limited competencies.

The socialization process leads to a set of sex-related personal characteristics. Femininity includes nurturance, warmth and expressiveness, emotionality, submissiveness, dependence, selflessness, and obedient cooperation. Masculinity is defined by rationality, logic, assertiveness and independence orientation, competence, and confidence (Broverman et al. 1970; Fabrikant 1974). Two aspects of the development of these sex-typed traits are problematic. One is that the latter set—the masculine characteristics—are more likely to be identified with adult mental health (Broverman et al. 1970) and are the characteristics deemed necessary to make one's way effectively in the world. The second problem is the exclusivity of each set to one sex when what is needed is a mixture, a balance, of the traits within any one individual, male or female. Individuals require both types of qualities, but current socialization educates for one or the other. As Rossi (1968) notes, contemporary adult women who score high on femininty scales "will be inadequate for the task of managing an isolated household with neither man nor kinswoman close by to help them through daily crises, for the assumption of leadership roles in community organization, or for holding down supplementary breadwinning or cakewinning jobs" (p. 38).

In two important ways there are also serious discontinuities for the woman related to the enactment of the expected role. First, there is a lack of preparation in formal education either for the main components of the home-related role or for adequate self-support in the event that the woman does not marry or her marriage ends. (Both of these prospects are becoming increasingly likely.) Second, in the traditional marriage there are serious discontinuities in the woman's progress through the life of the marriage. Her formal schooling does not educate her for her wifely or maternal role. Rossi (1968) has likened the sudden assumption of maternal responsibilities to an overnight shift from the status of graduate student to that of full professor. Should the woman work before the birth of a child, that work is usually not along a career line and will be interrupted by childbirth, perhaps with continued interruptions and continuations throughout the child-rearing years. Further discontinuities occur when the children are grown and leave home. For the woman who has worked continuously or intermittently, this means a lessening of home responsibilities, but usually without a fulfilling work role to substitute for them. For the wife who has not worked, there is a considerable and sudden emptiness in her life (Bart 1972). This last contingency can cover a significant period. Based on marriage at age 20 and death at age 80, the average woman will live through 45 years after her youngest child is in school full time and 32 years after the marriage of that child (Kirsh 1974:334). Unless she has consistently pursued a career, those years will be problematic for the woman. Added to this list of discontinuities is the fact that the effects of the woman's socialization—passivity, dependence, submissiveness, lack of initiative—do not provide her with the skills needed to cope with such disruptions. In contrast, the man will ordinarily use his formal schooling to prepare for his work—his major responsibility in life— and will pursue that work continually through marriage; the birth, rearing, and departure of children; and even divorce and the death of his spouse.

There is evidence that the "normal" events of a woman's life career are stressful. Seiden (1976) reports that "mental health statistics have shown that married women are more likely than unmarried to seek psychiatric help, to attempt suicide and even if non-patients, to report somatic symptoms indicative of psychological distress" (p. 1112).

In an extensive study Radloff (1975) reported a decided relationship between sex, marital status, and depression. "In the total sample, women are more depressed than men. When marital status is added to the analysis, an interactive pattern emerges. . . . Married women are consistently more depressed than married men" (pp. 254, 264). Bernard (1971) suggests that the "happy marriage" is a paradox and wonders whether the "qualities associated with marital happiness for women may not themselves be contrary to good mental health" (p. 157). Once out of that role, however, the separated or divorced woman also faces difficulties because of serious economic and psychological stresses of child rearing. The overall picture is that it is the young woman—age 25–44—who is most vulnerable to depression, and though the highest rates in that age group are among the separated and divorced, there is also considerable vulnerability in the married woman at home with children. In the married group, it is significant, too, that having work outside the home is useful for the alleviation of depressive symptoms (Mostow and Newberry 1975).

Limiting the roles that an individual can elect to assume has been suggested as a serious restriction of that person's social identity and a possible precursor of mental illness (Sarbin 1954). The woman's traditional role limits her to the major familial one, and even when a work role is undertaken in addition, as is true now for more than half of all married women, work has serious limitations for most women. Though more and more women are in the work force, and most work out of necessity, they earn less than men, have only minority representation in the higher-paying categories, and are clearly not in positions of power in the political, business, or academic worlds (Kirsch 1974). Havens (1973) offers an interesting commentary on the fact that females with high incomes are disproportionately represented in the unmarried category. "Such representation implies preparation for economic activity and perhaps an unwillingness to 'settle' for the alternative of marriage" (p. 218). This may be especially so when that alternative includes dysfunctional discontinuities for women. It may also be relevant to add that such discontinuities are not viewed as problematic by society; rather, they are seen as the natural consequence of a traditional marriage. Society is not generally open to the expression of negative feelings about the major roles it assigns to its members—work for men or home responsibilities for women (Rossi 1968).

Because the role of woman is so closely tied by society to the role of wife and mother, it is important to note that the absence of that status creates another set of problems for women. Some of these problems are discussed elsewhere in this book. in sections on the widow, the displaced homemaker, and the woman as a single parent. For women who are no longer in the marital role and for those who never marry, distinctive issues arise that we are only beginning to understand.

As its first purpose relative to depression, this review of aspects of women's socialization was intended to establish a connection between the traits and behaviors considered appropriate for women, on the one hand, and some conditions predisposing to depression, on the other. This will be done with reference to three personal qualities that are of significance to the cognitive–behavioral formulations concerning depression discussed earlier: negative cognition, lack of a sense of control, and inability to cope with stress. The argument is that characteristics in women that their socialization encourages may overlap with traits identified in the newly developing theories as triggers to the depressive syndrome.

If one assumes, as Beck does, that negative cognition is linked with depression, then it is of interest to observe that much of the socialization process of women, as discussed earlier, encourages negative self-views. The sex-typed traits for women—dependence, submission, self-denial, obsequiousness—can naturally lead to a restricted and depreciatory view of one's capabilities and expectations. Keller (1974) terms this a "primary impulse to self-effacement" and attributes its development to lifelong, societally imposed constraints on the development of abilities and opportunities.

Initially the inhibition comes from parents, teacher or other social authority, but later one's inner arbiter takes over and what was once second nature now becomes a primary impulse to self-effacement. Few find it possible to suppress ambitions at age three only to reverse this attitude at age twenty. (p. 428)

These negative self-evaluations are evidenced in schoolgirls' rating their own abilities more negatively and less realistically than boys,

(Maccoby 1972:37) and in studies indicating that generally women show less confidence in their expected performance on tasks and less sense of personal strength or mastery than men (Maccoby and Jacklin 1974).

There appears to be a strong conceptual rationale and some supporting evidence for the tie between negative cognition, discussed in a general way in the depression literature, and the specific consequences for many women of an intellectually and experientially restricted life. Society demands that the woman maintain limited horizons for her competencies and opportunities. It is not surprising that this translates into a negative view of her prospects and abilities. "The modesty, submissiveness and sexual conservatism which society expects of a married woman corresponds to the depressive's low self-esteem, dependence and libido loss" (Beck and Greenberg 1974:117). In their study of depressed women Weissman and associates (1971) found their subjects to be submissive, to have difficulty in asserting themselves, and to be dependent on their husbands.

The degree of control that women feel they have over their lives, particularly the limited extent to which they perceive that their actions can determine important consequences for their lives, relates to the learned-helplessness etiology of depression. Again, there is an important developmental chronology to this uncertain sense of control. The attachment behavior in female infants and the independent behavior in male infants described earlier presage adult sex differences. Boys, and later men, see that their own efforts lead to significant outcomes in work and social status; girls, and later women, look to the people on whom they are dependent to protect and provide.

Many female children are taught that their personal worth and survival depend not on effective responding to life structures, but in physical beauty and appeal to men—that is, that they have no *direct* control over the circumstances of their lives. (Beck and Greenberg 1974:120, italics in original)

The effect is evident in the school years, when girls are less likely to believe their success is a result of their own efforts (Maccoby 1972:17). In their continuing development, and especially in marriage, women are aware that in the very important areas of social status, income, and life style their lot depends on the standing and efforts of their husbands (Polster 1974:248). Rossi (1972) comments:

It takes no detailed inquiry into census data for a young woman to realize that no matter how well trained or competent she may be in her own field, most of her homemaker friends will enjoy a higher social status than she is likely to achieve by her own efforts. (p. 126)

There is the argument that in fact women do exercise considerable control, though this is indirect and operating through others (i.e., husband and children). Keller (1974) defines control this way and maintains that women exert considerable influence through the rearing of children, indirect pressures on the husband, and sexual power. This kind of control is, however, problematic. Its outcome still depends on other people; its exercise is often manipulative and sub rosa and, therefore, not associated with a positive sense of achievement; and its domain is restricted to the home, and therefore limited in its effects and the competencies it requires.

If we define the set of attitudes and skills required to obviate learned helplessness as the exercise of direct control over consequences through one's own efforts, then there is serious question as to whether women's traditional socialization provides for such traits. Women may very well come to believe (gradually and not necessarily through the traumatic events suggested by animal experiments) that they have little or no real influence over important circumstances of their lives. Added to the lack of a sense of control, many women do not experience the development of the skills necessary to exert direct control over life circumstances. This skill deficit is related to a third connection between women's socialization and the onset of depression.

Coping with stress is related to depression and includes elements of Lewinsohn's reinforcement model, but is more inclusive. The major point here is that depression symptomatology may very well result from the combination of a stressful situation plus a set of negative cognitions, lack of a sense of control over events, and deficient skills for managing difficulties. These latter deficits may very well include inability to secure sufficient positive reinforcement from the environment, but the emphasis here is on the question of range of resources for dealing with stress.

Two interrelated factors again raise the issue of the woman's predisposition to depression. The first is the importance of coping performance in the prevention and the treatment of depression. Much of the clinical experimentation conducted in the context of each of the three models discussed earlier show that taking initiative or action—to alter cognitions, to achieve control, to secure necessary reinforcements—has a beneficial effect on depressive symptoms. Successful performance appears to be a powerful antidepressant (McLean 1976:79), and it is also suggested that coping skills seem to separate the depressed from the nondepressed (p. 74). Related to this are Weissman and Paykel's findings (1974) that depressed women who work are less impaired at their jobs than depressed women at home in their daily activities.

The second factor is that many women have been socialized out of a wide range of coping skills. This occurs because of the encouragement of dependence in women and the connection between dependence and inactivity. "The dependent–conforming person is passive, waiting to be acted upon by the environment. The independent person takes the initiative (Maccoby 1972:40). This also occurs because we "not only tolerate but encourage women to work in jobs which are below their abilities" so as not to interfere with their central family role (Rossi 1972:125). It is significant that women who are found to be more resourceful and purposive are also less traditional in their sex role orientation (Kirsh 1974:331). The cost of the development of sex-typed female characteristics is the "renunciation of achievement and autonomy" (Block et al. 1973:338). Unfortunately, at times of stress a set of skills and attitudes subsumed under the heading of achievement and autonomy—initiative, action, use of resources, a range of skills, confidence, a sense of control—may be lacking, and depressive symptomatology may result.

To the extent that these connections between the traditional socialization of women and the etiology of depression find validity in further clinical studies and research, to that extent the onset for the individual woman patient will become better understood, and better-developed therapies for women will result.

As a second rationale for this review of the socialization of women and the etiology of depression, it was suggested earlier that some of this continuing research might take as its starting point the greater prevalence of depression among women than among men. To pursue this question, it is necessary to try to establish two positions: (1) that, in fact, a greater percentage of women than of men experience depression, and (2) if so, that the reasons for this difference are not spurious ones. As noted earlier, it is estimated that at any one time 15 percent of the nation's population is depressed and that within this group women outnumber men in a range from 2:1 to 3:1 (Seiden 1976:1115). Also, as mentioned earlier, women, both as hospitalized patients and as outpatients are more likely than men to be diagnosed as depressed (Guttentag and Salasin 1978). In other words, one can suggest to therapists that their typical depressed patient will be a woman (McLean 1976:84).

Even with these data, there would be a question as to whether these were true prevalence rates or artifacts of related conditions. Alternative explanations might include women's tendencies to express their feelings and to seek professional help or emotional problems more readily than men. There are indications that women will report more psychiatric symptoms than men when each group has a similar number of physical symptoms (Phillips and Segal 1969). A further explanation might lie in the mental health professional's greater likelihood, given similar symptoms in men and women patients, to diagnose depression in women. The greater tendency of medical journals to depict women as depressed and of medical personnel to dispense drugs to women for the relief of depressive symptoms would point to this sex-related diagnosis.

It would seem that these and related challenges to the reported data might be answered by epidemiological studies of the psychological condition of individuals in the general population who have not sought treatment. These reports would not be affected either by a propensity to seek the services of professionals or by the diagnoses of those professionals. Such epidemiological studies do, in fact, show women at a higher risk of depression (Goldman and Ravid 1978).

Certainly, further investigations for alternative explanations are indicated. For the present, though, mental health professionals responsible for treatment report depression as more prevalent in women, and it is proposed here that the condition of women might illuminate the etiological puzzles of clinical depression.

Most authors do not address the issue of sex-related prevalence. In a recent authoritative interdisciplinary report on depression, sex differences are mentioned only once in 317 pages (Friedman and Katz 1974). Most studies to date have ignored women as a distinctive group, even in view of the prevalence data and even when most if not all the subjects in a particular study are women. In many studies focusing on treatment, intervention therapies are often based on traditional conceptions of the options open to women (McLean 1976). When the woman as a depressed patient has been specifically considered, with a few exceptions (Beck and Greenberg 1974) the issues addressed have been related to biological processes specific to women. In Silverman's (1968) discussion of a sex as a variable in depression, she begins by stating that "there appears to be no exception to the generalization that depression is more common in women than in men" (p. 73). In commenting on that phenomenon she considers only such factors as menstruation, pregnancy, childbirth, and hysterectomy—processes belonging to women alone, but only in relation to their physiology (pp. 74–78).

There does not seem to be consistent evidence that depression is hormonally related in women, and in the case of postpartum depression there is a question of whether that condition can be interpreted on physiological or psychological grounds only (Klerman and Weissman 1978). In fact, if one were to pursue primarily an intrapsychic explanation for the prevalence of depression in women, with the exception of postpartum depression and without demonstration of clear etiological ties to other physiological processes to depression, it is evident that other psychological explanations (e.g., loss of a love object, internalized anger) are not sex specific.

The argument here is for a research approach that considers the socialization of women as an important component in the etiology of depression (Radloff, in press). The point was developed earlier, indicating that many of the outcomes of the woman's usual socialization overlap the responses and attitudes now being cited as etiological agents for depression. Lewinsohn *et al.* (1976) suggest that "it seems likely that many findings relevant to the etiology of 'abnormal depression' would result from investigation of the variables affecting mood among normals' (p. 92). An analogous suggestion based on the foregoing discussions is to look at what is "normal" behavior for women, how this relates to depressive symptomatology, and how a study of that relationship may provide potentially useful knowledge about the general condition of depression.

## Services to Women with
## Mental Health Problems

Seiden has reviewed the criticism by feminists of traditional psychotherapy for women, and part of her commentary introduces examples of nonsexist approaches. Much of feminist activity in the mental health field is intended to address the issues that Seiden (1976) cites.

The therapeutic relationships in a dyad may replicate rather than remedy the "one-down" position in which women frequently find themselves in life and marriage, thus encouraging the fantasy that an idealized relationship with a more powerful other is a better solution to life problems than taking autonomous action. . . . Therapeutic theories have more often supported rather than questioned stereotypical assumptions about sex roles, with different standards of mental health for women and men . . . including the assumption that dependency, masochism, and passivity are normal for women and the tendency to treat assertiveness and aggression differently for women than for men. . . . Women specifically, especially when treated as collaterals to their children, may be harmed by a "blame-the-mother" tradition in clinical psychopathology (vide the considerably greater and earlier literature on allegedly schizophrenogenic mothers than fathers, despite the clear evidence that either is specifically responsible for more serious disorders in their children). . . . There has been lack of realistic appraisals of the occupational hazards of the housewife role. (p. 1116).

The following selections cover a range of interventions for women. Cheryl Richey's contribution discusses in detail the interventive methodologies for depressed women based specifically on the cognitive and behavioral theories presented in this chapter. The two additional selections are of a more general nature. Carol Radov and associates contrast traditional and feminist therapy, including the specific applicability to an instance of depression. Reflective of the prevalence data cited earlier, other feminist therapists have reported depression as high among the concerns of the women they see (Moskol 1976). Consciousness raising, described by Annette Brodsky, represents a perspective on the mental well-being of women that emphasizes non-hierarchical group support among women, and sociological and political explanations for incapacity, rather than a medical model. The three illustrations reflect different nonsexist approaches, and each developed out of questions concerning the value of traditional therapies for the mental health concerns of women. Seiden (1976) offers a cogent characterization of current feminist therapy:

Major trends in feminist therapy appear to include a grounding in current research about women, a relative priority given to environmental interpretations rather than intrapsychic ones, and a trend toward greater egalitarianism between therapist and patient. Other characteristic trends include a careful avoidance of using the therapeutic situation to replace the one-down position that women often take in marriage or work, a hearty laugh at the idea that a healthy woman is characterized by passivity, and an attempt to provide a good role model in the form of a competent woman. (p. 1117)

# Cognitive–Behavioral Strategies for the Treatment of Depression in Women

CHERYL A. RICHEY

The typical learning histories of most women predispose them to depressive episodes. Female socialization appears routinely to result in women's being less able to cope with life stress in a competent, independent manner. Women's greater difficulty in handling stressful life events may be due to either actual or perceived deficiencies. In many cases women may not have the necessary skills to master stress, or they may underestimate or distort their capabilities and thus perceive themselves as helpless and ineffectual when in actuality they are not. The issue of why a woman is depressed or what factors contribute to her depression (e.g., actual or perceived deficits) is taken up in assessment, the first essential phase of any therapeutic endeavor.

Before a thorough assessment can be carried out, however, a beginning working relationship with the depressed woman client must be established. As in all feminist-oriented therapy, it is essential that an equal working alliance be developed between therapist and client. This is important in reducing the likelihood that the woman will experience in counseling the same one-down or low-status position that she often experiences outside of therapy (Seiden 1976). A "team approach" to therapy can be facilitated by the counselor as "demystifying" the therapeutic process, that is, sharing with the client her or his perceptions of women and mental health (e.g., emotional problems being largely the result of socialization and external stress rather than internal disease mechanisms), disclosing the anticipated timetable for assessment and intervention (Lewinsohn et al. 1976), and sharing with the client assumptions and hunches developed throughout assessment and treatment so that these can be acknowledged and/or corrected by the client.

In the presence of a supportive, coequal therapeutic relationship, assessment can proceed so that appropriate goals can be established and treatment strategies developed. During the assessment phase self-report and observational measures can be used to determine the range of "response modalities" involved in the client's depression (McLean 1976). Response modalities are areas of concern often pinpointed by depressed clients. These areas include the client's (1) overt, observable *behavior* (e.g., her work performance, social interaction, and degree of general physical activity); (2) *cognitions* (e.g., thoughts of worthlessness, helplessness, worry, etc.); (3) *affect*, or emotional indicators of her general feeling state (e.g., amount of crying); and (4) *somatic* complaints, or physical problems (e.g., fatigue, loss of appetite, aches and pains).

Most of the recent literature on the treatment of depression focuses on the behavioral and cognitive modalities, perhaps because these two modalities are emphasized in the main theories discussing the causation or correlates of depression (e.g., negative thoughts, perceived lack of control or helplessness, and environmental stress and loss of reinforcement (Beck 1974; Seligman 1975; Lewinsohn 1975). Although techniques for working directly with the emotional or affective aspects of depression have been discussed elsewhere (Lazarus 1968; Lazarus 1971; Taulbee and Wright 1971), most of the literature utilizes emotional responses or mood states as indicators of therapeutic change in the behavioral or cognitive responses areas. For example, many studies utilize questionnaires to ascertain the client's feeling states before and after direct efforts to change specific behaviors or cognitions (Beck 1967; Lubin 1965).

The somatic or physiological aspects of depression will not be dealt with in this chapter, since good reviews of techniques for alleviating common disturbances associated with depression [e.g., sleep problems (Gambrill 1977; Lewinsohn et al. 1976) and chronic pain (Fordyce 1976) are presented elsewhere. However, every clinician is urged to encourage clients to have a thorough medical checkup if physiological complaints are central and the counselor suspects any physiological basis for the depression (Wilcoxon et al. 1976).

Given that the behavioral and cognition aspects of depression will be highlighted, the following discussion will focus on specific intervention techniques applicable with depressed clients, the majority of whom are women. Since women's depression appears to be strongly linked with their female socialization experiences, techniques based on social learning theory will be emphasized as important therapeutic strategies in helping women alleviate depressive emotional reactions by relearning more effective behavioral and cognitive patterns. Each intervention strategy will be preceded by a brief discussion of assessment procedures, both self-report and observational methods, and will include an overview of treatment outcomes, when available. The treatment procedures described assume that a supportive working relationship has been developed between counselor and client, and that the client is encouraged to become as actively involved as possible in all phases of her own therapy (e.g., assessment, intervention, and evaluation).

The first series of intervention strategies to be discussed focus on the behavioral modality or observable problems of the woman client that may relate directly to her depression. The first treatment approach to be highlighted in this section is social skill training, which addresses the development and refinement of the skills necessary to initiate and maintain relationships through honest and direct self-expression. The second approach in this section emphasizes helping the depressed person increase her overall frequency of activities and pleasant events.

## Behavioral Modality

### SOCIAL SKILL TRAINING

*Basic Social Interactional Skills*
The social interactional skills of depressed women may be important to consider in an overall treatment plan because complaints of social isolation, anxiety in social interactions, and unrewarding social relationships are problems often mentioned by depressed people (McLean 1976). Women who experience few pleasant social contacts, excessive shyness, and loneliness achieve less reinforcement from their social environment than more skilled individuals (Lewinsohn *et al.* 1976).

The socially isolated woman who becomes depressed may be a widow who was dependent on her husband for social contacts and now finds herself not knowing how to make friends or maintain old acquaintanceships. Or she may be a single mother who, in maintaining the dual role of parent and breadwinner, has little time, energy, and skills to develop meaningful adult relationships outside of work. Or she may be a married woman at home with small children who has few social contacts with adults except for occasional dinner parties with her husband's business associates. These women often feel powerless over interpersonal events. They have learned to be passive and to wait for others (usually men) to take the initiative in establishing and maintaining social relationships. Women have generally learned to be reactive rather than proactive in routine social interactional situations.

If clinician and client suspect that a low rate of rewarding social contacts is a determinant in the depression, then a more thorough assessment procedure can be instituted that will delineate the nature and scope of the problem. Self-report measures in the form of questionnaires and record keeping are perhaps the easiest way to begin assessment. Various inventories and forms have been used to ascertain the extent of shyness, social anxiety, and withdrawal. For example, the Social Confidence Inventory (Gambrill 1973) is a 14-item questionnaire designed to determine how an individual views her social behavior—does she take the initiative in conversations, or worry about what others think of her when she is talking to them, more or less than other people? The Stanford Shyness Survey (Zimbardo 1977) is a 44-item questionnaire that assesses the history, extent, and consequences of a person's shyness.*

In addition to using questionnaires and rating forms, clients can monitor important features of their social contacts. For example, McLean (1976) asks clients to keep track of self-initiated social encounters, events participated in, degree of social anxiety, and satisfaction. Gambrill and Richey's (1976) self-help manual encourages individuals to complete two forms every week during training in order to highlight specific problem areas as well as each success. One form is used to note each conversation the person has that is more than a greeting and is not of a strictly service or business nature. Much relevant information can be gained by noting, for example, the overall percentage of conversations initiated; the percentage of positive, neutral, or negative reactions from others; and the average duration of each contact.

The clinician can also utilize behavioral or observational methods to gather relevant assessment information. In the literature on social interactional skill training, behavioral measures typically are taken from the client's responses to audio- or video-taped situations (Gambrill 1977; Rehm and Marston 1968). If the clinician does not have access to recording equipment, the client can be asked to role-play potential social encounters in the sessions with the counselor or an assistant. These simulations can provide valuable information on the client's strengths and deficits (Gambrill 1977).

Once assessment activities have highlighted the areas in need of change and specific goals have been established for improvement, intervention techniques can be utilized to help the client become more socially active and responsible for her own social environment. Sev-

---

* See also, for example, the Social Activity Questionnaire (Arkowitz 1975), the Situation Questionnaire (Rehm and Marston 1968), the Social Avoidance and Distress Scale (Watson and Friend 1969).

eral recent training developments in this area will be highlighted. One is the self-help manual by Gambrill and Richey (1976) already mentioned. It is designed to be used by individuals without the guidance of a professional counselor, although it could be a useful adjunct to therapy. This handbook provides a step-by-step program in the development and refinement of basic social interactional skills (e.g., where to go to meet people, initiating and maintaining conversations, arranging future meetings, having more enjoyable contacts, etc.). Zimbardo's recent work (1977), which addresses the problem of shyness and what to do about it, also contains specific suggestions for intervention that can be used by individuals alone or with the aid of a therapist.

The first concern of most shy and isolated women is how to begin, that is, where to go to meet people aside from singles bars and church socials. Gambrill and Richey stress the importance of taking advantage of the situations one is already in, such as work or school. They also urge the reader to locate promising places to meet people by satisfying two criteria: (1) The place should have people there that the person would like to meet, and (2) the situation should offer some activity that the person enjoys, aside from the potential social interaction. For example, if a person enjoys outdoor activities, such as hiking and bicycle riding, a first step could involve locating groups in her area that organize hikes and bicycle trips. Then she could call a representative of each group and ask about the people who usually participate (e.g., percentages of men and women, age range, whether individuals go alone or in couples, skill levels represented, etc.).

Once the issue of where to go to meet people has been addressed, the next critical step in training is what to do when one gets there (i.e., initial social behaviors). Zimbardo (1977) discusses the importance of beginning to practice smiling and saying "hello" to people in everyday situations. He also mentions starting out with "safe" conversations with strangers in public places (e.g., in a grocery line, a doctor's waiting room, the library). Gambrill and Richey discuss eight ways of initiating conversations with strangers and acquaintances, each differing to some extent in the amount of "personal risk" involved.

Once a social contact has been made, skills are needed to maintain an interaction, make it more enjoyable, and terminate it comfortably. Gambrill and Richey discuss several techniques for maintaining and enriching conversations, for example, changing the purpose or content of the conversation or creating a more personal atmosphere. Cotler and Guerra (1976) also discuss several conversational skills that can enhance the maintenance of an interaction (e.g., asking open-ended questions, attending to free information, and giving self-disclosures). These suggestions for social skill improvement can best be utilized in treatment (either individually or in groups) if the client is encouraged to rehearse them in the sessions and if sufficient modeling, explanations, feedback, and support are given by the counselor and/or other group members. Between-session assignments are also beneficial to motivate the shy client to begin moving in small steps toward her goals, thus increasing social and personal rewards and decreasing depressive moods.

Outcome research on social skill training to increase social contacts has indicated that it is generally successful in helping individuals improve interactional skills and increase self-esteem (Curran 1977; Gambrill 1977). However, even though prominent theorists on depression emphasize the importance of adequate social skills to ensure sufficient amounts of positive social consequences (Lewinsohn *et al.* 1976; McLean 1976), the empirical linkage between decreased depression and increased social interaction skills requires further verification.

*Assertion Training*
Aside from the skills necessary to establish social contacts, additional skills are needed to help individuals express themselves more thoroughly in ongoing relaionships with others. Assertiveness involves those behaviors which facilitate the honest expression of feelings and attitudes without undue anxiety or the depreciation of others (Alberti and Emmons 1974). Assertion is the "open, calm, confident expression of preferences by words or actions in a manner which causes others to take them into account" (MacDonald 1974:32). In contrast, the nonassertive or submissive person is self-denying, restrained, inhibited, and anxious. She allows others to make decisions or choices for her and generally avoids situations involving confronta-

tion (Alberti and Emmons 1974). The submissive person allows her rights to be ignored and yields humbly to the preferences of others. On the other hand, the aggressive person coerces others to give in to her preferences through the use of hostile words or actions (Mac-Donald 1974). The aggressive person attempts to achieve her goals by putting others down, by hurting or humiliating them (Alberti and Emmons 1974).

There is evidence that women may have more difficulty being assertive than men. A review of the literature on the female–male verbal interaction indicates that women are nonassertive when interacting with men in dyadic and group discussions (Richey 1974).

The client who is depressed and reports inhibitions in expressing wants and preferences or experiences negative reactions from others due to aggressive behaviors may be a candidate for assertion training. Many clients who might benefit from assertion training rarely request it as such. More often they complain they are "depressed" or "exhausted from being torn in a hundred directions," or that "nobody listens to me" (Bower 1976). Often the depressed person is unable to express anger in an appropriate way and avoids and complains about problematic situations rather than doing anything to change them (Gambrill 1977).

Initial assessment of assertive difficulties can be accomplished via self-report measures from questionnaires and record keeping. Several questionnaires have been developed for noncollege populations that measure reactions to a wide variety of interpersonal situations (Gambrill and Richey 1975; Gay et al. 1975). Numerous other forms have been developed for college students, and a few for adolescents and psychiatric populations. The reader is referred to Lange and Jakubowski's (1976) discussion of the format and merits of many of these forms.

The client can also keep track of her daily assertions or failures to assert on data sheets designed for that purpose. For example, the client can indicate the date, the type of situation, the sex and age of the other person, what she would or would like to have said, the other's reaction, her anxiety level, her degree of satisfaction with her reaction, and what she was thinking. All of this information can be useful in training sessions to help focus attention on particular areas of difficulty (e.g., higher levels of anxiety with males, excessive worries about being rejected, etc.).

Behavioral or observational measures can also be obtained before goals are established and training begins. Again, clients can be asked to respond to taped situations or role-play simulated interactions with the counselor. Counselors could use situations that have been developed (Eisler et al. 1973a; McFall and Lillesand 1971; McFall and Marston 1970) or develop their own. Lange and Jakubowski (1976) discuss how such situations can be introduced into the counseling sessions and how the client's responses can be analyzed.

In addition to having the client role-play simulated situations, the counselor can also use his or her skills of observation within the therapeutic sessions to determine whether assertive difficulties are a central problem in the client's depression. For instance, if the client is extremely reticent, engages in little or no eye contact, speaks in a low voice, and is overly agreeable with the counselor's interpretations and suggestions, nonassertiveness may be an important feature of the client's depression. However, such passivity and reticence in the treatment sessions may also be an artifact of the client's mood; that is, the client may typically behave in an assertive manner but is underresponsive because of the depression. Only a thorough assessment would shed light on whether the client's nonassertiveness was chronic and precipitated the depression, or whether her submissiveness was temporary and a result of her mood.

Another source of behavioral assessment information is home observations of the client and her significant others (spouse and/or children). Lewinsohn et al. (1976) utilize a verbal–interpersonal coding system in observations of depressed individuals in their own homes, usually around the dinner hour. These data can be used to determine the degree to which the client can give and receive positive and negative feedback from significant others. If home observations are not possible and if a group format is chosen as the principal vehicle for treatment, the client can be observed interacting with other individuals in group therapy sessions.

After assessment activities have highlighted individual assertive problems, training, conducted individually or in a group setting, can begin. Assertion training typically involves a number of techniques utilized as a "therapeutic package." These techniques usually include role playing, or behavior rehearsal of problematic situations either between therapist and client or among members in a group; modeling, or demonstration of alternate ways of handling interactions by the counselor or other group members; instructions, or verbal guidelines presented to the client that point out critical behaviors to perform if assertive success is to be accomplished (e.g., actually saying the word *no* when refusing an unfair request or demand); feedback and coaching from the counselor or group members regarding the client's performance during a simulation; social approval from the therapist or group members for any assertive success; and homework assignments between sessions to encourage the client to practice new skills in everyday situations (Alberti and Emmons 1974; Eisler *et al.* 1973b; Eisler *et al.* 1974; Hersen *et al.* 1973; McFall and Twentyman 1973; Rimm and Masters 1974).

An additional treatment element that shows promise when included with the above-mentioned techniques is self-reinforcement. Several investigators have demonstrated that people who are trained to praise their own assertive successes tend to show the greatest therapeutic gains after training (Gambrill 1973; Richey 1974; Richey 1975; Taylor and Marshall 1977).

In contrast to individual therapy with nonassertive individuals, group training for assertive difficulties is receiving wide recognition as an effective means for achieving behavior and attitude change (Field and Test 1975; Galassi *et al.* 1974; Hedquist and Winhold 1970; Lomont *et al.* 1969; Rathus 1972; Rose 1975; Shoemaker and Paulson 1976). Group training may be especially important for women who have problems being assertive (Osborn and Harris 1975). Because of their socialization, women may require more social support for being direct and independent, and more opportunities to observe assertive women who are still seen as appropriately "feminine" (Jakubowski-Spector 1973; Richey 1974). The reader is referred elsewhere for a detailed session-by-session description of a group assertion training format for women that utilizes the training variables discussed earlier, including self-reinforcement (Richey, in press).

Assertion training may also be successful combined with consciousness raising (CR) for women. Lange and Jakubowski (1976) discuss two benefits of utilizing both assertion exercises and CR experiences. First, CR increases the members' awareness that their problems are not individual failures but, rather, are common problems experienced by most women because of their feminity training. Second, CR is a way to help members view themselves and others differently. This change in beliefs and cognitions can facilitate the generalization of new assertive skills to a variety of interpersonal situations.

Since the relationship between thoughts and effective social skills is important (Gambrill 1977), direct attention to the cognitive aspects of assertiveness can also be included in routine training sessions, or members can be urged to attend to these between sessions. Clients can be encouraged to be more aware and keep a record of what they are saying to themselves before, during, and after encounters requiring an assertive response. The rationality of such thoughts can then be challenged (MacDonald 1974) and/or other techniques affecting client self-talk can be implemented (Meichenbaum 1975; Lange and Jakubowski 1976).

In addition to becoming aware of and changing covert self-talk, covert rehearsal can also be added to the typical assertion training package to provide clients with numerous opportunities to practice situations assertively before they occur. Kazdin (1975) found covert rehearsal, in which the client imagines herself or someone else dealing effectively with a problematic situation, to be as effective as overt rehearsal. Although this finding requires further evidence, preliminary research indicates that covert rehearsal has the potential for being an effective technique that can be used frequently and independently by clients in everyday situations.

After an extensive literature review on the effectiveness of assertion training with both individuals and groups, Rimm and Masters (1974) conclude that assertion training, primarily in the form of behavior rehearsal, is an efficient treatment procedure. Of further interest are two recent follow-up studies of group assertion training with women. The results indicated that assertive gains were maintained or increased even with women who had been out of training for one year or more (Mayo et al. 1975; Richey 1975). Again, the direct relationship between increased assertiveness and decreased depression needs further empirical validation, although many clients report improved self-concepts with increases in their assertive skills.

## INCREASING PLEASANT EVENTS AND
## GENERAL ACTIVITY LEVELS

In the preceding section the reduction in the amount of positive reinforcement due to social skill deficits was discussed. Depression can also be related to loss of reinforcement due to the reduction of daily activities and pleasant events (Lewinsohn 1974). That is, listlessness, dysphoria, and fatigue can result from a person's being on a prolonged "extinction schedule" in which few reinforcing events occur (Gambrill 1977). The client's work performance may suffer; routine duties may not be accomplished; she may engage in very little if any physical exercise and may sit and sleep a lot. Often these behaviors are maintained by the reactions of others. The woman's husband, children, or parents may be unduly sympathetic, interested, and concerned about her when she is depressed and, in turn, show less attention when she is functioning independently. Gambrill (1977) points out that a vicious cycle often develops to maintain low levels of activity and loss of further reinforcement. As others respond in a positive manner to the depressed individual, she becomes even more trapped in her depression, thus making it more and more unpleasant for others to be around her. Thus, significant others, although they are occasionally solicitous, begin to avoid the depressed person more often; in turn, the woman experiences a further decrease in social reinforcement, which facilitates additional depressive feelings. Several theorists believe that depression may be precipitated by a sudden change in the environment that is associated with a major loss of reinforcement and a resultant increase in stress, for example, divorce, the death of a significant person, or the loss of a job (Ferster 1973).

To determine whether loss of reinforcement from reduced activities or from few pleasant events is a major factor in a client's depression, assessment procedures can focus on the client's report of such variables as type and amount of physical activity, number of different places visited, and interest in and amount of work completed (McLean 1976). She can also complete the Pleasant Events Schedule, which pinpoints behaviors that may be incompatible with her depression (MacPhillamy and Lewinsohn 1975).

Behavioral or observational measures in addition to client self-report data can also be obtained on the client's daily activities and enjoyment levels. For example, as a measure of general activity level, the client could bring in her work record to determine loss of job time if this is indicated as a problem area; or significant others in the client's environment (spouse, children, parent) could be asked to keep track of the client's activities for a week. If the client is hospitalized, observations of her activities aside from eating and sleeping could be made by staff.

If assessment procedures verify that low rates of activity and engagement in pleasant events are correlated with the client's depression, intervention efforts can begin by having the client accomplish graduated task assignments (Burgess 1969; McLean 1976). This approach, which involves planning successful performances, however small, for the client, is based on the assumption that behavioral productivity is one of the most powerful antidepressants (Gambrill 1977). McLean (1976) discusses several steps for ensuring successful task completion: (1) The task must be broken down into small steps so that successful performance is guaranteed; (2) increases in task difficulty must be explicit; (3) attention must be focused on what has already been accomplished rather than on what has yet to be completed; (4) reinforcement must follow completion of each task and preferably consist of social reinforcement from important people in the client's environment (p. 80).

A clinical example may illustrate these procedures. The client, a 24-year-old white college graduate, was unemployed, single, and living alone when she sought counseling for depression, which had lasted for six months (Hodnett, 1977). The client indicated that the onset of her depression was associated with completing training as a travel agent and not being able to find work. She had called several travel agencies after the training but had failed to get an immediate response and had "given up." Assessment indicated that she rarely left her apartment and that she spent much of her time reading, watching TV, and writing poems. The intervention plan consisted of tasks devoted to job-seeking activities and engaging in more social contacts. Task completion was followed by self-reinforcement and therapist praise (there were no significant others in her environment who could become involved in supporting her successes). A list of simple, graduated tasks was developed and written on index cards. Examples of these tasks included looking through the yellow pages of the telephone book under "Travel" and making a list of prospective employers, including addresses and telephone numbers; calling an acquaintance from her training class and talking on the phone for ten minutes; calling the counselor from her former school to make an appointment to discuss tactics for locating a job. The client used self-praise and reading to reward herself for the completion of each small task. She monitored her daily moods (on a scale from 1, "very happy," to 10, "very depressed"), the number of tasks completed, the frequency of self-praise (via a golf counter), and the amount of reading engaged in as a reward for each task completed. The data kept by the client indicated that her overall mood rating was "8" before treatment and "4" during the intervention period. By the third session the client reported that she felt her depression "lifting." She had several job leads and felt that she would eventually get a job as a result of her efforts. She also had made a new friend who shared many of her interests. The client attributed her therapeutic gains to "taking it one step at a time" and to her new self-reward system.

Outcome research on the graded-tasks approach is generally of a case history nature. Lewinsohn et al. (1976) provide data that indicate that ten clients increased their activity levels substantially when therapy time was used as a reinforcer. In an updated review of the literature in this area, Lewinsohn (1976) cites other studies that indicate that increasing activity level and pleasant events enhance the client's overall mood and functioning. However, not all studies verify these findings. Hammen and Glass (1975) found that depressed students who increased the number of pleasant activities in which they engaged did not report a corresponding improvement in mood. Lewinsohn et al. (1976) suggested that these findings indicated that not all activities rated as enjoyable are related to one's mood. Rippere (1977) suggests that cognitive factors need to be considered when analyzing the relationship between activities and mood. That is, mood can affect the enjoyability of an activity as well as the reverse.

## Cognitive Modality

The second series of intervention strategies to be reviewed here deals with the cognitive aspects of depression, that is, the depressed person's negative views of herself, present and future experiences, thoughts of deprivation, self-blame, low self-esteem, and general inadequacy (Beck 1967; Gambrill 1977; Lewinsohn et al. 1976).

Because of their socialization, women may be particularly vulnerable to episodes of negative ruminations and the resultant depressive reactions. For example, there is some evidence that at an early age females engage in more self-critical or self-blaming behavior than males (Bandura and Whalen 1966; Davis 1975; McMains and Leibert 1968; Vann 1974).

To assess the extent of problematic ruminations, the therapist can observe frequently emitted negative verbalizations within the counseling sessions. Such verbalizations may be clues that similar cognitions occur with equal frequency. Negative verbalizations within the sessions may take the form of dysphoric talk, guilt, criticism, complaints, and discussions of personal inadequacies (Lewinsohn et al. 1976). Another indicator that cognitive behaviors may be a central problem with the depressed client is that she reports that such thoughts are intrusive and interfere with other activities (Lewinsohn et al. 1976).

If the therapist suspects that negative thoughts are an important component in the client's depression, assessment can proceed to delineate the extent to which these behaviors are a problem. Overt verbalizations can be monitored by the therapist within the treatment sessions, perhaps utilizing the codes developed by Lewinsohn et al. (1969). The client could also be asked to monitor her own negative verbalizations in conversations by counting them on a golf counter and/or writing them down soon after they are emitted. Observational measures could be augmented by having significant others in the client's immediate environment track negative or depressive talk as well as positive or health-related talk. Getting others involved in the assessment phase may help them become involved in intervention, which may be important if these significant others are maintaining trouble talk by paying particular attention to it (Lewinsohn et al.

1976). In addition to monitoring the frequency of negative verbalizations inside and outside the counseling sessions, the therapist, client, and others can also note when such verbalization occurs and what happens afterwards (e.g., the circumstances and others' reactions).

Observation of covert self-talk or cognitions is, of course, limited solely to client self-monitoring, since no one else can know what is going on inside the client's head. The client can be asked to note when she has a negative rumination, the situation, how she felt, how long it lasted, and what she did about it.

Once assessment activities have been completed and the content and conditions of the client's depressive self-talk (both overt and covert) have been established, several intervention strategies can be utilized.

## CHANGING OVERT VERBAL BEHAVIOR

If the client is engaging in a high frequency of negative verbalizations within the counseling sessions, even during attempts to offer alternatives and engage in problem-solving activities, then changing the client's talk within the treatment milieu may be an important first step. After a supportive relationship has been developed, it may be important for the therapist to utilize differential attention to consistently ignore the client's complaints and other negative self-talk while carefully attending to positive or coping statements (Wilcoxon et al. 1976). These procedures, usually called "verbal conditioning" activities, are based on the social learning principles of reinforcement and extinction, and they have received many years of investigation and verification. For example, Kanfer and Phillips (1970), after an extensive review of the literature on verbal conditioning, state that there are many areas of verbal content that can be affected in the interview situation by simple reinforcing cues from the therapist, even when these reactions are not deliberate or systematic. They stress that the therapist needs to be aware of her or his potential "influencing power" with the client so that therapeutic outcomes are enhanced rather than thwarted. Given that therapist reactions can influence client verbal behavior, the therapist can attempt to affect these verbalizations by reacting differentially to them. These differential reactions need not be kept from the client; in fact, client awareness of and participation in all aspects of treatment are encouraged. For example, the therapist could give the client feedback on the amount of "trouble talk" that occurs in the sessions, and inform her that such talk is self-destructive and, thus, will be ignored or pointed out, and that positive or problem-solving comments will be suggested and encouraged. The therapist could also attempt to regulate the amount of negative verbalizations emitted in the sessions by letting the client trouble-talk for several minutes after a certain amount of problem-solving or coping talk has occurred (Robinson and Lewinsohn 1973).

The therapist may also choose to encourage significant others in the client's immediate environment to differentially attend to her verbalizations, with the client's awareness and permission. In addition, the client could be asked to control her own verbalizations at home by limiting depressive verbalizations to situations in which she is alone and in which a fixed time limit can be implemented (Shipley and Fazio 1973). If the client is deprived of opportunities to engage in high-frequency negative verbalizations, other verbal behaviors are likely to increase (Lewinsohn et al. 1976).


## CHANGING COVERT VERBAL BEHAVIOR

In addition to helping the client change what she says out loud, it is important to alter what she says to herself, since self-statements and mood have been shown to be related (Coleman 1975; Velten 1968). Several techniques to alter covert verbalizations will be discussed. These techniques include challenging the rationality of the statements, increasing positive counterparts, establishing more reasonable criteria for self-evaluation, and stopping negative ruminations. All of these techniques may be used either alone or in combination. Undoubtedly, the more strategies are utilized, the more likely it is that change will occur.

### Rational Restructuring
The need to identify irrational cognitions and reevaluate them was first stressed by Ellis (1962). Recent authors have reinterpreted Ellis' writings from a more empirical standpoint (Gambrill 1977; Goldfried

*et al.* 1974). Typically, the client is asked to identify specific thoughts that accompany unpleasant emotional reactions, in this case depression. She is also encouraged to note the situations that prompt the thoughts and the beliefs that underlie the thoughts, for example, "One should be thoroughly competent, adequate, and achieving in all possible respects, if one is to consider oneself worthwhile" (Ellis 1962:63).

Gambrill (1977:500) discusses the steps involved in implementing a rational restructuring procedure. Briefly, these steps, as they might involve depression, include the following:

1. The client identifies feelings of anxiety, discomfort, and depression.
2. She then examines her thoughts about the situations that are associated with the change in her mood. The client asks herself, "What am I saying to myself that is making me depressed?"
3. The client then examines these thoughts for their irrationality—"Have I made a hasty negative judgment? Do I have irrational expectations?"
4. She then attempts to think of more rational and positive thoughts to replace the troublesome ones.
5. Finally, the client again becomes involved in the situation or task that initially cued the thoughts and feelings.

Several outcome studies have shown the effectiveness of Ellis' approach, rational emotive therapy (RET), with problems other than depression (Rimm and Masters 1974), but only a single case study can be cited in which the approach was used with depression (Geis 1971). Certainly, more research needs to be done on the effectiveness of this approach with depression, although the concepts and procedures seem worthy of clinical application as long as their effectiveness is monitored throughout treatment.

*Increasing the Frequency of Positive Self-Statements*
The depressed client can also be trained to increase the frequency of her positive self-referent statements or self-praise and thereby affect her mood and self-evaluation in a positive direction (Wilcoxon *et al.* 1976). Homme's (1965) coverant control therapy has been frequently

utilized in retraining depressed individuals (Wilcoxon *et al.* 1976)
*Coverant* is a term combining the words *covert* and *operant*. The
term reflects the assumption that cognitive behaviors or thoughts
function under the same rules of learning as overt behaviors or
operants. Homme's procedure utilizes high-probability behaviors
(HPBs) to reinforce the frequency of low-probability behaviors (LPBs)
(Premack 1965). In clinical practice with depressed clients positive
self-statements (LPBs) are arranged so that they have to occur before
the person engages in the HPB. Most studies using the coverant control technique incorporate HPBs that are routine for the individual
and are likely to occur at least several times a day, for example,
smoking (Mahoney 1971; Todd 1972), urination (Johnson 1971),
drinking liquids, or talking on the phone. Basically, the procedure
requires that the client, with the aid of the therapist, develop a list of
positive self-statements that are specific and believable, which are
then recited before each occurrence of the HPB.

The outcome studies on coverant control therapy are generally of a
single-case nature. However, the cases reported indicate that the
procedures result in positive changes such as reports of less depression, higher frequency of spontaneous positive self-statements, improved mood and self-confidence, and reduction of negative
thoughts. These gains have been reported after as little as two weeks
(Johnson 1971) and six weeks (Mahoney 1971) of treatment. Although follow-up data are not often reported, Mahoney (1971) reported that improvements were maintained after four months.

### Establishing Reasonable Self-Reinforcement Criteria
Several studies have attempted to directly alter the standards depressed clients use to evaluate their performance (Fuchs and Rehm
1975; Jackson 1972). Jackson (1972) discusses a 22-year-old depressed
housewife who was extremely harsh with herself and utilized excessively
strict standards for self-reinforcement. The intervention steps involved helping her lower her standards and set goals that were readily
attainable; to specify the performance necessary to achieve each goal;
to evaluate the extent to which she had met each goal; and to reinforce herself for goal attainment. Intervention resulted in an increase
in self-reinforcement and a decrease in depression.

### Decreasing Negative Self-Statements

When attempts to increase positive cognitions, establish more reasonable standards for self-reinforcement, and develop a more rational belief system are insufficient to decrease obsessive self-denigrating ruminations, then more direct means may be necessary. A thought-stopping procedure has been shown to be effective in helping individuals control their own obsessional thoughts (Wolpe and Lazarus 1966). Rimm and Masters (1974) provide a detailed description of the procedure. In summary, it includes the following steps: First the client is asked to relax and imagine herself in the situation that typically cues the troublesome cognitions. As soon as the client has the scene in her mind and begins verbalizing the negative thoughts out loud, the therapist produces a loud noise (e.g., by dropping some books) and yells, "Stop!" The reaction of the client is typically a startle response. The image and the negative thoughts are usually blocked immediately. Next the client imagines the scene again but says the negative thoughts to herself. She signals when she is ruminating, for example, by raising her index finger. After the client has signaled that she is ruminating in the scene, the therapist again shouts, "Stop!" Additional steps involve training the client to say "Stop" to herself covertly until she is able to block her own negative statements, and thus learns that she can in fact control her own ruminations.

Although the somewhat limited outcome research on thought stopping is encouraging (Rimm and Masters 1974), several authors point out the importance of training the client to think of positive counterparts after the negative thoughts have been successfully removed (Gambrill 1977; Hays and Waddell 1976).

## Summary

Certainly, a great many approaches to the treatment of depression in women can be formulated. Since depression is multifaceted, involving how a person feels, what she does, and what she thinks, techniques for change must be diverse and must be tailored to the individual constellation of problems presented by each client. The development of individual treatment plans requires a thorough assessment of each client's presenting concerns, including acknowledgment of such variables as sex role training and stereotyping, as well as the client's age, ethnicity, and social class. Shortcuts in the assessment phase generally mean reductions in treatment success. In addition, it is the responsibility of each clinician to evaluate the effectiveness of his or her therapy. Only in this way can the body of knowledge on effective strategies for alleviating depression among women be refined and documented.

# Issues in Feminist Therapy: The Work of a Women's Study Group*

CAROL G. RADOV, BARBARA R. MASNICK, AND BARBARA B. HAUSER

In 1973 a small group of women came together to form the Women's Center in Brookline, Massachusetts. The center was a response to the desire for a place where women could gather to share interests, concerns, and friendships.

As the center became established, a number of professional women with a primary interest in mental health services for women formed the Counseling Group of the Women's Center in Brookline (now known as Brookline Feminist Therapy Study Group). These professionals in mental health, social work, psychology, and psychiatry have met regularly for over two years. From the start they defined themselves primarily as a study group to consider issues in feminist therapy. However, members of the group felt that as affiliates of the center they had an obligation to provide clinical services to the com-

* Reprinted from *Social Work* 22 (1977):507–509, by permission;© 1977 National Association of Social Workers, Inc.

munity. In the early months they attempted both to provide such services and to formulate a model of feminist therapy.

It shortly became obvious that the dual focus divided energies so that the clinical services were minimal and theoretical discussions were often interrupted by administrative necessity. Priorities were reexamined, and certain conflicts became evident. Members of the group were reluctant to eliminate the services, in part because—as mental health professionals—they were oriented to respond to felt needs. Furthermore, if the services were dropped, what clinical material could be used as a basis for the theoretical considerations?

The conflict was resolved by adapting the clinical services so that they would serve as research components for implementing and furthering theoretical discussion. This meant that comprehensive clinical services were no longer provided to women in the community but, instead, specific groups for women have been offered—groups modeled on the developing theory of new approaches to feminist therapy.

While resolving the study–service conflict, the Counseling Group was developing a new model for its own functioning, which makes use of members' varied experiences as women in groups. Members have brought together skills and expectations from the following types of groups:

Peer supervision groups, which are formed to share clinical issues and refine skills.

Seminars, which are intellectually focused but have a hierarchical structure with a leader or teacher.

Consciousness-raising groups, in which personal issues are in the forefront in a supportive atmosphere.

The Counseling Group encompasses features from all the foregoing groups, but it is unique in that women are coming together as equals to focus primarily on an intellectual task. The model for women's behavior in groups has not been thinking but sharing, which lies within the realm of affective interpersonal relationships (Chodorow 1974; Rosaldo 1974). Traditionally, women have functioned most comfortably in this area. Intellectualizing, on the other hand, has been seen as more aggressive and hence unfeminine.

A paper by Pancoast (1974) and other members of the Feminist Counseling Collective of Washington, D.C., influenced early discussion of the study group. The philosophy and experiences of this collective contributed to the development of a model for feminist groups. Later discussions among groups around the country—including Berkeley, California, and Amherst, Massachusetts—further clarified thinking.

In conceptualizing certain aspects of feminist therapy, study group members began by asking the questions, "Is there a need for feminist therapy?" "If so, how does it differ from traditional 'good' therapy for women?" "Or from 'bad' therapy?" This article addresses these questions and gives specific contrasting examples of "bad," "good," and feminist therapy for women.

Clients and practitioners alike have felt the need for psychotherapy based on feminist models. To ensure receptive listeners in their struggles for self-awareness and growth, more and more women are specifically seeking out women therapists. During the current period of enormous change in women's roles and expectations, it is especially necessary for women to have therapists who are sensitive to issues highlighted by the women's movement. As therapists, study group members have become increasingly aware of how past models of female development and therapeutic technique have served to perpetuate sexist positions for their clients. They have felt the desire to translate their own increasing awareness and sensitivity into something benefiting clients. Consciousness raising is a gradual process for both clients and therapists, and therapists find a special excitement in growing in feminist awareness along with clients.

## How Feminist Therapy Differs

The Counseling Group has isolated five components that differentiate feminist therapy from more traditional therapy.

1. *Feminist therapy assumes that, in principle, all roles are open to women.* This is the most basic axiom under which the study operates. It seems self-evident, but has it been accepted by society or even by the mental health professions? Although study group members recognize that barriers still exist for women, they do not assign career or

life style according to gender or assume that pathology is associated with any particular choice. The opening of roles may move women into traditionally male spheres (Hennig and Jardin 1977). A cocktail waitress who is a client of one member is currently involved in court action to force her employer to train her as a bartender, as is done with all male employees working there a similar length of time. Therapy is a way for this woman to air her frustrations and conflicts without ridicule, harassment, or gratuitous interpretations, and to get the needed support.

As roles open up, women may also seek alternatives to traditional roles. For example, several study group clients have chosen not to become parents and are dealing with reactions to this choice.

Women may need to create new roles, especially in the area of relationships. A woman in one group was contemplating a second marriage and was concerned about how this commitment would affect her ability to be her own person. She realized that her view of marriage implied a dependent, submissive role by the woman. During group discussion it became clear that she had the freedom and power to influence the nature of her role in the marital relationship.

Changing established roles involves an element of risk taking for women. One task of feminist therapists is to provide support in this risk-taking process. They validate the woman's struggle as it relates to her not only as an individual but as a woman—and as women themselves, the therapists share in the struggle.

2. *Feminist therapists bring a sociological perspective to work with women.* In doing so, they help women sort out which roots of their behavior have been determined by internalized societal norms and which behavior is in response to current societal pressures. They also look at how these intrapsychic conflicts relate to outside forces that discriminate against women.

A CASE OF DEPRESSION

A 50-year-old woman with grown children is brought to therapy because of constant complaining, weeping, and inability to do her housework.

*Bad therapy:* The client is given a series of shock treatments or antidepressant medication and is sent back to her family with the message that she is "menopausal" or "sick."

*Good therapy:* The client is encouraged to talk out her feelings and relieve depression by expressing and thus dissipating anger. She is also encouraged to get involved in activities.

*Feminist therapy:* The client is approached not only with the understanding of the dynamics of depression and family relationships but with the understanding that her anger is an appropriate reaction when society's package for women has not lived up to its promised fulfillment. Her anger is kept simmering on the back burner, where it can be channeled into effective action. Feminist therapists ask themselves and the client: "Does your behavior reflect your own and society's view of a woman's role? Do you want such a role?"

The sociological perspective cautions against rapid diagnoses of psychopathology. This is in contrast to study group experience with traditional therapy, in which behaviors considered indicative of psychopathology were all too often those that did not fit the feminine stereotype (Broverman *et al.* 1970; Broverman *et al.* 1972; Chesler 1972). Thus, in traditional therapy women's taking on the roles of wife and mother was not questioned, but career aspirations were. Women's aggressiveness was explored; passivity was not. Identification with the father was suspect and with the mother was not explored.

3. *Feminist therapy develops with women a new feminist ego ideal.* When it was recognized that traditional theories of identity tend to ignore female development and concentrate on male development, a new feminist ego ideal began to grow. Women's development has been seen as analogous to or the obverse of male development (Miller 1973; Miller 1976). It is especially important for feminist therapists to acknowledge and value the assets of women—for example, nurturing, sensitivity, emphasis on relationships—which have hitherto been devalued, and at the same time to help women incorporate some of the more aggressive and assertive qualities that they have hesitated to develop.

This developmental process is helping to create a new ego ideal for which there are few role models. It is more difficult than many other change processes because women are remolding themselves in conflict with broader societal norms, which they have also internalized.

A CASE OF PASSIVITY

A young woman who says she is shy, quiet, and passive comes to therapy because of a divorce, a new relationship, and some dissatisfaction with work. She has a history of conflict with her parents and is clearly depressed.

*Bad therapy:* The therapist takes an authoritarian position and supports passivity as appropriate feminine behavior.

*Good therapy:* The therapist concentrates on the client's relationships to the men in her life, focusing on early familial relationships, especially that with the father.

*Feminist therapy:* The therapist picks up on the client's strivings for assertiveness and self-definition, focusing on what the young woman wants, who she is as a person, and what her concerns about career advancement are—as well as her relationships with men. She is encouraged to utilize such tools as a women's support group and assertiveness training.

4. *Feminist therapists strive to restore a balance in the emphasis on work and relationships.* Freud has said that the work of therapy is to help the person "lieben und arbeiten," that is, to love and to work. In practice, it seems, the emphasis in therapy has been to help the man to work and the woman to love. Feminist therapists who feel strongly about their work and are committed to professional development believe that treatment should give as much attention to women's work accomplishments and growth as to their interpersonal accomplishments and growth.

A CUSTODY PROBLEM

A client is contemplating giving up custody of her children to their father temporarily while she concentrates on professional school.

*Bad therapy:* By the tone and focus of the discussion, the therapist gives the client the impression that she is an unfeeling mother and somehow unwomanly if she follows this plan.

*Good therapy:* The therapist explores with the client her feelings and conflicts about this plan, avoiding any judgment as to its morality.

*Feminist therapy:* The therapist works with the client on the same issues but assumes that the client's own development, in a career or otherwise, is as important as her role as a full-time mother. It is assumed that the loss of an opportunity to fulfill oneself outside the family is often felt as keenly as the loss of family relationships.

5. *Feminist therapists reassess the value of women's relationships with other women as opposed to relationships with men.* (These relationships are not always, although they may be, sexual ones.) Leaning heavily on its members' professional experience and training, the Counseling Group has been left with the impression that nonfeminist therapists often stress heterosexual relationships. Nonfeminist therapists often take for granted the real strengths and opportunities for enrichment in relationships with persons of the same sex or, perhaps, do not question a dearth of them. Success of treatment is often thought to occur when the woman "resolves" her heterosexual "hangups" and enters into a stable relationship with a man. Feminist therapists take the position that a relationship with a man can be enriching but is not total or even central to a woman's mental health.

A woman in one group spoke at length about her extreme need for men's approval, exemplified by her radically changing her appearance and her interests for each man. After she had clarified her need to please men but clearly not women, another group member remarked, "You're really dumping on women." This comment enabled the woman to look for the first time at her feelings about women, about herself, and about herself as a woman.

### AN ATTEMPTED SUICIDE

A 20-year-old dropout came for therapy after a suicide attempt. Discussion revealed that she was having sexual relations with several men and with women, too. She did not manifest conflict about her homosexual activities, but was concerned about other ways she related to people.

*Bad therapy:* The therapist assumes that the client's sexual involvement with women indicates psychopathology and is a major issue to be explored in order to further the young woman's heterosexual growth.

*Good therapy:* The therapist explores the meaning of the same-sex relationships as they affect the client's heterosexual relationships, with the focus being on strengthening the latter.

*Feminist therapy:* The therapist seeks to help the woman understand and strengthen all same-sex relationships and to learn about qualities in other women and in herself that she values.

## Conclusions

Experience both in the study group and with clients has convinced members of the Counseling Group that a feminist perspective adds an important dimension to their professional lives.

The group has been instrumental in developing theoretical formulations. Within it, a conscious focus on intellectual issues can be combined with the affective interpersonal support of other women.

Although it is too early to assess the impact of feminist therapy on their clients, study group members have a real sense of the impact of their work on themselves as women and therapists. They have increased their understanding of themselves as women and also their self-esteem. The process has stirred them emotionally and challenged them intellectually.

As therapists, members of the group are more actively questioning traditional theories about women and the usefulness of these theories to women. They continue to be aware that they work within a profession and seek to influence it to be more accountable to women. They believe that the profession as a whole must begin to increase its responsiveness to the concerns of women and the issues of feminist therapy.

# Therapeutic Aspects of Consciousness-Raising Groups*

ANNETTE M. BRODSKY

With the reawakening of the feminist movement in the 1960s, women began to investigate what Friedan (1963) identified as the

* Reprinted from Edna Rawlings and Dianne Carter, *Psychotherapy for Women* (Springfield, Ill.: Charles C Thomas, 1977), by permission of the publisher.

"problem that had no name," the boredom and disillusionment of middle-class housewives with prescribed roles that provide little opportunity for individual talents and needs beyond the roles of "Kinder, Küche, and Kirche" (children, kitchen, and church). Later in the decade Bird (1968) discovered what women in the working world suspected but dared not voice aloud. She found that when a woman leaves the stereotyped roles she fights a battle against both subtle and blatant discrimination. The battle is a lonely one for those who must overcome the initial fears of loss of femininity, social disapproval, and disdain from men and women alike who resent her daring to compete in the male domain.

## Consciousness-Raising Groups

Consciousness-raising (CR) groups grew out of the sense of restless constraint in housewives and the awareness noted by professional women of being different and alone. In an important contribution to the women's movement, CR groups helped to develop the awareness among women that other women shared the same self-doubts. The present analysis focuses on the psychological impact of consciousness raising and its relationship to psychotherapy.

The small-group structure of the women's movement is ideally suited to the exploration of personal identity issues. The technique of heightening self-awareness by comparing personal experiences is as basic to the continuance and solidarity of the movement as any other tactic. Women find themselves eliciting and freely giving support to other group members, who often are asserting themselves as individuals for the first time in their lives. They gain strength from members who confront others, and they learn to ask for their own individual rights to adopt new roles and express new behaviors.

Women in CR groups do not react in the traditional female interaction patterns commonly seen in all-female therapy groups. For example, ask a therapist about the interaction patterns of an all-female group of mothers, of patients, or of institutional groups. Typically, the women are described as catty, aggressive, competitive, and much tougher on each other for digressions than they are toward men.

In their traditional roles women have been isolated from each other and from events in the larger political and economic world beyond their narrowly confined psychological space. The CR group offers a sense of closeness or intimacy with other women as opposed to the media-produced sense of competition and alienation. The development of the concept of sisterhood arises as a shared understanding of the unique problems of being a woman in a man's world.

There is evidence that all-women groups led by women produce greater levels of empathy than mixed-sex groups (Aries 1974; Halas 1973; Meador et al. 1972). The crucial difference between all-women relationships and those with men as therapists or group members is, in my opinion, primarily that men must overcome too much of the male perspective (socialization) in order to be aware of the ramifications of the social issues concerning women. Also, many women do not trust their knowledge of the situation and are inhibited by men's presence. This is not a condemnation of either the men or the women, but reflects that present level of consciousness in both sexes.

By education and training, women have been encouraged to be conformists and to be passive with men. In CR groups women must act as individuals. They are encouraged to examine their uniqueness apart from their roles toward others, such as wife, mother, or secretary. In this atmosphere it appears easier for a woman to reveal taboo subjects and feelings, such as not liking to care for young children, wishing one had never married, feeling more intelligent than one's husband or boss, or being tired of boosting a man's self-esteem at the expense of one's own. A woman who finds that her feelings are not abnormal but are common experiences of other women may undergo an experience similar to religious conversion in the CR group (Newton and Walton 1971). Another important aspect of an all-women group is the exposure to appropriate female models. (This is discussed in greater detail later.)

The exclusion of men from CR groups is often misunderstood (Whitely 1973). Most men, while sincere, do not realize the subtleties of the women's situations. Indeed, some men are feminists, but they are very few. Furthermore, feminism cannot always be determined by verbal report to that effect. Women's suspicion toward men's being included in their groups is natural at this stage of the women's movement. In therapy assignments I have seen this suspiciousness forced into confrontation by a staff member insisting that a woman participate in a mixed group or see a male therapist. Conversely, I have seen suspicion reinforced by the isolation of women (women's group, women's center, woman therapist, woman physician, etc.) from men so that these women have not yet learned to interact comfortably with men in any setting. It seems to me that the women-to-women setting can eventually lead to the handling of a woman-to-man setting. In training therapists I do not believe in assigning "hysterical" women to male therapists to work out their intense transference problems. A better solution is for the client to work out her identity as a woman with a same-sex model, and later to deal with how she can effectively relate to men in sexual and nonsexual ways.

In contrast with therapy groups, CR groups start with the assumption that the environment, rather than intrapsychic dynamics, plays a major role in the difficulties of the individuals. The medical model of abnormal behavior based on biological, innate causes is not acceptable to these groups. They are struggling to redefine the very concepts that have assigned women to a helpless patient role, destined to behave in certain ways as victims of their biological nature (Chesler 1971; Weisstein 1969).

The individual changes that women experience in the context of CR groups are quite different from the changes that they may have experienced in previous therapy. Occasionally the CR group may serve as a recovery from a sexist experience in therapy (Brodsky 1975). Some CR groups actually are more therapeutic than therapy groups. The intensity of feelings produced, the feeling of group support, the role modeling, and the empathy developed are often at such a level that therapeutic effects for the members are better than effects from the individual therapy sessions in which they are concurrently enrolled (Smith 1975).

However, while CR groups may be therapeutic, they are not therapy groups. Therapy is deliberately designed to be a corrective experience; CR groups are not. Of course, women may have corrective experiences in CR groups. The primary goal of self-disclosure in CR is not primarily individual change but the identification of problems facing women in a society that needs social reform. Thus, if a woman enters a CR group with great distortions about reality and poor coping skills with people, but emerges with a more realistic view of the world and her potential impact on it, she may well be said to have had a therapeutic experience in the CR group. On the other hand, a woman in the same group who discovers the commonality of her own views and feels a sense of relief that she has always been "normal" is now able to grow to a fuller potential, uninhibited by previous reservations and low self-esteem. Her experience is less a therapeutic one than a growth or self-actualizing one.

## Appropriate Candidates for
## CR Groups

CR groups are topic oriented rather than person oriented. They are geared to women who want role fulfillment but do not have major mental stumbling blocks. Perhaps the greatest distinction between CR and therapy lies in the intensity of the need of the individual and the response that results from that experience; while techniques from CR groups can be adapted to therapy with women, women who need intensive therapy cannot be served exclusively through the CR experience. The rise of feminist therapy as a specialty area has partially resolved the referral concerns of CR groups (Brodsky 1975).

Some candidates may be deemed inappropriate for a CR group if they appear too defensive about or too vulnerable to the issues, or if their position is so deviant from the group's values that alienation and lack of support might be an issue. Antifeminists are not converted to feminism by CR groups. The feeling of discontent with the status quo of traditional female roles is a necessary beginning point for facing the issue of the women's movement.

## CR Group Dynamics

A sense of trust in other women and a closeness based on common problems that arise from external sources as well as internal self-doubts serves to bind CR groups into continuing, relatively stable units. The attrition rate for the groups my colleagues and I have encountered as well as for those studied by Newton and Walton (1971) appears to be lower than those for typical voluntary therapy groups or sensitivity groups. Group members appear to move to an intimacy stage rapidly and to maintain a strong loyalty. Dropouts occur early, often owing to a woman's conflict with a man who is threatened by changes in her dependency behavior.

The processes that occur in CR groups are akin to those that occur in assertion training, personal growth groups, achievement-oriented training, and self-development groups. In assertion training, the key technique involves role models provided by other group members. Women as models are more convincing than male authoritarian leaders, for whom the assertive role is a cultural expectation. Likewise, achievement needs are raised more readily in an all-woman group. In CR groups as in Synanon, Recovery, Inc., or Alcoholics Anonymous, experienced members give strength to the neophyte.

I have seen faculty women return to long-forgotten dissertations and take advanced courses, and housewives confront their husbands for more rights or domestic help. Others have gotten divorces from marriages that were security traps, and childless women have stood up for their right to refuse to have children simply because others think they should.

Even with the empathy and support of the group, the process of translating skills discussed into action is a great hurdle but, if accomplished, is the greatest value of the CR experience. Difficulty arises when women try to transfer their new behaviors outside the group. In a fashion parallel to the sensitivity group member who expects others outside the group to respond as positively as the group, CR group members often find that the outside world has not changed to correspond to the group's level of awareness. It is at this stage that women tend to become angry with their employers, lovers, and old friends for continuing to act in chauvinistic, stereotyped patterns. Because the women are behaving in new ways that society usually does not condone, these women may be ignored, misunderstood, patronizingly laughed at, or subject to retaliatory confrontation. In frustration, the women may overreact and provoke just the response they fear to get. For example, loud demands for better treatment on the job by a previously meek woman may well meet with a backlash response terminating her job. Frustration with the outside world often leads to a period of depression, either in the individual or in the group as a whole. Group members feel that while they can become aware of their situation and make individual changes, they cannot make much of an impact on the outside world. There is little outside reinforcement to continue their motivation. At this later stage dropouts occur: The faculty woman gets pregnant instead of completing her dissertation; the potential divorcee decides that security is more important after all; the frustrated housewife announces that "Joe thinks this group is making me unhappy and he wants me to quit"; or the graduate student cannot find time because she is staying up nights typing her boyfriend's thesis.

If these regressive tendencies are weathered by the group, the most crucial, and often the most effective, stage of the group experience develops. The women plan to actively alter their environments in a realistic manner to make them more compatible with the developing growth needs of the members. The direction of the group turns from personal, individual solutions (except for occasional booster-shot sessions as the need arises) to some sort of group action. Actions that groups may take vary according to talents, age, and needs. They might consist of organized protests, political lobbying, educational programs, or missionary goals of helping to organize other groups to expand the population of the enlightened. The CR group works to give a sense of social as well as personal worth to the members and, as a by-product, serves to help modify an environment insensitive to the needs of a growing population of restless women.

In a four-year follow-up of women in one CR group in an academic setting, further growth from the impact of the group can be seen even when the original benefit was doubtful. Thus, in reference to dropouts, it is interesting to discover what the women eventually resolved at a later period. The graduate student whose attendance was inconsistent because of conflict with her husband over how the group was affecting her completed her degree, readopted her maiden name, and now has a professional position. The woman who decided to get pregnant rather than to complete her long-delayed dissertation or to fight for her job (which was threatened because of her feminism) also made surprising changes. She divorced her husband, filed a suit against her employer for discrimination, completed her degree, and is now applying for a position commensurate with her abilities and aspirations. Another member of the group who did not raise personal concerns about her job is gaining status in that job and feels free of peer pressures on academic women to get pregnant. She is now raising a baby without sacrificing her career to her child.

The pressures on women's roles come from two directions: a pull to remain with traditional ties even when they are stultifying, and a pull to move onward, even when aspects of the traditional role seem desirable. The ideal CR group raises the issues, the anger, the assertiveness, and offers group support for action. But it does not insist on actions, demean choices made, or become disheartened when a member's consciousness is lower than expected. Growth continues after the group disbands. The parallels to therapy are obvious. No one finishes therapy by attaining their ultimate goals. Therapy initiates a process of growth that must continue after the regular sessions terminate. The impact of a good or bad therapist may affect an individual years later. Investigations into the negative impact of therapy on individuals, and in particular women, are being pursued today (Brodsky 1975).

## Transfer of CR Values and Techniques
## to Individual Therapy

An implication of the preceding discussion is that the CR groups of the women's movement are relevant for the treatment of identity problems of women in therapy. The following suggestions are possibilities for transferring the CR group dynamics to individual therapy. First, in working with women on identity issues therapists should be aware of the increasingly wide range of roles and personality traits for healthy, functioning women (Maccoby 1971). For example, assertion should not be interpreted as aggression because the behavior occurs in a female. Second, a good therapist should be aware of the reality of the female client's situation. Many factors are beyond the client's control. She cannot realistically expect to attain achievement comparable to a man's unless she has greater intellectual and/or motivational abilities. Discrimination does exist (Amundsen 1971; Astin 1969; Bernard 1971; Bird 1968; Epstein 1970). Because of this discrimination, encouragement through training in assertion and independence is of paramount importance, counteracting the many years of discouragement through subtle cultural mores. The therapist can serve as supporter and believer in the client's competence throughout the regressive, dropout stages, and in the face of individual frustrations the therapist can also recognize the need for some direct and meaningful activity related to improving societal situations.

Working with women's CR groups offers a number of insights to a therapist about the particular problems women face in trying to resolve the difficulties of living in a world that revolves around men's work. For example, those women who report patterns of intrusive male behavior often appear to be oversensitive to slights and minor brushoffs. CR group experiences help women to confirm the reality of such slights, rather than denying their existence or passing them off as projections. A man can overlook such incidents as exceptional and not understand them as a frequent experience of women who are not taken seriously or accepted as thinking individuals.

For a woman, the experience is the rule rather than the exception (unless she is an exceptional woman). Her sensitivity to such slights comes out of an awareness of the situation and a concomitant frustration in being unable to defend herself without appearing pompous, "uppity," or paranoid.

The accumulation of experiences of being interrupted in conversations and having opinions ignored can severely affect a woman's feelings of competence and self-worth. Her desire to be assertive or to make an impact on the environment is continually weakened by the lack of affirmation of herself by others.

There are therapists who maintain that women act insecure or inferior in order to get secondary gains from such postures (using feminine wiles); therefore, they consider the woman's verbalizations of a desire for independence or responsibility as not genuine. Therapists often do not understand that, without role models or encouragement from the environment, these women have no real choice but to accept what they have been indoctrinated to believe about the capabili-

ties of their sex. There are other major themes that some therapists
are apt to misjudge or overlook when dealing with women clients.
Unaware therapists still tend to consider marriage uncritically as a
solution for women's problems without realizing that, as with men,
divorce or no marriage may often present the best available alternative for the individual. When a woman proposes such a solution, the
therapist may become more concerned with her nontraditional life
style than with her personal reasons for wanting such a life style.

Some therapists, who have not been exposed to the issues that a
CR group might raise, automatically assume that a woman's career is
secondary to her mate's career. The conflict over "having it both
ways" by wanting a career and a family is then seen as the wife's burden, not the husband's also. New patterns of division in household
tasks and child care are no longer stigmas that should label individuals as deviant. Therapists have been guilty of producing iatrogenic
disorders in women who felt comfortable with what they were doing
until the therapist suggested that they were selfish and unreasonable,
or pointed out how no one expected them to accomplish so much
because they would be loved and accepted without this unrealistic
drive to compete.

Perhaps related to the foregoing is the frustration women have experienced with therapists who can empathize readily with a man who
is stifled by a clinging, nagging wife, but interpret the same complaint from a woman as her being cold and unfeeling for not responding affectionately to her insecure, demanding husband. The
crucial point in such misunderstandings is that many therapists have
a double standard for men and women in mental health and adjustment (Broverman 1970). Their attitudes restrict their capacity to
allow their clients a free expression of the various available roles.
Women, after all, have needs for self-esteem, independence, anger,
and aggression, just as men have needs for security, affection, and
the expression of fear and sorrow. While both need greater freedom
in sex role expression at present, men have more diverse models in
our society for the development of an adequate masculine role. For
the most part, women's models have been restricted to housewives or
women in the narrow traditional feminine occupations (Block 1973).

Perhaps the strongest message in the success of CR groups is that women are capable of using other women as models. The identification of women with role models of their own sex has been largely limited to the traditional homemaker roles or the feminine occupations, such as teaching and nursing. The acceptance of more varied roles and personality traits in women will help to integrate a larger portion of women into the "mentally healthy" categories.

Until more female role models are available, perhaps, as Chesler (1971) suggests, only women should be therapists for other women. On the other hand, if it were necessary for therapists to have had the same experiences as their clients to help them, we would be very restricted. In the long run, whatever the situation or therapeutic format (individual, all-women, or mixed-sex group), it is crucial that the process not be sexist. No matter what the sex of the therapist, the values of the therapist about the role of women in society must be made explicit to the client so that she can make a choice about the goals of therapy before a therapeutic relationship is established.

Because male clinicians know women in their personal lives, they frequently assume that they know enough about women's conflicts to treat them. However, casual attention and personal relationships do not provide sufficient clinical data on which to base treatment. Many clinicians assume that women do not face different social conditions than men and, therefore, do not require *any* special treatment. Obviously, women do face a different world than men do; those different circumstances must be taken into consideration by the therapist.

The Freudians did assume that women were a special category and required special attention. However, they also assumed that women could not be trusted to report feelings honestly. Like children and psychotics, women needed analysts to interpret their actions accurately. Today, CR groups are demonstrating not only that women are capable of understanding their own motivations but that Freudian theories of female development served to discourage women from seeking legitimate goals.

Every clinician must be aware that the training she or he has received, and/or is receiving, does not sufficiently prepare her or him to treat women with role conflicts. *Any* therapist who has not kept abreast of current theories and issues relating to women is treating them from a position of ignorance and should disqualify himself or herself from treating women clients.

Studying CR groups is one way to learn alternatives to sexism in therapy. Workshops about women, supervision by feminists, and consultation with women colleagues are some other initial steps therapists can take to learn to eliminate their sexism. Not all therapists can or want to be "feminist therapists," but *all* should aspire to be nonsexist.

## Concluding Remarks

The thesis of this chapter is twofold. First, depression represents a mental health incapacity whose considerable prevalence among women and whose etiology, as seen from a cognitive–behavioral point of view, suggests a close relationship between women's social conditioning and the occurrence of the problem. The discussions have urged further study of that connection and have presented specific interventions based on that relationship.

Second, feminist therapists believe that women's mental health can be enhanced by assuming that the issues are political and social rather than intrapsychic. The hierarchy of the traditional therapeutic dyad is replaced by the support of other women, both as individuals and in groups. Women together investigate the social basis of their incapacities.

# 2. Women and Health Care

NAOMI GOTTLIEB

IN RECENT years many women have been increasingly vocal in their disatisfaction with health care delivery and have objected to the sexist bias evident in that care. That dissatisfaction has focused on the effect on women's health care of the physician's exclusive domain and autonomy, combined with a moral and evaluative stance that reflects society's stereotyped view of women. This chapter discusses the relationships between these concerns about the medical profession and the delivery of health care services to women, particularly services for the women's reproductive system.

As background to the specific focus of this chapter, a general demographic view is presented first—the nationwide picture of illness as experienced by women, the use women make of medical services, data on mortality among women, and how each of these compares with the experience of men. The discussion that follows describes factors of exclusivity, autonomy, and evaluative judgments that are evident in the medical profession. The circumstances that are distinctive for women—health care for the woman's reproductive system—are then presented both as an illustration of how such factors are played out in health care delivery and as background to the alternative services to be described.

In contrast to the other chapters of this book, this chapter does not describe specific tasks to be performed by social workers. However, the importance of both the contextual background of women's health care and the discussions of the new services can alert the many social workers employed in health settings to the need to rethink their roles in order to be more responsive to women. The alternative services describe settings in which a revised social work orientation would be effective, and also suggest revisions in the provision of health care for women in traditional settings.

## Women's General Health

Statistical accounts of morbidity and mortality rates among men and women usually reflect the apparent paradox between the greater number of illnesses recorded for women and their lower death rates. Erhardt and Berlin (1974:68) note that "the higher incidence rates of acute illness among women, like their prevalence rates of chronic conditions, are in contrast with their low mortality from the same conditions." Or, even more succinctly (Verbrugge 1976:388), "How can the sicker sex have greater longevity?" Before some suggested answers to this question are discussed, the health experience of women as compared with men will be documented: the extent of acute and chronic illness, the use of health care facilities, and mortality cases.

Various experts consistently indicate that women have both more acute and more chronic illnesses than men (Verbrugge 1976; Thomlinson 1965; Anderson et al. 1976). Verbrugge (1976) reports on a fifteen-year survey—1957 to 1972—of the morbidity experience of men and women:

Females experience more acute conditions than males do, their rate being 9–20 percent greater than males. . . . With two minor exceptions, females have higher rates for infective and parasitic diseases, respiratory conditions, digestive system conditions, and the residual category, "other acute conditions." . . . Removing rates for deliveries and disorders of pregnancy and the puerperum . . . the sex differential for the category narrows. But female rates are still 41–70 percent above male rates. . . . Females are about 6 times more likely than males to have genital urinary disorders and twice as likely to have headaches. . . . Their rates for musculoskeletal disorders (e.g., bursitis, bunions, headaches) and upper gastrointestinal problems often exceed males by 40–50 percent. (pp. 398–392)

The data for chronic conditions repeat the experience of acute conditions, with some sex differences as to the extent to which individuals are limited in their activities (Cole 1974:103). Though adult females are more likely to have a chronic condition than adult males, with the exception of the years under 17, "males, not females, are more likely to be limited in activity" (Cole 1974:75).

Verbrugge (1976) offers an explanation:

If we accept the data as diagnostic, we conclude that females are more vulnerable physically to chronic conditions, but have less severe ones. But activity limitation data cannot be taken to reflect physical severity of chronic conditions. First, roles can be altered to accommodate a chronic condition, thereby reducing or eliminating activity limitation. Females may be able to make this accommodation more readily. Secondly, if typical male roles at a given age require more physical effort than typical female roles, females can have equally severe conditions (or even more severe ones) but be less limited by them. (p. 395)

## Women's Use of Health Care

There is also consistency in the overrepresentation of women among users of health services. "Females are more likely to have a regular source of care, have a recent examination, seek a physician in response to symptoms of illness, and go to a physician for conditions classified as requiring a physician's care," and prenatal visits account for only a portion of the difference (Anderson *et al.* 1976:15, 32). When they get to the physician's offices (and their visits average 25 percent more than men's), doctors prescribe drugs for them 50 percent more than for men (Boston Women's Collective 1976:337). Except for their early (before 16) and later (after 65) years, women are also hospitalized more frequently. Even when deliveries are excluded from the reporting, Cole reports that during the childbearing years (ages 15 through 44) "Rates for females during this middle period are generally about 18 percent higher than those for men" (1974:89).

Given the large pockets of underserved rural and urban areas, there are marked differences in use of health care between white and nonwhite groups and between high- and low-income populations. Even with those variations in mind, women are still found to use health facilities more than men.

## Mortality in Women and Men

Women in the United States live, on the average, seven years longer than men. In 1968 the life expectancy for white females was 74.9 years and for white males 67.5 years (Spiegelman and Erhardt 1974:12). There are two important additions to these data. These life expectancies are lower than those of at least twelve other countries, and within the United States life expectancies are very different for the nonwhite populations. Though women in these nonwhite groups live an average of seven years longer than men, their life expectancies are seven years less than those of the white populations—for non-white males, life expectancy is 60.1 years; for nonwhite women, 67.5 years (p. 12).

Though women live longer than men, the leading causes of death are the same for both groups—in rank order, they are heart disease, cancer, strokes, accidents, pneumonia and influenza, and diabetes, the first three accounting for two-thirds of all deaths. Among women who succumb to cancer, breast cancer is the most frequent type of malignancy, and in the years between 37 and 55 breast cancer becomes the leading cause of death in women (Boston Women's Collective 1976:99). In all age groups, however, women have lower mortality rates than men, and this is reflected in the longevity data.

Still there is the paradox: "How can the sicker sex have greater longevity?" Higher female mortality rates in some less developed areas (Thomlinson 1965) contradict the notion of a biologically superior female sex. Suggested explanations focus on social–psychological variables. The first of these pertains to the collection of the data in which the paradox is based. Reporting of morbidity may be flawed because much of the data is in the form of self-reports and there can be differences in how individuals perceive and define illness. Also, there are implications in the preponderance of women among respondents in surveys. For example, the federally sponsored Health Interview Survey for the years 1957–1972 was conducted primarily with women at home, and Verbrugge notes (1976:398) two possible biases in the data: Women may show greater willingness to report their own physical ailments, and women may underreport the conditions of the absent men.

In addition, social expectations can affect the illness behavior of the sexes differently. Men have been socialized to ignore symptoms and not to admit weaknesses (Verbrugge 1976:389; Phillips and Segal 1969). Women "may be more sensitive to body discomforts and/or more willing to report their symptoms to others" (Verbrugge 1976:398). It is also suggested that women have fewer role obligations and may feel they have both time and social approval to slow down when sick (Verbrugge 1976; Nathanson 1975). A possible confirmation of this, cited by Rivkin (1972), is that working women (those with increased roles) report fewer sicknesses than unemployed women. There is also some contrasting speculation that the dual roles that women assume when they are employed—both work and home responsibilities—lead to greater vulnerability to illness (Verbrugge 1976:400). Writers generally acknowledge that these social variables are still to be tested (Cole 1974; Thomlinson 1965; Verbrugge 1976), but the systematic variations in morbidity reports, plus the theories about illness behavior (Mechanic 1962, 1966; Parsons 1951), suggest their importance.

As for mortality, other factors with social bases may play a part. Men's work roles plus their social behavior lead to greater risk of injury or illness resulting in death. Men smoke, drink, and drive more than women and are exposed to more risks in their jobs, in sports, and in some home-related activities (Verbrugge 1976:399). It may also be that women's socialization, which leads to early acknowledgment and medical attention for physical symptoms, results in early attention to illness, the care of conditions before they become serious, and therefore, greater longevity (Thomlinson 1965:126; Spiegelman and Erhardt 1974:11). As women's social roles change, it is possible that their susceptibility to illness and injury may mirror that of men.

As this review suggests, at present women are overrepresented in patient populations. Because of this factor and because they usually assume a more passive role in interpersonal relationships, women may be particularly affected by those characteristics of the medical profession which go beyond technical knowledge.

## Autonomy, Values, and the Exclusive
## Domain of the Physician

Some of the general observations about the effects of the exclusive domain and evaluative stances of physicians will be noted here and then illustrated by the example of physician attention to the health care needs of women. These illustrations make the point that physician autonomy has resulted in ineffective medical practice for women and that challenging the exclusive domain of the physician is warranted. This seems especially true in medical care for the woman's reproductive system.

Many examples illustrate that physicians define their domain broadly and that personal values affect medical decisions. Studies indicate that physicians prefer middle-class to lower-class patients and that their professional behavior varies with the class of the patient (Miller 1973; Roth 1962). It has been found that "physicians' attitudes about the legitimacy of prescribed psychoactive drug usage . . . were more strongly related to the social values and moral standards of the physicians than to their scientific backgrounds" (Prather and Fidell 1975:23). Cancer specialists make judgments about whether individual patients will know the full extent of their condition. Physicians will interpret physical symptoms as psychogenic in origin and refer or treat patients accordingly. Doctors will vary their treatment recommendations depending on the home circumstances of the patient. One might argue that some of these discretionary judgments show that doctors individualize patients (though systematic variation depending on class would not be such an indication), but whatever the rationalization, it is clear that physicians make a range of decisions about patients that vary not with the objective data about patients' conditions but with other considerations.

Along with other writers (Zola 1972; Miller 1973), Freidson (1970) has commented on the implications of the moral activities of the medical profession. He makes the clear distinction between medical decisions based on scientific knowledge and moral decisions based on personal values. He questions domains of experts accordingly.

We can justify removing decisions from the hands of laymen and placing them in the hands of experts only when experts have the special knowledge by which to make corrective decisions in the lay interest. . . . When decisions are at bottom moral or evaluative, rather than substantive, laymen have as much if not more to contribute to them than have experts. (p. 338)

Physicians, of course, enjoy professional autonomy, that is, society's acknowledgment that they have particular skill and a body of knowledge that others do not have (Greenwood 1957:46), but Freidson emphasizes the flaw in that autonomy. The flaw in this autonomous stance is "a self-deceiving view of the objectivity and reliability of its knowledge and of the virtue of its members" and "a rigid self-perpetuating mystique about its knowledge, jurisdiction, practice, prerogatives and its mission" (pp. 368, 369, 374). Thus, physicians rationalize their expertise in areas in which they are not experts, and are protected from having others point this out through the status they hold in society and the intraprofessional system of protecting their own members against challenge.

In its fairly brief history as an accepted profession, medicine has become a major and thoroughly entrenched institution. As their position has solidified, physicians have limited their own numbers (Bazell 1971), assumed central responsibility for treatment to themselves, and severely constrained the domains of others in the health care system (Boston Women's Collective 1976:340). They have also created an aura surrounding their own expertise that has been termed "an imperialism of knowledge" (Boston Women's Collective 1976:340), and many of their expert judgments are kept free from public scrutiny, an effective mechanism for precluding question and challenge (Zola 1972:501).

It is important to note that consumers of health care have, by and large, assumed a stance that is complementary to the physician's status. Physicians have assumed the role of expert director of health care delivery, and their patients have tended to assume a passive role in the face of this expertise. The result—an acquiescent patient and an authoritarian doctor—is the norm. Patients also believe it appropriate that the role of patient include, at the least, reluctant reliance on and, more usual, blind faith in the physician (Zola 1972:501; Wax 1962). We have accepted the physicians' definitions of both themselves and their patients, particularly with limited patient rights to question and participate.

Thus, there has developed a health care situation in which "supposedly morally neutral, objective experts" are making varied and encompassing judgments about patient care, "not in the name of virtue or legitimacy, but in the name of health" (Zola 1972:487). Physicians have also extended their domains of influence—Zola (1972:492) calls this the "medicalizing of society"—by expanding what they believe is relevant to good medical practice and maintaining absolute control over technical procedures. The public in general has accepted these terms.

## Women's Special Needs and the Health Care System

Medical care for the woman's reproductive system is seen as a distinctive issue and a crucial one for women. It will be argued that much of the medical care in this area can be seen as moral and evaluative, and to that extent, not necessarily appropriate for, if not distorted by, the medical domain. This theme is illustrated in the history of medical practice with reference to women, in the medical training currently offered for treatment of women's obstetrical and gynecological needs, and in the psychological interpretation of women's medical needs.

In the late nineteenth and early twentieth centuries, and parallel with the professionalization of medicine in the United States, there occurred the "cult of female hypochondria" (Ehrenreich and English 1973:17)—an emphasis on women (i.e., middle- and upper-class women primarily) as frail and sickly, an interpretation of both pregnancy and menopause as illnesses, and a pervasion of illness in upper-class female culture. There were, in fact, some real health hazards. Childbearing was dangerous—"in 1915 (the first year for which national figures were available) 61 women died for every 10,000 live babies born, compared to 2 per 10,000 today (1973) and the maternal mortality rates were doubtless higher in the 19th century" (p. 19). Tuberculosis was experienced in epidemic proportions, especially among younger women and in all classes. As a consequence of slum life, hazardous working conditions, inadequate public health measures, and inaccessible health care, low-income women suffered an entire set of other health dangers not known to the upper classes. However, the emphasis of a medical profession reaching for legitimacy was on the middle and upper classes, and stress was placed on the woman, particularly her supposed frailty. Ehrenreich and English contend that the cultivation of that frailty served the developing medical profession in two ways: "It helped them to disqualify women as healers and, of course, it made women highly qualified as patients. . . . In the late 19th century there was, by present standards, an excess of doctors in the cities. Competition was fierce, and there was a strong motivation to over-treat ill women and discover illnesses among well women" (p. 23). Women were seen as having limited energy; passivity was, in fact, a frequent prescription for illness; and women were viewed as being "governed by ovaries and uteruses" (p. 31). The portrait of the hysterical, bedridden upper-class woman surrounded by doting physicians and a perplexed husband may be a limited case in terms of numbers, but the pervasive notion of the weakness of the female affected a far greater circle. That historical view has changed only in kind—with the tendency toward psychological explanations of women's physical conditions. "The medical view of women has not really shifted from 'sick' to 'well'; it has shifted from 'physically sick' to 'mentally ill' " (p. 79).

Myths about the female character continue to be created and continue to affect women's health care. Doctors in general, and obstetricians and gynecologists in particular, develop a perspective on their women patients that derives first from their socialization as men (90 percent of all physicians are men, as are 96 percent of gynecologists and obstetricians) (AMA 1977:61, 371) and is further reinforced by their medical training. The man is viewed as inherently assertive, dominant, independent, the woman as inherently passive, docile, dependent, and nurturing. Medical training further socializes the male doctor into an authoritarian and elitist stance. An education for obstetrical–gynecological practice adds a further level of distortion about women's "inherent nature," especially concerning her sexual needs. A set of statements excerpted from recent obstetrical and gynecological textbooks reflects the official stance to which cohorts of women's physicians have been educated (Boston Women's Collective 1976; Scully and Bart 1973).

The traits that compose the core of the female personality are feminine narcissism, masochism and passivity. (Willson *et al*. 1971:43–44)

An important feature of sex desire in the man is the urge to dominate the woman and subjugate her to his will; in the woman, acquiescence to the masterful takes a high place. (Jeffcoate 1967:726)

It is good advice to recommend to the woman the advantage of *innocent simulation* of sex responsiveness and as a matter of fact many women in their desire to please their husbands learn the advantage of such innocent deception. (Novak and Novak 1952:572, italics added)

The findings of first Kinsey and later Masters and Johnson have had a mixed impact on medical textbooks. Following the Kinsey Report's challenge to the myth of the vaginal orgasm, a 1956 textbook reported that "investigators of sexual behavior distinguished between clitoral and vaginal orgasm, the first playing a dominant role in childhood sexuality and in masturbation and the latter in the normal mature and sexually active woman" (Rubin and Novak 1956:77). Scully and Bart (1973) report on textbooks published in more recent years (1963–1972) as follows:

Two-thirds (eight) of the books of that decade failed to discuss the issue of the clitoral versus vaginal orgasm. Eight continued to state, contrary to Masters and Johnson's findings, that the male sex drive was stronger and half (six) still maintained that procreation was the major function of sex for the female. Two said that most women were "frigid" and another stated that one-third was sexually unresponsive. Two repeated that the vaginal orgasm was the only mature response. (p. 286)

The importance of these views, promulgated as part of the basis of medical practice, is not only that they are used for inept and incorrect sexual counseling by gynecologists, though that is serious enough. They are significant also because they inform a set of psychological explanations for physical disorders of the reproductive system—explanations that are also inept and incorrect. Freidson (1970) suggests that medical practitioners' definitions of illnesses result in their receiving only limited and distorted knowledge about those illnesses from their patients. "In such cases, the practitioner is less informed and less qualified to evaluate the 'illness' than those who are able . . . to study the relevant behavior and responses that actually take place" (p. 273). Even as research provides new information on that "relevant behavior and response," several forces—including the general tendency of physicians to use firsthand individual experience rather than the shared knowledge of science (p. 347), but also the strength of socialization processes—hinder a revision of the medical profession's perspective on women.

Psychological explanations for women's gynecological and obstetrical difficulties illustrate the need for such a revised perspective. Those explanations, by and large, define women by their reproductive functions, expect that they will be passive in relation to men, and identify etiology of problems as difficulty in conforming to either or both of these norms. A few examples:

[Benedek on the basic nature of women] A woman has to have a personality which permits her to be passive, to be loved and cared for, so that she may give in to her physiological needs with pleasure, without protest and thus may enjoy pregnancy and motherhood. (T. Benedek, cited in Osofsky and Seidenberg 1970:612)

[Deutsch on the menopause] Woman has ended her existence as bearer of a future life and has reached her natural end—her partial death—as servant of the species. She is now engaged in an active struggle against her decline. (Deutsch, cited in Osofsky and Seidenberg 1970:611–612)

Lennane and Lennane (1973), in a review of four common problems related to women's reproductive functions—dysmenorrhea, nausea of pregnancy, pain in labor, and infantile behavioral disturbances—cite evidence that clearly implicates organic etiology, yet most medical practice attributes these problems to psychogenic causes and treats accordingly. Research such as this constitutes just the beginning of needed scientific inquiry into women's disorders. Such study has been hampered by a social–psychological set viewing women as primarily bearers or rearers of children, and considering only psychological causes when something goes wrong in that process. Thus, Bardwick's problem formulation (1972:259) for the study of contraception is stated as follows: "Physicians' impressions that an easy tolerance of the pill or severe discomfort and rejection were essentially psychological phenomena seemed a logical hypothesis." Inquiry has also been impeded by the tendency to apply to all women theories based on clinical cases, as has been done in the area of menopause (Bart and Grossman 1976:6), and to employ a sex-typed stance toward the linkages of biology and psychology. Osofsky and Seidenberg (1970:613), writing about menopausal depression, comment on the latter:

Whereas it is clearly recognized that male psychology must be differentiated from male biology, with awareness of the effects of one upon the other, no such differentiation has been allowed for females. Males are not governed by biological maturation processes related to aging. They can be abstract, external and worldly, and unconcerned with jobs, and events of the day. For whatever reasons, little attention has been given to the obviously similar dichotomy in the psychology and biology of women. Emotions and cognitions both have been viewed as being a part of, and controlled by, biology. Almost all research has proceeded from this obviously muddled hypothesis.

In summary, as women utilize the health care system their experience is affected by a set of pervasive social variables. The physicians who treat them act on other than medical facts and scientific evidence and are strongly affected by socialization factors defining women and men in certain sex-typed ways. This is especially evident in the treatment of disorders of the women's reproductive systems, where physicians show a propensity to interpret and treat problems within a traditional and psychological framework. Women themselves define ailments and incapacity differently from men and use medical facilities far more than men. In addition, as consumers of health care they are aware that most of the leadership positions in health care delivery are held by men, who for the most part treat both women patients and women subordinates in stereotyped ways. And in that milieu women are particularly handicapped in developing a more assertive stance in their use of medical care. Because the male doctor/female patient relationship is an exaggerated form of the sex-typed passive/dominant relationship between men and women generally, the distorted views of women's medical problems held by physicians, especially ob–gyn specialists, are rarely questioned. Women's passivity in physicians' offices has been identified as a major health problem (Boston Women's Collective 1976:98).

Examples from obstetrical and gynecological practice illustrate how these social factors in combination are manifested specifically in medical treatment of women's reproductive systems. For one, the use of estrogens for a variety of purposes, some nonmedical, continues unabated despite evidence of their carcinogenic properties (Weaver 1976).

Between 1962–1973, dollar sales of estrogen quadrupled in the United States in spite of the fact that the incidence of cancer of estrogen-dependent organs was observed to be rising in association with estrogen use. . . . Unlike many drugs, the majority of estrogen prescriptions are written for healthy women for non-medical purposes. Ten million U.S. women take the oral contraceptive, 8 million prescriptions annually are written to meno-pausal women for uses classified as "probably effective" by the F.D.A. and about 40 million women have been given the suspect DES to help their breast milk dry up, although the process would occur without the aid of the drug. . . . Historically, many of the decisions about how hormones should be used were based in value-ladened assessments on the part of one class (male physicians) about the normality of another. Today, estrogens are still used to alter female behavior, both physical and psychological (Weiss 1976:3).

Women are placed in this vulnerable position concerning estrogen partly because of the assumption, as in the case of the pill, that the burden of contraception is theirs. "They are taught that women are responsible for fertility or conception: they are responsible for any or all consequences of sexual relations" (Weaver 1976:9). The compara-tively little research attention paid to contraceptives for men as con-trasted to women is further evidence of this. Women are also vulner-able when estrogens are regularly prescribed for menopausal symptoms. Research on menopause has clearly been inadequate, and understanding of women's menopausal experience has for the most part been based on studies of clinical samples. A more general survey has found that comparatively few women suffer severe symptoms (Boston Women's Collective 1976:335). Bart and Grossman (1976) suggest that "the failure of medical researchers fully to investigate the side-effects of estrogen therapy as well as possible alternatives to it may very well stem from its apparent effectiveness in reducing the symptoms (and therefore the complaints)" (p.4). The attitude of the

physician toward the menopausal woman, who is popularly stereotyped as tired, irritable, and irrationally depressed, may very well be
reflected in the advertisement in the medical journal picturing "a
harassed, middle-aged man standing by a drab and tired looking
woman. The drug advertised is 'for the menopausal symptoms that
bother him most.'" (Boston Women's Collective 1976:327). Not
only may physicians be seeing only the minority of menopausal
women with serious symptoms, but there are indications that the
causes of the difficulties are neither in the inability of women to accept "mortification of menopause," as postulated in the psychoanalytic literature (Osofsky and Seidenberg 1970:614), nor in inevitable
hormonal dysfunction. Studies indicate that women who have skills
that enlarge their options in life have fewer menopausal difficulties
(p. 614). In contrast, women who have a singular tie to mothering
and suffer the loss of role associated with the end of child rearing are
more vulnerable to menopausal stress (Bart and Grossman 1976).
Present medical treatment of the menopause, which includes heavy
emphasis on symptom-associated use of problematic estrogens, does
not take into account that the problem may be in limited social roles
and in the inability to see the woman as appropriately in conflict
about those limits and not suffering only from hormonal imbalances
(Osofsky and Seidenberg 1970:614).

Restricted perspectives based on inadequate research also obtain in
treatments for difficulties of infertility and pregnancy. In each, stress
is placed on the psychological barriers to the woman's fully accepting
her maternal role. For example, infertility is often assumed to be the
psychological problem of the woman even before complete physical
testing has been accomplished (Decker 1972). Nausea in pregnancy is
also held to be partially or completely psychogenic, although "the
type of nausea and its usual duration are exactly mimicked by estrogen therapy and such nausea is a recognized side effect of es-
trogen-containing oral contraceptives. Estrogen has been shown to be
excreted in large amounts during pregnancy (Lennane and Lennane
1973:289). Lennane and Lannane comment on the illogic of classify-
ing the nearly 88 percent of women who experience nausea in pregnancy as neurotic. They also note that if one assumes that nausea in
pregnancy reflects conflict about being pregnant, similar nausea from

the use of contraceptives could hardly be explained by women's being "resentful, ambivalent or inadequate because they are not pregnant." These authors similarly question the psychological explanation for dysmenorrhea and infantile colic (pp. 288–291). There may also be other than medical factors operating in the surgical termination of childbearing capabilities, since several reports assert that from one-fifth to one-third of the hysterectomies performed are unnecessary (Frankfort 1972; Lester 1973:18).

Clearly, abortion is a far more complicated matter than the obstetrical and gynecological conditions already discussed. Unlike some of the others, it has political and religious implications, though interestingly, they have only a recent history. It was in the nineteenth century that legal sanctions against abortions were first promulagated, and a number of sociopolitical reasons have been advanced for the designation of abortion as a "crime" at that time.

The first [reason] is quite legitimate: abortion was a dangerous operation—methods crude, antiseptic scarce, the mortality rate high. It was in part the mid-19th century wave of humanitarianism that brought in abortion laws to protect women. Secondly, it was during this time that medical care for women passed out of the hands of midwives, who had almost certainly performed abortions as part of their services, into the realm of male doctors, who did not necessarily respect the woman's right to end a pregnancy. Thirdly, new understanding of the biology of conception made it clear that the fetus is alive before its movements can be felt, so an abortion before quickening became for some a more serious matter. Fourth, just at a time when women's increased understanding of conception was helping them to avoid pregnancy, certain governments and religious groups desired continued population growth to fill growing industries and new farmable territories. Abortion saw to it that women took their place alongside the other machines of the developing economy. Last and perhaps most insidious, a highly moralistic group obsessed with banning "sex for pleasure" struck up a campaign against both abortion and birth control. Sex was for marriage and marriage was for making babies. Sex outside of marriage was immoral; pleasurable sex inside marriage was somewhat immoral; and unwanted pregnancy was the punishment for such indulgences. (Boston Women's Collective 1976:217)

Abortion remains a volatile political issue. Recently, federal funding for abortion was the subject of a major debate in Congress, and citizens' groups have proposed an antiabortion amendment to the Constitution.

Though abortion had and still has ramifications beyond the doctor's office, physicians have all along been centrally involved in the issue—some as participants in the lucrative abortion industry (Frankfort 1972) and many more as both proponents (somewhat) and opponents (mainly) of abortion on demand. Physicians still have much to say about the treatment of unwanted pregnancies. This becomes a clear example of the earlier-discussed influence of moral and evaluative attitudes in the delivery of health care. Doctors have incorporated and reflect social attitudes about the women's responsibility for the consequences of her sexuality, even though society's double standard on sex constrains women from feeling comfortable about having a free and equal sexual life and, concomitantly, hinders her from purposefully planning effective use of contraception (p. 39). Physicians have also been highly protective of the woman's childbearing capacity. As illustration, the stance of the American College of Obstetrics and Gynecology is that a woman may have a sterilization procedure if at a certain age she has had a specified number of children (for example, 5 by age 25). "By contrast, the requirements for voluntary sterilization of a man are that he be 21 years old" (p. 50).

Physicians, lawmakers, and religious leaders are, in the main, men and will have limited ability to understand abortion from the woman's perspective. They may have difficulty accepting very different and female-oriented ways of posing the question of abortion, for example, one by Shainess (1970):

After the act of procreation [man] is free to continue his life course. If he becomes diseased as a result of coitus, or if he breaks an arm in taking a walk, we ask that he be treated to restore his former state as closely as possible. Nor would we assert that his venereal disease or his broken arm is best for him. But with woman, we insist that she will be damaged physically and psychologically if *her* former state is restored, if her body integrity is restored. I say that if a pregnancy is regarded as an unfelicitous happenstance and is aborted, the abortion restores the former state of integrity, and there is no innate connected sense of damage or guilt, except as the collective social superego, the prevailing attitude fosters this and confuses the woman. (p. 211, italics in original)

Another example, by Hardin (1968):

The question "How can we justify an abortion?" plainly leads to great difficulties. It is operationally unmanageable; it leads to inconsistencies in practice and inequities by any moral standard. All these can be completely avoided if we ask the right question, namely: "How can we justify compulsory pregnancy?"

By casting the problem in this form, we call attention to its relationship to the slavery issue. Somewhat more than a century ago, men in the Western world asked the question: "How can we justify compulsory servitude?" and came up with the answer, "By no means whatsoever." Is the answer any different to the related question: "How can we justify compulsory pregnancy?" Certainly pregnancy is a form of servitude: if continued to term it results in parenthood, which is also a kind of servitude, to be continued for the best years of a woman's life. It is difficult to see how it can be argued that this kind of servitude would be more productive of good if it is compulsory than if it is voluntary. (p. 249)

Hardin (1968:249) includes two pieces of data as support for his perspective: (1) that the accepted failure of the pill results in 250,000 unwanted pregnancies in the country annually and (2) that data from a Swedish study indicate that unwanted children, compared with their controls, exhibited a greater range of social and psychological problems.

This review of selected aspects of women's health care has focused on obstetric and gynecological issues because these are central concerns of women and are, of course, unique to them as a consumer group. This is an area of medical practice in which nonmedical opinions and stereotyped thinking among health care professionals, mainly men, have exerted a significant influence on the care provided. Women have focused on these medical needs in the creation of alternate health care services as they have sought to gain control over the health aspect of their lives. (Marieskind 1975). All of the previously discussed issues—medical care partly based on evaluative judgments, the special history of the American doctor and the American woman, obstetrical and gynecological practice informed by ste-

reotyped perspectives—have converged to create a special set of circumstances in which alternative health care services for women have
developed.

## The Rationale for Alternative
## Health Care

The descriptions of new health care programs to follow will demonstrate specifically how revised medical services can be offered. There
are certain themes that pervade these innovations in care, themes
that strengthen the base of all the services.

First, there is an intent to build a sound basis for the new programs. The call is for not only "dignified, non-patronizing, non-sexist care, but also medically sound care that takes into account the latest scientific knowledge" (Frankfort 1972:xvii). Research efforts are
reported in the established literature (see, for example, Lennane and
Lennane 1973); annotated bibliographies summarize the developing
knowledge (see, for example, Ruczek 1975); and a new journal,
*Women and Health,* is devoted exclusively to this field, providing a
forum for original research and reviews of issues. The publication
*Our Bodies, Ourselves,* developed by the Boston Women's Health
Book Collective (1976) and providing both a feminist perspective and
a wealth of sound information, much of which is based on recent
research, is widely consulted. This network of female-oriented publications supplements the established medical journals as an outlet for
new knowledge.

Second, major emphasis is placed on consumer participation in
the use of health care services. Instead of, on the one hand, patient
dependence in and physician control of medical care, or, on the
other, the mixed messages of some care [e.g., breast self-examination
but not participation in breast cancer treatment; regular PAP smears
but not regular self-inspection of one's own cervix (Boston Women's
Collective 1976:98)], the call in the new programs is for a complete
and active role by the consumer. This is operationalized by full information to women about normal physiological processes as well as illnesses and the encouragement of a series of consumer activities to

prevent and treat disorders. The assumption is made that most people can understand a good deal about their own bodies and, with that understanding, can take an active role on their own behalf. The focus is on promoting health, not treating illness. The mystery is removed and the patient, not the doctor, is seen as the key to good health. The emphasis is on "cooperative care: one in which health is a common concern to patient and professional alike; where self-knowledge replaces mystery, where orders bow to instructions; where self-help is regarded as a matter of common pride and not as stubbornness; where decisions are made by all involved and not passed down from on high" (Frankfort 1972:xxv).

Third, there is concern for restructuring the personnel configuration in health care delivery in order to equalize the importance of each member of the health care team and to increase the percentage of women physicians in all specialties. Women have been at the lower rungs of the traditional medical care hierarchy (Navarro 1972), and the new programs attempt to counteract this by increasing the responsibilities of people at all levels (e.g., nurses, paraprofessionals). Though the number of women physicians has increased, they are specialized mainly in the fields of pediatrics, anesthesiology, and psychiatry (Frankfort 1972:42), and there is concern for more varied representation. Women have been effectively barred from obstetrics and gynecology through the designation of that specialty as surgical practice and through the parallel bias in medicine against female surgeons (Boston Women's Collective 1976:309). The presence of women in all branches of health care is desired, though the greater emphasis is on equality among all care givers. Marieskind (1975) comments that the women's health movement "rejects the power considerations which place the physician at the apex of the health care pyramid and recognizes all health workers as integral to the structure, process and outcome of health care delivery" (p. 220).

Fourth, there is clear recognition that nonwhite women, who are often poor as well, are affected by medical racism as much as by medical sexism. They are faced with "poor quality care, unavailability of services and the alienation of the largely white medical personnel they have to deal with, who have little comprehension of their situation or of the community from which their needs arise" (Boston Women's Collective 1976:337). For poor women—white and non-white—the question may be how to get medical services at all, over-shadowing concerns about the quality of that care. There has also been a historical shift in the attitudes of women in different socioeco-nomic classes. Whereas the middle-class reformers of the nineteenth century acted purely as missionaries to reorganize health care for poor women, such women are now aware that their own needs are also distorted by the medical system. While nonwhite and poor women have special and serious complaints to be lodged against the health care system, middle-class and white women are becoming aware that their medical care has frequently been depreciatory of them as well.

The raising of awareness among all groups of women about the deficiencies of the health care system has, in fact, been one of the main effects of women's work for better medical care. Along with in-novating services and trying to alter established medical care organi-zations, consciousness raising has been an all-important intent (Marieskind 1975:220). In fact, some writers see this increased aware-ness among varied populations of women as a potential and potent political force (Weaver 1976; Frankfort 1972:xxvi). The participation of working-class and middle-class women and of nonwhite and white women in the present movement has undoubtedly enhanced this ef-fectiveness.

As indicated earlier, the alternative health services to be discussed here do not specify particular roles for social workers. However, the four considerations listed previously—a sound program for service, consumer participation, an egalitarian team approach, ethnic minor-ity concerns—are areas with which social work values are congruent and in which social work competence can be most appropriate. As examples, the social work advocacy role can be utilized to encourage more consumer participation; social services can be more effective when the social work component of the health care team is given equal weight with other professionals; social workers have a particular commitment to ethnic minority women. The hope is that social workers will join other groups whose awareness has been heightened about the need for changes in health care delivery for women.

## Alternative Health Services
## for Women

In recent years efforts have been made by various citizen groups to have an impact on the health care delivery system. Such efforts have included groups organized for fund raising (e.g., the American Cancer Society), information and referral services, environmental impact, mutual help (e.g., victims of cancer), and health education (e.g., childbirth and breast feeding groups). Some citizen activities have also been shaped by a feminist perspective (e.g., consciousness raising discussions centered on body functions, self-help groups focused on health issues, home birth movements). However, alternative health delivery systems constitute an approach that is qualitatively different from these efforts.

As the ideas and actions of referral, mutual help, Know Your Body courses, self-help, paramedical training, home birth and patients' rights groups gain momentum, the challenges to the existing health care system fall into two categories. One directs itself to consumers, helping patients as individuals or in groups to try to gain knowledge and alter their individual experiences or to reform the system. The other is deeply influenced by the limitations and failures of efforts to reform health care (some of which go back over twenty years) and is coming to believe that women will have to take over their own health care and the system of women's health care in order to return a sense of dignity and adequacy to these services. (Boston Women's Collective 1976:367–368)

The service to be described first is in the second category and represents both a political stance against the present medical care system and the direct provision of health care.

## The Feminist Women's Health Center

The Feminist Women's Health Center in Los Angeles is part of a national network of seven such centers. Though there are over 1,200

groups in the country identified with women's health activities
(Marieskind 1975:218), the Feminist Women's Health Centers are
used as examples of a small number organized to combine a political
and educational commitment to effect changes in health care delivery and also to provide a set of services including basic gynecological
care, self-help, and paramedical training.

The description of the Los Angeles center starts with an adaptation
of the statement of philosophy and purpose of this women-controlled
organization and proceeds to a discussion of the various ways women
may use the center, including illustrations of specific health care services. The statement of purpose touches on a number of issues raised
earlier in this chapter. Further information about the center will appear in a publication by the Federation of Feminist Women's Health
Centers (Berkeley: Putnam).

Why have women-controlled clinics arisen in the past few years to
provide well-woman care, including abortion? Social conditions affecting a woman's growth and development stem from misleading
and mystified notions about women by men. Childbirth, abortion,
menstruation, and menopause are life processes that have been under
women's control until the very recent past, in fact, until the past 100
years. Women-controlled clinics, although seen as a recent phenomenon, are just a current expression of the general agreement of
women of all times and places that they should have control over
their health care and lives.

Women-controlled clinics have developed because: (1) Women are
denied knowledge of our own bodies so that treatment of everyday
conditions seems mysterious; (2) the branch of medicine known as
allopathy, a disease-oriented system, has taken over the practice of
medicine and the education of physicians and has encroached on
many normal functions, such as birth, menstruation, death, and
mental processes; (3) widespread use of dangerous birth control
methods and reckless use of hormone-like drugs have created illness
in an otherwise healthy population; (4) even though the practice of
abortion has been sanctioned by the Supreme Court, the medical
profession still regulates its practice, women still lack access to abortions in many areas, they still lack information about early abortion
because of the mystification of abortion, and they lack the support

necessary to overcome feelings of stigma, sin, guilt, and fear attached to abortion; (5) venereal disease is epidemic in the population owing to the reluctance of people to seek help except from people they trust and feel comfortable with.

A major goal of a woman-controlled clinic is equal access to information about our bodies. Self-help is a process that allows for sharing of information in a group setting. Women learn in groups to do their own cervical and breast examinations and uterine checks. Since women learn from one another, observe one another, and practice skills with one another, the foundation is laid for exploring health questions in a much more knowledgeable way. Education, development of skills, and research, the cornerstones of enlightened health care, are being pursued by women in a peer-oriented, nonprofessional context.

The focus of well-woman clinics is the well woman. Well women may or may not use birth control, may or may not have babies, may or may not have vaginal and bladder infections, may or may not need abortions. Well women have to relate to menstruation, reproduction, sexuality, maternity, and old age. By sharing experiences, women are redefining the range of what is considered normal. Many so-called conditions, such as "tipped uteruses" are now seen to be normal variations.

Well-women clinics are prevention oriented, in contrast to medical facilities that are disease oriented. They are concerned about preventing the most common vaginal and bladder infections, since the causes are easily understood and once they are understood the woman can easily take action. (For instance, understanding the connection between vaginal infections and fecal contamination makes a woman aware of hygiene practices that will prevent future infections.)

Current gynecological practices cause disease in an otherwise normal population. Thus, women come into the well-woman clinic with complications from birth control pills and IUDs, and are concerned about the risk of cancer from indiscriminate use of estrogen-like drugs to alleviate anxiety at menopause. The failure of our government or our medical profession to deal effectively with venereal disease has permitted such disease to become epidemic. Women come into the women-controlled clinic for testing for venereal disease. Thus health workers in a well-woman clinic have learned what is healthy through participation in self-help clinics, participatory clinics, workshops, and reading. When a health worker recognizes that a woman's problem is outside the range of what is healthy or when she explains a positive result of a screening test, she advises the woman on ways to find a solution to her problem. The nurse or physician is generally accessible to the woman at the clinic, or the woman may decide to go to another specially equipped facility to seek another opinion. Or, she may decide to take other measures that she may know about or have learned about through discussions with the health worker and other women in the group.

One way in which physicians have maintained their power is through the mystification of the process of diagnosis. Groups like the American Medical Association or state boards of medical examiners have made it a criminal offense for anyone besides a licensed physician to diagnose a condition of the body. Yet all people, at one time or another, make decisions about how they will deal with certain familiar conditions such as colds, diarrhea, a sore throat, or a headache.

A diagnosis is a hypothesis, a tentative conclusion based on common sense and signs and symptoms that are present either in oneself or in someone else. The process is the same for a layperson as it is for a physician. Sometimes people are unfamiliar with symptoms or do not have special tools to detect signs of illness, and a diagnosis cannot be made. If a physician has difficulty making a diagnosis, a consultation with another physician may be made. Sometimes they do not admit to the patient that they do not know what is going on. Even after consultation physicians do not always know how to diagnose a condition. When physicians act as though the diagnosis were an established fact, not a hypothesis, the patient misunderstands and attributes almost magical significance to the diagnosis. Women-controlled clinics promote an educational process in which women can make their own diagnoses of common body states, and health workers do not make diagnoses. In fact, even the physicians and nurses in a women-controlled clinic strive to give the woman the information that will allow her to arrive at her own conclusion.

Medical regulating agencies attempt to control treatment totally; it is a criminal act to treat anyone unless you are a licensed physician. If this law could be wholly enforced, the jails would be filled with our mothers and grandmothers. We learn health maintenance at home. We learn what to do to prevent dental cavities, for example. We also learn what to do to relieve the symptoms of sore throats, colds, flu, and other widespread ailments. Women-controlled clinics promote a cooperative effort on the part of the individual woman, the other women in the group, the health worker, and the physician. The process of treatment is demystified by sharing with women the experience of treating common and recurring vaginal and bladder infections at home.

## The Self-Help Clinic

The Women's Center acts on its educational commitment by staffing self-help clinics for interested women in the community. These are informal gatherings of women held at the center, in someone's home, at a school, or at some other community facility. They are meant to provide information and to foster discussion and the sharing of experiences among the women. The focus is on gynecological issues as an area of distinctive concern for women; but the emphasis on self-knowledge, prevention of illness, and demystification spills over into other health areas.

The staff person who leads the discussion stresses the importance of the woman's knowledge of her own body, the awareness of normal physiological processes, and the promotion of health. A major focus is the cervical self-examination, which serves several purposes: (1) In a slide presentation women see other women examining their own cervices. This demystifies both the process of examination and the physical attributes of the cervix. Following the presentation, or in continuations of such self-help clinics, interested women will learn how to do this self-examination. (2) By seeing a range of cervices, the women develop a sense of what is normal, and particularly how normal changes occur cyclically (e.g., during ovulation, menstruation, pregnancy). (3) They have a sense of the appropriateness and possibility of examining one's own cervix in the same say one examines any other body organ, in order to be aware of changes and to make one's own decision about the need for medical consultation. Women are encouraged to consider natural remedies for disorders and to be aware of the iatrogenic effects (i.e., caused by medical treatment) of some physician-prescribed medications.

The same approach is taken with other gynecological issues (e.g., use of hormones, vaginal infections, childbirth procedures). In each instance facts are offered to dispel myths, experiences with the medical system are shared openly, and suggestions for further reading are offered. In many different ways the women are encouraged to know about their bodies and to know how to promote their own health. They observe a nonmedically trained person speak knowledgeably about physiological processes and illustrate by her presence and approach that women can know more about their health and their bodies. It is made clear that certain disorders call for a medically trained person but that much can be done by the woman herself. Even when direct medical care is sought, the woman is encouraged to know enough about her physiology to ask appropriate questions and to expect clear answers.

A discussion of menstrual extraction also serves the demystifying purpose well. Menstrual extraction is a procedure in which women trained in advanced self-help clinics learn to extract one another's menstrual linings. The women present see that a procedure has been developed by women for women so that they may have control over an important bodily process, and they learn that, with training, a nonmedical person can carry out this procedure safely. Though most of the women present would probably not use the procedure, interested women may join advanced self-help groups outside the center to pursue this women-controlled research. The women have had presented to them an approach, developed by women, through which they can control menstruation, decrease severe menstrual pains, and end unwanted pregnancies. Another illustration has been offered in which dependence on an esoteric expert has been reduced and women can see the possibility of women having both control and competence in health care.

## The Participatory Clinic

The self-help clinic has a clear community education purpose. The participatory clinic held at the center provides women with specific attention to their own health needs and an alternative to traditional health care.

The participatory clinic consists of a group of five or six women and two health workers. Often women who have similar health concerns are scheduled for the same group. When a woman calls to make an appointment at the clinic, its participatory nature is fully explained and there is an attempt to schedule women with similar needs at the same time.

Whenever a woman visits a women-controlled clinic, she and the health worker discuss information about her body that might affect her health care. She and the health worker fill out a form, often along with other women in a group. The questions deal with such matters as her menstrual experiences, her experiences with birth control or with health problems or diseases that she or her family have had (e.g., diabetes), and what drugs or medication she is taking.

The focus of the discussion will vary from one woman to another, depending on the reason she has visited the clinic. Certain basic types of questions, such as the pattern of menstrual periods, are similar to those asked in standard history forms used by hospitals, physicians, and clinics. Many, however, have evolved out of the practical experiences of women and health workers in a women-controlled clinic.

If the woman has visited the clinic for a specific problem, she will be asked her experiences in relation to that problem, how long the problem has existed, what she has done about it, and how the problem has changed, if at all. Unless race, marital status, or sexual orientation are directly relevant to the woman's health needs, such questions are not included in her case record. Financial information and identification are not included unless a financial arrangement is necessary.

After the routine questions have been asked and the routine areas of discussion gone over, the sharing of information between the

woman and other women in the group, as well as the health workers
and the physician or nurse, continues. Thus, information on each
patient is added to throughout the visit as other facts come to light
that are pertinent to the woman's health care.

Careful and thorough "herstory" taking* is emphasized in a well-
woman clinic. Health workers and, on occasion, the physician evaluate whether or not conditions exist that exclude the woman from a
well-woman setting and might necessitate her seeing a physician or
going to another facility that is specially equipped to deal with the
condition. For example, a woman who reported pain during menstrual periods or during coitus would be asked to describe the pain,
when it started, and any other changes she noticed in her body. If the
woman's experiences seem to be all unusual, she might decide to see
the physician at the women-controlled clinic or another specially
equipped facility.

The information gained through the information-sharing process at
a women-controlled clinic is a major factor contributing to the excellence of health care provided in a women-controlled clinic. The
woman's subjective reporting is given full attention, and all her perceptions are regarded as valid. This is contrary to the traditional medical situation, in which the physician's observations, particularly so-
called objective observations made with measuring devices, are given
much more credence than the woman's self-reports.

The informal, egalitarian atmosphere of a women-controlled clinic
enables women to fully remember their health care experiences and
facts about their bodies and to fully share this information. The nonjudgmental approach of the health worker enables women to bring
out doubts, fears, and speculations that give the health worker and/or
physician the opportunity to explore these to the depth that is desired
by the woman.

Skills in information gathering are developed in training sessions
provided by the clinic that teach health workers why certain questions
are important and give them ways to present information in a clear,
easy-to-understand manner. Also, precise language is used so that the
information received is consistent from one patient record to another.
Listening to the woman's self-reports is a skill that health workers de-

* The Clinic's choice of this term reflects a feminist position on the use of language.

velop as a result of their profound respect for each woman's experiences.

The taking of a complete account for each patient, which involves extensive discussion, information sharing, and education in a group, is the hallmark of the women-controlled clinic. This process is an extension of the everyday dialog between people about their bodies and their health. Family members and coworkers typically talk about their health problems, describe the signs of problems, share solutions, and speculate about possible cause–effect relationships. Each person is an expert on her own body. Good herstory taking draws on each woman's knowledge of her own body.

Each woman in the group discusses her reasons for visiting the clinic. At this time the women can discuss the significance of each question on the record form.

The health worker explains that if at any time a woman feels uncomfortable doing self-examination in the group she should make her feelings known and can do the self-examination with a health worker at the end of the group session.

The group does screening tests such as blood pressure and hematocrit (a test for anemia). Common screening procedures, such as pap smears, uterine checks, and blood pressure, are demystified when women are able to observe and perform them themselves. They do breast and cervical self-examination. Uterine checks and other educational procedures are done by health workers and often by other women in the group. Home health treatments are shared. The group sessions usually last two to three hours. If at any time the woman requires medical care, or for any reason wishes to see the physician, she is referred appropriately.

The participatory clinic combines well-woman health care and health education. Women in the group, through group examination, have an opportunity to gain an idea of the range of "normal" among well women.

The woman is actively involved in learning about and discussing her own health care every minute that she is in the clinic. This is in contrast to the situation at most health facilities, where a person may spend hours reading a magazine in a waiting room or sitting alone in an examination room.

The participatory setting offers a unique and safe environment for the training of new health workers. The trainee learns along with all of the women in the group, sees women with a variety of health needs and problems, and has the security of the more experienced health worker as well as the backup of a physician, if necessary.

In the medical model, a physician uses her or his knowledge and instruments to make objective measurements to arrive at a diagnosis of any malfunction. In a participatory clinic in contrast, the group setting ensures a more egalitarian process. Input into decision making comes from more than just one person, and women can make educated decisions regarding their own health care. A woman's subjective symptoms provide her with information, and she arrives at conclusions based on subjective data, objective measurements, and others' observations. The conditions are met for true informed consent.

## Clinic Procedures

The following sections describe some of the situations that commonly arise in women-controlled clinics. These descriptions, developed by the Los Angeles Center,* specify the health care activity and, in most instances, also include the training of the clinic health care worker for that procedure. In this sample of procedures, as is true for the entire manual of procedures, the demystifying philosophy is clearly evident.

### BREAST SELF-EXAMINATION

When a woman comes into a well-woman clinic, a health worker and women in the group may discuss what is usually felt during self-examination of the breasts. Women discuss changes that they have felt in their breasts during their monthly menstrual cycles. The health worker demonstrates by doing her own self-examination. Other women in the group follow along by examining their own

* These procedures appear in a manual developed by the Feminist Women's Health Center, *Well Women Health Care in Women Controlled Clinics* (1976).

breasts. There is usually a discussion of the differences and similarities in the breasts of healthy women.

If a woman notices anything unusual during the self-examination, she may question the health worker or other women in the group to get their opinion and suggestions for referrals. Other women in the group observe and feel the place on the breast that is being discussed. If there are unanswered questions, or if an unusual condition is found, the woman or the health worker will get the opinion of a more experienced health worker or the physician, and if necessary, suggestions for further testing will be made.

Health workers are trained to teach breast self-examination by routinely examining their own breasts and attending ongoing in-service training, sharing experiences with women in self-help clinics, and having the opportunity to see the wide variation in the breasts of well women in the context of groups in women-controlled clinics. Health workers can also take advantage of the many community resources providing further information about breast self-examination.

Breast self-examination has been widely accepted as an important screening technique. It has been demonstrated on television and widely discussed in popular magazines. Studies have shown that women are usually the first to notice any unusual changes in their breasts.


DIAPHRAGM FITTINGS

When a woman gets a diaphragm from a women-controlled clinic, she begins by participating in a discussion with a health worker and other women about how the diaphragm works, how to determine the correct size, women's experiences using diaphragms, and the effectiveness and safety of the diaphragm. Actual fitting is done in a group with the assistance of a health worker. Someone in the group shows the woman how to insert a diaphragm and where to place the spermicidal jelly when actually using the diaphragm. The health worker inserts one or two fingers to estimate the length of the woman's vaginal canal from under the pubic bone to under the cervix. Having determined the general range of sizes that she will probably use, the health worker has the woman try on a series of diaphragms or fitting rings to determine which is the largest she can comfortably wear with no sensation of its presence within the vagina. After putting in each diaphragm, she stands up and moves around to see how it feels and whether or not it slips out of place. During this process the woman is learning how to insert and remove the diaphragm and discussing its use with the group. Questions can be answered at this time. Each time a woman tries on a different diaphragm, she and the health worker assess, by inserting a finger into the vagina, whether the rim is snugly behind the pubic bone and whether the cervix is covered. The appropriate size is the largest one that the woman cannot feel inside her vagina, which does not gape at the pubic bone but fits snugly against it.

If the woman is unsure of the fit or has difficulty removing the diaphragm, she might decide to ask for help from a more experienced person.

A health worker should know how the diaphragm works, be able to describe its use, be able to insert and remove it, and know how to help a woman determine a correct fit. She may learn this by attending self-help clinics and training sessions, inserting a diaphragm in her own vagina several times, reading, checking other women's diaphragms in training sessions, or assisting a more experienced health worker.

A woman should be able to fit her own diaphragm, with the assistance, if needed, of other laywomen, and should be able to obtain one without a prescription. A diaphragm is not a medical device. It is a simple mechanical means of blocking and killing sperm before they can reach the cervix, and works on the same principles as the condom and spermicidal preparations, which are available without prescription. Its use has nothing to do with the diagnosis or treatment of disease. Diaphragm fitting is a process similar to trying on shoes and is viewed differently only because it involves the vagina. A woman cannot seriously injure herself with a diaphragm. If it does not fit properly and causes discomfort, she will know what the problem is and will get another size.

References that a woman might use to learn about diaphragms and that health workers use in training include *The Birth Control Handbook; Our Bodies, Ourselves; Woman to Woman; Contraceptive Tech-*

*nology*; articles describing the recent Planned Parenthood study on the effectiveness of the diaphragm; manufacturers' packaging inserts; posters depicting diaphragm insertion; and plastic pelvis models designed for demonstrating fit and insertion.


## PREGNANCY SCREENING

In many women-controlled clinics pregnancy screening takes place in a group containing two to six women with a health worker. The goal of each woman in the group is to determine whether or not she is pregnant and, if so, how many weeks pregnant she is. The health worker acts as a facilitator in this process in a women-controlled clinic.

The woman considers the following: late or missed or unusual menstrual period, subjective signs of pregnancy such as morning sickness, exposure to sperm at a time of possible fertility, and other possible causes of a missed period (jet travel, birth control pills, anxiety, etc.). The health worker must have information on early signs of pregnancy and on the menstrual cycle.

The urine chorionic gonadotropin (UCG) test is a laboratory test that screens for a particular sign of pregnancy two weeks after a missed period. A drop of urine is mixed with a drop of UCG and a drop of latex coating solution, which shows the interaction of the urine and the serum. Two minutes is allowed for the reaction. If the hormone is present in the urine, the mixture will remain milky and smooth. This hormone is associated with the building up of the lining of the uterus in early pregnancy.

The health worker explains the mechanics of the test and possible causes of false results. Each woman performs the test herself and compares her results with the other women's so as to see for herself the difference between positive and negative readings. In order to do the test a woman must have the ability to follow simple instructions.

Another sign of early pregnancy is a blue or purplish color of the cervix. A woman can easily learn how to insert a plastic speculum to observe the color of her cervix. She can compare the color of her cervix to that of her own vaginal walls and to that of the cervices of other women in the group. The training required for sharing self-examination is having used a vaginal speculum for self-examination in a group and having seen the cervices of healthy women.

In early pregnancy the uterus softens and enlarges. The health worker can check the uterine size and tell the woman what she feels. The woman can feel the other women's uteruses. The woman can add this information to the information she already has in coming to her own conclusions. If she determines that she is pregnant, the woman is referred, if necessary, for abortion or prenatal care.

Health worker training involves experience in feeling the size and consistency of the uteruses of healthy women, both women who are pregnant and women who are not.

Early signs of pregnancy—including nausea, especially in the morning, change in appetite, frequent urination, swollen and tender breasts, cramping, sleepiness, a bloated feeling, and mood changes—may be felt by the woman before she misses her period, before anyone could detect uterine enlargement, and before the UCG test would be positive. When a woman comes to a women-controlled clinic for pregnancy screening, the group process of information sharing allows her to put confidence in her own perceptions and experiences and come to her own conclusions.

A recent investigation at a women-controlled clinic showed that of the women who came for pregnancy screening and chose to have preemptive abortions, almost 100 percent were pregnant (based on laboratory examination of the uterine contents). This illustrates that the person most qualified to draw conclusions as to whether or not a woman is pregnant, the person with the most information, is the woman herself.


TAKING A PAP SMEAR

The Pap smear is a laboratory test that screens for cancer of the cervix and vagina and for vaginal infections.

An open speculum exposes the cervix and the vaginal walls. The cells from the cervical os are taken by putting the tip of a cotton swab into the os. A woman usually doesn't feel it, but she may have a feeling of slight pressure on the os. The cells from the cervix are taken by gently picking up the cells on the surface in a 360-degree circle with a wooden spatula. The woman may have a slight feeling of pressure that is not uncomfortable if the spatula is applied gently. Cells from the vaginal wall are taken with the other end of the spatula by gently wiping the vagina, under the cervix, where secretions have pooled, or on either side at the back. The woman does not feel it, but she may have a slight feeling of pressure. The secretions are smeared on a microscope slide and set with a fixative. The slide is then sent to a laboratory for testing.

In a women-controlled clinic a health worker may tell the women in the group how the laboratory reports the results of the Pap smear and how the women can interpret the results for themselves. The women are told that the results of the Pap smear will be made available to them.

The training required of a health worker to do Pap smears is to have observed an experienced person take the secretions with the wooden spatula and cotton swab and place them on a slide. She is supervised by an experienced health worker the first time she does it, and usually has a Pap smear herself. Women who have Pap smears taken in a group setting in a women-controlled clinic, after seeing how easy it is, sometimes take each other's Pap smears under the supervision of an experienced health worker.

Many people remember being in a high school biology class and scraping the insides of their cheeks with a toothpick, putting the cells on a slide, and looking at it under a microscope. Taking a Pap smear is no different, except for the taboos surrounding the vagina.

The equipment necessary for collection of a Pap smear is simple. The major obstacle to women's doing their own Pap smears is the fact that generally laboratories will send test results only to physicians.

## VAGINAL SELF-EXAMINATION

A woman has the option of learning vaginal and cervical self-examination any time she visits a women-controlled clinic, usually in a group setting. A health worker or another woman who has done self-examination demonstrates how to use a speculum, and the group discusses the advantages of knowing how to perform self-examination. The woman inserts the speculum herself, opens it, and looks at her cervix and vagina, and the group discusses their appearance. Once all the women in the group have done a self-examination, they have an idea of the common variations among healthy women. Having done self-examination in a group, they have a good basis for further observation of their own cervices. A woman learns how to teach vaginal and cervical self-examination when she herself is taught by another woman.

Any time someone looks at a woman's cervix, she should have the option of seeing her own cervix and vagina. In women-controlled clinics women can learn self-examination and obtain a speculum for home use. If she inserts her own speculum in a clinic, she will be more relaxed and comfortable than when someone else inserts it. Self-examination demystifies women's bodies and many of the procedures performed during examinations. A woman who learns what is normal for herself is able to detect changes, to learn what these changes mean, or to seek the advice of a trained person when necessary. Knowing the normal condition of the cervix and vagina is no more a medical concern than knowing the normal condition of the mouth and throat. A woman has the right to look at and learn about her own body.

Currently, most women learn self-examination from other women rather than from books or articles. No medical textbooks teach self-examination, but popular health books are beginning to include instruction in it. (It is included in *Our Bodies, Ourselves.*) Women's clinics usually have printed material on self-examination and speculums available for purchase. The film *New Image of Myself* also explains self-examination.

The Feminist Women's Health Center has been presented as one example of a women-controlled health center. Different procedures and different emphases have developed in other clinics and centers elsewhere. Common to all, however, is a stance that encourages women to have control over and knowledge about their own bodies and health care needs. Certain programs, such as the Los Angeles Center, have pioneered these efforts. In fact, the center has as one of its purposes providing consultation for other groups about the establishment of similar services. There is also general acknowledgment of the important contribution of the Boston Women's Health Book Collective in the publication of the widely used *Our Bodies, Ourselves*. Recent years have seen the greater development of women-controlled clinics in the country, paralleled by legal battles to answer the medical establishment's charges of encroachment on physician autonomy.

Two other services are presented here to illustrate additional approaches to nonsexist health care for women. One represents an attempt to train medical and paramedical personnel in greater sensitivity to the needs of women, but with the close collaboration of the medical profession. The second is an attempt to contribute to the training of medical students, but with a clear challenge to traditional medical education.

## The Gynecorps Project

The Gynecorps Project in Seattle, one of ten such programs in the nation, was established with the close cooperation of physicians and physician groups, but has the clear aim of extending the training of health care specialists so that they will be particularly responsive to the needs of women. The rationale for the project is that women can benefit from obstetric and gynecological services that are preventive, oriented to the woman's right to understand her own biological processes, enhanced by women as service deliverers, and provided in an empathetic, unhurried atmosphere; and that registered nurses and others can be trained to offer these services. The program participants are all women—women patients, women students, and women instructors—and in this health care specialty that is distinctive for women, the training and services recognize women's special needs.

A further purpose is to provide these enhanced services to particular groups of women—high-risk, low-income, and underserved populations. The sponsoring organizations (initially the Regional Medical

Program of the University of Washington and now the National
Cancer Institute and DHEW) require that graduates of the program
return to practice at sites previously identified as serving these special
groups.

Students in the program will become women's health care specialists. To enter training, a student must be either an RN with some experience in obstetrics/gynecology or a woman with a B.A. and at least
two year's experience (e.g., as a nurse's aide) in the ob–gyn field.
About 20 percent of the students are members of ethnic minorities.
The women are trained in small groups, with no more than ten in a
class. Probably as a result of the all-women educational experience,
with its emphasis on raising women's consciousness of their health
needs, there has developed in each group a supportive, noncompetitive sense of sisterhood that is very different from the atmosphere of
traditional medical or nursing training.

The 18-week didactic and clinical training emphasizes cancer
screening and detection (proficiency in performing pelvic and limited
physical examinations, pap smears, and breast examinations); routine
prenatal and postpartum care; contraceptive care and family planning
assistance; patient education in cancer signs, symptoms, and breast
self-examination; timely and intelligent referrals to sponsoring backup
physicians when abnormalities are suspected; and community outreach, aimed at educating and motivating women toward preventive
health care. The program provides both classroom and clinic experiences, and students rotate through four clinic settings, each of which
provides exposure to particular client groups. In the Public Health
Hospital they are more likely to see menopausal and postmenopausal
women; at the University of Washington Hospital and in the maternal and infant care clinics they see low-income and ethnic minority
women; and at Planned Parenthood clinics they see a greater proportion of adolescents.

The three main aspects of training include, first, classroom lectures by a wide range of medical specialists and, in supervised clinical
experiences, education for well-informed, skillful practice. Students
are exposed to the latest in medical knowledge in the ob–gyn field.
Their medical training is supplemented with presentations by community self-help groups such as groups of mastectomy patients. They
are expected to become highly skillful in clinical practice, first by ob-

serving the work of the four primary instructors and then by practicing information taking, breast examination (including the teaching of breast self-examination), and pelvic examination. They must complete 100 pelvic examinations with 90 percent agreement by the instructor that they have been done successfully. The students must show similar expertise in prenatal care, contraceptive counseling and service provision, and patient counseling. In all, they are trained to deal with most outpatient gynecological services and, following an initial physician visit, to provide prenatal care up to the time of delivery.

Second, students are educated to become knowledgeable in encouraging women to engage in self-care and prevention. They are trained and urged to give women ample time in their clinic visits, a commodity frequently lacking in physicians' offices. They encourage women to ask questions about their health and health care, and try to give patients complete answers to their questions. In their pelvic examinations they explain each step of the examination process and encourage women to observe their own cervices by mirror. They emphasize preventive health care and, when indicated, recommend natural remedies such as the application of yogurt directly to the pelvic area for certain disorders. They assume that the patient is the major decision maker in the choice of birth control methods, and they are educated to provide full information about the advantages and disadvantages of each method. Because of reported side effects of both the pill and the IUD, they encourage the use of the diaphragm; similarly, because of questions about the carcinogenic consequences of estrogen, they discourage its use. For adolescent patients as well as other women, when sexuality becomes an area of concern, as it frequently does, they are trained to offer counseling within a non-stereotyped view of female sexuality. Students are educated to offer pelvic examinations with the woman's sexual partner present so that the woman and her partner can understand normal female anatomy. Through the use of ample time and the intent to establish an empathetic relationship with the woman patient, and by evidencing a clear respect for the woman's right to know, for her ability to care for her own body, and for the appropriateness of her role in decision making, the students are educated to educate others, in turn, for prevention and self-care.

The third aspect of training is for the role of advocate. When referrals are made to traditional, patriarchal medical systems, the students teach patients their rights—to have sensitive health service, to ask questions, to know what modes of treatment they are receiving, and to change practitioners if need be.

The experience of the patients who have been seen by Gynecorps Project students supports the intent and rationale of the program. There is one specific piece of evidence of this and many more impressionistic, anecdotal, but consistent indications. The specific experience has occurred when the women patients have had two pelvic examinations—first by the student and then, for corroboration of findings, by the instructor. Among the 5,000 women who have been examined in this way since the project began, only three have objected to the double procedure. In fact, the patients have commented on their preference for being examined by women and expressed their appreciation for the concurrent careful explanation of the process. In general, women patients will say that these visits are the first time they have felt comfortable in a gynecological examination (many report a sense of intimidation in interaction with a male gynecologist), the first time they have felt free to ask questions and receive clear and understandable answers. No one had explained normal processes and disorders to them previously. The students and instructors both report that when time is taken to encourage questions, the lack of knowledge among women about their own anatomy and physiology is appalling. They find not only that the patients are eager for knowledge but that many are ready to participate in decision making about birth control and in a program for self-care.

The Gynecorps Project is an example of a program that is supported by the traditional physician yet encourages a nontraditional approach to women's health care. Because the project was developed in close cooperation with physicians and physician groups, has continually sought the endorsement and recognition of physicians and their associations, has been supervised by physician staff, and requires of all candidates for training that they have a physician sponsor for backup during their practice, the project has enjoyed strong physician support and cooperation. On-site visits to graduates of the project and interviews with their physician sponsors have established that no significant professional conflicts exist between project-certified women's health care specialists and physicians. Indeed, these working relationships have proven mutually supportive and beneficial. Many of the patients seen by the women's health care specialist are unmotivated patients who are not seen regularly by physicians. Most physician sponsors have greatly appreciated being freed from routine,' screening types of examinations.

Nonetheless, there are two nontraditional aspects to the program: First, women health care specialists are educated in a non–sex-stereotyped way to expand their own capabilities and to have more control and autonomy in their own practice; and second, patients are provided with a nonsexist service that encourages self-care, self-knowledge, and greater participation in prevention and decision making. Both sets of women expand their competencies and sense of self, while better health care is provided.

The following reports from the Women's Community Health Center, Inc., of Cambridge, Massachusetts, represent three stages of development of an innovative program intended to train Harvard Medical School students to conduct pelvic examinations. They describe the rationale for the program, the initial experience of its implementation, and a plan for its subsequent revision.

# A Pelvic Teaching Program

### WOMEN'S COMMUNITY HEALTH
### CENTER, INC.

## Proposal for the Program: Fall 1975

For most women a pelvic examination is an unpleasant experience at best. At worst it can be painful, humiliating, mystifying, and sexually charged; furthermore, like most other doctors, gynecologists are in the habit of making decisions in the name of "the patient's best interests" or "efficiency" without more than the most superficial explanation and consultation with the woman. The women's health movement has grown around a desire to change this situation.

For most instructors teaching the pelvic exam to medical students also seems to be an unpleasant experience. Various Harvard Medical School courses have found it necessary to use anesthetized women, prostitutes, or uneasy clinic patients; in the last case logistics may involve hurried instructions outside the patients' hearing and one-minute visits by a medical student who later assures his or her instructor that he or she did indeed feel the upper end of the uterus, not a situation permitting adequate learning.

We have three purposes for the following proposal:

1. To teach the parts of a routine well-woman pelvic and breast examination; and to introduce a few ob-gyn subjects of special concern, for example, comparison of birth control methods, common disorders (vaginitis, pelvic inflammatory disease, etc.), treating the rape victim, DES, sexuality.

2. To give medical students some interest and insight into the point of view of the patient; to create a situation in which the patient is a colleague, teaching and giving feedback herself (this is a much mentioned but little practiced ideal—that the doctor learns from the patient!).

3. To encourage medical students, including the great majority who will *not* become gynecologists, that the pelvic examination can be mutually positive when the doctor is interested in teaching the woman about her body. We believe that many women like to see their cervices, that breast and speculum self-examination can be important screening procedures and teach familiarity with one's own body; and a pelvic examination need not be uncomfortable if the woman is relaxed and in control.

### *Experiences of a Pelvic Teaching Group:*
### *June 1976* *

The Pelvic Teaching Program of the Women's Community Health Center, Inc., was developed by a group of women who are members

* Women's Community Health Center, Inc., "Experiences of a Pelvic Teaching Program," *Women and Health* 1 (1976): 19–20. Reprinted by permission.

of an advanced self-help group which instructed Boston area medical students in the pelvic examination in 1975–1976. The Pelvic Teaching Program contracted with interested teaching hospitals to carry out the instruction of pelvic exams to medical students as part of the students' second-year course, the introduction to clinical medicine. Our program has changed radically in purpose, scope, focus, and structure since its early beginnings in the spring of 1975. What follows is a statement of the program's goals and structure; it also places the program in a full historical and political context.

In mid-1975 members of the Women's Community Health Center, Inc. (WCHC) were approached indirectly, through a member of the Boston Women's Health Book Collective, by women medical students to discuss the possibility of WCHC members serving as paid "pelvic models" to aid in the practical instruction of the pelvic examination as taught in medical schools. These women medical students were displeased with the ways pelvic exams were being taught, using anesthetized women, unsuspecting clinic patients, prostitutes, or plastic "gynny" models. These students felt the time was ripe for women to assume a more active role in the instruction, primarily as educated models who could give the students feedback as the exam was being performed. This use of feminist pelvic models, the students thought, would greatly improve the learning process and would do much to provide an active counterbalance to previously held and institutionalized attitudes toward women as passive recipients of health care. Both the students' feminist liaison and WCHC collective members thought the program would be a good way to channel funds from the medical establishment into the women's health movement, to demonstrate our expertise, and to establish contact with sympathetic women medical students.

There are other prototypes in the USA for this pelvic model approach to instruction. Programs usually involve "informed women of the community," recruited by doctors, who serve as "simulated patients" while the instructors, the physicians, coach the students on the particulars of technique.

After the first session we began to see the shortcomings of the pelvic model concept. Although we gave active feedback as the exam was being performed, the physicians were the major instructors and the students looked to them to handle the "tough" problems and to field questions regarding pathology. We had very little control over the teaching session. The students were pleased with the experience of having "talking pelvises" to guide them; the physicians were pleased because the program enhanced their status within the medical community; but we were severely displeased. We did not agree with their approach to health care as looking for disease. We felt exploited: We were being paid for the sessions but the scant monetary payment was a condescending, patronizing sort of recognition. The unspoken agreement was that our bodies were valuable but our information and skills were not. We were encouraged to have overweight women with hard-to-find ovaries in the sessions so as to be "challenging," but any information beyond an immediate response (such as "You're hurting me" or "Yes, that's my cervix") was thought distracting or trivial.

The original protocol agreed upon included, in addition to the practical session, a session in which topics germane to women's health care would be discussed and information compiled by women's health activists (*Our Bodies, Ourselves*; handbooks; fact sheets) would be distributed. These sessions were deemed superfluous and too expensive by medical schools and consequently were not held. We are women with valuable information about anatomy and physiology, common gynecological concerns, health care delivery, antisexist practitioner–consumer relations, self-help, etc., but it was apparent that our conceptual framework of well-woman–oriented gynecological health was not welcomed.

When we realized this we began to discuss and implement ways to gain complete control over the program. We did not discard the pelvic model idea out of hand, but we unanimously decided to alter the program substantially as a direct result of the untenable circumstances in which we found ourselves.

The structural and procedural changes we instituted were both internal and external. Internally, we channeled our energies to become a stronger, ongoing self-help group. New participants whose only affiliation with WCHC was through this program (i.e., the women were not WCHC collective members) joined the group and were trained. They are not volunteers; they receive fees for the sessions they instruct. We began to meet weekly, with time divided equally between practical training, information and skill sharing, and business. The group began to evolve a specific identity, facilitating unity of purpose and strength.

We found it necessary to have a legally binding contract to clarify the mutual responsibilities between the Pelvic Teaching Program and the medical institutions. Among the stipulations were

1. There are always at least two women from the group acting as instructors.

2. Medical personnel (if present at all) are limited to one per session and assume only the role of silent observer. These two provisions demonstrate the biggest change in the program: that we are *the instructors* in the session. The concept of pelvic model is no longer accurate to describe our position as instructors; it implies that we are passive recipients of the pelvic exam, which is no longer true.

3. Each session includes no more than five students, at least one of whom is a woman.

4. We review all publicity about the program before it is made public.

5. Each teaching institution agrees to reproduce and distribute to the medical students *How to Do a Pelvic Examination*, the copyrighted manual in which we have presented a healthy way to perform a well-woman gynecological examination with nonsexist, nonheterosexist, nonelitist assumptions.

6. Payments arrangements must be confirmed in advance of the sessions.

7. The contract must be signed prior to the first session.

The logical question which arises is, If all the preceding controls are necessary, and if the situation has been so oppressive, why would we want to continue the program? Why, indeed.

While we had few illusions about the program's ability to effect sweeping changes within the medical establishment, we reasoned that as long as there are physicians doing pelvic exams, pelvics will be taught to them. We thought that individual women might have better experiences and more complete care with individual physicians as a result of better teaching. There are several potentially positive but limited aspects to the program:

1. We formed an ongoing self-help group in which we shared skills with each other about well-woman care. Our training was based on the concept of self-help and, thus was accomplished in noncompetitive information and skill-sharing sessions, relying on experience rather than credentials as the basis for expertise. We approached health care from the point of view of *health*, as opposed to the disease finding that medical students are taught.

2. The teaching sessions themselves were models for the process that a well-woman gynecological examination in particular, and practitioner–consumer encounters in general, should follow. We emphasized that both common and scientific language must be used; that women are competent and should participate fully in the exam; that every woman can be an expert about her own body. The woman being examined, and not the examiner, has full control over the examination. This session is probably the only time that the medical students will be exposed to this self-help approach to health care and education.

3. The program gave us access to and information about the medical training process. This demystified the medical education process for us firsthand.

4. We learned about current trends in medical schools, such as the push for chaperones during pelvic exams to protect the physicians from charges of rape or malpractice (!) and the interest in "patient management" techniques.

5. We learned how to negotiate with medical schools.

6. The program enabled us to contact women medical students and encourage them to implement changes in the medical establishment that are consonant with demands in the women's health movement. At any rate, we confronted them with their responsibilities as women to make conscious choices about women's health care.

7. We made some money from the medical schools to fund our ongoing self-help projects.

(Points 6 and 7 are reiterations of initial reasons for setting up the Pelvic Teaching Program. They continue to be positive, but limited, reasons for the program.)

One of the basic assumptions by both parties (PTP and medical schools) was that this program would give medical students better, more humane instruction; therefore, they would be more comfortable with the pelvic exam as physicians, and better health care for women would result. This approach assumes that by changing the attitudes of professionals, who come in contact with many health care consumers, the benefits will automatically be widely shared; in other words, that better training for physicians is a worthy way of ensuring better health care delivery for women.

Our experiences with this program caused us to question its potential for achieving change. Although we had wanted to exemplify a skill- and information-sharing, well-woman approach in our teaching sessions that physicians could incorporate into their practice, we found that medical students reacted by reinforcing the traditional division between health care providers and consumers. Medical professionals have a vested interest in perpetuating the general system while making palliative, individual changes in it. The consumers, on the other hand, have an interest in changing the basic relationship between practitioner and consumer, which oppresses and alienates the latter and provides inadequate medical care.

The Pelvic Teaching Group of WCHC believes that programs involving pelvic models and even pelvic teaching as we have developed it are doomed to creeping liberalism, contributing to the support of a health care system that needs *radical* change. We have discontinued the program as it now stands, and we *strongly* discourage other groups of women from participating in similar programs. We are devising a protocol for an acceptable program to teach pelvic examinations in medical schools—a program that would contribute to the goals of the self-help movement.

### Report on the Pelvic Teaching Program: September 1977

During the spring of 1976, a self-help group consisting of Women's Community Health members and affiliated women taught pelvic examinations to Harvard medical students at four major hospitals in the Boston area. We attempted to teach within a well-woman context and with women, not the doctors, in control. Two women from our group met with four to five medical students at a time, demonstrating how to do a pelvic exam, including speculum insertion, pap test, external genital exam, and bimanual exam. Each medical student then had an opportunity to do the exam on one of the instructors.

We included discussion of the concept of self-help: that every woman has the right to information about her body and the right to control her body.

We decided to discontinue this program in favor of one more consistent with self-help. We realized that the original program was not conducive to change: It did not challenge the fundamental hierarchical power relationships. Instead, it encouraged fragmented health care, since we met with each group of students only once and offered limited and isolated information. It left many of us with a sense of victimization, a sense that our bodies were being used only for financial recompense and convenience. We wanted to develop a program to challenge the existing medical structure, which teaches hierarchy, oppression, and fragmentation.

The new program includes medical students, consumers, and other health workers. The intention is to cut through the inherent elitism that encourages some groups to maintain a monopoly over health information. Sharing between individuals with different medical and health information, experience, and skills establishes a priority of sharing information.

The new program we have devised corrects some of the previous problems. We feel it is a radical and exciting plan for sharing health information and challenging the current system of medical education and health delivery. The new program is for women only. Only when we exchange roles—that is, when everyone receives as well as gives exams—can we step beyond the roles of active doer and passive receiver.

Another change is the extension of the program to three or four sessions. The sessions include the politics of women's health care; health information of special relevance to women; what a good whole-woman, well-woman gynecological exam should include; self-examination; and skill sharing. This places skills learning in a broader context and more directly meets our goals of challenging fragmentation of health care.

Finally, the fee for the program was increased. Because we are women and because we do not display traditional credentials, we can easily become undervalued and underpaid. We demand recognition of our self-help skills and appropriate compensation for our work, compensation equal to that received by other consultants and commensurate with Harvard's ability to pay.

In the spring of 1977 Harvard again approached us to conduct our program for teaching pelvic exams. When we submitted our revised program and the reasons for the changes, none of the hospitals wanted to participate. It seems that the hospitals were more interested in a readily available supply of women's bodies rather than the opportunity to participate in an experience that helps to reduce the fragmentation of health care.

The politicizing and integrating content of the original program was mild enough for the hospitals to accept, but with increased political content they have been threatened enough to seek another source of women's bodies to use as teaching tools.

We remain interested in the training of medical students and all health workers for women's health care. For too long women have been denied access to information about their bodies. We choose to reverse this by focusing on women doing women's health care.

## Concluding Remarks

It is clear that the new programs described here do not include service tasks by social workers or similar helping professionals. The value of the stance of these programs is to encourage the many thousands of such professionals associated with an extensive array of medical facilities to question the definitions of women and their medical problems currently in operation where they work. Implicit in the new services is the assumption that women can receive more effective health care if they have a more proactive posture vis-à-vis the medical profession. The establishment of alternative health facilities is the clearest statement of that position. Even within regular medical environs, the philosophy of the staffs of these new programs and of the feminists who are concerned about health care suggests that women's physical and mental health can be improved by a redefinition of the patient–doctor relationship and by women assuming greater control over their own bodily welfare. The discussion of the health care issue in general and of these innovative programs in particular is intended, in part, to encourage social workers and others in medical establishments to consider these alternatives.

# 3. Women and Chemical Dependency

## NAOMI GOTTLIEB

THE ABUSE of drugs and alcohol is a persistent and perplexing contemporary problem. A variety of treatment programs and vast sums of money are used annually in attempts to rehabilitate drug addicts and people with drinking problems. Chemical dependency as a serious social problem is reflected not only in the number of people addicted but also in the deleterious effect on others in the addict's immediate environment—family and friends, coworkers and employers, victims of addiction-related accidents and crimes.

This chapter builds on the central observation that as professionals and others have dealt with this major social problem, the distinctive problems of women who are drug addicted or alcoholic have only recently been addressed. There has been a lack of careful research with respect to sex differences and a lack of responsiveness to the special treatment requirements of women. The newly developed programs for women described here illustrate the potential efficacy of separate consideration of women's needs.

To provide the context for descriptions of these new services, three issues are discussed. First, until recent years treatment personnel and scientific investigators made no clear distinction between the chemically dependent man and the chemically dependent woman. Second, research in this area has been based on theoretical contexts that stereotype men and women, and the research methodologies employed reflect related biases. Finally, the limited amount of new research knowledge developed in recent years indicate clear ties between overall traditional assumptions about men and women and the specific problems of the chemically dependent woman.

The intention in this discussion is not to present a comprehensive review of the literature in this area; rather, it is to indicate through attention to selected issues where that literature and related interventive methodologies have been influenced by traditional, and now changing, views of men and women. Specifically, the issues reviewed are the implications of a historical perspective for an understanding of the contemporary scene, the documentation of the lack of attention to the special needs of women, evidence of the use of stereotyped views of women in some research, and finally, the new and potentially useful insights derived from recent studies.

The incidence of chemical dependency in the United States over time reflects distinctions between men and women. The history of the prevalence of drug addiction should have alerted investigators much earlier to the probability that women's use of drugs is different from men's. Reviewing the data from 1850 to 1970, Cuskey *et al.* (1972) make two points. First, they state that "America had more addicts during the last half of the nineteenth century than it has today, despite the tremendous and frightening increases since World War II and the skyrocketing rises in the past few years . . . no other Western nation has such a history of drug abuse" (p. 8). Further, "during the entire period, from before the Civil War until immediately following the First World War, female drug addicts outnumbered male addicts two to one" (p. 9). Writers generally acknowledge that the enactment in 1914 of the Harrison Act (which made narcotics illegal and shifted regulation of drug use from the doctor's office to the law enforcement agency), coupled with the reluctance of many women to procure illicit drugs, caused the shift to the present predominance of men in the addict population. Recent figures (1971) indicate that probably about 250,000 people are addicted to drugs in the United States and that of these about 20 percent are women (p. 16).

Writers also generally acknowledge that the higher prevalence of women addicts in earlier times was related to the rather free prescription of opiates to women patients. The tendency of nineteenth-century physicians to relieve many distresses by the administration of an opiate may very well have a contemporary counterpart in current addictions among women. The prevalence of addicts among women may be lower today than it was a century ago, but the medical profession's continuing perspective on women's complaints still contributes to women's addiction problems. It has been reported that 60 percent of all drugs prescribed in 1967 were for women. Seventy-one percent of all antidepressants and 80 percent of all amphetamines prescribed in 1967 were for women (Brecker *et al.* 1972). In the face of this high rate of drug usage, particularly prescribed usage, research dealing specifically with the woman addict has been significantly sparse until very recently.

The same indifference to the particular problems of women occurs in relation to the woman alcoholic. "Women were either ignored or their experiences as alcoholics were considered to be identical to those of male alcoholics until the late 1960's. Between 1929 and 1970, only 29 published studies in the English language dealt with women alcoholics" (*Women and Drugs* 1975).

The general neglect of the chemically dependent woman is exemplified in two recent publications. In June 1974 the Department of Health, Education and Welfare published the monograph *Alcohol and Health*, "a comprehensive review of the *new* directions that are being taken to understand and deal with alcohol misuse and alcoholism" (Chafetz 1974:ix, italics added). Throughout the monograph there are statistical reports that reflect differential occurrence of certain alcohol-related problems by sex, and there are statements, such as the one related to the economic cost of lost production, indicating difficulties in obtaining reliable estimates of the number of women alcoholics. However, there are no statements indicating that there may be important differences between men and women alcoholics that should receive special attention. Further, of the references for three of the chapters in which specific attention to women might be expected—"The Economic Costs of Alcohol-Related Problems," "Trends in Treatment of Alcoholism," and "Problem Drinkers on the Job," only 4 of the 209 studies cited refer specifically to women.

In a series of comprehensive annotated bibliographies concerned with drug abuse published by the National Institute on Drug Abuse in 1975, the same phenomenon occurs. By and large, the articles reviewed there either deal exclusively with male subjects or make no special distinction between men and women when both sexes appear as study subjects. In the monograph devoted to drugs and employment, the professions selected for emphasis are medicine, sports, and aviation, with little reference to those women who are at least part of these groups. The one article that concerns a female group, that of nurse addicts, makes no reference to the distinctive problems of women.

The first point, then, is that most research investigators and treatment professionals have not addressed the special needs of the chemically dependent woman (Waldorf 1970). As will be indicated later, there have been some recent changes in research and treatment emphasis, beginning in the early 1970s (Levy and Doyle 1974:2). The practical implication of this is that when "treatment for women has been typically based on what works for men, poorer success rates for women have resulted from this treatment" (*Women and Drugs* 1975:4).

The second point is that some studies and treatment interventions that have acknowledged women as a separate group have, at the same time, been based on stereotyped assumptions about women. As examples, two studies of alcoholic women (Parker 1972; Parker 1975) employ the concept of femininity measured by scales that use traditional masculine–feminine polarities and tend to view women's substance abuse problems primarily as mental health problems. This tendency to consider alcoholic women psychologically sicker than alcoholic men, has hindered the treatment of female alcoholics, for as Curlee (1970) suggests, the public is more willing to classify women as mentally ill than to classify them as alcoholic. The moralistic view that bemoans the female alcoholic or addict's fall from a set code of conduct distinctive from the code for men is of the same cast as the research instrument that classifies women according to long-held views of women's role behavior. Both have impeded a useful approach to the chemically dependent woman.

Even as this literature accumulated, there were indications in some studies that special consideration of the chemically dependent woman was warranted, though within a nonstereotyped framework.

In Bateman and Peterson's study (1972) of the outcome of treatment of alcoholics, it was found that only 2 of the 13 variables under consideration had prognostic value for both men and women. When Miller and associates (1973) looked at value patterns of drug addicts, they found dissimilar value hierarchies between the two groups, leading to their conjecture that these differences might mean that the same interventive techniques would produce different treatment effects in men and women. Such studies give additional rationale for a distinctive and systematic approach to women's problems.

Once the need for separate consideration is accepted, and particularly as that consideration occurs in a nontraditional perspective, new understanding of women develops. For one thing, the knowledge accumulating from recent research is affording an increasingly clear picture of how and why women become chemically dependent. In both drug abuse and alcoholism, the routes to and the patterns within these addictions appear to be distinctive for women as compared with men, and the differences derive in large part from the traditional roles of men and women.

As indicated earlier, women, who constituted the majority of drug addicts in the last century, developed their addictions through the widespread prescription of drugs by physicians. The phenomenon of drug taking by women at the recommendation of physicians to relieve every ache and pain continues today. Two recent studies document this. Cooperstock (1971) reported that 67 percent of all mood-modifying drugs were dispensed to women, and Backenheimer's (1975) data indicated that in 1974, 67 percent of the Valium and 71 percent of the Librium dispensed was prescribed for women. Backenheimer also reports that in 1974 there were 76,000 emergency room episodes involving Valium or Librium and that in 73 percent of these episodes women were the patients. Glaser's (1966) characterization of narcotic addiction with the pain-prone patient as an iatrogenic disorder (i.e., a condition precipitated by treatment) appears to be an apt one. Moreover, the particular character of the iatrogenic experience repeats the theme of this book—the relationship between women's role in this society and their consequent difficulties.

A number of authors (Cooperstock 1971; Mellinger et al. 1971; Mitchell et al. 1970) have developed this theme well. To begin with, women are more likely than men to view their problems within a medical model. They define themselves as sick, believe it is culturally acceptable to admit weakness or deficiency, and seek professional advice and direction readily. They visit doctors' offices more frequently than men and often appear there with diffuse symptoms.

In a study of the use of a wide range of drugs, all the women queried, compared with 40 percent of the men, reported stress as their primary reason for drug use (Mitchell *et al.* 1970). When women do seek help with generalized complaints (e.g., anxiety, depression, stress), physicians by and large do not understand the reasons for these diffuse disorders. Cooperstock (1971) cites a study in which 73 percent of physicians, when asked to describe a typical complaintive patient, referred spontaneously to women.

Physicians may treat each woman as an individual, and often with compassion, but they are dealing with her own specific situation and not seeing her as one of many women affected by the commonality of a restrictive social role. They turn to mood-modifying drugs as an answer to baffling problems, although serious questions have been raised about the appropriateness of treating such problems and anxieties in this fashion (Chambers and Schultz 1971; Whitlock 1970).

The advertising of mood-modifying drugs by the drug industry is one more indication of society's attitude toward the female patient and constitutes a further exacerbation of the problem. A content analysis was done of drug advertisements in several leading medical journals over a five-year period (Prather and Fidell 1975), and the findings are instructive.

1. The sex stereotypes were confirmed virtually without exception in the advertisements.
2. There was a strong tendency to associate psychoactive drugs with female patients.
3. Nonpsychoactive drug advertisements usually showed a male as the patient, despite the fact that women also take more nonpsychoactive drugs than do men. . . . this difference [is] particularly insidious because it indicates that "real" illnesses are had by men while mental problems are shown by women.
4. The symptoms listed for male and female users of psychoactive drugs were significantly different, with men usually presenting specific and

work-related symptoms while women complained of diffuse anxiety, tension, and depression.

5. Male patients were shown as older on average and at a wider variety of ages than female patients.

6. There were also tendencies to show women as recuperating from mental illness when they reassumed sex-stereotypical attitudes, as irritating significant others by their illnesses, and as suffering from socially embarrassing symptoms. (pp. 25–26)

These advertisements fall on receptive ears. Physicians, like much of society, see women's usual role, particularly the homemaker role, as less important and less demanding than others, and the use of drugs as therefore appropriate. One study found that physicians thought tranquilizers were indicated for homemakers "since they can always take a nap and needn't be mentally alert" (Fidell 1973:9), and in another study 87 percent of the physicians queried judged daily use of Librium as legitimate for homemakers, though only 53 percent held the same view for students (p. 9).

Several negative consequences follow from this widespread prescription of mood-modifying drugs. Perhaps the most important is that the solution does not address the problem. Physicians and their women patients do not understand the causation of this endemic and pervasive difficulty, and in fact the prescription of medication encourages women to continue to see their diffuse complaints as evidence of personal maladjustment to what is supposed to be a satisfying life situation. And, as indicated earlier, there are serious and life-threatening episodes involving medically prescribed tranquilizers. Further, there is some evidence that there is a relationship between maternal use of mood-modifying drugs and drug use by children. One study found "that children whose mothers used tranquilizers daily, when compared with children whose mothers used no drugs, were three times as likely to smoke marihuana or use LSD, six times as likely to use opiates, five times as likely to use stimulants and other hallucinogens, and seven times as likely to use tranquilizers and barbituates" (Women and Drugs 1975:3). In sum, the ready prescription of mood-modifying drugs for women has consequences beyond the well-meaning attempt to alleviate a particular set of generalized and perplexing anxieties.

A look at women's use of hard and illegal drugs reveals a different set of circumstances but a significant connection to stereotyped roles for women. Rosenbaum's data (1973), supported by evidence that is beginning to accumulate (Eldred and Washington 1975), portray the female heroin addict's induction into and continual abuse of the drug as characterized by the same passivity and dependency that is shown by her nonaddicted counterpart.

With respect to what is considered "feminine," the woman addict is not considerably different from the straight woman. Overwhelmingly she is introduced to the drug by a spouse, boyfriend, lover, etc. After having been introduced to heroin by a man, the woman tends to immerse herself into his world and become an addict in faster time than it takes for most men. . . . Whereas a man may brake his habit in order to maintain it at a level at which he can function to support it, the woman, who does not see herself as a financial provider, does not exert control over the growing size and cost of her habit. She does not limit amounts of use and becomes a heavier user than her male counterpart. . . . Sex roles are also reflected by the nature of women's hustles. Though they participate as frequently in two of the same hustles as the men (theft and dealing narcotics), the nature of their participation reflects the woman's role. They may do lightweight theft such as shoplifting, but are not highly represented in burglary or grand theft. They may sell narcotics, but are not the big "connection." There are two hustles which we have called women's hustles due to the ease with which women succeed in them: forgery and prostitution. The success in both is due to sex roles. Women can pass checks because they are assumed to be innocent. They can sell their bodies for money because spontaneous sex is a social taboo. (pp. 25–26)

It would appear that even in one of the most deviant segments of society (i.e., heroin users whose waking hours are totally consumed in supporting their addiction) there are differences between men and women, and that those differences are heavily influenced by sex-typed roles.

Now, also, with preliminary data on the female alcoholic seen as distinctive from the male alcoholic, women seem to have distinctive onsets and different continuing patterns of alcoholism as compared with men. Much of this developing knowledge repeats the connection to societal expectations of women.

There is some evidence that the onset of alcoholism for a woman is related to a crisis situation and frequently tied to her family roles (Curlee 1969). Though there are conflicting data (Morrissey and Schuckit 1977) some studies report two vulnerable periods for the onset of alcoholism—the late twenties (James 1975) and middle age—and two important triggers—the death or desertion of the husband or the maturity and departure of the children (Senseman 1966). "Without their children or husbands to depend on for their identity or sense of worth, these women turned to alcohol" (*Women and Drugs* 1975:4).

James (1975) found in her study that women with alcohol problems waited an average of twelve years before seeking outside assistance, and the reasons for that wait further differentiate the woman alcoholic. The woman tends to be a hidden drinker. She drinks alone, and because so many women do not work, it is possible for her to remain at home, drinking clandestinely, with few people aware of the extent of her difficulty. The shame and stigma of the alcoholic are greater for women than for men, possibly because of the inappropriate idealization of the behavior expected of women. The further shame she imposes on herself may very well be because the personal failure she feels relates to her central or only role as wife and mother. Men can either blame other sources, such as work situations or bad luck, for their alcoholism, or find satisfaction in other arenas. The woman at home drinking quietly and secretly has no other outlet to explain the difficulty or balance the sense of failure. An already low sense of self-esteem is further decreased by alcoholism.

When the woman does begin to make some efforts to find help, those around her, as James reports (1975), are frequently reluctant to acknowledge her alcoholism for what it is. Clouding the response of others is society's need to see the female alcoholic as more abnormal than the male alcoholic. Ironically people are more ready to diagnose a woman's condition as mental illness than as alcoholism (Curlee 1970). When she finally does seek professional help, the physician she consults is likely to see the problem as a psychiatric one, often prescribing mood-modifying drugs (Fraser 1973). As a consequence, the severely alcoholic woman is frequently dependent on more than one drug.

In addition to distinctive onset patterns, drinking behavior, and societal pressures, developing research is showing that female alcoholism is a complicated entity psychodynamically (Wilsnack 1976). Schuckit and Winokur (1972) describe three diagnostic categories for the female alcoholic: (1) the primary alcoholic, in whom no psychiatric illness antedates alcohol abuse; (2) the secondary or affective disorder alcoholic, in whom alcoholism is associated with a history of depression; and (3) the sociopathic alcoholic, in whom a sociopathic personality is present prior to the onset of alcoholism. Commenting further on the affective disorder alcoholic, they note the similarities between alcoholism and depression, and observe that each of these conditions may mask the other. Greater success is reported in the treatment of the affective disorder alcoholic, and Schuckit and Winokur make the case for both differential treatment based on appropriate diagnosis, and further study of this insufficiently researched area.

This discussion of the chemically dependent woman has emphasized two general points. First, the specific and nonsexist attention to the alcoholic and drug-abusing woman as distinct from her male counterpart has only a recent history. Women have been either ignored as a separate group when chemical dependency has been studied or treated, or approached, without thorough research or therapies, in a sex-stereotyped manner. Second, when looked at as a distinctive group, women have been found to have patterns of chemical abuse that are different from those of men. The woman drug abuser both now and in the past is clearly connected to the drug-prescribing physician. The patterns of onset and continued use, in addition, reflect the traditional dependence on men as the primary actors. The woman alcoholic also has a distinctive history, characterized primarily by hidden drinking, and is much more likely to be diagnosed as mentally ill than as alcoholic.

Newly developed services for the chemically dependent woman have been based on the premise that such women have distinctive needs and problems and that in order to be effective, services have to be delivered within a nonstereotyped framework. These programs present an alternative to the traditional medical model of treatment and also to the now almost traditional therapeutic community approach exemplified by the Synanon/Daytop models. The new programs for women place emphasis on the full development of the woman, that is, not only resolving the problem of drug abuse and/or alcoholism but widening her nonsexist life style and work options. Also, and to varying extents among these programs, emphasis is placed on the needed reeducation of the program staffs to a nonsexist orientation.

The programs described here are presented in a variety of formats in order to emphasize different aspects of each. None of the programs is discussed in its entirety, though, depending on the purpose, some are presented more fully than others. Stressing one aspect of the program (e.g., special staff training) in a particular instance does not imply the absence of such service aspects in other programs.

The treatment program of TODAY, Inc., of Newton, Pennsylvania, translates a philosophical base of radical feminism into services for drug-abusing women, and for men as well. Women, Inc., of Dorchester, Massachusetts, a center to which women can bring their children, has developed a carefully documented review describing their clientele (women with drug addictions), the women's use of services, and outcome data. The Alcoholism Center for Women in Los Angeles has pioneered services for the lesbian alcoholic. The Women's Program of CASPAR (Cambridge and Sommerville Program for Alcoholism Rehabilitation) in Massachusetts has a specially designed training program for the development of a nonsexist approach to alcoholic women.

An important aspect of an introduction to these services planned specifically for the chemically dependent woman is their sparse number nationally, in contrast to those for men or for mixed populations. For example, NIAAA (The National Institute for Alcohol Abuse and Alcoholism) funded "542 alcoholism treatment programs, only 14 of which are designed specifically to serve women. The monetary breakdown is slightly over 2 million dollars for women's programs as compared with close to 75 million in total funding (Finkelstein *et al.* 1977:2). Not only are these services for women a recent phenomenon, but their small number is a reflection of a continuing reluctance to acknowledge the need for separate attention to women. Finally, by way of transition to the programs, these descriptions and the scholarly papers that accompany them will serve to supplement the introductory review and provide further refinements in understanding the chemically dependent woman.

# TODAY, Inc.

TODAY, Inc. (Treatment of Drug and Alcohol Abuse Among Young Adults) is a Newton, Pennsylvania, center for the treatment of drug addiction and alcoholism for men and women between the ages of 15 and 30. The material that follows describes the program as it operated in the middle 1970s, until late 1976. Though the program has changed considerably since then, this description is included because it represents a particular approach to the addicted woman that has its counterpart in other such services. The fact that the service has changed reflects the fact that shifts in programming do occur as new personnel or new ideas enter the scene (see Doyle *et al.* 1977).

The program as described used radical feminism as the philosophical base for its programs for women, and extended that rationale to a nonsexist approach to male addicts as well. The description that follows is adapted from two reports authored by Ardelle Schultz, former director of therapy. The two papers, dated 1974, are "TODAY, Inc.'s Non-Sexist Approach to its Treatment Modalities" and "Special Treatment and Service Needs of Women Drug Abusers."

The history of TODAY, Inc., is a study in the evolution of a community-based program from the one-dimensional approach of the Synanon/Daytop model to its present and continuing search for a more total approach to people who happen to have a problem with addiction. TODAY opened in March 1971, and for the first six months it imitated what seemed to be the most successful model for treating drug addicts at that time: the self-help, encounter-oriented, therapeutic community, with all its various structures and basic techniques. Admission to the program was gained through a high-stress interview, usually preceded by "sitting on the bench" for hours, sometimes days, at a time. The interview itself was an intense situation in which prospective residents had to prove their motivation, usually by means of an exaggerated expression of feelings. Those who passed through the interview were assigned to the "punk" squad—the lowest rung of the status system that was utilized to incorporate the work aspects of the program.

Therapy groups fell into two categories. One was the "slip group," which was held twice a week and was designed to help facilitate understanding of the uses and abuses of anger. The other was the encounter therapy group, which was held three times a week. The groups were composed of both male and female residents led by a male therapist. It should come as a surprise to no one who is familiar with the self-help model that the director and all the therapists were males, nor that the women in treatment were receiving, basically, a new set of behaviors designed to make them more acceptable to males.

"Learning experiences" were being used in their most rigid and punitive form—for example, head shaves, diaper and playpen experiences, and so forth. It was the indiscriminate use of these techniques that brought the original administration to an end after the first six months.

## First Steps in Reorganization

When the program changed directorship in November 1971, one of the main concerns in evaluating the status of the program and defining new directions was concern for the women and the failure of most treatment programs to relate to the needs of women in treatment. The first order of business was to hire a female therapist and to separate the groups by sex. The rationale for this was arrived at through a prior successful experience in trying to establish an effective treatment program for women within a male–female program. Basically, the rationale was as follows.

### AN ALL-WOMEN GROUP

If self-worth is a given for successful recovery, then caring about oneself as a human being and as a woman is crucial. How can a woman see herself as worthy if she cannot identify with other women in a positive way? Society has kept women isolated from each other through competition and superficiality. Women themselves do not trust each other. They see other women as dangerous to their own search for male approval. Older women are threatened by the unlined faces and nubile bodies of younger women. Younger women do not want to be reminded of aging to come by the presence of sagging breasts and varicose veins. The moralistic suburban woman alcoholic decries the immorality of the young, promiscuous woman drug addict. The younger drug addict attacks the phony value system of the married older alcoholic, seeing her as the biggest prostitute of all, and a drunk at that.

## A WOMAN ROLE MODEL AS THERAPIST

The rationale for having a woman therapist as role model focused on the need for the therapist to provide genuine empathy, honest self-disclosure, and broadly based accpetance of the conflicts of womanhood. The difficulties the average male therapist faces in meeting these criteria are multitudinous. The average addicted female has had extensive experience in learning the advantages of giving males the answers and behaviors that will please. It is hard for the male therapist not to relate to the woman addict as a benevolent Daddy, demigod, or protective big brother. While any of these suggested relationships may *feel* mutually good to therapist and patient, they are fraught with potential destructiveness for both.

When women have constituted a minority of the patients within therapeutic communities for drug abuse treatment, reports indicate that they are used—for sex itself, as hostesses at community gatherings, for kitchen work, and, mostly, as sex role models for the men in therapy groups. If a male group was planning an extended therapy session, such as a marathon, women were included to act out the mother, sister, lover roles for the male resident. The average woman in the average institution would simply accept this kind of treatment and leave with a further reinforcement of the identity/worth conflicts that brought her there in the first place. A women's group, therefore, should be led by a woman, a woman who has resolved her own identity/worth conflicts and can be a role model providing strength, compassion, and competence.

A 24-year-old woman drug addict talks about the effect of such a woman role model:

> I had seen her before on the grounds of the therapeutic community where I was trying to recover from my addiction to heroin. . . . I knew she was the Director's wife, a recovered alcoholic, and a qualified therapist in her own right. One day I happened to overhear her having a loud verbal argument with her husband, the Director. Her voice, clear and distinct, angry and unwilling not to be heard, stating her demands, taking a stand, telling him where it was at, and what she was worth. To me, this was unheard of, practically unlawful, from the kind of suburban background I had come from. No woman dared to speak to her husband like that. As I came to know her in the coming months, she did dare to speak. . . .
>
> When this woman took over our group, it was like an end to a spiritual famine. She gave to myself and the other women a very real conception of what a successful, well-directed woman is, something none of us had ever seen in the flesh.

With the all-women group led by an appropriate woman role model, the self-help concept at TODAY offered several components that were of particular benefit to women.

## Self-Help Techniques Applied for Women

### SLIP GROUPS

The self-help concept at TODAY had several components that are of particular benefit to women. One was the mixed-sex *slip group*. Slip groups emerged from the Synanon/Daytop encounter model of treatment and are based on the "hold-and-dump" theory. No moral judgments are made about feelings, but it is held that what you do with your feelings is important. Hence, residents may not *dump their feelings* within the course of the day, but are strongly encouraged to deal with them in slip group. There are many advantages to this technique. People learn that anger can be controlled. They learn that anger does not have to destroy, but can be used in a positive way to defend oneself. They also learn that they can survive other people's anger—that they will not be destroyed.

For women, slip groups offer one of the most important learning experiences. Many, for the first time in their lives, are in an atmosphere where they are allowed to be angry. Many more find, for the first time, they they can survive anger directed at them, especially male anger. Slip groups provide women with the awareness of the power that anger can generate. They see how it has been used to keep them frightened and in their place, and they also see how they have used their own anger against themselves. With the support of other women, they learn to survive the charges of "aggressive, angry bitch" and to believe that their womanhood is not dependent on sweet passivity. It is in the slip groups that men begin to perceive that something very different is happening with women.

It was also in the slip groups that the attempt to develop a single standard of mental health can be observed most clearly. Broverman, Broverman *et al.* (1970) point out in their paper, *Sex Role Stereotypes and Clinical Judgments of Mental Health,* that a double standard of mental health does predominate. The standard for the healthy male correlates with the standard for the healthy adult. However, the standard for the healthy female differs significantly from that for the healthy adult. This places women in the conflictual position of having to decide whether to exhibit those positive characteristics considered desirable for males and adults and thus have their femininity questioned (i.e., to be deviant as a woman) or to behave in the prescribed feminine manner, accept second-class status, and possibly live a lie to boot.

It is possible that women who abuse drugs and alcohol, a seemingly male disease, are making a strong statement about their need to find an outlet for their so-called "male traits." For treatment purposes, it is enough to know that women must learn to develop honesty and integrity in order to feel the self-worth necessary to live sober lives. For most addicted women, that means learning to be independent and self-confident, and to do this they must have an environment that will not then question their femininity or call them deviant, but will support their right to first-class adulthood.

In the slip group women confronted others with their anger. They risked the rejection inherent in showing their true selves to men. Men, of course, did not like this at first, but as they changed and grew, and as they saw that they are given the same rights as regards the feelings society has not allowed them to express (tenderness, tears, and trepidations), they began to prefer the "honest" woman to the game players they have known most of their lives.

## THE WORK STRUCTURE

Another aspect of the program that offered women a vast opportunity for growth was the work structure. The professional staff directed the therapy, but the day-to-day operation of the house was taken care of by the residents themselves. People were assigned duties and promoted through the status system on the basis of ability rather than sex. Therefore, there could be a male resident in charge of housekeeping and a female resident in charge of maintenance. Learning to be resourceful and competent in areas formerly regarded as "man's work" (driving a tractor, fixing a sink, etc.) gave a woman confidence and independence.

This kind of breaking down of stereotypic sex role behavior did not happen without confusion and conflict. The woman feared rejection for being "too masculine"; the man resented and was severely threatened by this intrusion into his domain. Hostility often erupted and the men attempted, through coercion and intimidation, to put the woman "back in her place." It was then that the women relied heavily on the solidarity of the women's group, where they got the message that it was "all right" to be aggressive, competent, and independent and still be a woman. As the men themselves grew, they learned to respect and to appreciate the women's honest efforts to be self-reliant and realized they were being released from the male stereotype of Mr. Fix-It.

## THE LEARNING EXPERIENCE

The learning experience, used with a context of support and concern, proved to be a most effective tool in helping the addicted women cut through years of conditioned response to society's expectations of womanhood. For example, a good number of addicted women relied on their sex object image to survive and succeed in the drug world.

This leaves the woman with the feeling that her primary worth is dependent on her physical looks and sexual desirability.

In the role of sex object a woman becomes overly concerned with her looks. When a woman has a poorly defined ego, as well as a low self-image to start with, she relates to her sex object image in an exaggerated way. Many found temporary self-worth and power in the drug world on the basis of this identity. A 19-year-old heroin addict related the following story:

> I met a heroin wheeler-dealer from Philadelphia. He took me as His Girl. He wined me and dined me, and dressed me up in pretty clothes, and most importantly, he supplied me with junk. Of all my identities, it gave me the most reward. I had status, a sense of power, I was adored by an important person and any conflict that even started to surface could be easily deadened with heroin.

If she is to discover that there are other parts of herself that have worth and meaning, she must be temporarily withdrawn from self-exploitation of her sexual personality.

Another manifestation of the feminine sex role concept is the "little girl" syndrome, outwardly expressed via girlishly long, straight hair and overly juvenile attire. The learning experience here would be a simple cosmetic approach with a shorter, more grown-up hairdo and clothing more commensurate with the woman's actual age and personal style.

Since women in treatment have spent a good deal of time seeking approval through male attention and male relationships, it was sometimes necessary to enforce a communication ban with the male population. The goal of the ban was to provide the woman with the experiential knowledge of her ability to sustain herself without male feedback. And, at the same time, it forced her into more supportive, noncompetitive relationships with women.

## THE SPORTS PROGRAM

As women began to break out of their dependent roles as little girls and sex objects, they began to discover parts of themselves that had been denied. In the transition from adolescence to adulthood, many young "tomboys" who may have become competent athletes were discouraged from that "unfeminine" activity. Athletic competition has long been viewed in a very positive light for men. In school it is seen as a healthy outlet, even an integral part of the specific physical and psychological development of a healthy male. The status of athletic achievement at the high school and college levels opens many an employment and social door for men. That these obvious values are denied to women seems unjustified in view of the data that are beginning to flow out of research studies regarding the strength and capabilities of women vis-à-vis men.

Specifically, in the TODAY program not only had an unusually high percentage of young female addicts been identified as "tomboys" in adolescence, but a number had had active athletic careers during high school. In more than one case there was an obvious and direct relationship between the cessation of athletic activities and the ensuing involvement in the drug culture. In one case, a change of residence and school left one young woman with no athletic tenure at the new school and seemingly no way to penetrate the caste/clique system that surrounded the sports program. In another, leaving one school that had provided a good sports program for women and entering another where there was little or none had the same effect. Without sports activities that had provided not only an outlet for competition, aggression, and physical fitness but also a means of identity and recognition, both girls became involved in drugs, which offer their own recognition and power/status rewards.

At first competing somewhat tentatively across the ping-pong table, and then finding some small success in that, women residents at TODAY began to want more opportunities to play at other games and were willing to risk competition with the men. They participated in ping-pong, volleyball, softball, swimming, basketball, and bowling. Their athletic endeavors produced results almost immediately, and the sports program was clearly an important and healthy outlet for their competitiveness and aggression, an opportunity to develop confidence in their bodies, and a source of pride in their achievements.

## Special Problems of Women

Other problems had to be faced regarding the special concerns of women. This was particularly true with the problems of black and other minority women, who have experienced the double oppression of being black or Puerto Rican and being a woman. In a therapeutic community minority men, both staff and residents, put tremendous pressure on the minority women to identify only with the minority struggle and to see women's issues as relevant just to upper-and middle-class white women.

Ideally, a minority woman therapist who has dealt with these conflicts is best equipped to work with and help women who are caught in this sociocultural double bind. White women can try to use the empathy of womanhood and be sensitive and open to experiences that they have not shared. Most important, a white woman therapist should not become an instrument of conflict for the minority woman by creating more pressure, trying to have her identify totally with the women's movement without allowing her to seek a sense of worth at her own pace and in her own way.

Motherhood also presents special psychological, social, and economic concerns for women that cannot be compared to men's roles as fathers. Motherhood is one of the only career identities open to women in our society that promises power, prestige, and prominence. Addicted women quite naturally seek that role, probably more than most women, as some insurance against their feelings of inadequacy and self-hate. As a 23-year-old woman addict said,

> Even though I met my husband over a drug deal, and even though we married while still on methadone, for the first time in my life I felt respectable. My feelings of being a woman blossomed in marriage, and then I was desperate to have a baby. Now that I was truly a woman, motherhood would be the ultimate fulfillment.

This drug-blinded search for fulfillment as a mother leads all too often to further disgrace as a woman. It is impossible for an addict to play out the mother role, and children are either left to fend for themselves or given over to relatives or public agencies.

When an addicted mother reaches a point of abstinence, after physical withdrawal from the drug, she is overwhelmed with feelings of shame and guilt about her children. The feelings must be dealt with therapeutically. However, this cannot be done successfully in a vacuum of inaction, for the woman must also be assured that her children are being cared for in an appropriate and acceptable way. Few programs have addressed themselves to the need for temporary foster homes and child care facilities. One solution found was setting up a network of foster homes near the treatment center where the woman's children could be housed with families and she could begin to visit them and move toward accepting the full responsibility of motherhood as she was able to.

Older women with grown children face different problems related to motherhood. Often their drinking and drug use have taken place through the years of their children's adolescence and young adulthood, and in many cases the children have turned away in disillusionment and harbored great hostility toward them. Sometimes reconciliation could be effected, sometimes not. Nevertheless, the issue for the addicted women is still learning how to forgive herself for one of society's biggest crimes—failure at motherhood.

As noted earlier, the program of TODAY, Inc. has shifted considerably. The rationale and specifics of this program, however, remain useful alternatives.

# The First Two Years: A Profile of Women Entering Women, Inc.*

PAMELA J. SCHWINGL, DARLA MARTIN-SHELTON, AND LAURA SPERAZI

Women, Inc., is one of the small number of the nation's residential drug treatment programs for women that are staffed by women and allow residents to bring their children into treatment with them.

* This investigation was supported by Grant no. 5-H81-DA-01651, National Institute on Drug Abuse. The report is dated July 27, 1977.

The initial impetus for the program arose primarily from the experience of women working and being "treated" in residential therapeutic communities. "TCs," as they are commonly referred to, have been modeled primarily after Synanon, a self-help program formed by ex-addicts in the early 1950s. They are typically based on confrontation and hierarchical work models; residents in these programs usually work up a ladder in the house hierarchy and earn basic rights and privileges as they climb. Most of these programs have been run by men, and the status of women in these programs has been reflective of the second-class status of women in the larger society. Women usually represent a minority in these programs, and they are generally known to stay for a very short time in treatment and to have a very low "success" rate.

The failure of TCs to be an attractive treatment alternative for women has been described recently. Labeling, stereotyping, sexual abuse, and failure to provide such services as child care and health care have been cited by an increasing number of authors (Wynn and Clement 1977; Soler *et al.* 1974). In the early 1970s, with the strength of the women's movement behind them, women from all over the country decided that women would not be adequately served until women themselves started forming and running programs that focused on developing new ways to treat addicted women.

To encourage this effort, the National Institute of Drug Abuse (NIDA) funded five demonstration programs for women across the country. A range of modalities ranging from methadone maintenance to drug-free residence are represented by these programs, although Women, Inc., is one of only two models that are run by women. To facilitate the task of coordinating ideas and research from these programs as well as others, the Women's Drug Research Collaborative was also funded by NIDA. Throughout this report we will be referring to research prepared under their auspices.

The Women, Inc., demonstration model focuses on self-help within a supportive, collectively governed atmosphere. There is less emphasis on group dynamics and hierarchical work structure than exists in traditional TCs, and more concern with advocacy, education, and skill development. As part of our larger effort to describe this treatment approach, we have prepared the following description of the treatment needs of women that arise from their survival experience as working-class and minority women, mothers, and addicts within the drug subculture and within the larger socioeconomic system.

This report provides basic demographic data as well as the drug use, survival, and child-raising histories of the 54 women who entered Women, Inc., between June 1, 1975, and May 31, 1977. Although additional studies will incorporate comparisons of residents of Women, Inc. with female residents of local co-sex therapeutic communities, the importance of the current findings alone is considerable for the program itself, and provides a base of comparison for other drug treatment programs, particularly other all-women programs.

## OVERVIEW OF RESEARCH AT WOMEN, INC.

During a two-year period 54 female residents voluntarily completed a structured interview prepared by the Women's Drug Research Collaborative (WDR) and an unstructured social history interview compiled by the Women, Inc., research staff. Both interviews were administered by two trained professional interviewers on the Women, Inc., research and admissions staff. In addition to these data, 15 women from this group and 15 from local co-sex programs completed an open-ended interview, administered at two times, that aims at assessing the learning of self-sufficiency skills by clients in women's programs and co-sex programs. A third group of 20 women who have treatment histories from Women, Inc., and local co-sex therapeutic communities are currently being interviewed to investigate women's needs and situations after leaving a treatment program, and to evaluate the differential impact of all-women and co-sex programs on female participants.

## METHOD

Interviews were conducted in privacy during the first week after a woman entered the program. These interviews required 60 to 90 minutes to complete. The group interviewed included all but two women, who left before they could be interviewed. There are several women included in these data who stayed less than the full six- to nine-month program period, and a sizable percentage who stayed in the program less than one month (24 percent). We have included all the women in this report, however, and have correlated length of stay with several other variables in the final section of the report.

## Demographic Description of
## Women Entering Women, Inc.

Women entering the program come primarily from the inner city of Boston (78 percent). Women coming from outside this area (22 percent) come mainly from large industrialized towns and cities outside the Boston metropolitan area. Most of the women (76 percent) have voluntary status and have been referred either from local drug treatment programs (24 percent), through the court referral system (13 percent), or through other social service agencies (13 percent), or are self-referred and have heard of the program through family or friends (26 percent). Only 24 percent have been assigned to the program by the courts. This may be somewhat different from the status of women in traditional therapeutic communities. In a sample of women entering residential treatment programs in Connecticut, an overwhelming majority were reported to be involuntary admissions (Soler *et al.* 1974).

However, the majority of women entering Women, Inc. (80 percent) are involved in some legal proceedings at entry. Women are either on probation, on parole, awaiting trial, or have cases pending. In a WDR report (Binion 1976) based on data collected from the five demonstration programs, this was not shown to be the case for the larger group of women. Binion reports that 72 percent of women entering programs were not involved in legal proceedings at entry. This suggests that women entering Women, Inc., may be representing quite a different population from the general sample included in Binion's data.

Women, Inc., was created for the "older woman" with children. The minimum age for entry into the program is 19; in the two years of data collection and treatment, women up to the age of 34 have entered and received services. In a small sample of outreach clients who are not included in this description, there have been women receiving services who are in their 40s and 50s. The average age of women is almost 24, and over 75 percent of the women are age 26 or under. A smaller percentage, 22 percent, are between 27 and 34 years old. Other studies report the average age of various populations of addicted women to be from 2 to 13 years older than our data show (Ellingwood *et al.* 1966). Since we do not have corresponding figures from these data that compare the number of years women in these samples and women in our sample have been addicted, it is difficult to determine whether women are using drugs at an earlier age, whether they are seeking treatment and termination of their drug careers earlier than women did previously, or whether women's programs attract younger women. There may also be a difference in the ages of women who enter therapeutic communities, women's programs, and methadone maintenance programs, as is suggested by the research of the Women's Health Advocates. Their study indicates that women who are older are likely to use methadone maintenance programs and nonresidential programs. However, given the different approach and services of women's residential programs, more older women may be attracted to them over time.

Women, Inc., has also focused on serving a multiracial, multiethnic population. There has been a clear need in the commonwealth of Massachusetts for a program to serve the needs of minority women who have been underrepresented in drug treatment programs throughout the state.* Our data reveal that Women, Inc., serves primarily black women (72 percent) and smaller percentages of white (22 percent) and Latin women (6 percent). The location of the program in the predominantly black and Third World areas of Roxbury–Dorchester and the South End, and the presence of a multiracial staff, has in a small way begun to close the gap in treatment needs for minority women in the city and state.

Among the sample of women entering Women, Inc., 93 percent cited heroin as their most frequently used and favored substance of

* Data from the Division of Drug Rehabilitation, Department of Mental Health, Commonwealth of Massachusetts, indicate that white women account for over 80 percent of their sample in state-funded drug and prevention programs.

abuse. The remaining women either favored alcohol or were primarily "polydrug" users. Of the women favoring heroin first, 44 percent claimed a second preferred drug; the drugs reported were alcohol, marijuana, other opiates, amphetamines, and barbiturates. The period of time in which women have been involved in drugs or alcohol when they enter the program is anywhere from six months to thirteen years. The average length of addiction and serious drug involvement is almost five years. As might be expected older women (27–34) appear to have longer addiction histories, 6.9 years, than younger women (19–26), 4.1 years. For women who are primarily heroin users, the mean age at their first use of heroin is 18.7 years, with 71 percent of the sample starting to use heroin before the age of 20.

The vast majority (85 percent) of women entering Women, Inc., are mothers. They have between one and four children, with most (69 percent) having one or two children and the smallest group (7 percent) having four children.

## Women Surviving:
### The Alternatives and Choices

Several authors in the field of drug abuse refer to people's involvement in a drug subculture as their participation in a "deviant social career" (Rubington 1967; Becker 1967; Becker 1963; Coombs et al. 1976). They propose that drug abuse can be explored as a social career in the same way that other career patterns can be investigated. Coombs et al. suggest four "career stages": (1) initiation into drug taking; (2) escalation of drug taking behavior, motives, etc.; (3) maintenance of a deviant life style; and (4) a successful discontinuation of drug use (Coombs et al. 1976). They also urge identification of the "structural preconditions" from which drug abuse careers arise.

In an unpublished paper on women and deviant careers, Reed and Herr (1977) use this model and suggest several advantages for it, one being the ability to develop strategies for intervention into a woman's addiction cycle in order to terminate the drug career earlier and less destructively. They also point out that if women have patterns of deviant careers, they also have special issues that are likely to influence "career development," including multiple roles, need for support networks, responsibilities of child rearing, and lack of occupational opportunities.

In the following sections of this profile, we will borrow from Coombs' model of careers and will examine from our data how the particular issues of working-class and minority women modify and affect their career choice and development. Using this model, we have been able to generate a set of questions and line of inquiry to draw a somewhat different picture of the needs and circumstances of female addicts than has heretofore been developed. We feel, however, that the term *career* needs to be used with caution. The term implies choice, and young women rarely can be said to "choose" either motherhood or addiction out of a range of alternative choices. In fact, these may be the only feasible alternatives for young inner-city women, as will be shown by our data.

## TURNING TO DRUGS

Much of the research on addicted women has investigated the psychodynamics of the families of addicted women as a predisposing factor, if not a causal explanation, of their entry into drug addiction. It has been suggested that drug abuse and child abuse/neglect in the families of female addicts create a cyclic pattern that operates to bring women into addiction careers and to continue patterns of poor parenting (Blum 1972; Densen-Gerber *et al.* 1972; T. Freedman *et al.* 1975; Braucht *et al.* 1973).

Other investigators seek physiological or psychosomatic predispositions of female addicts to explain their drug use. The "pain-prone female" has been identified as one type of woman who is likely to become addicted (Glaser 1966; Glaser 1968). However, important work is also suggested by a sociological and economic discussion of the predisposing factors of addiction among women.

Given the increasing presence and availability of heroin and other opiates in the black community since the 1960s, there has been evidence to suggest that the number of women using narcotics as well as alcohol is increasing and that women are starting drug use at earlier ages (Thure and Moore, 1977). The employment options available to a woman growing up in these communities continue to be limited at the same time that social mores restricting behavior are loosening and the availability of illegal drugs is increasing. It is not surprising that more women are becoming involved in "addiction careers."

The lack of employment opportunities has been suggested as cause for initial and continued drug involvement of addicted men and women (Yankowitz and Randell 1976:20). In studies that have examined the variable of employment, it has been found that addicted women have lower rates of employment than addicted males (Curtis *et al.* 1974; Levy and Doyle 1974) and higher rates of unemployment than males in general (Binion 1976). Addicted women, of course, are subject to the alternatives, or lack of alternatives, that are available to women throughout society and to minority and working-class women in particular. Many of the jobs these women are able to find are sex typed and low paying. In a survey of women entering the five women's demonstration programs (ibid.), the occupations women report having been engaged in prior to treatment are largely in service and clerical categories, while very small percentages of women (4 percent) are engaged in professional, technical, or management job categories. It has been suggested elsewhere that for many addicted women, choosing a male-linked life style and drugs is an attractive and somewhat glamorous alternative to the available options. This fact, combined with the perception and reality that other kinds of work are less open to them, provides some explanation for the lack of employment of addicted women.

In the sample of women entering Women, Inc., all were unemployed at entry, while 93 percent reported having had some occupational history; 7 percent reported never having worked. Most of the jobs women have held fall into the clerical, sales, and semiskilled or unskilled labor categories.

Curtis *et al.* (1974), in a report on data collected through the network of the Drug Abuse Reporting Program (n.d.), find that the majority of addicts have less than a high school degree and more than an eighth-grade education. Of the women in our sample, 66 percent have attained a high school diploma, although 72 percent have had at least some high school and 34 percent have a diploma and some years of college. The extent of vocational training received by ad-

dicted women has not been described, although analysis from the
Client Oriented Data Acquisition Process system (U.S. Dept. of
Health, Education, and Welfare, n.d.) tells us that women are less
likely to be involved in vocational training at admission than men.
Women in our sample are more likely than not to have had some
vocational or skill training. Fifty-eight percent have had some training, and an additional 4 percent have completed their GED. While
these figures on vocational training are somewhat encouraging given
the employment picture, particularly in the last half-decade, these
educational levels still do not give addicted women an advantage in
getting employment, particularly in careers offering mobility and opportunities.

If there is a range of social and economic preconditions pushing
women into addiction, there are also preconditions pulling women
into a child-rearing role. For many women, becoming a mother isn't
a choice; pressure within black and Spanish families, as well as in
white families, for women to become mothers puts additional bur-
dens on women. Availability of birth control information and attitudes toward abortion and child rearing vary throughout both black
and white communities; however, it has been reported that addicted
women tend not to choose abortion once they become pregnant, and
often do not use birth control to prevent pregnancies (Back *et al.*
1976). There are many reasons offered for this, from psychological
ones to political ones. In any case, there are cultural, racial, and
class issues behind the decision to have children that need to be described, not only for addicted women but for nonaddicted women as
well.

Some insights about the alternatives that poor and working-class
women have are suggested by an analysis of when women start using
drugs. We divided our sample into women who used heroin or alcohol prior to the birth of their first child. Results indicated that, of the
women in our sample who had children, 45 percent started using the
drug prior to the birth of their first baby and 48 percent started using
it after the birth of their first baby. (Information was incomplete for
4 percent of this sample, and 3 percent of the women in the sample
reported starting drug use the year their first child was born. We did
not have enough data to determine which event occurred first.)

Upon investigating the differences between these two groups of women, a pattern emerges suggesting that between the ages of 16 and 17, or around the latter part of high school, women in this sample "choose" between two alternatives: becoming engaged in the drug culture or becoming mothers. For the women who "choose" to have their babies first, their average age at the birth of this child is 16.8. Their entry into drugs is delayed by an average of another three or four years to about age 20. For women who enter the drug scene first, their average age at the time of their first child is 20.4, while their entry into addiction occurred about three years prior, when they were about 17 years old. There is also some indication from our data that these patterns may vary according to race. Of the white women with children in the sample, 29 percent had their babies first, while 47 percent of the black women and 100 percent of the Puerto Rican women followed this pattern. This might suggest different pressures on black and Spanish women to bear children; however, these percentages and interpretations are tentative.

What these data suggest is that two "career options" are available to women in this group, those of child rearer and addict. Data on the level of skills, educational and occupational history, and entry into addiction illustrate that women are limited to narrow choices at a very early age, if we can permit ourselves to call these "choices."

It has been suggested (Eldred and Washington 1976) that women might begin addiction careers because of lack of support, feelings of role failure, or child care responsibilities. While we do not have complete data on this, in a subsample of women (N = 14) asked about what they see as the relationship between their drug use and their responsibilities as a mother, all women answered that they did not feel that their children were responsible for the onset of their drug use, but almost 50 percent reported that their child care responsibilities accounted for the continuation and escalation of their drug use.

Other literature suggests that women begin drug use in small groups and are usually introduced to drugs by men, often their husbands (Eldred and Washington 1976; Cuskey 1972). Women in this sample are introduced to drugs primarily by male and female friends and their husbands, and through the use of legal prescription drugs. It appears that an almost equal number of male and female friends or lovers introduce women to the use of drugs (35 vs. 31 percent). This is somewhat surprising, given the literature's emphasis on males as initiators of females into drug use. As women increase drug use, however, the number of women introducing other women to drugs is likely to increase. Forty-four percent of the women who have been married ($N = 18$) were introduced to heroin by their husbands. Women who had their first babies prior to their addiction were slightly more likely to be introduced to heroin by close male friends or husbands (55 percent) than women who did not have their babies until after they began using drugs (30 percent). Women who started using drugs earlier (about 16 or 17 years old) were more likely to report female friends or peer pressure as motivation to start using drugs.

## PATTERNS OF USE AND THEIR EFFECTS

The processes of moving into a drug career and establishing patterns of drug use have not been described, particularly for women. Factors affecting changes in patterns of drug use and descriptions of the various espects of the woman's life that are affected by drug use are virtually absent from the literature (Reed and Herr 1977). Women's use of drugs during pregnancy is one area of investigation in which there are some data, however. Samples of women from drug programs for pregnant addicts show high percentages of women who are addicted during pregnancy and at the birth of their babies (Stern 1966; Stone *et al.* 1971), while surveys of addicted women who are not involved in such drug programs indicate that a much higher percentage of women control or interrupt drug use during this time (Mayer and Black 1976). While we do not have comprehensive data in this area, a subsample ($N = 11$) of women entering Women, Inc., who were asked to report on whether any of their children were addicted at birth indicated that only 9 percent had given birth to addicted babies. This may suggest that women interrupt their drug use during pregnancy. However, our present data do not provide details of the type and amount of drug use during pregnancy for us to be sure that this is the case.

Literature on the physical condition of women addicts and the effects drugs have on their health has been limited primarily to descriptions of women's reproductive systems, although research efforts currently are under way that investigate a broader range of symptoms among women addicts.* In general, despite the physiological nature of drug use and addiction, issues of the health care of addicted women often have not been given sufficient attention. Whether this arises from a tendency to label the female addict as "hypochondriac" or from limitations on resources, the health problems of female addicts go unnoticed unless they are associated with pregnancy or gynecology (Soler et al. 1974).

Studies of the effects of alcohol on women and men have indicated that in fact women may be more debilitated by alcohol and at a faster rate than men. While there are no comparable data for methadone, heroin, or the range of drugs that users may take throughout their lives, attention is being drawn to the fact that women may not be complaining simply to "get attention." Other medical studies have also shown that in times of stress individuals show physical signs of change and disability (Rahe 1968; Adler 1975). Given the fact that the life style of the addict is somewhat unstable and stressful, it is not unlikely that addicted women may suffer a range of symptoms associated with stress. The extent of health problems in this population might arise, then, not only from drug use, poverty, and poor nutrition but also from repeated life crises. To use a concept borrowed from sociology, the poor health of the addict is likely to be overdetermined.

Given this fact, however, relatively few women in our sample report medical and gynecological problems. Fifty-three percent report the presence of medical problems that are currently being treated at entry and 23 percent report the presence of problems that they feel should be treated. Women cite such disorders as abscesses, dental problems, thyroid disorders, hepatitis, gallstones, urinary tract infections, venereal disease, chronic headaches, phlebitis, abdominal pain, edema, and hypertension. Many of these disorders have been shown to be associated with drug use, stress, or poor diet.

Data on the presence of gynecological disorders, however, give

* Current research is being conducted under the auspices of the Women's Drug Research Collaborative, Ann Arbor, Michigan.

some insight into the woman's perception of her own physical well-being. Sixty-six percent of the women in the sample reported having no gynecological problems; 26 percent of the women mentioned "problems" having to do with obstetrical conditions, such as being pregnant, just having had an abortion, having had miscarriages or tubal pregnancies, or having trouble becoming pregnant. Eight percent mentioned venereal disease, pelvic inflammatory disease, vaginal discharge, or not having a period as problems. Only one woman mentioned amenorrhea as a problem. This is surprising, given that counselors report that the overwhelming majority of women who enter the program have not had their period for several months. They also report that when asked about it, women do not perceive lacking a period as a "problem" requiring medical attention. That many women did not report amenorrhea or other problems as frequently as might be expected may be due to the fact that many women probably learn to live with a range of disorders and do not perceive them as problems, or that our interview schedule is not differentiating medical problems as well as might be expected.

## MAINTAINING INVOLVEMENT WITH DRUGS

Maintaining involvement with drugs requires that one have a source of drugs. It has been reported that women often depend on a man to support their drug habit (Chambers 1971). Given that a smaller percentage of women in our sample are introduced to drugs through their partners than is reported elsewhere, it is not surprising that women report that they do not procure drugs on a regular basis from them, either. Eighty-seven percent of the women in this sample who use illegal substances report that they get drugs primarily from "the street"; women in this group who also use prescription drugs report getting these through legal and illegal prescriptions. Only 9 percent report getting drugs through their lovers or "friends" and 40 percent report receiving drugs as gifts.

Maintaining a habit requires money, and women need to have a source of income to support it. Data from women entering Women, Inc., indicate that 52 percent of the women have not held a job in the last two years and an additional 34 percent have worked only

1–12 months during this period. Only 6 percent of the women in this sample have worked 18–24 months in the two years prior to entering the program. We have already discussed the fact that women in this sample have not held particularly high-paying jobs. Thus, we are led to ask how women maintain their habit financially and support themselves and their families.

A very large percentage (71 percent) of the women in this sample rely on welfare for at least part of their income. However, a large percentage report supplementing welfare payments by stealing, prostituting, or passing checks or stolen goods. Twelve percent report that they rely on jobs, family members, or spouses in any way. Many studies indicate that high percentages of women engage in prostitution to support their habits. Ellingwood (1966) cites that 40 percent of his sample of addicted women are prostitutes; Chambers *et al.* (1971) report that 47 percent of a sample of addicted women had said they had prostituted; Cushman (1972) reports up to 70 percent of addicted women in his sample reported utilizing prostitution for support. Forty-two percent of women in our sample report prostitution as a source of support. Thus, not all women in our sample prostitute, but several women report arrests and convictions for property crimes and victim crimes.

Weissman and File (undated) suggest that addicted women fall into at least four categories: (1) women who engage in serious property or personal crime as well as prostitution, (2) women who engage in serious property or personal crime only, (3) women who are strictly prostitutes, and (4) bag followers, or women who neither prostitute or engage in serious crime. Our data indicate that 93 percent of the women in our sample report engaging in prostitution or serious crime. Only 7 percent report arrests for drug dealing only. Twenty percent engage in prostitution only; 31 percent combine prostitution and victim and/or property crime; and 42 percent report engaging only in victim and/or property crime. The largest groups, then, are women who prostitute and engage in crime or engage only in crime (73 percent). It is interesting that a large percentage of women are involved in crimes other than prostitution. James (1974) and Adler (1975) both suggest that as women become more involved in criminal activities, the idea that there is some unique relationship between addiction and prostitution becomes more tenuous. This suggests that alternative criminal sources of getting income are opening to women and that women are not "limited" to using prostitution as the only illegal source of income.

For many addicted women "hustling" and illegal activities are a source of substantial income. Almost half of the women reporting income in our sample said they were making well over $10,000 a year. Binion (1976) reports that addicted women are primarily dependent on others (94 percent), including families, welfare, and illegal activities. However, it is clear from our data that while women are not legitimately employed and do receive welfare, they are also actively earning income to support themselves and their households. In a subsample of women who were asked about their financial responsibility for living arrangements, cost of food, bills, child care, etc., 29 percent reported that they have total responsibility for all costs, while another 42 percent said they shared expenses with roommates, spouses, or families. Only 29 percent reported that they have no financial responsibilities.

## ENDING INVOLVEMENT WITH DRUGS AND ENTERING WOMEN, INC.

Deciding to terminate drug involvement can involve detoxification from heroin or alcohol under medical or psychiatric supervision, entering a methadone maintenance program, a therapeutic community, or a drug-free day program, or any combination of these. Women joining Women, Inc., have extensive drug treatment histories involving participation in several types of treatment modalities. Eighty-four percent have been in at least one other program; 52 percent have been in three or more.

Forty-nine percent of these women have psychiatric histories that evolve from contact with detoxification and methadone maintenance programs. Since psychiatric evaluation and chemical therapy is standard procedure in many clinics, a wide range of legal therapeutic substances, such as Elavil, Thorazine, or Librium, has often been prescribed for women participating in such programs. Many women have been also hospitalized while receiving such treatments. In this sample of women receiving psychiatric help, 76 percent have been treated with chemical substances and 67 percent have been hospitalized. Addicted women, as well as any women who choose to step out of traditional life styles, have often been labeled "crazy" (Chesler 1972). For women who have become involved in drugs and must deal with the medical model of treating addiction, which assumes that such behavior is "crazy" (as is suggested by the practice of routine psychiatric referrals), a triple problem is created: (1) The addiction itself has not been confronted and treated; (2) the use of drugs as an "answer" is perpetuated; and (3) the label and fear of being mentally ill are reinforced. The system intended to terminate drug involvement instead perpetuates it.

Running from the street, keeping clean in the eyes of the legal system, or just wanting to stop drug use and get straight have all been suggested as motivations for entering treatment. Eldred *et al.* (1976) report that the responsibilities of child rearing may motivate women to begin drug use. They report that women more often than men live alone or with children at the time of onset of drug use. It also seems worth considering a woman's living situation just prior to entering treatment to suggest pressures or responsibilities that she might experience before seeking help.

Twenty-three percent of the women who had children prior to entry were living with their children prior to entry into the program, and 16 percent were living with their children and other related or unrelated adults. Forty-two percent were not living with their children at all, but were living either alone (26 percent) or with other adults (16 percent). (Missing information accounts for the remaining 19 percent.) Thus, almost half the women were living alone or with children at entry into the program. While we do not have figures that would place this figure in context, it appears that a large percentage of women are living with very little support at entry. In addition, the fact that 42 percent of the women who had children were not living with them prior to entry indicates that they had gone through some stress or separation with respect to their children.

A recent study conducted by Eldred and Washington (1976) also suggests that a woman's children or her relationship to those children may be a motivation for her to enter treatment. Data on this sample of women indicate that all women who have children at entry cite them as a motivation to enter treatment. Because the program is so openly geared toward women and their children, however, this tells us less than it appears to. Many women in our sample enter Women, Inc., to keep from losing custody of their children or to gain custody of children they have already lost through the courts. State laws and tracking systems currently exist within the commonwealth of Massachusetts that enable the state to remove addicted babies from their mothers at birth and keep track of addicted women with children. This fact is likely to affect motivation to enter a program that is geared to advocacy around this issue.

Generally, throughout this section we use the phrase "having custody of all her children" to mean that the women has all the children in her care or a relative has taken temporary, short-term custody of one or more children without taking legal action. A woman is not considered to "have custody" either when her child/children have been taken from her through legal proceedings initiated by the state or by relatives or when relatives have taken permanent responsibility for raising the children.

Many women in this sample (41 percent) do not have custody of all their children when they enter the program. Either they have lost one or more of their children though legal proceedings, or they have given our custody of one or more of their children to relatives on a "permanent" basis. Women who come from the South or from other parts of the country may have left their children with their families; other women, who had their children at a very young age, will allow their parents or families to take permanent responsibility for raising the children.

Fifty-seven percent of the women in the sample have custody of their children. That is, they have either been living with their children (37 percent) or have been pregnant with their first child (4 percent) or have allowed family to take short-term custody of their children in the months prior to entry until they "get it together" (16 percent). (The 2 percent not accounted for is missing information.)

The women who enter Women, Inc., can be divided into four groups based on how they and their children use the facility: women who enter and who are pregnant or have newborn infants, women who enter the house with children over a year old, women who enter the program without bringing in their children, and women who do not have children.

### Group 1

The first group of women consists of those who are pregnant at entry and intend to have their babies, and of women who have just given birth. This group represents 15 percent of the sample. Women in the group are at various stages in their child-raising histories: There are women who have lost custody of their other children, women having a first baby, and women having third or fourth babies. The one thing all have in common appears to be their use of the facility during a period of transition or pregnancy. All the women who were pregnant at entry $(N = 4)$ had interrupted or stopped their drug or alcohol use at the early stages (first three months) of their pregnancies. Three of these women stayed in the program during their full term and remained approximately two more months with their newborns; the fourth woman stayed in the program only two weeks, but remained drug-free throughout her pregnancy and remained in contact with program staff on an out-patient basis throughout her term. Women who brought infants in with them appeared to use the program for support during the crisis period after the baby's birth, usually two to three months. The support the program provides to pregnant women and new mothers is probably a central motivating factor in their decision to enter Women, Inc. Because women who are addicted and who give birth in the commonwealth of Massachusetts are liable to lose custody of their babies at birth, in entering a program such as Women, Inc., these women are able to stay drug-free after the births and reduce the risk of having their babies removed from them by the state.

### Group 2

Women who have brought children over a year old with them into the program represent 20 percent of the population. Sixty-four percent of these women brought their children into the program during the first six weeks of their stay, while the remainder of this group (36 percent) stayed in the program several months before their children came to stay on a regular basis. The women in this group by and large (73 percent) have custody of all of their children. The average age of this group is the same as that of Group 1, 25.4 years; this is a somewhat higher average age than that of the total sample (23.7).

### Group 3
The women who have entered Women, Inc., and have not brought their children into treatment with them make up the largest group, half the population (50 percent). It bears mentioning at this point that a large percentage of the women in this group stayed in the program less than a month (56 percent); thus, they did not stay long enough to bring their children with them into the program. This group is characterized by the high percentage of women who do not have custody of their children (54 percent). The average age of the women in this group is about 23.

### Group 4
The average age of women in the fourth group, those without children, was the youngest (21 years) of all the groups. It appears that this is the group of young women who have become addicted prior to the birth of their first baby. The oldest woman in this group is 25, while most of the women are 19 to 21 years old ($N = 5$).

## Staying in Treatment

Traditional therapeutic communities have been known to have difficulty keeping women in treatment. Many reasons have been offered to explain this, including the fact that these programs rarely offer child care or other services to women or that these programs do not speak to the experience or lives of women. Length of stay in treatment, then, is one indicator, although probably not the best, of "program success" with women. Length of stay has been shown in several studies to be one indicator of a client's success after leaving treatment; that is, length of stay positively correlates with being drug-free, having no criminal record, and being employed (Katz *et al.* 1975). However, in this report on length of stay, we will be more concerned with program impact, as represented by length of stay, on various groups of women, than with a woman's "success" after she leaves Women, Inc. Current Women, Inc., data collection speaks to this latter issue more directly.

Length of stay was correlated with age, voluntary status, custody status, and use of the facility by the four groups of women defined in the preceding section. Results indicated that women in the oldest age group (31–34 years) were likely to stay in treatment longer than any other group, while women in the youngest age group (19–21 years) were likely to stay for the shortest time. There has been discussion that suggests that maturity has a lot to do with successfully terminating a drug career (Winick 1962). It is not surprising that from our data Women, Inc., has a more positive impact on older women, given that they are more likely to quit or to be more stable anyway. However, because many programs do not attract an older group of women,* these women are likely to terminate their drug careers with little support from established programs. Thus, in attracting this group Women, Inc., is providing support at termination that may not be available to women elsewhere in the area.

In correlating length of stay with voluntary status, we were surprised to find that there was no difference between women with voluntary and involuntary status in terms of the number of weeks they stayed in the program (12.0 vs. 12.6). Women who were involuntarily placed in the program were as likely to remain one or two days or several months as women who were referred on a voluntary basis.

The custody status of the women was somewhat more interesting. Those who had custody of all their children tended to stay longer (16 weeks) that those who had lost custody of at least one of their children (9.9 weeks). While we did not run tests of significance, we find this difference to be somewhat important. Since the average length of stay is 12.3 weeks, women who have custody of their children tend to stay longer than the average for the group.

However, the most interesting correlation appears to be between length of stay and use of the facility. We investigated length of stay for the four groups of women defined in the preceding section. The women who had children and brought them into treatment stayed on

---

* Commonwealth of Massachusetts, Division of Drug Rehabilitation. Data suggest that 87 percent of women in treatment are under age 24 and only 4–7 percent are over age 29.

the average over six months, while those who did not bring their children into treatment with them and those without children stayed an average of less than two months. Women who were pregnant at entry or had just had a baby stayed an average of about four and a half months. As we suggested earlier, the program appears to provide support for women just before or just after the birth of a baby.

It appears from these data that if a woman is interested in or is able to be with her children (i.e., if she has custody) during treatment, the program provides strong support for her. However, for women who do not have custody of their children or are not ready to be with their children for one reason or another, it appears that an environment of women working and living with their children is not as supportive, and these women will tend not to stay in the program as long as others. That women without children stay a relatively short time bears out this interpretation.

## Conclusions and Recommendations

1. The preceding report offers a description of women entering one of the nation's few drug treatment programs for women and their children. Data in this report suggest that Women, Inc., may be serving a population of women that has not been served before in existing traditional therapeutic communities. The high percentage who have been involved in criminal activity suggests that women in this sample may have had more street experience than women who tend to enter male-dominated TCs. The high percentage of black women included in our sample is also somewhat unique and may contribute to the existence of a different legal/criminal composite than has been described for women entering other therapeutic communities. The high percentage of women who voluntarily admit themselves to the program also suggests that Women, Inc., is drawing in a different way than traditional TCs.

The idea that Women, Inc., may be drawing a unique population is also substantiated by the fact that women in this sample are as likely to be introduced to drugs by female friends as by male friends and are likely to get drugs themselves on the street rather than through gifts or through men. That such a low percentage of women qualify as "bag followers" also indicates that these women operate somewhat independently and possibly in a different way than women who would enter co-sex programs.

It is also the case that Women, Inc., is drawing women who have custody of their children and have been living with them prior to entering the program. This means that these women are able to enter programs without having to be separated from their children. Given the crises that have already occurred in many of these women's lives, avoiding a major separation from their children in order to enter treatment is a positive step in stabilizing families.

Women who are pregnant or have newborns can also stabilize during a crisis period and are able to receive valuable information on pregnancy and drug use and on prenatal and infant care from program staff. These women would probably not otherwise have such support during this transition in their lives.

From length-of-stay data we see that Women, Inc., has its most positive impact on women who have custody of all of their children, are over 25 years old, and bring their children into treatment with them. The support that the program offers women and their families in a transition phase from drug involvement to being drug-free is not currently available to women in traditional co-sex programs.

2. The existence of a drug-involvement career pattern, which has usually been described with male addicts in mind, appears to be modified for women by the experiences of childbirth and child rearing. The description of the interface of drug involvement and child-raising histories has important implications for both research and treatment. In understanding the major shifts in a woman's involvement with drugs from onset through termination, it is essential to explicate the intertwining variables of childbirth, child rearing, and expectations for women in working-class and minority communities.

In order to assess addicted women's needs in treatment, it is critical to describe the experience of women's lives within a social, economic, and cultural context. Working-class women clearly have different needs and expectations than middle-class women; black and Latin women experience different pressures than white women. It is also the case that the "needs of addicted women" cannot be addressed only with psychodynamic interventions. Addicted women live in a society with unequal distribution of resources and opportunities. Drug treatment needs to address the broader prevention issues of unemployment, institutional classism, racism, and sexism. Training and education that provide some opportunity and mobility for women must be made an integral part of the treatment and prevention strategies. In addition, programs must not stop at giving training only for narrow, sex-typed occupations that guarantee no mobility or opportunity.

If we are to provide a viable treatment experience that truly terminates involvement in drugs, we must think out career and life style alternatives for women and change the opportunity structure so that all women (and men) can have a life worth living without drugs.

## OUTCOME SUMMARY[*]

The rate of "success" of clients going through a drug program is something everyone wants to know about. Funding sources, the media, and evaluators want to know what they are getting from such large expenditures of time and money. However, program administrators are often hesitant to give "success" rates because they know how relative such a concept is and that the criteria for success can be based on hard-to-pin-down attitudinal changes as well as on the more concrete behavioral development of the client. They are also reluctant because of the intense competition that goes on in the funding of programs, and they are afraid that decisions can be based on something as simple as a "rate" or a number.

Women, Inc., is based on a number of assumptions, as are all social service programs. The primary assumption is that drug addiction is a social and political symptom and that people who are poor and need some hope are the most cruelly victimized by drug and alcohol use. "Success" for us is being free of the drugs and alcohol; but it also means being able to feel one's own success by accomplishing the goals that are important to oneself and by feeling one's own autonomy and power within a drug-free existence. It means surviving in a self-respecting way and seeing how the forces in the inner city and in the United States impinge upon us as women,

[*] October 31, 1977.

as Third World people, as poor people, and as working-class people.

To help women "succeed," our strategies follow from these assumptions and goals. We have set up a structure that makes it possible for women to move out of the street and their drug-using life style: to learn how to go about getting something as simple, but as important, as a social security number; to write a resume and turn street skills into marketable skills; to get a driver's license; to understand welfare rights or insurance policies; to use day care facilities; to be able to negotiate with bureaucracies; to lose some of the fear of all the "no's" and "shoulds."

Other residential programs operate on different assumptions and have different goals. They assume that women and men (particularly women) have deep psychological problems that have to be worked through and be rebuilt before a person can stay straight. Their therapeutic emphasis is on rebuilding personalities—a rather ambitious task.

In an article on treatment and rehabilitation, James V. Delong (1972) suggests that probably about 5 percent of those who come into contact with "TC"-like programs can lead a reasonably drug-free, socially productive life. He quotes statistics from programs that suggest that there is a large turnover of people in TCs and that only a very small percentage of people stay, much less finish and maintain a drug-free life. We know from experience and from some recent studies that the number of women who stay in treatment is even smaller.

In talking about "success" there are tremendous drawbacks; some evaluators suggest that we cannot even begin to talk about success until we have done thorough follow-up studies on individuals for five or ten years after they leave treatment. On the other hand, evaluators sadly add that under the present funding structure such studies are not expedient and we have to settle for much less, that is, for studies that follow clients who have been out of treatment for only six months or less.

It is in this context that we are presenting some preliminary figures about what has happened to women coming through our program. Our information has been gathered through formal interviews as well as from informal street information, which is continually gathered by staff and residents of the program. The women we have "followed up" have been out of the program from five months to two and a half years.

### The Women We Know Are Drug-Free

We know that of 50 women who have come into our program and left, 21, or 42 percent, are now drug-free. Most of these women (76 percent) have been out of the program more than 6 months; 5 have been out over 18 months, and another 5 have been out between 12 and 18 months.

Of these 21 women, 15 were either working full or part time or were enrolled and participating in a training program or school when we talked to them. Two were actively looking for work, and three were at home caring for infants. It was not clear to us what the one remaining woman has been doing.

These women did not necessarily all stay in the program for an extended period. The length of program residency ranged from 1 to 46 weeks, or 11 months. The average length of stay, however, was 22 weeks, or 5½ months. Two-thirds of these drug-free women stayed in the program longer than 3 months, while one-third of them left sooner.

Thirteen of these 21 women came into the house with their children or were pregnant at entry. The remainder either did not bring their children with them into treatment ($N = 4$) or did not have children of their own ($N = 4$). Right now, 16 out of 17 of the women who have children have custody of their children and are caring for them.

The average age of women in this group is 25, and they range in age from 19 to 34.

### The Women We Know Are Not Drug-Free

We know of 14 women who are back "on the street." These women are not working or in training programs or in school. Thirteen of these women stayed in the program less than 4 months; the remaining women stayed as long as 8 months. The average length of stay in the program was only 8.4 weeks, or 2 months.

Only 3 of these 14 women brought their children into the program with them; the others either did not have children or did not have custody of their children. Only 3 have custody of their children now and are currently with them.

Half of the women in this group left over 18 months ago; 4 left between 6 and 18 months ago; and 3 left less than 6 months ago.

The average age of these women is 23, and their ages range from 19 to 28.

### The Women We Cannot Find

This is a group of 15 women. Over two-thirds of these women stayed in the program less than a week. Three of these women stayed three or more months. These were overwhelmingly "revolving door" clients. We have conflicting reports on the drug use of two women in this group who stayed for over three months. One woman is out of state and we are not able to contact her. Two of the women in this total group did bring their children into the program with them for some time.

The average age of women in this group is 23, and they range in age from 19 to 24.

### CONCLUSIONS

From this very early report we can see that length of stay as well as bringing children into the facility may be related to success after treatment, or at least success in the early stages after treatment. While we have not conducted correlation analysis on some of these variables, it does appear that age alone is not a particularly strong predictor of how a woman will do when she leaves the program. We are currently collecting formal follow-up data on a sample of women who have left co-sex drug treatment programs, and will soon be able to determine to what extent the program itself can be said to directly affect success after treatment.

The Alcoholism Center for Women, Inc., in Los Angeles was funded on October 1, 1974, by the National Institute on Alcohol Abuse and Alcoholism to provide relevant and effective alcoholism treatment services for women, with a particular emphasis on the needs and concerns of the lesbian alcoholic. The primary purpose of the center is to substantially reduce the serious problem of alcoholism among women by using both traditional treatment techniques and innovative/supportive ones. In the past two years of center program services, the integration of these two treatment processes has been found to be highly effective. The problems of women alcoholics are closely related to the problems of being a woman, and traditional alcoholism treatment, specifically geared to the male alcoholic, does not deal with these problems in a relevant and effective way.

The center utilizes traditional treatment processes such as one-to-one counseling, groups, vocational rehabilitation services, social services, and social/recreational alternatives. Program services include a fourteen-bed recovery home as well as nonresidential services. Nontraditional treatment processes include CR groups, lesbian awareness raps, and assertion training. Perhaps most important, the center has created an environment of safety, an environment of nonjudgmental caring and support that allows participants the freedom "to be me." It is this feeling of safety permeating all program services that allows even traditional treatment processes to become more effective.

The problems of the lesbian alcoholic are similar to those of non-gay women but are exacerbated by society's prejudices, stereotypes, misunderstandings, and hostility toward lesbians. The lives of many gay women are characterized by fragmentation, compartmentalization, isolation, and desperation. A common strain running through these women's experiences is self-doubt, low self-esteem, and feelings of inadequacy. Effective treatment processes must begin with a staff that is not only sensitive and aware but has a positive understanding of lesbian behaviors, attitudes, and life styles. The creation of an environment of caring and supportive safety is especially crucial to effective treatment of lesbian alcoholics, since much of their lives have been spent hiding an important part of themselves. It is important to provide services that allow lesbian alcoholics, as well as non-gay women alcoholics, to grow in self-esteem, confidence, and self-integration. This can be accomplished only with an agency and staff attitude that is positive, sensitive, and aware.

As background to the center's services, Brenda Weathers, the center's former director, has outlined in the following article the particular issues for the lesbian alcoholic.


# Alcoholism and the Lesbian Community

## BRENDA WEATHERS


Recent studies have indicated that alcoholism is reaching pandemic proportions within the gay community, with an estimated 25 to 35 percent of that population directly affected (Fifield 1975). Given such startling statistics on the extent of the problem and of the individual suffering involved, it is incumbent upon those in the field of alcoholism services to begin increasing their awareness of this community's problems and special needs with the goal of providing quality alcoholism services to members of this minority group.

This examination of issues will be confined to those problems, issues, and alternatives as they relate to the lesbian community. It is of great and increasing importance to recognize the woman-identified community as separate from the male homosexual community and to view it as one with its own identity, heritage, life styles, and special problems. It is not surprising that the communities continue to be categorized together under the label "homosexual," as volumes have been written about homosexual males, with lesbian women receiving little or no attention. Sociological/psychological researchers, then, have perpetuated the "single community" myth and misnomer, with the all-too-usual assumption of women's secondary importance. (Given the bias of much of this "research," the lack of attention to lesbians might also be viewed as a disguised blessing.)

## Lesbians: Myth and Reality

Before examining the problems at the core of the lesbian woman's alcohol abuse and her unique treatment needs, it is important to explore some of the many myths and stereotypes about lesbianism that continue to inhibit knowledge and awareness. A lesbian woman is as individual as a single member of any other population segment, for lesbian women are found in all socioeconomic strata, ethnic groups, and religious and cultural backgrounds. She is a woman wearing overalls, driving a tractor in a farming commune; a stylishly dressed professional; a blue-collar worker struggling to make ends meet; a college student; a welfare mother fighting for survival; the "girl" next door; masculine, feminine, or androgynous in appearance; an ex-con or a belly dancer. Whoever she is, she has probably found it unsafe to be herself in all but very limited environments and may have found alcohol a mighty balm for soothing the pain of loneliness, fear, and alienation. Thus, it is impossible to carve out a strict definitional niche for the lesbian woman: The only consistent characteristic is that lesbians are those women whose primary or highly meaningful emotional and sexual relationships are experienced with other women.

As mentioned earlier, there are numerous myths and misunderstandings that surround lesbianism, too numerous to be addressed in this brief work. There are, however, three major myth categories that should be examined: negative choice myths, sexuality/pornography myths, and child molestation myths.

Negative choice myths stem from the belief that lesbianism has been chosen as a life style because of one or more negative factors associated with relationships to males. Either males were unavailable (e.g., to "homely" women or because of the isolation of women's schools and jails, etc.) or they were feared and despised, whether owing to misandry in and of itself or as a result of traumatic experiences with males. These theories are clearly rife with male arrogance and the male supremacy syndrome, containing more than a pinch of Freudian hangover. Studies currently under way are indicating that past traumas with males are no more prevalent among lesbians than among heterosexual women, and that crimes of violence against women—incest, rape, and beatings—are our common problem, not a determining factor in our emotional/sexual life style preference. Statistics obtained in gay community groups engaged in prison/parole programs throughout the country show that lesbian relationships are often formed by heterosexual women while they are confined in prisons, although the great majority of these women revert to heterosexual behavior upon release. The "ugly duckling" myths are easily discounted by observing the wide range of physical characteristics exhibited by heterosexual women *with* male partners. Essentially, as Tripp (1975) points out in *The Homosexual Matrix,* to approach an understanding of lesbianism/homosexuality from the perspective of negative choice is self-defeating, since choices for emotional and sexual satisfaction are, by nature, positive choices.

Another major misconception concerning lesbianism stems in large measure from the pornographic literature. This literature portrays lesbian women as highly erotic, engaging in bizarre acts of sadomasochistic behavior often culminating with heterosexual "salvation." It is interesting to note that, conservatively estimated, 95 percent of the pornographic literature is written by heterosexual males for the reading pleasure of heterosexual males. Through the ages men have made it their perogative to define *all* women, usually in terms of their own fantasies and needs. The lesbian woman has been no exception. Another perspective on woman-identified women in literature could be obtained by reading the works of Colette, Willa Cather, Elizabeth Bowen, Gertrude Stein, and more recently, Jane Rule, Rita Mae Brown, and others.

The myth of the lesbian woman as child molestor also continues in our society, but a look at the statistics will again show that 90 percent of all child molestation is committed by heterosexual males. Interestingly, few negative sanctions or internal control mechanisms are exercised upon this population segment in their ongoing violent crimes against women and children. In fact, one might suspect that there is cultural support for the mistreatment of females.

M. Friedman (1975) observes:

My research on lesbians found them scoring higher than a control group on autonomy, spontaneity, orientation toward the present (as opposed to being obsessed with the past or anticipating the future), and sensitivity to one's own needs and feelings. A comparable experiment by June Hopkins in 1969 compared lesbians and matched controls on Raymond B. Cattell's 16 Personality Factor test. Among the adjectives that characterized the lesbian group were: independent, resilient, bohemian, and self-sufficient. In 1972, Marvin Siegelman compared a non-clinical sample of lesbian and heterosexual subjects on similar personality inventories, and the lesbians scored higher than the controls on both goal direction and self-acceptance.

## The Lesbian Woman and Alcohol: A Statement of the Problem

Lesbian women drink for the same reason anyone else drinks— alcohol is there and it works! Why, then, the high alcoholism rate in this community? There appear to be three major factors at the core of the problem: (1) The community is an oppressed minority; (2) the lesbian bar is the traditional setting for its social activities; and (3) alcoholism service agencies are unresponsive to the lesbian alcoholic.

### THE COMMUNITY AS AN OPPRESSED MINORITY

As is true of all minority groups that have been victims of ongoing and systematic discrimination, the dynamic of oppression manifests itself in that community as low self-esteem, alienation, despair, self-destructive behavior, and high rates of alcoholism and drug addiction. Many of these characteristics (e.g., low self-esteem, a sense of inadequacy, loneliness) are felt by informed professionals in the field of alcoholism to constitute the profile of an "alcoholic personality." When these feelings and behaviors are intensified by widespread and systematic societal oppression, the alcoholism rates of the communities involved take on a new and more understandable perspective. As a result of this oppression, lesbian women often find themselves living compartmentalized, often fractured, and sometimes less than full lives. As with anyone else under those circumstances, alcohol is found to relieve anxiety, soothe tensions, produce a sense of euphoria or well-being, and generally provide the temporary coping mechanism necessary for living in the oppressing society. The stages of addiction and progression of alcoholism are identical for the lesbian

woman and for any other alcoholic, with alcohol in time becoming
the problem rather than the solution. The critical point is that the
adverse societal conditions that act on the lesbian community encourage greater usage of alcohol as a coping mechanism and produce
a higher alcoholism rate than in the heterosexual community.

## THE TRADITION OF THE LESBIAN BAR

Lesbian women vary widely in their sense of connection with the lesbian community. Many women, for example, who come to identify
themselves as lesbians describe themselves as having felt unique in
the world, isolated from other women whom they perceived to be like
themselves. A woman then who comes to feel she is a lesbian encounters a real problem in finding others with whom she can identify
and relate (Ponse 1976).

Bars for lesbians, then, have taken on the characteristics and significance of the community center, the coffee break, family gatherings,
clubs, societies, and the church picnic. In a society that has openly
oppressed the gay minority, has condoned police harassment, and has
fostered an atmosphere of secrecy, mistrust, and hatred, lesbian
women usually are forced to socialize in very limited environments.
Traditionally, these environments are bars, and lesbian women look
to them as places for meeting friends, finding partners, relating with
peers, and performing most other human social functions. Bars provide the atmosphere where "it is OK to be me," even if only for a few
hours a week.

By nature, bars are alcohol-related environments, and consump-
tion of alcohol and sociability become strongly interrelated in the lesbian woman's experience. The Gay Community Services Center
study indicates that current gay bar users spend an average of 80 percent of their gay social activity time in bars and at parties where
alcohol is served (Fifield 1975). The study also showed that 63 percent of the sample go to bars alone in the hope of meeting friends,
and that the typical bar user has spent an average of ten years going to
gay bars. While the relationship between drinking and socializing is a
common thread running through the American culture, this relationship is exacerbated in the lesbian subculture owing to lack of

alcohol-free alternatives and the limited social options available to lesbians in the larger society.

## AGENCY ATTITUDES TOWARD THE LESBIAN ALCOHOLIC

Responsibility for the effectiveness of an agency's services program rests, ultimately, with its staff and staff attitudes. Most of the alcoholism agency staff questioned in the Gay Community Services Center's survey demonstrated judgmental and restrictive attitudes toward lesbians and continued to view lesbianism as a pathology (Fifield 1975). Their negative attitudes, even considering occasional attempts at disguise, seriously hinder the lesbian alcoholic's progress toward recovery. The following are examples of these attitudes as they affected the recovery of lesbian alcoholics:

> I was only one week sober and new to the clinic. I needed lots of support and understanding; instead, I felt as though others were sneering at me behind my back, as if I were a leper. Eventually the rejection became too much, and I drank again—for five years.

> I felt that my counselor wasn't concerned about my drinking problem, but he was really tripped out on my lesbianism.

> I was so grateful to be admitted into recovery home treatment, as I knew my drinking was killing me and I wanted help. I was assigned to a room alone (although there were empty beds in other dorm rooms). Then, a few hours after admission, the house manager took me aside and said I was just lucky to be there at all—and that if I even looked like I might "cause trouble" I would be asked to leave immediately. I decided to leave the house that night, and it was several months later before I again had the courage to ask for help.

In general, there appear to be three major types of negative interaction that can characterize the lesbian alcoholic's experience with alcoholism agencies:

> Refusal of services if the woman's lesbianism is known or suspected.

Provision of services on a limited basis or with negative attitudes that are not conducive to support, growth, self-disclosure, or sobriety.

Provision of services directed toward isolating and "curing" lesbianism as the primary problem, with little or no attention directed toward alcoholism.

Given these factors, the lesbian woman's chances for recovery in many alcoholism agencies may range from poor to nonexistent.

In addition to examining staff attitudes as they relate to the lesbian alcoholic, it is critical to examine the lack of specifically designed outreach to this community. The lesbian community, with its increasingly high alcoholism rate, is a difficult community for outreach owing to its often closed and secretive nature. According to one researcher, the stigma and negative imagery that accrues to lesbianism in the larger society has led to a separation of the lesbian and heterosexual worlds, under the protective cloak of secrecy. However, the protection that secrecy affords also has negative consequences in that it can render outreach to this community particularly problematic (Ponse 1976). While this is generally true of the country as a whole, the advent of lesbian and women centers, plus a slowly decreasing stigmatization in many urban areas, have to some extent reduced the secrecy aspects of the lesbian community.

## TREATMENT NEEDS OF THE LESBIAN ALCOHOLIC:
## SPECIALIZED SERVICES
## AND EVALUATION OF EFFECTIVENESS

During the early developmental stages of the Alcoholism Center for Women, attempts were made to isolate the unique treatment needs of the lesbian alcoholic and then to design treatment services relevant to those needs. Inputs were obtained from observations made by the gay community service workers, recovered lesbian alcoholics, and concerned alcoholism professionals. On the basis of experiences, inputs, and observations of this group, the following major treatment needs were defined:

The need for a safe and nonjudgmental environment in which to share honestly and receive support.

The need for a peer support group, both during treatment and to facilitate community reentry.

The need for full access to a wide range of services, including alcoholism-focused groups and counseling, vocational development, social welfare, and recovery home services.

The need for nontraditional support services to facilitate self-esteem, positive identity, and self-development. These include lesbian issues raps, CR groups, assertion training, and alcohol-free social alternatives.

Responses to all of the preceding services and environmental/attitudinal needs were built into the Alcoholism Center for Women's program, which was funded in October 1974 by the National Institute on Alcohol Abuse and Alcoholism. The program provides a full range of services to all women who apply and makes a special outreach to and is concerned with the special problems of the lesbian alcoholic. All program services are provided for women by women, creating an immediacy of connection and safety for self-disclosure in a supportive, noncategorizing atmosphere.

Recent studies have demonstrated the importance of all-women treatment groups and women staff in positively affecting the percentage of women who complete treatment programs (Schultz 1974). In accordance with a philosophy of peer orientation, the all-women staff of the Alcoholism Center for Women is approximately two-thirds lesbian to one-third nonlesbian, with the participant population reflecting approximately the same ratio.

After nearly two years of services delivery, some data have been obtained on the effectiveness of center's programs. Of the women who completed intake, only 7 percent did not participate in a program of services and reported no change in their drinking patterns. Of the remaining 93 percent, dramatic intervention in drinking patterns was reported, as follows:

*Months of Sobriety Attained*

| | |
|---|---|
| Fewer than 3 | 10 percent |
| 3–5 | 19 percent |
| 6–11 | 42 percent |
| More than 12 | 22 percent |

SUGGESTED GUIDELINES FOR ALCOHOLISM AGENCIES
IN PROVIDING SERVICES FOR LESBIAN CLIENTS

1. *Recognize the individuality of the client.* Each client in an agency
must be viewed as an individual, with individualized stresses, sets of
problems, and capabilities. As with representatives of any other population segment, no two lesbians are identical in their history, problems, and needs. While this paper has focused on issues specific to
lesbians, it cannot be overemphasized that individuality must always
be recognized and honored.

2. *Provide a full range of services.* Each client must be assured full
access to available services. Isolation and alienation are painful realities for lesbian women, and these feelings, if experienced in the treatment process, can only impair chances for recovery.

3. *Increase staff awareness of and sensitivity to the lesbian alcoholic.* As was noted earlier, the effectiveness of services rests largely
with staff attitudes, and these attitudes also influence the "safety" of
the environment. Staff attitudes concerning lesbian women can be
greatly enhanced through an ongoing process of in-service training.

Most urban areas have organized lesbian, gay, and lesbian feminist
organizations that are available to provide panels and speakers for staff
training. Gay student unions at colleges and universities as well as
Alcoholics Together (a national, gay A.A.) and the Metropolitan
Community Churches are also valuable resources.

In addition to providing in-service training, these groups or individuals could make valuable inputs into the development of program
services, and they may also be highly effective as referral sources and
in providing for community reentry and follow-up services.

4. *Implement specialized treatment groups.* The experience of the
Alcoholism Center for Women in services delivery, as well as data
provided by other researchers (Schultz 1974), indicate the importance of the connection and safety provided by the peer counseling
group. Where the number of clients permits, a lesbian group can be
a valuable asset in the lesbian woman's recovery experience. Where
there are too few lesbian clients, an all-women group or a gay group
with women and men will also provide an effective peer group support and sharing system.

## The Work of the Center

The Alcoholism Center for Women in Los Angeles is housed in two adjoining buildings—old, rambling houses adapted to the center's activities but retaining the sense of homey comfort—and is organized around two interrelated programs: the Recovery House, with fourteen beds for acutely alcoholic women referred from detoxification services, and a center for activities for recovering alcoholic women living in the community. Within any one month 150 participants (their preferred term) use the various services of the Alcoholism Center. The women's ages range from 19 to 63; they are of varied ethnic backgrounds; and approximately two-thirds are lesbian. All participants are alcoholic, but many are polydrug users as well.

Several themes pervade the center. First, there is an overall accepting atmosphere for participants—as women, as alcoholics, and for many, as lesbians. The staff is composed solely of women, many of whom are lesbians and many of whom are recovering alcoholics, including former Center participants. There is a manifest intent to accept the participants wholly and to extend much caring along with specific therapies. There is also a gradual but purposeful exposure to a full acceptance of the lesbian woman and to nonsexist ideas for all women, including a wider range of life styles and work opportunities for women. For many participants, their time at the center is their first experience with these perspectives. Third, the center provides a continuing, caring environment for women as they reenter the general community and try to remain sober.

In the Recovery House, where women stay for 60 to 90 days, the primary early emphasis is on physical recovery from acute alcoholism. Gradually in these early weeks, in one-to-one counseling and in groups, as the participants are working on the resolution of their individual drinking problems they also begin to hear nonsexist and feminist ideas. This can simply be the notion that there are options for women other than a return to an unsatisfying and depreciatory marriage and/or low-paid, dead-end work, and that women can be achievers at work, often in nontraditional occupations. Most women have little understanding of feminism at the outset and are often initially hostile to these ideas. This can also be the first time

that lesbian alcoholics begin to sense acceptance of their sexual orientation and that heterosexual women know and begin to understand
lesbian women.

These themes, along with others that stress women's full acceptance of themselves as capable individuals, continue to be part of
what the center terms Phase II. This is the period when, with provision of specific support services, women return to live and work in
the community but continue to use the center. Women utilize one-
to-one counseling and/or group experiences while, at the same time,
referrals are made to A.A., N.A. (Narcotics Anonymous), vocational
rehabilitation or career planning services, etc. The participants
engage in intense personal work on their alcohol problems and on
the development of new behaviors to handle stress, but this is done in
the context of an equally intense caring environment that emphasizes
new understandings of themselves as women, with clear alternatives
as to sexual preference.

An important factor in this purposeful environment is the continual work done by the staff on their personal reactions to the stresses of
the job and to their development as women. This staff work is based
on three principles: (1) They, as women, face the same societal pressures on and expectations of women as do the participants. Since
some of the staff are recovering alcoholics and some are lesbians,
they know precisely the special pressures experienced by the participants. (2) They will not place themselves in the role of martyr in
meeting the needs of the women participants. This means an overt
admission to themselves and to the women participants that they
know personal miseries and "face the same demons" as the women
who use the center's services. (3) They acknowledge that they must
continue to work on their own personal growth as women and as service givers. This means a combination of in-service training (both
didactic and experiential), consciousness-raising experience, and personal therapy, if indicated. This also means recognition that the differences that exist among the staff—in age, ethnicity, and gay and
straight orientations—inevitably lead to interpersonal conflicts and
that these need continual efforts at resolution. Though decision making is based in a hierarchical structure within the staff, conflicts
among the staff are made overt and are worked on, and all members,

whatever their hierarchical position, work within the principles just outlined.

The center also emphasizes liaisons with community resources, particularly with lesbian and feminist organizations. These connections provide a community support system for women in treatment and serve as resources for in-service training. The center is also concerned with improving the relevance and effectiveness of alcoholism treatment services for lesbian women and offers the following suggestions for non-gay alcoholism agencies and staff: )1) Utilize a program of traditional as well as innovative/supportive treatment processes; (2) provide in-service training for staff to upgrade understanding, sensitivity, and awareness to the needs, concerns, and life styles of both lesbian and non-gay women alcoholics; (3) develop a staff that includes lesbian women and screens out homophobic people; (4) create an environment of caring, supportive safety; and (5) develop liaison communication with local community lesbian and feminist organizations, which can then be utilized for staff in-service training, outreach, and community support for women in treatment.

Finally, the center has had an unplanned impact on a more circumscribed community. Center residents have experienced no hostility from their immediate residential neighborhood, and in fact their relations with the surrounding residents have led to a healthy acceptance of the center's purposes and clientele by that limited but important community.

## CASPAR: A Women's Alcoholism Program

The Women's Alcoholism Program of the Cambridge and Somerville Program for Alcoholism Rehabilitation (CASPAR) offers a variety of services: out-patient women's groups, including child care services; in-patient and family treatment at a detoxification center; and Womanplace, a recovery house. However, this discussion focuses on its innovative outreach, educational, and consultation program, which has a three-faceted rationale. The first is the realization that offering special services to women is not sufficient to draw them into treatment. Many forces in the community "protect" them from getting help, and the cooperation of local agencies and organizations is needed to help find women who require treatment. Because of the stigma attached to alcoholism in women, those who are alcoholic, their familis and friends, as well as helping professionals share in the denial of the alcoholism. Many people, lay and professional, define the alcoholism in other terms, and one of the major purposes of CASPAR's educational efforts is to encourage these people to recognize the alcoholism for what it is and urge the women to seek help. The second rationale is that, once in treatment, women need care and attention that recognizes their particular needs as women. The third is that the recovering alcoholic needs a community support system that encourages her efforts to remain sober.

Within the foregoing context, the program has these specific purposes:

1. To draw more women into the treatment services offered by CASPAR.
2. To draw different kinds of women into treatment—young, old, Third World, lesbian, professional, women with dependent children.
3. To reach out to women in the earlier stages of alcoholism, when there is a better chance of recovery.
4. To develop an awareness in the community of the extent of alcoholism as a problem for women and to dispel the myths and stereotypes many people have regarding alcoholic women.
5. To develop an awareness of alcoholism resources for women—as the only program for alcoholic women in the Cambridge–Somerville area, CASPAR serves as a referral/information unit for various alcoholism treatment resources.
6. To stimulate and support the development of additional resources for women alcoholics.
7. To increase and constantly stimulate the sensitivity of the CASPAR staff to the issues particular to the alcoholic woman.

8. To form links with other women's organizations—with collective support, the intent is to reach out to more women as well as serve the women seen at CASPAR in a more comprehensive manner.

## Community Consultation

A major target of these efforts is the network of community agencies and groups: health clinics, women's centers, counseling programs, welfare agencies, nurses' associations, high school girls' groups, college counseling centers, home health care organization centers for the aging. In meeting with members of such groups and agencies, the Women's Program staff first encourage the individuals to explore their own personal attitudes toward and experiences with alcoholism. Then

they are presented with factual information on alcohol and alcoholism, the special issues affecting alcoholic women, and the effects of alcohol abuse on a woman's family and friends. Lastly, they are introduced to some practical skills: how to identify a possible alcohol problem in a woman client, how to approach her about her problem, and where and how to refer her to treatment. Throughout the training, the lecture–discussion format is interspersed with role-playing sessions to help participants practice new ways of dealing with possible problems among their clients. (Sandmaier 1977:23)

The intent in planning the educational efforts is to contract for five to six sessions of two hours each, but a compromise in time is often necessary. Given such time limitations and the fact that confidence in working with alcoholic women comes through repeated exposure and practice, consultation services are offered as a follow-up to all training. This is done on an on-call case consultation and/or regular group consultation basis.

As part of this consultation commitment, the Women's Alcoholism Program developed an on-call consultation service to the staff of the Alcoholism Out-Patient Department at Cambridge Hospital (also a CASPAR facility). When a woman came to the Walk-In Service there, a staff member from the Women's Alcoholism Program was called to conduct a joint interview with the out-patient counselor. This consultation service had three purposes: (1) It introduced the client to a Woman's Program staff person so that the program would be familiar to her; (2) a Women's Program staff member would be on hand to advise the client as to the availability of specialized services that the out-patient counselor might have overlooked; (3) assistance would be provided to the out-patient counselor in the interview to ensure that she or he would be attuned to the unique aspects of the woman's alcoholic situation.

The Out-Patient Department staff was resistant to this service at times, since Women's Program staff were often viewed as "outside" consultants. There were also logistical problems; it occasionally took a Women's Program staff member from ten to fifteen minutes to respond to the consultation call from the hospital. While the consultation service was not totally successful, it accomplished some of its goals. The out-patient counselors learned about some of the women's resources with which they might never have come into contact. Furthermore, the willingness to make a special trip to see a client was an indication to clients that the program cared about the services women were receiving. Given the fact that many more women were using the out-patient services and that the consultation service was not consistently meeting the need for more specific and individual out-patient treatment for women, it was decided that it would be more appropriate to have a Woman's Alcoholism Program staff member regularly located at the Walk-In Service, and this plan was put in operation.

## Staff Training

A second aspect of the educational program is training of the CASPAR staff itself. The staff felt the need to focus some training efforts on its own Alcoholism Program staff, since it is the newest program of CASPAR and the only one devoted solely to women.

The Women's Alcoholism Program conducted a six-week training series on the alcoholic woman for the entire CASPAR staff. Attendance ranged from 35 to 50 female and male staff at each session. The primary purpose of the series was to help people realize that they have different attitudes toward men and women and that these attitudes and differences can be reflected in treatment. Another purpose was to sensitize the staff to women's special issues and needs. The first three sessions were devoted to issues for women in this society and the last three to issues for the alcoholic woman. Various exercises and materials were used in the series. As an example, a "word association game" was devised in which people were asked to say what words came to their minds when thoughts of women, women alcoholics, men, and men alcoholics were suggested to them. They also developed and performed a role play of women in a halfway house to portray various issues in treatment of women, such as self-identity, perception by others, relationships, motherhood, and sexuality. Both of these methods were challenging and generated considerable discussion.

There have also been follow-up seminars for CASPAR staff on issues for alcoholic women that have included such topics as women's history, the alcoholic lesbian, battered women, and self-help health care. Some of these presentations were done by women's agencies, reciprocating for the alcoholism education they had received from the Women's Alcoholism Program.

In addition, the program conducts a two-hour training session on women and alcoholism for all new CASPAR staff as part of a regular ten-week training course entitled "Drinking, Drunkenness, and Alcoholism." These sessions are conducted about four times a year. One of these sessions is also led by the family counselor for the program, with the families and significant others of alcoholic women. A variety of materials are used for these sessions, including: (1) opinion questionnaires, musical selections depicting different views of men and women in society, and attitude statements and surveys; (2) a word association exercise to draw out the trainee's stereotypes and attitudes toward women alcoholics; (3) a guided experience exercise through which trainers explore the feelings of a woman alcoholic from the time she discovers she has a drinking problem to her entry into the Walk-In Emergency Service; and (4) a packet entitled "Issues for Women in Treatment" as well as a videotape of a role play of women in a halfway house that depicts these issues.

## Community Support Networks

Finally, the staff of the program has worked to form relationships with all parts of the local women's community in an attempt to form various support networks for alcoholic women. For example, a core group of women who have achieved and maintained sobriety with the help of the Women's Alcoholism Program formed the first feminist Alcoholics Anonymous group in Massachusetts, called the Sisterhood Group, with weekly meetings at Womanplace. Also with assistance from the Women's Alcoholism Program, a collective has been formed, called Amethyst Women, that sponsors drug-free dances, meetings, and special events for alcoholic lesbians. Approximately 100 women have attended these events.

Through the alcoholism training done with various agencies and through the growing recognition of a woman's alcoholism program, various cooperative projects have been arranged. For example, Women's Enterprises, an organization for women that does vocational counseling and education, has agreed to present a vocationally oriented class for the residents of Womenplace. Similar arrangements have been made with the Rape Crisis Center and the Women's Community Health Center. Organizations for battered women and a woman's music collective have participated in mutual fund-raising efforts with the Women's Alcoholism Program. In these and other ways (e.g., presentations at professional conferences, local workshops on women and alcoholism) the programs build a solid network of interested and knowledgeable individuals and groups to help alcoholic women achieve and maintain sobriety.

## Program Outcomes

Evidence of the attainment of the goals of these outreach and educational efforts is seen in several ways. The growing number of women using treatment services is a primary example of the success of the outreach program. Prior to the inception of the Women's Alcoholism Program, women accounted for only 10 to 15 percent of the population using out-patient services and less than 10 percent of patients in the detoxification units. This number has increased considerably, so that women account (in 1977) for 35 percent of those using out-patient services, 22 percent of those using the Emergency Walk-In Service, and 25 percent of those in the detoxification units.

More women coming to the program are in the early stages of alcoholism, or perhaps just beginning to question their drinking. This is considered to be a direct result of the consultation and education efforts with nontraditional service organizations and agencies that serve primarily women. Referrals have also increased from the staffs of traditional agencies, which women are more likely to approach before they even consider alcoholism tratment agencies. As the number of women increases and more women are reached in early stages of alcoholism or alcohol abuse, the range of general characteristics for women using the services has also broadened.

## Concluding Remarks

Because attention to the chemically dependent woman as separate from her male counterpart is so recent, investigators are only on the threshold of understanding the complexities of her condition. The systematic differences that have become evident suggest that this attention is long overdue. As is true for other circumstances addressed in this book, research and demonstration are needed to test, within service centers, the intervention ramifications of research studies.

The experiences of innovative programs for the chemically dependent woman caution that this will not be an easy task. As indicated in the report of Women, Inc., it is not from lack of interest that new programs may not conduct careful studies; rather, it is a matter of survival. The congressional testimony cited earlier reflects the continual fight for needed financial support, even for the comparatively few women's programs currently in existence. The intraorganizational difficulties in maintaining separate feminist services, as indicated in the changes of TODAY, Inc., and in Doyle's commentary (1977), suggest that there may be issues distinctive to this field that make such progress problematic. This may be in the nature of the incapacity itself, carrying as it does the onus of a stigmatized deviance and a historical resistance to treatment. Further, when the treatment of women has been combined with the treatment of men and women's distinctive needs are thereby blurred, sexist stereotypes of women are likely to be evident in those treatment procedures. The scattered, inconclusive, but intriguing results showing considerable effectiveness in treating women in separate feminist services provide a compelling reason for more systematic attention to outcomes based on increasing knowledge.

# Part Two

*Violence Against Women*

# 4. Battered Women

## TROVA HUTCHINS AND VEE BAXTER

THE PHYSICAL abuse of women by men is among the most extreme manifestations of sexism. The social and cultural roots of abuse are deep, complex, and ultimately related to two basic realities: the longstanding subjugation of women and the irrevocable fact that most women are physically smaller and weaker than most men.

Violence against women is, in one important respect, a *social* problem. For it to be eradicated to any significant degree, major changes at an institutional and societal level must occur. Research is also needed if understanding of the problem is to move beyond a superficial level. In the meantime, however, as with so many of the problems discussed in this book, women who are victims of abuse need help, and often their need is desperate. Moreover, it does *not* require extensive research to identify what such helping services should entail. Battered women cannot afford to wait for the results of "need assessment surveys" or studies on the etiology of violence, and certainly it is unrealistic to ask them to wait for the emergence of a nonsexist society.

The services described in this chapter were begun, for the most part, by feminist people who not only recognize the sexist roots of men's assaults on women and are appalled at the lack of awareness and knowledge about the problem, but also know that widespread understanding and prevention will take time. They believe that abused women can and should be helped now, and in diverse, tangible ways. Through action, the pioneers of service for abuse victims are not only helping thousands of individual women; they are also documenting the need for services and increasing the base of knowledge about abuse. They are documenting the need, perhaps more clearly than any scholarly researcher could, because virtually all services for abused women are deluged with requests for help as soon as they are established and publicized. They are increasing knowledge because they have direct contact with those who know most about the problem through personal experience.

Services for battered women, then, can be viewed as much more than stopgap measures of outreach to a few women. It is likely that the impact of such services will be increasing and far-reaching, for a number of reasons. First, as has been noted, the services themselves have demonstrated the extent of demand for them. As services are publicized, the demand increases and the extent of the need is further illustrated. The people providing services often regard publicity and public education as part of their charge. They are also concerned with gathering and pooling statistics, because they know the importance of factual information if others are to be convinced of needs and problems.

Second, the services that can benefit abused women tend, of necessity, to pervade all aspects of the health, welfare, and legal systems. The consciousness of those who work throughout these systems is being raised in proportion to the demands of assault victims for legal protection, medical care, shelter, and social services. Such awareness, however reluctantly acknowledged, is crucial because it is those who run the system (physicians, lawyers, judges, social workers, and police officers, for example) who have the power to change it.

A third reason why the impact of services for abuse victims will grow relates to the feminist context out of which the services have sprung. The developers of these services have available to them the rich network of resources and communication that is part of the women's movement. The signs of support and exchange among the coterie of service providers throughout the United States—and between the United States and other countries—are heartening. Those involved in service delivery tend to keep in touch. They help each other and learn from each other. It is somewhat easier today, for instance, to start a shelter for abused women than it was a few years ago simply because information on the experiences (and mistakes) of others starting such services is available and, to a great extent, willingly provided. The importance of this multileveled climate of awareness and support is stressed throughout this chapter.

## AWARENESS OF ABUSE

Men have been regularly beating up their wives, ex-wives, and girlfriends for centuries. There is no evidence that the incidence of woman battering has either increased or decreased over recent decades. What has changed, at least in the past few years, is the level of public awareness and social consciousness about the physical abuse of women. This change is dramatic, and it is indicative of how consciousness raising is necessary for a phenomenon to be identified and legitimated as a true social problem.

The sudden and widespread publicity being directed toward wife beating is, perhaps, a mixed blessing. Although public apathy has been shaken and more support of services for battered women has resulted, there are indications that the topic is being exploited by the media for its sensationalist value, and there is a danger that the public may soon tire of hearing about it. There has been a spate of television dramas on wife abuse, as well as a series of documentaries. Some of these programs have provided sensitive overviews of the problem, while others can be characterized as cheap, cliché-ridden, and factually inaccurate; however, even the best of them will, given the constraints of television entertainment, offer portrayals that are much too simplistic and superficial.

Popular print media—including "women's" magazines like *Ms.*, *Ladies' Home Journal*, and *Woman's Day* as well as general-audience periodicals like *Time* and *Newsweek*—have recently had features and articles on battered women. Ann Landers has, with disturbing and characteristic glibness, addressed the problem in her column. Newspapers throughout the country have been flooding readers with dramatic accounts of incidents of wife abuse and with articles on new services for battered women.

The popular media are cited frequently in this chapter because such articles provide at least some factual information on the subject. The information tends to be anecdotal and sketchy, but, with some exceptions, it is all that is available. Hard research and statistics are sparse; the studies that have been done are of limited generalizability. While some scholarly research on family violence is emerging, the results so far offer few concrete suggestions having implications for either understanding or preventing wife abuse. Other aspects of family violence, particularly child abuse, have received much more attention and research funding.

In short, accurate and in-depth knowledge about wife abuse, including why it occurs and what can be done to stop it, is lacking. There is a sense, in reviewing the literature, that the researchers and writers have reached a stalemate. They seem unclear about where to go or what questions to ask next. Hence, the literature conveys, again and again, the same bare facts, and researchers continue to confirm what is already known: for example, that men frequently beat up women but that women rarely beat up men ["widespread violence . . . between American couples is virtually always perpetuated by men against women" (Kremen 1976:1)]; that wife beating is not a rare event; that abuse occurs at all socioeconomic levels; and so forth.

A feminist analysis offers promise for understanding the wife abuse syndrome, and feminist people have rallied to promote both social services and responsible research. It can only be hoped that their efforts will be sufficient to retain the momentum so recently achieved and to counteract any backlash that may occur in the future.

This chapter presents, first, a discussion of definitions of wife abuse, a description of what abuse typically involves, and a summary of what is known about the current incidence and patterns of abuse. A brief discussion of historical roots and myths pertaining to wife beating is offered, with examples of how current thinking is inconsistent and tends to result in blaming of the victim. Some more persuasive explanations of the abuse syndrome are then presented, followed by examples of societal obstacles that have militated against effective help for battered women. Finally, there is an overview of new services that have been developed for battered women. Emphasized are new training for police officers, the availability of shelters or havens for abused women, approaches to counseling, and legal alternatives. Other work being done in behalf of battered women is mentioned briefly.

## Definitions, Incidence, and Patterns

The terms used to label the problem (and used interchangeably here) are many: *battering, wife beating, wife abuse, wife assault, wife thrashing, domestic violence.* The physical acts involved are as varied as the strength, imagination, and inclination of the abuser. A man may use his hand to slap a woman, his fist to sock her, or his foot to kick her. He may hit her once, several times, or a hundred times. He may strike any part of her body, although the face, head, and abdomen are particularly common targets. Depending on his size and hers, an abuser may pick her up and throw her to the floor or against walls and furniture. A frequent pattern is for the physical abuse to begin with slaps and shoves, to progress to hitting and throwing, and once the woman is down, to advance to kicking, choking, and a literal "battering" of the woman's head against the floor or wall.

Some men also use implements for beating women. Knives, guns, clublike objects, belts, bottles, and pieces of furniture are among the most familiar, but women have also been hit with telephones, potted plants, books, rocks, musical instruments, coathangers, golf clubs, and toys. Women are strangled with cords or scarves; smothered with pillows or blankets; burned with lighters, cigarettes, or stoves; drenched in water or other liquid; forced to eat, drink, crawl, or beg. In some cases women are tied up and mutilated, frequently about the genitals and breasts. Women have also been thrown down stairs and out windows as well as locked up in rooms and closets.

There is no shortage of vignettes about the experiences of abused women. The literature contains many examples of horror-filled stories and countless variations as to the forms of assault. The following examples (Katz 1975) reflect *typical* incidents:

Mrs. A was dragged across the floor by the hair; when she screamed she was slapped in the face.

Mrs. B was tied to a chair in the basement, her mouth was taped, and her breasts were burned with lighted cigarettes.

Mrs. C was thrown down a flight of stairs and, as she tried to dial the telephone to summon help, was punched in the mouth.

Mrs. D was knocked to the ground, kicked, then locked in the trunk of the family car.

The injuries most frequently sustained by battered women are bruises, contusions, and broken bones, particularly ribs, fingers, and collarbones. Concussions, burns, and wounds requiring stitches are also common. Miscarriages resulting from abuse of a pregnant woman are not unusual.

The definitions as to what constitutes abuse vary from one community to another, as do the legal categories under which an abuser can be prosecuted. But virtually everywhere an informal distinction is made between assaults involving strangers and those in which the parties have a "primary relationships." "Primary relationships include legally married couples, common law couples, divorced or separated couples, and boyfriend/girlfriend relationships" (Fojtik 1976:19). If the assaulter has (or has had) any such ongoing relationship with the woman, the police are likely to refer to the incident with such euphemisms as "family dispute" or "domestic conflict." *Legally*, assault is assault no matter who the perpetrator is.

Unfortunately, and for reasons discussed later, when the assault occurs within a primary relationship arrest and prosecution are unlikely. As one woman noted, "If a man hits me over the head with a brick in front of People's drugstore, he goes to jail. If it's my husband, he goes home" (Newman 1976).

Another problem is that the media tend to cover the most sensational abuse incidents, creating the impression that only extreme cases of violence and injury constitute "real" abuse. Women who see these stories may feel that they are not true victims of abuse simply because they are not abused as severely as others. In fact, almost any behavior that they would not tolerate from a complete stranger need not be tolerated from a boyfriend or spouse.* It is important that this simple guideline be kept in mind. The debate over establishing definitions of abuse and categories with regard to "stages" or "levels" of

---

* Or any acquaintance or relative. It should be noted that women are also beaten by their fathers, brothers, uncles, neighbors, and family "friends."

abuse can detract from the basic issue, namely, that any physical injury or abuse inflicted on one person by another is illegal.

There are two qualifications to this general criterion. First, most courts are guided by a minimum definition of abuse as having to involve a blow with the clenched fist (not open hand) repeated over time. If and when such definitions are literally adhered to, many cases in which a woman has been severely injured might not qualify legally as abuse. The difference between a "slap" and a "sock" is also extremely difficult to prove in a court of law.

Second, at this writing only two states recognize rape of a wife by the husband as a crime; therefore, if the attack is "sexual" and does not involve other abuse it is not assault. Feminists have challenged the lack of these laws for some time; however, it is only recently that signs of possible change have appeared. For example, in March 1976 a Michigan woman was acquitted of the murder of her husband because he was trying to rape her at the time. The judge instructed the jury "that although a husband cannot be convicted of raping his wife, the woman has a right to refuse and resist what in fact may be a rape by him" (Ms. 1976:95). Self-defense is sometimes used as a successful legal argument for women on trial for murdering a spouse or boyfriend; however, in most cases it is difficult to convince the courts that a woman's life was threatened. Many women in jail for such murders allege a history of abuse and anticipation of assault as the reason for their own violent act; rarely is this accepted as legal justification.

Wife abuse is probably the most underreported crime in the country. Even with reported incidents, accurate statistics are hard to obtain because a high percentage of complaints are never prosecuted and others are not recorded as instances of wife beating.

It is virtually impossible to get an accurate estimate of incidence basically because wife beating is a tolerated act, rather than a crime or a social problem. Procedures and recording systems of the police, the courts, hospital emergency rooms, traditional and even nontraditional social service agencies systematically ignore and obscure incidence. Many battered women do not report beatings out of fear, shame and ambivalence and often their previous experience with a "system" designed to "help" them. As a result, the true incidence of wife abuse, however narrowly or broadly defined, is unobtainable. (Kremen 1976:1–2)

Few national statistics have been compiled; however, the statistics available from various specific communities, when considered together, suggest an alarming and widespread problem. A few examples:

New York State family courts handled 14,000 cases of wife abuse in 1973. (Gingold 1976:51)

A study of 600 couples applying for divorce in Cleveland revealed that 37 percent of the women gave physical abuse as the cause. (Newman 1976)

About 60 percent of the night shift calls to police in Atlanta are for domestic disputes. (Warrior n.d.:26)

Thirty-five percent of all assault cases reported in one Michigan county involved wife assault. (Resnick n.d.:1)

Boston police receive 45 wife beating reports per day. (Mybans 1975)

Although it *appears* that wife abuse is more common among people of lower socioeconomic status, these groups are also more likely to become known to the police for acts of violence (Stark and McEvoy 1970). The research of Gelles (1974) has established that abuse occurs at all socioeconomic levels as well as among all races, occupations, and educational levels.

Abuse can also happen to all women regardless of family size and age, although violence appears to be most prevalent in the 41- to 50-year-old age group. The average age of the beaten wife is in the late thirties. There is evidence that beatings tend to occur during the first year of marriage and to escalate in frequency and intensity thereafter (ibid., p. 1).

As the abuse becomes progressively worse, it may culminate in the homicide of either spouse. FBI statistics indicate that one out of eight of the 19,500 murders in the nation in 1973 involved a spouse killing a spouse. A study in Kansas City, Missouri, revealed that over 85 percent of the city's family homicides had been preceded by at least one "domestic disturbance" call to police (Gingold 1976:54; Kremen

1976:10–11). The newspapers contain numerous accounts of men who repeatedly beat their wives or girlfriends and eventually killed them.

The reverse is also true. Micklow and Eisenberg (1974) found that of the 13 cases of homicide occuring in one county during 1974, 6 involved women charged with the murder of their boyfriend or husband. In at least 5 of the 6 cases, there had been years of wife beating prior to the murder. In addition, wife abuse frequently leads to, or is associated with, child abuse perpetrated by the husband, the wife, or both.

Violence usually erupts on the weekends, at night, or during the early morning hours. It almost always occurs in the home, with no witnesses other than the children. That children frequently witness abusive scenes between their parents is known, and it is suspected that the effects on them may be decisive and lasting. Many of the men and women involved in abuse situations were themselves raised in violence-laden homes. It appears that habits of violence can be transmitted from one generation to another. One wife beater described his background to an interviewer for Ms. magazine (Geracimos 1976):

I was . . . the middle one of nine kids. My father used to beat my mother at home, in front of us. We kids would intervene so she wouldn't get hurt. You grow up thinking you ought to protect a woman, but still you've seen the beatings. I got confused signals. (p. 53)

While wife battering does occur at all socioeconomic levels, it is often true that, whatever the level of the husband, it is somewhat less than that of his friends and acquaintances, and less than what he aspires to. Over 80 percent of the violence-prone families studied by Gelles (1974) were of lower occupational status than their immediate neighbors.

Both partners caught up in abuse situations tend to be isolated and alienated from others, with few friends or social activities. There is a lack of communication between the partners, and often a lack of basic verbal skills on the part of the man. Frequently the female is more articulate and better educated than the male. O'Brien (1971) found that the violent men in his study "were characteristically underachievers in the work/learner role . . . deficient in certain status characteristics relative to their wives" (p. 692).

The immediate factors precipitating a man's battering his wife appear, in many cases, to be trivial. An abusive man may become violently angry if dinner is not ready, or there is not enough beer in the refrigerator, or the television set is broken.

After one occasion when [an abused] woman couldn't think of anything she'd done to provoke the attack, she asked her husband (when he returned to the house three days later) what, in fact, she had done to irritate him. His answer was that he "hadn't seen her in a skirt in months." (Myers 1975)

Opinions differ as to the association between drinking and incidents of abuse. The founders of one shelter for abused women state that "even when a woman denies that alcoholism is involved, we find that in nine out of ten cases drinking is still a factor" (Ms. 1976:97). Gayford (1975b) cites evidence suggesting a relationship between "regular and frequent" drunkenness and violent behavior in 52 percent of men arrested for violence. Wolfgang and Ferracuti (1967), in their discussion of the subculture of violence, report a consistent association between acts of violence and alcohol use.

However, in his study of 100 battered women Gayford (1975a) found that drinking was reportedly involved in only 44 percent of the cases. Marsden and Owens (1975) note that the battered wives they studied did not "place the major blame on drink, which had precipitated the incident in a minority of instances" (p. 334).

Bard and Zacker (1974:281) believe that prevailing assumptions about the salience of alcohol use in family disputes reported to police are false. In fact, they found that "disputes are not usually influenced by alcohol use; and, indeed, assaults are less common when alcohol has been used." Scott (1974) echoes the views of many when he states that alcohol or drug abuse "seems to be just another expression of the tension within the relationship and not necessarily directly causative" (p. 438).

Although it is true that alcohol releases inhibitions and that some abusers are alcoholics who may undergo extreme personality changes when drinking, the exact role that alcohol plays in any one abuse syndrome is difficult to determine. Both partners are very likely to reify the effects of alcohol, as though it alone were responsible for the abusive behavior, rather than seeing drinking as another behavior that follows from, or is associated with, lack of control. Gelles suggests that some men automatically begin drinking when they feel like beating their wives. He calls the drinking a "disavowal technique." "Husbands know they will be released from responsibility both by their wives and by the rest of society" if they are drinking (Gingold 1976:54). After beating up their wives or girlfriends, many men will express remorse and promise to stop drinking, implicitly defining the drinking, not the abuse, as the presenting problem.

It appears, then, that excessive drinking, when it does occur, is simply another part of the abuse pattern that develops between couples. The abuse becomes a ritual, a learned sequence of events, with each partner assuming familiar roles. It becomes, in the words of one abuser, a habit:

There isn't any particular thing that would set me off. Drinking had a lot to do with it. The alcohol justifies any action. After you've slapped a woman around a few times it's no big deal. . . . My second wife and I got into the habit from the beginning of the marriage. It always happened in the bedroom and it usually ended up with us making love. (Geracimos 1976:53)

## Historical Roots and Entrenched Myths

The expression "rule of thumb" has been traced by historians to the ancient right of a husband to beat his wife with a stick no thicker than his thumb (Gingold 1976:94). An old Pennsylvania law states that it is illegal for a man to beat his wife after 10:00 P.M. and on Sundays (Warrior 1976:4). Wife-beating jokes and proverbs have existed since marriage began, as has the habit of equating women with domestic animals (who are also seen as deserving a beating from time to time). Many organized religions have tolerated wife abuse and reinforced the subservience of females, admonishing women to stay with their husbands no matter how cruelly they were treated. ("Wives, submit yourselves unto your husbands . . . for the husband is the head of the wife"; Ephesians 5:23–24.) During the Middle Ages, and again during colonial times in America, thousands of women were tortured and burned for being "witches." For centuries women were regarded as the property of their husbands—an idea that was sustained by powerful cultural and legal norms.

As the world became more civilized, women were given more formal and legal recognition as human beings rather than possessions, and overt or public violence toward women became less tolerated. The abuse of women continued unabated, but it went underground and came to be viewed as a private matter—a family's own affair. Society had no business interfering in the sanctity and integrity of the family unit. A man's home was still his castle, and he could do anything he wanted there, including beating up his wife, as long as neither husband nor wife burdened others with the facts of their situation.

Eventually various forces, including the growth of cities and neighborhood living, made it increasingly difficult to ignore the occurrence of family violence. Wife beating tends to be a noisy event, carried on at odd hours and often accompanied by conspicuous destruction of property. The physical results of abuse—that is, the women's cuts and bruises—are also highly noticeable. Moreover, abusiveness is sometimes associated with other occurrences like crime, unemployment, and drunkenness, all of which were recognized as social problems long ago.

It became difficult, therefore, to deny the existence of wife abuse, and most people had to admit that it was a distasteful phenomenon. Gradually it was acknowledged that wife beating might indeed be a problem, but only in some cases and not, it should be emphasized, as a social problem of widespread occurrence. As is so often true of problems rooted in sexism, there emerged a set of beliefs and attitudes about wife beating that were erroneous, often contradictory, and that managed not only to enforce the status quo of permissiveness toward wife abuse but to exacerbate it. These attitudes and beliefs persist today.

First, the traditional idea that a little beating is acceptable, and even "good for her now and then," remains strong. In one recent survey 25 percent of the male respondents and 16 percent of the women said that they would approve of slapping a wife under certain circumstances (Fojtik 1976:32). The continuing popularity of jokes about wife beating also reflects a determination to relegate the issue to a lighthearted, inconsequential level (An example is a cartoon that shows a man in a restaurant choking his wife and a waiter, rushing to intercede, saying "Here! Here! There's a place for that, sir." Another is an advertisement that reads "Have some fun—beat your wife tonight.")

At the same time, extreme beating is not widely tolerated, although there are no definite norms as to when a beating has become excessive. Usually a high degree of both social disturbance and physical injury must occur before it is acknowledged that a problem exists. Only then, perhaps, is the response likely to be one of concern or outrage rather than amusement. The problem is seen, at best, as a moral or psychological one. In addition, the extreme incidents of abuse are viewed as rare, abnormal, abhorrent, and above all, wholly different phenomena than "a little beating now and then."

Problems need explanations. The simplest explanation in the case of a battered woman is that pathology exists in the parties involved. Sometimes it may be suggested that the man is deranged or psychotic. But more frequently, in line with blaming-the-victim logic, it is suggested that something must be wrong with the woman and that she is at fault.

The final irony in such thinking is that, as extremes of wife abuse have become regarded as deviant acts, the pressure on both the abuser and the abused to hide such acts has increased. They know, or at least suspect, that what is occurring is wrong, and their shame and humiliation are considerable. So they strive to conceal the abuse, and the belief that such incidents are rare and atypical continues to flourish.

That wife beating has not been seen as a social problem but as a joke or as a psychological and moral dilemma has led to the promulgation of peculiar and devastating ideas about why it occurs. Freudian psychology must assume part of the responsibility for the dissemination of these ideas.

The psychoanalytic premise that some people are basically "masochistic" while others are inherently "sadistic" is one pervasive example. This view purports that women allow themselves to be abused because they unconsciously wish to be victimized and that men become abusers because of an uncontrollable sadistic drive; when the female masochist meets the male sadist, an optimum climate for wife beating is generated. Many of these psychoanalytic ideas have been elaborated with an array of complicated concepts and theories; however, they are all essentially reducible to tenuous, unprovable assumptions about the basic character of men and women. Behavior is seen as instinctually determined and biologically derived; cultural and social influences are ignored. The development of the female is seen as a "biological process, essentially unaffected by social pressures and paralleling the same course in most cultures and times" (Nichols 1976:29). Freudian ideas also offer little insight into how to ameliorate the problem behaviors involved.

Other psychiatric theories are equally notable for their sexist premises. As recently as 1964 a study of the personalities of wife beaters and their wives, conducted by three psychiatrists, was reported in *Time* Magazine (*Time* 1964:82). The research was based on thirty-seven cases of wife abuse in Massachusetts. The researchers reported that both the husbands and the wives in these cases "fell into a definite pattern." The men were characterized as "hardworking and outwardly respectable" but as inwardly "shy, sexually ineffectual mother's boys." The women were described as "aggressive, efficient, masculine, and sexually frigid." Once again the woman is blamed (here the man's mother as well as his wife) and the socially imposed nature of definitions of masculinity, aggressiveness, and frigidity are ignored.

Further, the researchers concluded that the fighting among the couples they studied had "helpful overtones." It tended to ensue only when the man had been drinking, and it allowed him to release the frustrations and anxieties he felt over his wife's dominance. The fighting, they said, could also be beneficial to the woman because it gave her "masochistic gratification" and relief from the guilt she felt over her castrating behavior. The psychiatrists viewed the domestic violence as necessary in these situations because it allowed the couples to achieve a "working equilibrium" and thereby to counter and neutralize their differences.

The images of the abused woman as the nagging wife who has driven her husband to the limit or the masochist who craves abuse are as misguided as the idea of the rape victim's teasing and leading on her assailant. On a simpler level, abused wives may be regarded as stupid and incomprehensible. One judge was quoted as saying "Any woman dumb enough to marry such a jerk deserves what she gets" (Durbin 1974:65).

Such views, though extreme and amply countered by more responsible journalism and research, are still disturbing because they continue to receive popular distribution and because they are often shrouded in the trappings of pseudo-scientific persuasion. Most important, they are completely contradicted by the facts that have recently emerged about the wife abuse syndrome.

## Understanding the Abuse Syndrome

The two most frequently asked questions in the literature and research on battered women are "Why do the men do it?" and "Why do the women stay and take it?" The most logical, straightforward answers to the latter question—answers that are verified by the experience of those who counsel battered women—are that the women stay because they are frightened of retaliation should they leave; they have nowhere to go; they are as socialized as anyone else to the idea that there is something wrong with them and that they are to blame for the situation; and consequently, they are too guilty and humiliated to admit to their situation. They are desperate, panicked, trapped, and ashamed.

The fear of retaliation is justified. Thirty-five percent of the women in one sample reported that their beatings were more severe if they resisted (Micklow and Eisenberg 1974). Women who leave face the possibility of being charged with desertion. Many are afraid for their children as well as themselves—afraid to take them away but equally afraid to leave them behind.

The men will be free to retaliate in most cases. As has been noted, police are reluctant to arrest wife beaters and rarely do. Ironically, among the reasons police give for not arresting is that they believe most women will not file a complaint or, if they do, will fail to pursue it. In 1974, 751 women filed abuse complaints in one Michigan county, but only 1 or 2 percent of these were prosecuted (Zintl 1975). Too often, the woman is blamed for this failure to follow through, even though she is motivated by fear and overwhelmed by a law and justice system that is cumbersome, recalcitrant, and hostile. Abused women say that they want to do nothing more to provoke their husbands. Many stay, or return home after leaving for a short while, because the prospect of hiding out and being found by an enraged husband is more frightening than taking their chances at home.

Until recently there has been literally nowhere for battered women to escape to. Kremen's (1976) description of the services in New York City during September 1976 is typical of most cities at that time:

At the present time there are no shelters for battered women and their children in New York City. There is a municipal shelter for homeless women who wander the city streets during the day. There is a shelter for children who need to be removed from their homes on an emergency basis or who are abandoned. There is a residence for mothers who abuse their children and a companion shelter for abused children. There is emergency housing available for families including mothers and children who have become homeless through fire or eviction. There are several small residences operated by religious groups offering shelter to women without children. But there is no refuge or shelter specifically for battered women and their children in New York City today. (p. 15)

Economic necessity is also a factor. Many abused women have led a basically traditional existence as homemakers and mothers. They have little likelihood of supporting themselves and their children, and they know it. For some, and this seems particularly true of middle-class women, the decision to stay is calculated and resigned. The trade-off for the inevitable battering is a degree of economic security and material comfort that they could never achieve on their own: "it's often a choice between taking an occasional beating or living in poverty. And that's a tough choice to make" (Guthrie 1976).

While fear and economic dependency are the salient reasons why women stay in abusive relationships, certain psychological factors may also contribute. Abused women tend to have exaggerated apprehensions about the loneliness they would feel if they were on their own, as well as stubborn hopes that their situation and their husband's behavior will change: "the periods of calm between the violent episodes are genuine and may lull a woman into a false sense that the crisis is past" (Durbin 1974:67).

Women may also feel they are responsible for the abuse because they have been reared to believe that it is the woman's duty to maintain peace and stability in a marital or other primary relationship. To them, divorce or separation would represent inexcusable failure: "she will take great pride in a good marriage, and often take full responsibility for a bad one" (Martin 1976:81).

Gelles (1976) has identified four clusters of variables that interact to influence a woman's decision to stay or leave. First, a woman is more likely to stay and not seek outside help in relation to the severity and frequency of the abuse. The less severe and frequent the violence, the more likely she is to remain at home. A second factor is how much abuse she experienced as a child. Gelles emphasizes that violence is viewed as normative in many families—an event to be expected and perhaps even mandated. "The more she was struck by her parents, the more inclined she is to stay with her abusive husband. It appears that victimization as a child raises the wife's tolerance for violence as an adult" (p. 667).

A third set of variables relates to the resources and skills a woman has available to her. Less educated and less employable women have fewer alternatives to marriage and are more likely to remain in an abuse situation. The number and ages of her children, and the extent to which the children have become embroiled in the violence, may also be factors, although the patterns here are not as clear. However, Gelles does cite evidence suggesting that "the presence of an older child motivates a woman to take her husband to court." He also notes that some wives will take action more to protect their children than to protect themselves.

A final factor concerns what Gelles calls "external constraints," namely, the inaccessibility and unresponsiveness of the police, courts, and social agencies.

Gelles qualifies his conclusions by noting the complexity of the forces that will influence any one woman to stay, leave, or seek help. "It is not simply how hard or how often a wife is hit, nor is it how much education or income she has. The decision of whether or not to seek intervention is the result of a complex interrelationship of factors" (p. 667).

The following accounts from battered women reflect the immobilizing effects of fear, hope, and guilt:

I stayed for the sake of the children . . . I had no working record to fall back on; I got married right out of high school . . . it's hard to venture out. And I'd get paralyzed with fear. My husband would threaten to do things to me if I left, and I had no reason to doubt him. And I felt it would be immature to walk out on my marriage. I was trained to think a woman should cater to a man. (Myers 1975)

I always told myself, "I'll leave when Little League is over . . . I'll leave when school is out . . . I'll leave when the wash is done." But the next day he'd be so sorry and promise never to do it again, and I'd believe him. You believe. You want to believe. I still want to believe. (Mybans 1975)

I kept thinking it must be my fault. He wasn't like this before we got married. What did I do to provoke him? Then one night I was in bed asleep and he came in and started hitting me, and I said, "Boy, I didn't provoke this." (Mybans 1975)

Answers to why men become abusers are more elusive, but at least a few have been suggested by research and experience. In part, men beat their wives because they are frustrated and angry. A woman with whom they have a relationship is the most accessible target on which to vent these emotions. There is evidence that abusive men learn violence as a behavior—from their families of origin (Gelles 1976; Marsden and Owens 1975; Straus 1974) as well as their own later experiences with it. Learning theory would also explain why their violence tends to both repeat and intensify itself. It intensifies because it is never particularly satisfying as an outlet and, like many compulsions or addictions, multiplies in response to the continuing lack of satisfaction. It is repeated because it is rarely, if ever, punished sufficiently or consistently enough to be extinguished. In fact, most wife beaters know that women are not only available, accessible targets but safe ones as well. There have been few repercussions, social or legal, for wife abusers. Also, the lack of outside rewards in these men's lives has enhanced their isolation and anger. Their wives become, in many instances, the only people they relate to with any regularity at all.

A social and cultural perspective is needed to understand why abusers become so enraged in the first place. Most seem to have rigid, stereotyped ideas about what a truly masculine and successful man is like, and most, of course, are never able to achieve these ideals. Most are insecure and immature enough for this lack of achievement to become infuriating. Male abusers are also typically unable to perceive their own inadequate backgrounds as contributing to their behavior.

But they have to blame someone. They are likely to blame their wives—take it out on their wives—because that is the only remaining alternative. The wife is there, probably possessed of real and observable faults, and not likely to strike back.

O'Brien (1971) postulates that family violence and violence at a societal level can be similarly explained. He relates his theory to his finding that the achieved status of abusive men (i.e., their achievements in work, educational, and social areas) is so often less than that of their wives, neighbors, and coworkers. Since in American society the *ascribed* status of males is regarded as superior relative to that of women, the result for these men is a strongly felt "status inconsistency." Citing the work of others, O'Brien notes that violence in larger society "is typically intended either to bring about some needed change in the social order or else to reaffirm, in a ritualistic sense, the existing structurally differentiated status quo."

O'Brien applies these ideas to the husband–wife relationship and hypothesizes that "one should find that violence is most common in those families where the classically 'dominant' member (male–adult husband) fails to possess the superior skills, talents or resources on which his preferred superior status is supposed to be legitimately based" (p. 693). Thus, violence will be prevalent in "families where the husband–father [is] deficient relative to the wife–mother in achieved status characteristics" (p. 694). O'Brien's research findings support this hypothesis.

Certainly the average wife beater is a frustrated, pitiful human being. Efforts have been made to provide clinical descriptions and classifications of the abusive male personality (Scott 1974; Faulk 1974); however, wife beaters are rarely psychotic or otherwise blatantly deviant outside the home. One person who has treated violent husbands offers the following profile of the typical abusive male:

There's a good chance that the husband was abused as a child. He's an unhappy person with a poor image of himself. He feels that he's a failure both in his career and his masculinity. Often, he's an intemperate drinker, and later, feels remorseful and guilty about things he has done while drunk. Physical abuse is a desperate, last-resort form of behavior. . . . The man who beats his wife feels weak, vulnerable—trapped and helpless in a situation he can't get out of. (Katz 1975)

Wife beaters tend to be inordinately jealous of their wives and girlfriends, suspecting infidelity when none exists (Marsden and Owens 1975). It has also been found that abusive males are under daily stress from outside problems with which they are unable to cope. Failing job performance or unemployment, family health problems, and severe debt or other financial trouble are among the most common stresses faced by these men. In attempting to explain why men so frequently are abusive when their wives are pregnant, Gelles argues that impending parenthood is perceived by these men as a crisis. The stress and strain of the forthcoming family transition are further exacerbated by the man's sexual frustration and by irritability of the wife due to biochemical changes. A woman is also more defenseless during pregnancy (Gelles 1975).

Both the abusive man and the abused woman are mired in a destructive, ritualized relationship that becomes more violent and uncontrolled over time. The only immediate solution is to sever the relationship; however, until recently there have been few resources to assist the woman—or the man—in escaping the abusive syndrome.

## Societal Response and Service Needs

A battered woman may need a range of emergency and long-term services: police protection, medical care, shelter, legal counsel, personal and employment counseling, public assistance, and child care. The obstacles that abused women have faced and still face when attempting to seek help are many.

The stereotype of the battered woman as one who is apathetic and submissive and neither wants nor seeks help is not completely accurate. Nearly half the women in one sample had sought help from some source at the time they were being beaten. Most had, at some point, called the police for physical protection. Over two-thirds had received personal counseling, and over half had consulted lawyers (Fojtik 1976).

Unfortunately, the women who sought help did not necessarily receive it. In part this is because there have been few, if any, services specifically for abused women, as well as no workable theory or strategies for providing help. Most service providers have incorporated the general view that wife beating is a private matter in which society should not interfere. When the police, the courts, or counselors have become involved, they have tended to emphasize goals of appeasement, mediation, and conciliation. The following excerpt from the international association of police chiefs' training bulletin indicates the attitudes and guidelines of many police departments:

Avoid arrest if possible. Appeal to the woman's vanity. Explain the procedure of issuing a warrant . . . and the cost of the court. Explain that [women's] attitudes [about pressing charges] usually change by court time. Attempt to smooth feelings, pacify the parties. Remember, the officer should never create a police problem where there is only a family problem existing. (Krolik 1975).

The courts, if they act at all, are more likely to refer one or both parties to mental health centers than to press for divorce or prosecution. Prosecutors balk because wife beating cases have little status and are hard to prove, especially if the injuries were not severe or are no longer visible. The lack of witnesses also makes prosecution difficult. Kremen (1976) reports the laxness of emergency room personnel in keeping records of wife assaults. Few general practitioners pursue the matter even if assault may be suspected. "It requires a conscious effort to remember to ask irritable, bad tempered, and aggressive people whether anyone in the family has been physically harmed" (Dewsbury 1975:290).

Counselors are likely to approach abuse cases as a form of relational therapy, with goals of maintaining or rebuilding the relationship. In addition, traditional therapy emphasizes inner psycho-logical processes rather than environmental stresses or the impossible demands of stereotypical sex roles. The abuse will be seen as a symp-tom of underlying conflict and not as a problem in its own right.

Wilson (1975:294–297) notes that social workers have historically been reluctant to view battery as a discrete problem. Instances of bat-tered women were "usually perceived as one particular way in which marital malfunctioning manifested itself, rather than as a special kind of problem." Social workers have been trained to view the family as the dominant instrument of socialization, and to work always for its maintenance. Also, as "guardians of the states's resources," social workers (as well as the courts, the police, and others) are constantly aware that family breakdown creates further expenses for the state.

Nichols, whose article on wife abuse appeared in *Social Casework* in January 1976, was unable to find any coverage of the problem in past professional literature. Among the other reasons she cites for social workers' reticence to recognize abuse as a primary presenting problem are the fear "of being judged as too allied with feminism," the continuing influence of Freudian theory on social work practice, reluctance to assume an advocacy role, and lack of knowledge about legal and other alternatives (Nichols 1976).

Social service practitioners who have written about the need to help battered women continually emphasize that helping profes-sionals both reflect and perpetuate prevailing sexist assumptions and stereotypes, particularly the belief that abused women provoke vio-lence and the idea that abuse is a private matter. The intense awk-wardness and embarrassment that social workers feel when con-fronted with an abuse problem contrasts sharply with the forthright way they are able to deal with equally complex problems, including child abuse.

The caseworkers do not laugh outwardly; but there is usually embarrassment which appears as an avoidance of the issue. This reaction is due in part to the acceptance of a philosophy which tolerates the normalcy of male aggres-sion in whatever form it takes. (p. 28)

Another fundamental reason why acknowledgment of wife abuse has occurred so slowly relates to a theme that emerges repeatedly throughout this book: *All* forms of physical suffering experienced uniquely by women tend to be minimized, ridiculed, or denied by helping professionals as well as generally.

Few attempts have been made to help women with menopausal symptoms; scant regard has . . . been given to the often avoidable pain of childbirth; menstrual cramp is regarded as simply trivial. So, the sufferings of women who have been beaten, raped, and assaulted by the men they are living with, have also been minimized. (Wilson 1975:297)

When an abusive male receives therapeutic attention, it is more likely to center on his drinking than on his violence. Moreover, abusive men are characteristically unwilling to seek counseling and almost never do; consequently, there are few data on whether these men can be helped or on what counseling methods are effective for curbing their violent behavior. The abused woman in therapy is, by definition, the client or patient and is usually seen as the focus of the problem. In all probability she will be counseled to adjust to her situation or to change her behavior in order to provoke less violence. Thus, women who are unusually passive from both fear and years of socialization are made more so by the services system.

## Services for Battered Women

Many recent developments are of import for the needs of battered women. Among these are the growing recognition that traditional police tactics are ineffective and resulting experimentation with alternative approaches; the establishment of shelters or refuges for abused women and their children throughout the country; and the emergence of specific strategies for legal and personal counseling of abused women. Programs and services related to each of these three developments are discussed here.

### POLICE TACTICS

Police officers are the first and most likely outsiders to become involved in incidents of family violence. They are most frequently called to the scene by neighbors or by the abused woman and, if they respond promptly, will arrive while the abuse is taking place or shortly thereafter. Their role in halting the violence and providing immediate protection for the woman is crucial. They can also make a significant contribution to later developments. Their counsel, coming at the peak of the crisis, can influence a woman's decision to take or not take further action. They have power to decide whether the man should be arrested or otherwise separated from the woman. In addition, the police become eyewitnesses; their testimony in subsequent courtroom proceedings can be decisive.

It has been noted that the usual goals of the police in responding to wife assault calls are to effect appeasement and reconciliation. They aim to restore quiet and peace as quickly as possible and to minimize the degree of official involvement or follow-up. They rarely arrest anyone, and if they separate the couple at all, it is most often for a brief time only; for example, they will talk to the man and the woman in separate rooms or will have the man take a walk around the block.

Traditionally, the police do not intervene in the ongoing problem. They do not provide the woman with permanent protection. They do not help either the man or the woman explore alternatives to their situation. In their approach the police both reflect and reinforce prevailing norms about wife abuse as well as sexist stereotypes about the marital roles and responsbilities of men and women.

There are two reasons why police forces are beginning to consider ways of altering their approach to domestic violence situations. The first is that it is becoming increasingly apparent that traditional approaches are ineffective. Repetitive calls to the same residences, the eventuality of homicide in some instances, and complaints from abused women and their advocates about police procedures are among the most tangible signs that the usual routine is not working. The second reason, and perhaps the most influential one, is self-interest.

Police dread domestic violence calls. Such situations are volatile, unpredictable, and dangerous. More police are killed or injured on these calls than in any other line of duty. The FBI reports that 149 police officers were killed responding to domestic disputes between 1965 and 1974 (Gingold 1976:94). About 22 percent of the police

officers who die on duty are killed in such instances (Kremen
1976:23).

Although conventional police procedures can be severely criti-
cized, the dilemma they face when responding to domestic calls
should not be underestimated:

The clear reality that emerges from a look at police activity is that whatever
he may do at the scene of the "crime"—soothe, coax, threaten the parties
without arrest, or arrest one or both of them—the police officer will not get
to the bottom of the problem or effect any sort of lasting detente. Even if he
were to . . . emphasize support rather than control functions, no course of
action he might adopt would be suited to the demands or needs he faces.
The inevitable result is that he is forever called on for stop-gap solutions to
permanent problems. The officer is caught in a dilemma in which arrest
may trigger homicide as surely as the failure to arrest. (Field and Field
1973:230)

Kremen (1976) notes that police departments are "stimulated by
the high rate of injury and death which follows intervention in family
disputes" and are beginning to show "an interest in training police to
deal with family violence."

The introduction of special training for the police may serve to diminish
conflict which has resulted from the police officer's own actions. The element of self-interest may provide an opportunity to modify police procedures
in dealing with wife battering. (p. 10)

In addition, some police departments are learning that female
officers are more adept than male officers at dealing with family violence. Attempts have been made to train and use male–female teams
specifically for domestic violence calls. Interracial teams of police
officers have also received training to deal with family violence. Bard
(1970) reports on a training program for selected policemen in an
inner-city area with a population of 90,000. The purpose of the training program was to provide officers with interpersonal skills for intervening effectively in deteriorating family situations (Bard and Zacker
1971). The program is summarized as follows:

The preparatory phase of the program involved the selection of eighteen
officers, nine white and nine black, all of whom had three or more years of
service and evidenced motivation and aptitude for the training they were to

receive. The initial block of training entailed an intensive 160-hour, on-campus training course involving the entire Unit. In addition to lectures and field trips, there was active participation in "learning by doing" through real-life simulations. These involved specially written plays depicting family crisis situations enacted by professional actors and in which the patrolmen actively intervened in pairs. The teaching methods centered on repeated run-throughs of plays written without conclusions. That is, upon intervention by the officers (who had no knowledge of events preceding their intervention), the actors engaged in improvised, non-scripted performances keyed to the behavior of the officers. By this method, each run-through had a different outcome; a telling demonstration of the fact that an officer's behavior is a critical determinant of a crisis outcome. Practice interventions were subjected to group critique and discussion. Finally, self-understanding workshops were conducted to sensitize the patrolmen to their own values, attitudes and automatic responses.

The operational phase [in which the officers were in the field responding to actual calls] of the program lasted for twenty-two months. . . . During this twenty-two month period, discussion groups of six men met with civilian, professional group leaders, familiar with the work of policemen. . . . In each, the main consideration was current crisis situations as these involved assumptions, preconceptions and misapprehensions about human behavior and family relationships that may have been implicit in the attitudes and performance of Unit members. In addition to continuous group experience, each family specialist was assigned an individual consultant for at least one hour's weekly consultation. . . .

To facilitate evaluative procedures, a neighboring police precinct with a population composition somewhat similar to that of the experimental precinct served as a basis of comparison. Comparisons were made based on changes in the total number of family disturbance complaints, differences in recurrence of complaints by the same families, and changes in the number of homicides and assaults involving both family members and policemen responding to family complaints.

The demonstration in police family crisis intervention was evaluated primarily in relation to a police function as it affects certain categories of crime. In relation to the comparison precinct, the demonstration precinct reported a significantly greater number of interventions (1,388 vs. 492). Comparison with statistics prior to the Unit's operation within the demonstration precinct showed that while there was an increase in the total homicides (12 vs. 42), none of these occurred during the study period among any of the 962 families seen by the Unit, and there were no injuries to any Unit members despite a high statistical probability of injury. There were three injuries to patrolmen who had not been trained.

It should be emphasized that the family officers were clearly policemen and not social workers or psychologists. However, their training and organizational structure permitted them to do effective screening interviews with families, provide immediate counseling services and, if necessary, to make referrals specifically related to the problems as *they* defined them. (pp. 678–79)

## SHELTERS, REFUGES, AND HAVENS

Other countries have had shelters specifically for abused women for years. France, Canada, West Germany, Ireland, Australia, and Holland all provide various forms of short- and long-term housing for battered women. There are over fifty shelters in England and plans for the development of still more. Repeatedly, the experience in these countries has been that the shelters are filled to capacity shortly after they open.

Warrior (n.d.) notes that there have long been sanctuaries to which women living in intolerable situations could flee. But there are crucial differences between the shelters of the past and those of today:

Most sanctuaries for women in the past were affiliated with religious bodies, charitable organizations or community governmental groups. Some of these refuges still exist today. Often convents, hospitals, asylums, charitable institutions, poor houses, etc., offered women in extreme crisis a place to go temporarily or permanently. These refuges functioned to serve the needs of the family unit, the community, the governments and the status quo, rather than the long term well-being of the women who sought shelter there. In this respect they served as a safety valve for the social institutions with which women were in conflict. They bound her immediate wounds, gave her advice on how to adjust and cope with her situation and sent her back or kept her forever within their confines.

During the Middle Ages, many women entered convents to escape from the harsh realities of feminine life: constant childbearing, drudgery, poverty and male violence. Many women in crisis, though, were loath to enter the strict confines of these sanctuaries, whether convents, hospitals, or charities. Others felt they would receive no real understanding or sympathy there. For many women the streets became their refuge and even brothels their sanctuary from the family or community. Indeed, most refuges for women weren't refuges at all, but were merely forced to serve as such for lack of better alternatives. (p. 1)

The first shelter for abused women in the United States, Rainbow Retreat, was established in Phoenix, Arizona, in November 1973. Since then numerous refuges have opened around the country, particularly in urban areas. Most were begun by small groups of dedicated women, often women who themselves had once been victims of abuse. The majority of these women had little, if any, financial backing, and many had to deal with powerful community resistance. A common response of potential funding sources is to deny support on the grounds that a need for the service has not been demonstrated. It is frequently suggested that research and surveys of need be conducted before a shelter is established.

The demand for such surveys is, first of all, an unrealistic one, since the women involved are unlikely to have either the expertise or the resources to undertake research. More important is the fact that in recent years the need has already been amply demonstrated. Calls for further research are delaying tactics reflective of the community's reluctance to acknowledge an uncomfortable problem and, perhaps, to deal with women who are not part of the established services network.

Invariably, the founders of shelters for abused women have proceeded despite community resistance and ambivalence. In most cases the refuges have survived, through the hard work of a few and because the need for shelters for battered women is so great. As it becomes increasingly difficult for the community to ignore the existence of and demand for shelters, eventual support, financial and otherwise, may be offered. "Rainbow Retreat started with $50 and 11 dedicated and determined individuals. Today they have an annual budget of $110,000 to shelter up to 13 women and children at a time" (Ms. 1976:97).

It is impossible to describe a typical or representative shelter. The programs vary noticeably in terms of philosophy, purpose, and nature and extent of services provided. Philosophically, two major trends are apparent.

On the one hand are those who view the problem of abuse as

primarily situational and interactional, and as a temporary crisis in the ongoing relationship between the man and woman involved. Separation of the couple is seen as an emergency expediency that is useful until the problems in their relationship can be resolved. Counseling or other treatment for both the man and the woman is encouraged. It is assumed that eventual reconciliation of the couple is inevitable and, in most instances, desirable. There is emphasis on traditional male/female roles and on the sanctity of marriage. Both parties in the relationship are regarded as responsible for the abuse.

Many of the refuges espousing beliefs like these are affiliated with organized religious groups. The services they offer are more likely to be limited and of a short-term nature, encourage involvement of and contact with the husband, and rely on referral to outside sources for ongoing treatment (e.g., counseling for the woman and alcoholism treatment for the man).

Such viewpoints are, of course, largely incompatible with the stance assumed in this book. It is important to recognize, however, that the shelters eschewing feminist beliefs are, in many instances, the only shelters available or the only ones acceptable to the abused woman (e.g., because of her association with a particular church). While most of these shelters cannot be viewed as either feminist or innovative, as defined in this book, they do provide an alternative and often life saving service for many battered women.

At the other philosophical extreme are the shelters with a feminist orientation. Wife abuse is seen as a social problem, rooted in sexism and manifested in the suffering of countless individual women. The women are regarded as victims in need of immediate protection and long-term life change. Some of the refuges with this philosophy actively encourage permanent separation of the couple. They also make concerted efforts to attack the apathy and sense of helplessness that abused women tend to feel. Others avoid taking any stance with regard to separation, preferring to give the woman support and information about available alternatives until she is ready to make her own choices about her future.

Nearly all the feminist-based shelters discourage contact between the man and woman, at least at first. Some offer assistance to the man in seeking counseling or other help from himself, but for most the focus is primarily on the needs of the woman. Many shelters have elaborate security precautions to prevent the abusive man from seeing or contacting his wife (e.g., walled yards, locked and barred doors, unlisted phone numbers). Some do not even reveal the location of the shelter; instead, other places where the woman can call or go for help are publicized and she is picked up there and taken to the refuge.

Many shelter services have philosophies that lie somewhere between these two extremes or reflect elements of both. However, they all have in common the central goal of providing a physical place where a woman can flee for protection from a man who has beaten her. Another commonality is that the refuges have made their existence widely known: to the public (e.g., through media publicity and community organizations) and to potential referral sources (e.g., crisis lines, police, hospital emergency rooms, doctors, social service agencies). The aim is to ensure that women in need will eventually reach the haven, whether through direct contact or through referral.

The differences and similarities among the shelters can be described in terms of four salient factors: nature of phsysical facilities, target population served, extent of ancillary services, and number and kind of house rules.

*Physical Facilities*
Most shelters for abused women are houses, usually fairly big houses, located in residential neighborhoods. The capacity of a house can range from a few women to twenty or more women and their children. Attempts are usually made to provide privacy, particularly when a woman first arrives, though this may be difficult because of overcrowding. Typically, women are assigned to beds and bedrooms when they arrive. Livingrooms, dining rooms, kitchens, and bathrooms are communal rooms available for the use of all. Some shelters also have one or more of the following: a nursery or playroom for children, rooms for live-in staff, an office, and an examining room or other facilities for emergency medical treatment. A few shelter services have grown to include several houses. Occasionally, nonresidential buildings have been converted into shelters.

Another approach to provide emergency housing for battered women is the use of volunteers who are willing to take women into their homes. The volunteers are on call, with referrals made from a central location established either specifically for that purpose or in conjunction with other social services.

Food and clothing are also available at most shelters. Clothing is important because few abused women are able to pack before they flee. Many arrive dressed only in nightclothes. Most have little or no money.

In some communities nonemergency assistance for battered women is provided in a manner analogous to traditional outpatient or drop-in services. These shelters are places where a woman can come, if only for an hour or two, to rest, obtain information or counseling, and rap with others.

### Target Populations

The primary charge of the majority of shelters is to serve women who have recently been beaten, that is, women who are escaping from an immediate abusive encounter. However, women without tangible signs of having been beaten will usually be accepted if they are in fear of abuse. Most women who seek refuge have experienced a history of abuse. The current crisis—whether an actual beating or the anticipation of a beating—has finally pushed them to obtain help.

Some shelters assert that emotional and psychological abuse (e.g., verbal threat from a husband or boyfriend) is also dangerous, and therefore serve women who may not have been physically injured at all. Few services have rigid guidelines as to the extent of injury that must occur before a woman is taken in. The major criterion is the woman's fear.

Some refuges accept children; some do not. Those that do not will usually take children temporarily and help the woman make arrangements to house them elsewhere. Geographic stipulations are common; that is, a woman must reside within a defined catchment area. Many avoid taking in women who are violent or are under the influence of drugs or alcohol; others see dealing with alcohol or drug involvement (of the husband, the wife, or both) as a primary part of their service. Some have been established specifically to serve particular racial–ethnic or religious groups. A few require that a woman be legally married. Some stipulate that an official referral from the police or another community agency is necessary.

These and other criteria about the populations to be served are evident in official statements and publications provided by shelter services. Such criteria clarify the service priorities of a shelter and help guide its outreach to particular groups of women. However, it should be stressed that shelters, by and large, do not turn away *any* woman who is in need, even though she may not fit the population criteria.

### Ancillary Services

In addition to the basics of food, transportation, and shelter, refuges may provide other services. Often available are information and referral pertaining to many of the needs of abused women: housing, welfare and financial aid, alcoholism and drug abuse treatment, legal services, employment and employment counseling, medical aid, and so forth. Some shelters provide on-site first aid or other medical attention. Peer and professional counseling is sometimes available, as are opportunities for group discussion and therapy. A few shelters are affiliated, directly or indirectly, with community agencies providing an array of specialized services.

### House Rules

Almost all shelters have an explicit routine and set of expectations for the residents. The expectations tend to reflect the shelter's basic philosophy, its particular mission, and the extent of its resources. Shelters with fewer staff and resources, for instance, must depend on the residents to assist with such tasks as cleaning, food preparation, and child care. Many require a fee or donation, usually whatever the woman can afford. There also tend to be definite stipulations as to the length of time a woman can remain at the shelter. These time limits range from one day to several weeks.

Most shelters recognize that initially a battered woman is usually unable to plan constructively for the future. Her immediate needs are for rest and medical aid. Often a woman will sleep throughout most of the first twenty-four hours.

Subsequently the woman may be expected to contribute to the running of the shelter as well as to begin anticipating her transition out of the house. Staff members are usually available to assist in planning for the transition. Many women return to their former living situations; with others, a decision is made to plan for a new life away from the abusing boyfriend or husband.

Shelters tend to have a variety of specific rules designed to make the environment as safe and pleasant as possible. Among the most common rules are prohibitions against visitors and use of alcohol or drugs on the premises, and requirements regarding standards of hygiene and attendance at certain house meetings.

Most providers of shelter services for battered women gradually develop a philosophy and operating guidelines that are suitable for their particular community. All are offering a service that is long overdue. All recognize that the suffering of a battered woman is real and that her needs are many and immediate. A bulletin from one refuge sums up the enormity of these needs: "Just imagine what a woman would need to have done for her if she appeared on the doorstep at 3:00 A.M. clad in a bloody nightgown and with three crying children . . ."*

## Personal and Legal Counseling
## for Abuse Victims

The following section is excerpted from *Wife Beating Counselor Training Manual No. 1*, by Mindy Resnik, M.S.W. The introduction to this manual states that it is

Part One of a three part series of manuals for peer counselors of domestic violence and spouse assault victims. These manuals were prepared to assist volunteer counselors working with the Ann Arbor Washtenaw County Chapter of the National Organization for Women (NOW) and their Wife Assault Project. This manual is not an exhaustive, in-depth training manual, but rather an introduction to a practical, basic counselor-client relationship. The legal information written herein is from a layperson's point of view and is not meant to be a formal interpretation of the laws, but only a

* Shelter for Battered Women, Seattle, Washington.

guide to help victims through their counselors to understand the system generally. It is hoped that this manual will assist volunteer peer counselors and professional counselors alike. (p.i)

In addition to the passages quoted here, the manual contains an introduction to the nature and extent of the problem, suggestions about how to organize and structure services for abused women as well as how to train counselors, a glossary of legal and advocacy terms, a bibliography, and examples of a questionnaire and forms that can be used to deal with the multiple problems faced by battered women.

The advice and alternatives set forth in the manual stem from the experience and situation of women in the state of Michigan. Some of this information may not coincide with the laws and resources existing in other states. However, the basic ideas presented are adaptable to any locale.

# Counselor's Roles

## MINDY RESNIK[*]

### 1. Practical Helper and Educator

Many victims may be uninformed as to where and how to go about seeking the kind of help they need. Counselors can provide them with the information they need to take action on their own behalf, especially in the legal, medical, and social services areas, and can help them to arrange the necessary appointments with appropriate personnel. In some cases, there may be several options in agencies or persons that provide the same or similar services. Those who are being counseled should be informed as to all of their options.

[*] Reprinted from Mindy Resnik, *Wife Beating Counselor Training Manual No. 1.* 1977 AA Now/Wife Assault, Ann Arbor, Michigan. This manual was developed and is copyrighted © 1976 by the NOW Domestic Violence Project, Ann Arbor, Michigan.

## 2. Advocate

The victim may well be unfamiliar and therefore uncomfortable with medical, legal, and social service agencies and authorities. Often in proceedings (particularly legal) she will become lost in the action and her needs may well not be fully met. As her advocate, the counselor should keep in contact with medical, legal, and social service authorities in order to keep her informed about what is happening, and in order to insure that the appropriate personnel are taking as much action as is possible in her case. Advocacy should be done tactfully but with resolve and persistance if necessary. Counselors will not just be functioning as a personal or peer advocate, but also as a representative and advocate from their parent organization.

## 3. Counselor–Supporter

The role here is to provide the victim with emotional support, to encourage her to talk about her experiences and to help her to identify and understand her feelings. The presence of a concerned person will help her to realize the importance of her feelings. Support can be a tremendous help to her at all stressful times.

## INITIAL INTERVIEW/INTAKE

### 1. Victim Anxiety

In the first contact with a new client, it is important to remember that there is most often a great deal of anxiety involved in initial help-seeking efforts. The following are some of the possible reasons for this anxiety. The client may mention her concerns. If she does not, the counselor might explore the following sources of anxiety with her, because she might feel reticent about initiating such a discussion.

### a. Worries About How to Communicate with Counselor

The victim may see her life as so chaotic that, in anticipating her meeting with the counselor, she may worry about where to begin talking, what to say, and how to say it.

The client should be assured that there is no rush for her to tell all that is on her mind. She should, further, be reassured that she need not feel compelled to tell anything that she doesn't feel comfortable confiding.

### b. Fears That Counselor Will Be Judgmental

Especially if the beatings have been going on for an appreciable period of time, the client may be worried that her counselor will be critical or judgmental in attitude.

The client must be assured that the counselor will not be critical or judgmental and understands that motivations for any action or lack of action are complex. It is very important when counseling to be aware of personal feelings about the client. In order to be an effective counselor, one must not allow feelings to color one's work. Not all of the victims encountered will be likeable, nor may the counselor agree with their way of thinking. A counselor must face these negative feelings about the victim or her case honestly. If they are ignored and counseling continues as if they didn't exist, these feelings will most likely be poorly hidden and the negative attitudes will leak out in nonverbal communications with the victim.

Some of us may have more difficulty than others in accepting the fact that some clients that we see may not want to leave the man who physically abuses them, let alone press criminal charges against him. This is the client's decision to make. She should be advised of her options, made aware of the support that she can expect from you, from your organization, from legal authorities, etc., and she should be encouraged to follow through on legal proceedings if she is so inclined. She might not want to do so at present but may change her mind in the future. If she does decide to stay with a physiclly abusive man, the counselor can help her clarify why she has made the decision.

### c. Embarrassment in Labeling Self as a "Battered Wife"

Because of society's attitude toward the victims of wife assault (They must like it—they are getting what they deserve—if they were better wives their husbands wouldn't have to beat them, etc.), the client may feel embarrassed to identify herself as a "battered woman." It is important to assure the client that she need not feel embarrassed at being a victim, that it is not a reflection on her character or her worth as a human being.

### d. Confidentiality

The victim may be concerned about her assailant finding out about her visit to you and, thus, be worried about physical retaliation.

The client should be assured that everything that she says and the very fact that she is seeking help is to be held strictly confidential. She is to be assured that the counselor will release no information to anyone without her consent. . . . Further, if her assailant should find out or if she is worried about physical abuse for any reason, if she has no place to go for refuge, she should be assured that temporary safe housing is available to her.

### e. Commitments

The victim may be worried about what kind of commitment to action she is making by seeing the counselor. She may be worried that, against her inclination, she will be pressured into filing for divorce or pressing criminal charges.

The client must be assured that her needs will be met as SHE defines them, that the counselor has no intention of pressuring her to do anything. Encouragement to follow through on her intentions, yes—pressure, never!

Some or all of the above-mentioned fears may be so overwhelming that the client may not show up for a scheduled appointment. Having a client not show up for an appointment is always a frustrating experience for a counselor. A telephone call in which the counselor helps to identify and alleviate the concerns that kept her from coming can often open or reopen the channels of communication. Above all else, it is important to stress that anxiety when seeking help is normal, and that as rapport builds, her anxiety level concerning your meetings should decrease. Also, there may well be reasons other than those mentioned that caused her to miss her appointment. Some real detective work may have to be done to ferret them out, and it is quite possible that the client herself cannot label the concerns that prevented her from coming to the appointment. Caution: The obvious should not be overlooked, such as, Was transportation or child care a problem? Did the husband or boyfriend prevent the client from coming? (For infants and younger children, the use of a nursery which has cribs and beds that a client can use during counseling sessions [should be] provided.)

## 2. Practical Aspects

### a. Where to Meet

It must be made clear that at no time will the counselor be able to visit the client at her home, or for her to visit the counselor at his or hers. This is for the counselor's safety. Remember that more police die when intervening in domestic violence situations than they do in any other crime.

### b. Assailant

As a policy rule, the counselor will not meet with the woman's assailant anywhere. There may be some few exceptions to this, but you should never make this decision without discussing it with your supervisor beforehand.

### c. Setting Limits

The counselor must set personal limits as to time and energy commitments to the clients seen, e.g., how long session will last, whether or not it is desirable for her to call the counselor at home or at work. When seeing a woman for an appreciable time period, she should be advised if the counselor is going out of town for an extended period of time. . . .

## 3. Range of Emotional Reactions

The following is a list of feelings victims typically experience. . . .

### a. Loss of Control, Helplessness

Feeling at the mercy of someone's mood fluctuations and outbreaks of temper is a very frightening and frustrating way to live one's life, and can easily lead to a feeling of having no control over one's life. In [one] study it was found that abused women said that most of the attacks were unwarranted and totally unexpected. Some were even attacked and beaten while sleeping.

Efforts at seeking help have often proved to be dead ends for many of these women—again leading to feelings of helplessness.

Tremendous fear may result and/or a sort of emotional paralysis, so that the victim feels passive and experiences all that happens around her as being done *to* her. It is important to help the victim get back in control of the situation, and this can be done in many ways. Helping her to identify her feelings is one way to calm down her chaotic state of mind. Getting her to seek medical, legal, and social service attention she needs helps her to take action on her own behalf. . . .

### b. Fear

It is important to reassure the client of the confidentiality of her help-seeking contacts (except for filing a criminal complaint against the assailant). She should be helped to make a realistic assessment of her imminent danger. If she is not living with the assailant, suggestions can be made about changing locks on the doors, locking windows, etc. If she is living with the assailant and is in imminent danger, suggestions should be made as to at least temporarly alternative housing; legal measures such as divorce, prosecution, restraining orders may be the route to take, but the client should never feel pressured into this route. Legal processes should be thoroughly explained.

### c. Anger

All victims will be experiencing anger at some level about their situation. Some victims will be able to express their anger directly on or at the assailant, but others will not. It is very important to help the victim to express the anger and to get it focused in the proper direction, that is, at the assailant. If this is not done, the victim may well internalize the anger, getting angry at herself instead of the assailant; this leads to feelings of guilt and self-blame. At other times the victim may ventilate the anger toward police, medical, or social service personnel or at the counselor.

### d. Guilt

As mentioned previously, guilt often has its roots in misdirected anger, anger turned inward. Guilt also arises from some all too commonly held beliefs that if a woman gets beaten she deserves it; therefore she must be a bad woman, wife, or mother. Another belief is that women are by nature masochistic and thus expect and enjoy physical abuse. It is important to explore these beliefs and misconceptions with the victim to let her know that her counselor doesn't believe these things are true.

### e. Embarrassment

A woman may well feel embarrassed to admit that she is a battered woman. She may well be ashamed of her scars. She may feel foolish to have made a domestic commitment to a physically abusive man as well as ashamed of herself to have put up with repeated beatings. Considering the embarrassment that a victim of domestic violence might well feel, she may never have discussed her problem or feelings with anyone. In such cases she will really welcome the opportunity to ventilate in a supportive atmosphere. . . .

### f. Doubts About Sanity

Some women have fears of insanity, particularly if they have strong feelings of lack of control. Living in constant fear of physical assault can have many emotional ramifications which may lead a victim to isolate herself socially. Once socially isolated, she has no one to confirm her sanity. Her only input is from her assailant and from herself.

### 4. Counseling Skills and Techniques

### a. Listening and Summarizing

The most fundamental aspect of good counseling is the ability to listen. Good listening demands intense concentration. Effective listening also demands not only that the interviewer hear and understand what is being said, but that she or he also hear and understand what is being communicated through silence. Frequently the impact behind what was not said suggests clues about sources of difficulty. Again, a client should never feel pressured into discussing anything that she doesn't want to talk about. The counselor should be aware of topics that are emotionally stressful for the client. After trust and rapport have had time to build up, the counselor may want to gently pursue these areas. Body language (the way a client sits, whether she looks the counselor straight in the eyes, whether she rocks, wrings her hands, etc.) should be carefully observed, as it offers important data to the counselor. Discrepancies between verbal and nonverbal communication should be noted by the counselor, and if the atmosphere is appropriate, the discrepancies should be pointed out to the client.

For example, a woman is discussing how terribly angry she is at her husband, but is smiling as she speaks. This could be purely a nervous reaction or it could be an indication that she has difficulty in expressing her anger or dissatisfaction. . . .

It is often a very helpful technique to summarize the salient aspects of what you have understood from a client's verbal and nonverbal communication. Such a summary should never be put forth as a statement of fact. In other words, it is not appropriate to say, "I can see that you are very angry," but rather to say something like, "It sounds to me like you are feeling very angry." We must never assume that we understood or that a message came through clearly, without first verifying it. . . . Ascertain whether the client has listened attentively and understood what you have said by asking her to summarize your communication to her.

### b. Sorting Aspects

A victim may feel so enmeshed in her problems that there seems no logical way to begin fighting her way out. It is important to help the client dissect her problematic life—to segmentalize different aspects of the problem, to label each aspect of her problematic situation. A problem will usually not appear as overwhelming and unwieldy if its components can be identified and labeled.

Especially if the client is planning to make dramatic changes in her life, such as leaving a man whom she has been with for a long time, there are many decisions to be made and changes to plan. Labeling and discussing each category of change can often help reduce anxiety. A client in this type of situation may need help in prioritizing. Her options should be fully explored and discussed.

### c. Labeling a Client's Feelings

The range of feelings that a victim often experiences has been previously mentioned. As an outsider, the counselor will be able to hear her feelings more clearly . . . and can help her label her emotions.

Very often, simply getting her feelings named will relieve her greatly. It will bring some order to the chaos she is experiencing. A client may be feeling a good deal of ambivalence. She may feel that she both loves and hates her assailant. In such a situation, it can be useful to ask the client to enumerate or list the positive aspects of her husband or boyfriend, and the negative ones. . . .

### d. Ventilation

With good listening and labeling skills, the counselor can provide the client with a supportive atmosphere in which to ventilate her problems, anxieties, fears, etc. She may need the counselor to function primarily in this role for the first few sessions. After a reasonable period of time, the client must be offered direction and encouragement to take positive steps to solve her problems. Ventilation is important but is usually not enough. It won't do the client any good to center her happiness on her counseling session, if no other steps are being taken to make her life a better one. Warmth, kindness, and sympathy are very important, but unless the client is also encouraged to take charge of her life and improve her situation, we are handing out bandages when we are prepared to assist with surgery.

### e. Appraisal of Strengths and Assets

Many of the clients whom we see feel weak, defeated, and helpless. It is important to help them get in touch with and believe in their strengths and assets. It is often therapeutic to ask a client to list her assets and strong points as a person. This may sound like an easy question to answer; experience will show it to be quite the contrary. Most of us would probably have difficulty answering such a question ourselves. The client will probably need a lot of encouragement and patience to get started. It is quite possible that she will be unable to say even one positive thing about herself. In such a case, it would be a good idea for the counselor to give her an honest and realistic appraisal of what some of her strengths and assets appear to be. If she sees that the counselor believes in her, it may well be a first step to her believing in herself. The very fact that she came for help shows that she has not given up, and has the strength, the will, and the resolve to work for her own happiness.

The counselor should also emphasize the client's external strengths, such as family and friends.

### f. Realistic Goals and Subgoals, Defining These Behaviorally

At all points in the counseling experience both the client and the counselor should be clear on the goals toward which the client is working. Since domestic violence is a multidimensional problem, she may be working with several long-range goals. The client sets her own goals, with the counselor's assistance in objectifying and offering support and assistance in meeting them.

Objectifying a goal means putting it in behaviorally specific terms. For example, a non-behaviorally specific goal would be "I want to start a new life." A behaviorally specific goal would necessitate defining "new life," as in "I want to get public assistance until I can find a job," "I want to move to Ohio to live with my sister," etc.

Especially with behavioral goals, it is tremendously important to help the client set up short-term subgoals so as to prevent a sense of discouragement. Behavioral and life style changes take a long time, and the process can prove frustrating if one keeps measuring their progress in relation to the meeting of such a long-range goal. The setting up of realistic short-range goals gives more direction and allows for more immediate gratification. For example, if a client sets up the goal of obtaining a job, some subgoals may be

1. Investigating day care facilities.
2. Choosing and enrolling her children in such a facility so that she can begin job hunting.
3. Going to Employment Security Commission and employment agencies, etc.

Even if the long range goal is, by its nature, behaviorally objective, such as obtaining a divorce, subgoals, such as engaging an attorney, filing, etc., must be stressed so that the client can see and internalize progress on a more immediate basis.

### g. Plan of Action

Once goals and subgoals have been set up by the client, plans of action to achieve these goals must be decided upon. Again, all options should be presented to the client. Caution: Our values should never color the emphasis that we place on the presentation of an option. Some of us may be pro- or anti- religion, abortion, welfare, etc. We must be in touch with these feelings, but we must always remember that they are our personal beliefs and not universal truths.

Once plans of action are decided upon, the client may be particularly apprehensive about certain contacts or conversations that she will be having in the future. Role playing can be a very helpful technique to allow the client an opportunity for behavioral rehearsal. Also, if it seems appropriate, the counselor can play the client's part, perhaps giving some suggestions, by modeling, as to how to get the information that she wants across.

### h. Record-Keeping

In the initial interview, it is necessary for the counselor or the client to fill out our intake form. The counselor will have to use judgment as to the best time to do this. Sometimes it may be appropriate to have the client fill out the form before you begin talking, so that the counselor can read it over and know some of the significant areas to be dealt with. The language of the form may be difficult for some clients to comprehend, so that, for some, it might be more appropriate to ask the questions and fill out the form for the client. Again, the counselor will have to decide the appropriate time to do this.

Beyond this initial intake form, counselors are expected to write up detailed notes at the end of each contact with the client. Ideally, domestic violence counselors will never have more than two ongoing cases at any time, and most probably will have only one, so that the record keeping will not be time-consuming.

Notes should be relatively detailed as to impression of the client's needs, goals, problems, improvements, assets, etc., as well as counselor's reactions, input, assessment of her goals, plans of action, and the direction that counseling is taking.

### i. Terminating Hour

It should be made clear to the client, at the beginning of each session, how much time you are planning to spend with her that day. A one-hour counseling session is recommended . . . It is often advisable to offer reading material on the subject of domestic violence and wife abuse.

## THE LAWS: CRIMINAL AND CIVIL

Wife beating or husband beating is a crime in the state of Michigan and in most (if not all) of the United States. However, it is a crime that often goes unresolved and, sometimes, unrecognized by the authorities. Usually, police, attorneys, prosecutors, public defenders, and even judges feel that they should not get involved in "family squabbles" for fear that they are invading people's privacy. If a battered wife desires intervention by legal authorities, she must be prepared to insist that she be allowed to sign a complaint. It is her legal right to sign a complaint against an assailant. It is important that she realize that signing a complaint is only the first step of a process which may take months, and in some cases, years to complete. The complainant should also realize that nothing may come from her complaint because prosecutors are not compelled to issue a warrant and charge a person with a crime. In some cases, the complainant may have to insist that the prosecuting attorney or district attorney issue the warrant. This may require her to call the attorney or visit in person to verify the complaint and express a firm desire to follow through with the legal procedures necessary.

A victim of assault needs to understand that, within the legal system, her alternatives are few . . . three in number. First, she may choose to prosecute her assailant under the criminal laws of the state. Second, she may choose a divorce. Third, she may choose the possibility of a mental illness commitment. If she chooses the criminal route, she should familiarize herself with district and circuit court procedures. If she chooses the divorce route, she must retain a private attorney or legal aid services, and be prepared to go to circuit court. If she chooses the possibility of mental illness commitment procedures, she must familiarize herself with community mental health services and the probate court commitment procedures. A victim may use all the resources available to her. She may in fact do "all the above" in an effort to end violence perpetrated against her, or she may decide to do one, two, and/or three of the above.

THE AGENCIES:

SOCIAL SERVICES AND MENTAL HEALTH

In most communities, agencies such as legal aid societies and community mental health services can be very helpful during times of crisis and stress, especially if a person is on a limited income. Legal aid societies can provide the necessary services for obtaining a divorce, at little or no cost to a victim of domestic violence. Feminist legal service organizations and private attorneys may be receptive to the special needs of victims and may be called upon for legal advice and opinions. It is wise to form a list of private attorneys and psychologists who are especially empathetic to victims of domestic violence and share this information with all volunteer peer counselors.

Emergency housing facilities may be available through the YWCA, church groups, the Department of Social Services, Catholic Social Services, and/or the Salvation Army. In some communities, the community mental health agency may have "emergency admissions" beds which can be used by wife assault victims. It is necessary to survey all the social service agencies in your community to see what is available.

Emergency food, clothing, shelter, and financial aid may also be available through such programs as the Community Services Agency (CSA, which is the old OEO programs), or through Catholic Social Services or special community agencies designed for this purpose. If medical help is necessary, many community hospitals are beginning to offer "walk-in" clinics. If "walk-in" clinics are not available, the emergency room may be the only location for primary medical care.

Special agencies such as a women's crisis center or interdenominational church services or special crisis hot lines may be available in your community . . . Of course, all referrals should be well planned and followed up to see if the client has received the desired services.

A complete referral list should be made available for each and every counselor, with the names, addresses, and telephone numbers of all reliable contacts for referrals. If you are fortunate enough to have a system of volunteer emergency housing, the names and addresses of all the volunteer homes should also be readily available to all counselors.

## Step by Step After the Crime

### THE POLICE

The first person at the scene of a crime after it has been committed is usually the police officer. (Victims should be encouraged to file a complaint with police agencies.) Upon the arrival of the police, if the police officer witnesses a felony or misdemeanor in progress, she or he may arrest. If the officer does not witness a misdemeanor, but the victim wishes to file a complaint, the victim has a legal right to do so. After the arrest, the officer will interview the victim to obtain information concerning the incident: date, time, location, suspect's name, description, etc. The victim should cooperate with the officers, giving as much information as possible. Sometimes a police agency will have a "five day cooling off period" which will not allow the victim to be interviewed until after five days. Some police agencies may instruct the victim to come into the office in the morning to fill out the report. The victim should always see to it that a report is taken by the officer even if it is five days later.

### THE WARRANT

After the police officer's investigation and after the victim has signed a complaint, a warrant will be sought for the arrest of the suspect. The officer will show the complaint report to an assistant prosecuting attorney. To be sure of the facts, the prosecutor may want to interview the victim again. The assistant prosecutor must decide if criminal charges can be brought. A warrant will be recommended if the facts show that a crime has been committed under the laws of the state, that there is enough proof to show probable cause to believe that the person accused is the one who committed the crime, and that it is in the best interest of justice and the public to take the case to court. The prosecutor decides exactly which criminal law has been broken and fills out a form which she or he signs. The officer takes the signed paper to the district court judge in the district where the crime occurred. The victim may be asked to answer questions about the crime and the accused by the judge. If the judge decides to sign the warrant, the police will begin to look for the suspect. An arrest may follow.

## THE ARRAIGNMENT IN DISTRICT COURT

The defendant (assailant) is brought to district court for arraignment. The judge advises the defendant of the charges against him and his legal rights. If the defendant cannot afford to hire a private attorney to represent him, the court will appoint a public defender. At this time the judge may also set the terms of release from arrest. The judge sets bail at the amount he or she believes will make sure the defendant will come back for the next court appearance. A date is set for a preliminary hearing or examination if the charge is a felony. If it is a misdemeanor, the case will go to trial either the same day as the arraignment or at a later date. For a felony, by court rules, the preliminary hearing must be held within twelve days after arraignment. The victim need not be present for the arraignment, but for her information, it is advisable for her to attend. The defendant may plead innocent or guilty at the arraignment.

## PRELIMINARY HEARING

The purpose of this hearing is so that the defendant can exercise the right to know the evidence and witnesses against him or her. The defendant has the right to waive the preliminary hearing. Unless the victim has been told that the defendant has waived it so she or he need not appear, *the victim/witness must be present for the hearing.* If not, the case will be dismissed and the defendant will be released. The prosecutor handling the preliminary hearing is usually not the person who authorized the warrant. The prosecutor may ask the witness to take the stand after taking an oath, to tell who she or he is and what she or he knows about the case. The defense attorney usually cross-examines the witness also. The counselor must prepare the victim for this experience, especially in light of the fact that it occurs soon after the crime and the victim may have many unresolved feelings. The counselor should take notes throughout all court proceedings. If the prosecutor can show enough proof that a crime has been committed, and probable cause . . . that the defendant committed it, the judge will order the defendant to go to trial. The district court judge binds the case over to circuit court. If probable cause is not found, the judge will dismiss the case and set the defendant free.

## PLEA BARGAINING

The prosecutor may meet with the defense attorney after the preliminary hearing to discuss the possibility of a plea. The defendant could plead guilty so that the case could be settled without taking it to court. The plea can be guilt to the crime as it was first charged, or guilty to a related crime with a lower penalty. If the defendant, through his attorney, offers to plead guilty, the assistant prosecutor considers the seriousness of the crime, the strength of the proofs, and the defendant's criminal record. Often, if the prosecutor believes she or he has a good case, she or he will not authorize a plea of guilty to a lesser charge. If the defense attorney believes she or he has a solid case, no plea is offered since the defendant could be acquitted after trial. However, to insure a conviction, the prosecutor may attempt to obtain a guilty plea on another charge. If the prosecutor accepts the plea offer, the defendant and attorney take the authorization form to a judge. If the judge is satisfied that the defendant is guilty, the plea is taken and a date is set for sentencing. Plea bargaining can occur any time between when the crime is reported and the trial date. Theoretically, defendants who plead guilty are sentenced to prison or probation as if there had been a trial. The idea behind plea bargaining is that since there is such a backlog of cases and the courts are so overloaded, lots of time, energy, and taxpayers' dollars can be saved by not holding a trial. *The victim is usually not present or consulted during plea bargaining.* The counselor and victim may want to restate to the prosecutor firm intentions of following through on the case so that the prosecutor knows the case will not be dropped even if there are delays.

## THE ARRAIGNMENT IN CIRCUIT COURT

This is when the defendant again hears the formal charges against him and a plea is entered into the record. The defendant may plead guilty, not guilty, "stand mute," or "no contest." If he stands mute the judge automatically enters a plea of not guilty and asks if he would like a trial by jury. Bail is set again at this arraignment, and since it is a different court and judge, the bail may not be the same as that set in district court. A trial date is set next.

## THE TRIAL

The victim will be notified by the court of the date of the trial. However, the actual trial date may be postponed several times. The adjournments are usually due to overloaded court dockets and defense attorneys asking for more time to prepare the case. Often, the underlying reason for the delays requested by the defense attorney stems from his or her belief that if there are enough delays the complaining witness will drop the case (or remove herself or himself as a witness). The defendant chooses to have either a bench trial (before the judge only) or a jury trial. If a jury trial is chosen, jury selection will occur the morning that the trial actually begins. The prosecutor assigned to present the case probably is not the same person who presented the case at the preliminary hearing. Often, assistant prosecutors are assigned by court and jurisdiction, not by defendant, crime, or victim. The complaining witness may be called to the stand several times and will be questioned by the prosecutor and the defense attorney. At the beginning of the trial, both attorneys will briefly explain what they will try to prove to the jury, what witnesses will be called, and why they think the jury should render a particular verdict. At the end of the trial, both attorneys offer arguments summarizing their perceptions of the trial and again which verdict they hope the jury will render. It is a good idea for witnesses in upcoming trials to observe part or all of another assault case to become accustomed to the procedures in the courtroom. Usually witnesses are sequestered outside the courtroom during the testimony of other witnesses so that what is said does not influence their version. But after a witness has finished testifying, she or he may remain until the trial is over. In a jury trial, twelve jurors must decide, beyond a reasonable doubt, the guilt or innocence of the defendant. It must be a unanimous decision. If the verdict is guilty, the judge sets a date for sentencing, usually two weeks later. If the verdict is not guilty, the defendant is acquitted and set free.

## THE PREPARATION FOR COURT AND THE PENALTY

The notes about the incident taken by the counselor and/or the victim will come in handy when preparing for testimony in court. Each detail should be gone over in sequence so that the facts will be straight in his or her mind. Important things to keep in mind when preparing are the *time* of each event and approximately *how long* it lasted. Many victims have been intimidated by defense attorneys insisting on a step by step, movement by movement account of the incident, and each should be warned of the possibility of this occurring. It is generally reassuring for the victim to understand court procedures, the setting, where to sit and stand, the sequence of events in a trial, who will be present, etc. The best way to accomplish this is to attend another trial.

Honesty is the best and only policy when under oath. If the victim is unsure of an answer, it is better to say "I don't know" than to say something which could be used to confuse or impeach her later. Although the victim should be prepared, her answers should not sound too well rehearsed or without emotion. It is good to caution her not to answer questions immediately since the prosecutor may want to object after the question is asked and before an answer is given. Witnesses can take as much time as is necessary to answer.

The victim should be instructed to talk to no one about the case except the prosecutor and the counselor while in the court building. Clever defense attorneys can convince unknowing witnesses to tell them about the incident, and later use the information against them.

In the preliminary hearing the witness should relate only those events which are relevant to the crime. Questions such as "Miss———, could you tell the court what happened after that?" can lead witnesses into spilling more details than are necessary to prove "probable cause." Defense attorneys may try to obtain as many tiny details as possible in this hearing to be used later to confuse the witness or damage her credibility. Also, before the preliminary hearing the judge may clear the courtroom. If the witness wants the counselor to be present in any case, the prosecutor should be told this in order to pass the request along to the judge.

A victim may begin to doubt herself and question the worth of her actions in terms of putting the assailant in jail. Reinforcing the fact that she was the victim of a crime, and that the system was established for victims to seek justice, may give her confidence and help her become a more forceful witness. The counselor should use any means to work out the doubts and guilt feelings, but the victim must be clear that she wants to prosecute and convict before the trial begins. There will generally be at least two months between the preliminary hearing and the trial. There may be as much as a year between the two.

One of the best preparatory actions for trial is reading the transcript of the preliminary hearing. A copy is available from the court services of most courts. Look up the defendant's name in the standing file on the counter for the file number, and then give that number to a clerk, who will allow you to read the transcript. It is important that the witness be credible. She should be prepared for her courtroom experiences and be honest about the crime.

If an assailant/defendant is found guilty, the penalty in many cases is probation and/or a fine. If the assault is particularly severe, the assailant may spend time in jail, but seldom is the maximum penalty administered. If probation is the sentence, this will give the assailant an excellent opportunity to receive counseling and learn to control and change his violent behavior.

## Others Working for Battered Women

*Working on Wife Abuse* is a directory of people, services, organizations, and resources concerned with battered women. While the emphasis is on sources within the United States, there are also listings for Canada and abroad. There is a separate section on publications and films pertaining to battered women as well as a forceful introduction highlighting the longstanding needs and problems of these women.

The directory was prepared by Betsy Warrior. At this writing, the directory is being updated and revised for the fifth time. The following statement appears on the title page of *Working on Wife Abuse:*

The names in this directory represent thousands of hours of womanpower spent in an effort to expose and combat the physical and psychological terror women are threatened with and subjected to daily.

For the most part, this effort has been put forth without thought of pay, career considerations, or academic recognition.

The existence of this directory is a tribute to the growing strength and determination of women to control their own lives.

A number of multipurpose task forces aimed at alleviating the problems faced by battered women have been established throughout the country. Many of these task forces are affiliated with local chapters of NOW, which was one of the first organizations to recognize and protest the widespread occurrence of wife abuse. Such task forces tend to have a number of goals, including public education and community consciousness raising, provision of both emergency and ongoing support services, and political activity geared toward eliminating violence against women.

Task forces can help not only to develop new services but also to coordinate existing ones. They can serve as a focal point to which diverse service provisioners can turn, and as a clearinghouse for facilitating exchange of resources, reducing duplicative efforts, and minimizing the fragmentation that so often characterizes the service network for battered women. Moreover, the work and goals of locally based task forces can be adapted to the special needs and circumstances of particular communities.

The following is excerpted from *Wife-Beating—How to Develop a Wife Assault Task Force and Project*, by Kathleen M. Fojtik. This publication is a product of the Ann Arbor–Washtenaw County National Organization for Women (NOW) and Women Against Violence Against Women.

### HOW TO ORGANIZE
#### A WIFE ASSAULT TASK FORCE AND PROJECT
*First*

CALL A MEETING of your NOW chapter to discuss "battered wives" using John Stewart Mill's *On the Subjection of Women,* 1969; Erin Pizzy's *Scream Quietly or the Neighbors Will Hear,* 1974; or *The Assaulted Wife: Catch 22 Revisited,* by Pat Micklow and Sue Eisenberg [or other sources], as resource material. Or, contact a police agency, a social service agency, a women's crisis center, and a psychiatrist/psychologist to participate in a panel discussion of the topic "Wife Beating." From the interest generated at this meeting . . . form a Task Force on the assaulted wife . . .

### Second

Using volunteer homes SET UP A SYSTEM of emergency housing for temporary shelter for beaten women and their children. Be sure to discuss the pros and cons and get a firm commitment from your volunteers. We suggest a maximum of three days of emergency housing for victims and their children. Coordinate this system carefully. This takes a lot of time and dedication. Contact women's crisis centers and help lines when your system of volunteer emergency housing is intact—advertising your service to the community—and be prepared for more than you can handle or house.

STOP. If you do the above, and do it well, you will be overwhelmed with very complicated, serious cases of women with economic problems, religious problems, social problems, physical problems, psychological problems, etc. . . . just remember, no one else is helping these women. Someone must point out that there are great numbers of these women out there that need and will ask for help, if they know that help is available to them. For centuries, battered women have been told to "grin and bear it"; it is now time to assist them in "helping themselves." To prove that no one else is offering services to these women, go on to number three.

### Third

CONDUCT A SURVEY (telephone) of the social service agencies in your community, e.g., community mental health programs, crisis centers, etc. Ask questions concerning the types of services they provide for battered women. The results of the research in Washtenaw County show that many agencies recognize the problem but do not have the "resources" to provide adequate services, except referral.

### Fourth

DOCUMENT THE INCIDENCE OF WIFE ASSAULT in your community. This will arm you with data not available any other place. The social service agencies and the police agencies do NOT keep statistics on domestic violence, or wife beating. Therefore, you must do this research yourself, today (and demand that the agencies do it tomorrow).

### Fifth

PROVIDE COUNSELING AND FOLLOW-UP SERVICES with volunteer laypersons, or get your local community mental health agency to do it. This is an extra service that is necessary for beaten women, but very difficult to deliver on a volunteer basis. One hour a week counseling is minimal.

### Sixth

For a long-term, more realistic WIFE (SPOUSE) ASSAULT PROGRAM, write a grant application using the information collected through your research of the social service and police agencies, and your experience with the volunteer emergency housing. Apply to local foundations, governmental bodies, and state and federal law enforcement agencies. The safety havens are a mechanism to prevent crime; therefore, crime prevention money should be available for this purpose. The grant applications should include adequate funding for a permanent shelter with necessary support services. Use known existing shelters as models.

The following is the text of a resolution adopted by delegates to the National Women's Conference held in Houston, Texas, November 18–21, 1977:

The President and Congress should declare the elimination of violence in the home to be a national goal. To help achieve this, Congress should establish a national clearinghouse for information and technical and financial assistance to locally controlled public and private nonprofit organizations providing emergency shelter and other support services for battered women and their children. The clearinghouse should also conduct a continuing mass media campaign to educate the public about the problem of violence and the available remedies and resources.

Local and State governments, law enforcement agencies and social welfare agencies should provide training programs on the problem of wife battering, crisis intervention techniques, and the need for prompt and effective enforcement of laws that protect the rights of battered women.

State legislatures should enact laws to expand legal protection and provide funds for shelters for battered women and their children; remove interspousal tort immunity in order to permit assaulted spouses to sue their assailants for civil damages; and provide full legal services for victims of abuse.

Programs for battered women should be sensitive to the bilingual and multicultural needs of ethnic and minority women.

## Concluding Remarks

Throughout this chapter the fact that wife abuse occurs at all socio-economic levels and among all racial–ethnic groups has been noted. In many respects the service needs of battered women, no matter what their race or socioeconomic status, are similar. Although some services are geared toward particular groups by design and others by legal constraint (e.g., some legal services are available only to women on public assistance), the vast majority of services developed for battered women are intended to serve all women who are in need. Most have done so effectively and with sensitivity to the individual circumstances of each woman.

Nevertheless, the special situation of battered women from racial–ethnic minority groups should be recognized. Minority women are much more likely to come to the attention of the police or other law enforcement agencies for abuse complaints. Field and Field report that of the 7,500 women in the District of Columbia who sought help from the prosecutor's office in 1966, the majority were black (Field and Field 1973). At the same time, minority women are less likely to seek help from established social service agencies such as mental health centers, hospitals, or feminist groups. Organizations providing services for battered women may need to make a special effort to ensure that their services are known, available, and accessible to minority women.

In addition, social service practitioners need to be aware of the impact that culture can have on the way abuse is perceived. Some minority groups have strong patriarchal traditions that go beyond the issues of sexism that prevail in the majority culture. Nichols observes that often "the problems that beset a family suffering cultural shock are defined in terms of how the men have fared. The male's role as head of the family and his prestige as protector and wage earner, are considered crucial to the family's well-being, while at the same time they are related to its misery. . . ." It is especially important "for a social worker to find a point of intervention that does not in some way threaten or violate the cultural norm" (Nichols 1976:30).

# 5. Rape Victims

## DORIS A. STEVENS

LIKE BATTERING, rape of women by men has occurred consistently and frequently throughout recorded history. Susan Brownmiller has documented this historical fact in the most definitive history of rape to date, within a frame of reference stating that rape is "nothing more or less than a conscious process of intimidation by which *all* men keep *all* women in a state of fear" (Brownmiller 1975:15) Rape is not an aberration but part of a historical drama that involves all men and all women.

For most of these thousands of years, women who were raped (although certainly experiencing these acts as terrorizing and undesirable) were in the position of having to accept this brutalization and dehumanization as inevitable, as a part of women's station in life. There were certainly many women who resisted in spirit (and through any physical means available to them); however, until very recent times society's rules proscribing rape were either nonexistent or, where they did exist, defined totally as one aspect of men's property rights (pp. 16–30).

Indeed, by the end of 1978 only four male-dominated legislatures throughout the United States had revised state laws to protect married women from rape by their husbands (and one of those revisions has already been repealed) (Geis 1978:285 and *Newsweek* January 1, 1979:55). The first case to be prosecuted under such a statute was reported in Salem, Oregon, in late 1978. Ultimately, the husband was acquitted of the crimes. However, the history of the relationship between the victim and her spouse was jokingly treated as a soap opera story in the national media because of her decision to try fighting back legally against her husband for what she reported as a rape (*Newsweek* January 22, 1979:26). In spite of the Oregon law, it was implied that a report of sexual coercion—or rape—within the context of a marital relationship cannot be taken very seriously. Through laws and court procedures, men are still allowing and supporting the definition of women as sexual property.

In the past ten years the rape crisis center movement in this country has worked very successfully toward a societal (and legal) redefinition of rape as an act of destructive violence against an individual, regardless of the victim's life style, her relationship to the offender, or the political or social context. The rape crisis movement, as part of the more global women's awareness movement, has been responsible for creating a new understanding of rape as a violation of individual human rights rather than property rights. This was accomplished primarily by women helping women.

Beginning in the early 1970s, "speak-outs" on rape were held during which brave women shared with each other (and with the public) their individual horror stories of how it felt to be raped and, just as important, how it felt to be blamed for those rapes by family, friends, and society's helping institutions (e.g., legal and medical) (Largen 1976:69). A result of these speak-outs was the establishment of rape crisis support groups in which women who understood helped other women who had recently been raped to endure their personal traumas. Many of these self-help groups expanded to rape crisis centers, including an emergency telephone service for rape victims, an informed, supportive network of women who were available to advocate for rape victims in medical and legal systems, and an educational program aimed at changing the local community's response to rape victims. For the first time women had validation and a source of support for directly fighting against rape and its effects as a major destructive influence in their individual and collective lives. It became possible to learn about the true extent and effects of rape in this society, as defined by the victims—women.

## Definition and Incidence

The word *rape* is a popular term usually used to describe a forceful sexual act. *Rape* is also a legal term, and as such, it is defined somewhat differently from one jurisdiction to another. Traditionally, the legal definition of rape has connoted forceful penetration of a vagina by a penis. Recently revised statutes, reflecting the crime more accurately, have included nonconsensual—as well as forceful—intercourse in the legal definition. Also, some statutes have substituted "sexual assault" for "rape" in order to recognize and criminalize a variety of possible types of abuse (e.g., penetration of anus and mouth as well as vagina, and penetration by fingers and objects as well as by penises). Some of the revised rape laws are not sex specific, thus recognizing the fact that males as well as females are victims of sexual violence. Other legal terms commonly used to define acts of sexual abuse are *sodomy, statutory rape, indecent liberties,* and *incest.* (Examples stated here are from former and present Washington State law 1974: Chapter 9-79 Revised Code of Washington.)

Throughout this chapter the terms *rape, sexual assault, sexual violence,* and *sexual abuse* will be used interchangeably—all in the sense of describing women's experiences of these attacks. Specific physiological acts or exact legal definitions are not what one should use in determining whether or not an act of sexual violence has occurred. A person experiences sexual assault when she is coerced (physically or verbally) to have sexual intimacy with another person. Often acts of sexual assault involve forced penetration of several body orifices. But sexual assault can also include other types of forced sexual contact that do not involve penetration: forced fondling, forced masturbation, verbal sexual harassment.

Like the battering of women, rape can and does occur in the context of marital relationships. In addition, all women face the possibility of being raped (in public places or in their own homes) by complete strangers or by extended-family members, coworkers, neighbors, or acquaintances. In a population of 800 people of all ages who reported to the Sexual Assault Center (a hospital-based, city-wide medical, crisis counseling, and legal advocacy service for sexual assault victims) during 1978, 67 percent were attacked by individuals known to them prior to the assault (39 percent by friends and acquaintances, 28 percent by relatives) and 32 percent by strangers. Among the child victims (age 16 and under), only 15 percent were assaulted by strangers whereas 43 percent were abused by immediate-family members (usually fathers) and 42 percent by acquaintances and friends of the family (Sexual Assault Center 1979).

Burgess and Holmstrom (1974:4–6), who studied 146 victims reporting to the Victim Counseling Program at Boston City Hospital in 1972 and 1973, concluded that victims experienced "blitz rapes" (no prior interaction between assailant and victim) as well as "confidence rapes" (assailant obtained sex by using deceit, betrayal, and violence).

Sexual assault is inflicted on members of all geographic, socioeconomic, ethnic, and age groups. A preschool girl diagnosed as having gonorrhea of the throat and the 92-year-old resident of a nursing home who was found to have lacerations resulting from forceful penetration of her atrophied vagina are real examples of the demographic scope of rape victimization (Sexual Assault Center 1979). Males are also subjected to sexual abuse, but in all statistical reports surveyed by this author the large majority of reported victims are female, and virtually all were sexually abused by male offenders. Realistically, therefore, fear of rape among *women* is a generalized, collective experience.

When an adult woman is raped, physical violence is usually the offender's mode of accomplishment. In addition to forced vaginal penetration, there is often anal and oral penetration. It is not unusual for these acts to be repeated over a period of hours, sometimes even days. In addition to brute force, weapons (guns and knives) are often used. The assailant may hold a victim down, choke her, burn her with cigarettes, scratch her with a knife, or mentally abuse her by threatening her children or forcing her to say and do repulsive things to please him.

In a national survey of 208 police agencies conducted in 1974, approximately two-thirds of adult rape victims experienced threat or use of weapon(s) during the attack. More than one-quarter of these reported rapes involved two or more rapists, and the victims generally sustained some type of injury (Battelle Law and Justice Study Center 1977:21–22).

### CASE EXAMPLE #1

A 23 year old woman had been attending a spring street celebration in the downtown area of a large city. She left a restaurant alone, around midnight, in order to catch a taxi cab home. Before she could find a taxi, two young males grabbed her, dragged her to a deserted building several blocks away, and assaulted her sexually and physically. They hit her with their fists and beat her with a belt. When the males were through with her, they let her go.

### CASE EXAMPLE #2

A 29 year old woman had been steadily dating a man for approximately one month. When she told him that she wished to discontinue their relationship, he became very upset and threatened to kill her. He forced her to have vaginal and anal intercourse and held her captive for four hours before she was able to escape from her home (where the assault took place) and call the police.

### CASE EXAMPLE #3

A 20 year old woman was on a date with a man she had met through a good friend. She did not know him very well, but they had had a pleasant evening together. On their way home, he drove her to a deserted area, where he became very angry with her, threw her around, choked her, tore her clothing, and threw her into the back seat of the car. He assaulted her orally and vaginally, and then drove her to her home.

Children who are sexually abused are also most often female. Although some children are forcibly raped by strangers, in most cases they are molested by someone they know and trust, and verbal coercion, bribery, or sheer authority are used by offenders to carry out the sexual abuse (Berliner 1977:331; Peters 1976:416). The sexual abuse of a child is often a series of rapes that continue until she finds the avenue to understand and extricate herself from the adult male's secretive abuse of power. Although this chapter will not attempt to review specific needs and services for child sexual abuse victims, it is important to remember that sexual victimization of many women began when they were young children.

### CASE EXAMPLE #4

A seven year old girl reported to her mother that her girlfriend's father had tried to hurt her. Upon questioning, it was learned that during a time when she was staying overnight with the man's daughter, he had coaxed her to sit on his lap, had taken his penis out of his pants and attempted to insert his penis into her vagina. The man told the seven year old girl not to tell anyone, threatening that she would "get in trouble" if she did. The girl reported that this had happened three other times, with the same man. (Berliner 1977:315)

Over the past few years there has been much emphasis in the popular media on the incidence of violence against women as an escalating phenomenon in our society, as if it were a new discovery of the "terrible times" in which we live. FBI statistics (the only national data about rape that are collected uniformly) indicate that the number of rapes reported to law enforcement authorities increased by 11.1 percent from 1976 to 1977 and by 23 percent from 1973 to 1977 (*Uniform Crime Reports* 1977:14) In 1977, 63,020 different rape offenses were reported to law enforcement agencies (p. 13). For the purpose of these reports rape is defined in a specific legal, narrow sense. However, there are many other types of sex offenses reported to police throughout the nation that are not included in this count. In addition, all rape crisis centers and other victim service agencies know that many rapes occur that are not reported to law enforcement (or other) authorities. For example, Seattle Rape Relief (1969), a rape crisis center providing a confidential hot-line service for rape victims, reports that only 50 percent of the women they serve have reported the rape to a law enforcement agency. Data on sexual assault of children (involving illegal acts other than rape) are not collected in a uniform way in most jurisdictions and are not collected at all on a national basis.

Although the present incidence of rape is certainly abhorrent, it is probable that this rate of sexual assault has occurred for some time. It is clear that victims of rape are more willing than ever before to share their experiences (officially and unofficially). Over the past ten years women have come to understand the meaning of sexual assault more fully, and they have begun fighting back by obtaining post-rape services for themselves and/or attempting to prosecute their offenders. Where a relatively full complement of sexual assault victim services exists (e.g., in Seattle, Washington), the per capita reporting rate for rape is significantly higher than the overall national rate (Law and Justice Planning Division 1978:161).

## Victims' Experiences

In order to understand the effect of rape on women, it is not enough to be generally aware of the fact that rape does occur and that it is a statistically significant social problem. These facts do not tell us the pervasive human and political effects of rape. Hearing the victims' experiences is the only way to understand the truth about rape, because

Most of us . . . share myths about rape. It's something that happens to *other* women. *Other* men do it. Those who do it are crazy. A woman cannot be raped by someone she knows or is married to. A woman who does not want to be raped cannot be raped, so most women who are raped must have asked for it. (Russell 1974:inside front cover)

A number of authors, among them Diana E. H. Russell (1975), have provided vivid, personal documentations of how women are affected by rape and its aftermaths. Following are the partial experiences of a 55-year-old woman raped seven years before her account quoted here. She is one of ninety women who agreed to be interviewed by Russell and her colleagues in the hope of feeling less isolated as a victim, correcting ignorance about rape, and achieving change in the treatment of rape victims. In the seven years since the rape, the woman had told only one other person about the experience. Ms. X's account specifically addresses the myth that "nice" women cannot be raped.

It was a Sunday morning around noon. I had gone up the road to get the newspaper and had come back into the house and was reading the paper. Then I went into the bathroom. I opened the door to the bathroom from my bedroom, and he was standing there with a gun. I just froze. I went into shock.

He kept me prisoner for two nights and two days. With a gun at my head, he made me call my school district on Monday to tell them I was sick . . .

He was very sadistic. His sexual assaults went on constantly, and I was forced into perverse activities—the whole ugly mess—gagging, choking, vomiting. He cleverly didn't black my eyes or leave marks. There were some bruises from where he threw me into furniture, but mainly he would twist my arm and choke me. I found that if I fought him very hard, he came to orgasm more quickly, and it was over for a while, which shows his sadism. I was wondering, "What can I do to get out of this horror?" I would try to submit, thinking, maybe that would get it over with, but I found that it infuriated him if I submitted without fighting him. . . .

I found out how a woman can be totally immobilized. He was a heavy man. He was probably two hundred pounds, and very strong. He would lie on one side of my body, pinning down one leg and one arm, and he'd get his other arm up under my knee, and he'd be twisting my other arm, so that I just couldn't move. He would do it three or four, maybe five times, and then he would sleep. I did escape once from his grip, and I got some clothes on, and I was heading out a window as quietly as I could, but he caught me. . . .

I felt that I was outside my body, watching this whole thing, that it wasn't happening to me, it was happening to somebody else. It was a strange feeling, absolutely unreal. I was terrorized, but it's very hard to describe the shock of what was happening. At first, I went into a state of shock where I just shook and shook and shook and shook and shook. And I was freezing cold. Just freezing cold. And he kept the gun on me all the time. He showed me the bullets in case I should think it unloaded. . . .

When I realized he was gone, I wanted to pour Lysol all over me. I wanted to be cleansed. I took a bath, and then I thought about calling the police. And I thought no, I can't do that. It's too much of a horror story. People would look at me differently. If it's so horrible to *me*, it must be horrible to other people. I don't want anybody to know what happened to me. I thought that they would see me differently if they knew about it. . . .

So I assumed that if I told people, they would think I had consented, because they would think as I had thought before I had the experience. Also, I remember reading something that stuck in my head about how you have to press charges, and you have to go to court, and you have to do all this stuff. I just couldn't do it. I'm basically a rather retiring person, and the thought that I would have to be in a roomful of people who knew what had happened to me made me sick. . . .

I called my friend, because I knew I couldn't go to school the next day. I didn't know how long it would be before I could face people. She came up to the house and stayed with me, and I poured the whole thing out to her, and we cried together, and held each other. She never told her husband because she said she knew his attitude toward me would change. He also thought a woman couldn't be raped. . . .

INTERVIEWER: So what did you do after talking to your friend?

MS. X: I stayed home and kind of healed. Then I went to school Friday. It was very hard. Very hard.

INTERVIEWER: Did you have bad dreams after the rape?

MS. X: Oh, yes. And I would relive it. It became almost an obsession. I thought I was being punished for something. And I kept wondering, why did this happen to me? What have I done that this thing would happen?

INTERVIEWER: Did you blame yourself?

MS.X: I was trying to find ways to blame myself. Trying to think, what did I do? What brought this on? Later I knew that this was ridiculous, because I hadn't done anything, and it had just happened. . . .

All through the time he was there, and then afterwards, there was a heavy discharge, a bloody discharge, and that's what scared me. I thought, gee, maybe I have venereal disease. I went to a doctor who I never saw before or since, and he made a joke of it as though I was a really hot number. He acted as though I was a swinger or a prostitute. I didn't tell him I'd been raped. I just said that I had had relations with a man I didn't know, and that I was worried. . . .

INTERVIEWER: Did you seek counseling?

MS X: I wanted to so badly! I was so tempted! I knew some good counselors, but I never was able to do it. I would come so close, because I badly wanted to talk it out, but I couldn't do it. I'd just say, deal with it yourself. Cope with it in your own way. I found out that I am very strong, which surprised me. I wondered if all the protective, loving, bringing up that I had had made me strong.

I learned to cope with the obsession by myself. I'd start to fall asleep at night, and the whole thing would come back. Also, I had a number of headaches. Tranquilizers don't do much for me but depress me, so I just took simple medicine. But I would get so discouraged. Sometimes I would get very depressed. I'd think, I'm never going to get this out of my head. When is this garbage going to get out of my head? Because I would be in the most harmonious situation, and bang, there it was again. It was like a flash, and then I'd have to just wrench it away again. (Russell 1975:17–23)

In an early case study of a group of thirteen young women, Sutherland and Scherl (1970:503–511) were among the first to note and describe a common pattern of responses by rape victims. They presented some insights into the actual content of the post-rape responses of these women, but even more important, they gave beginning credence to the fact that it is normal and usual for rape victims to have strong emotional responses, and that it is legitimate and helpful to provide crisis intervention counseling specifically because a woman has been raped. Prior to that time almost all the psychiatric and social work literature has dealt with the needs of rape victims, if at all, only in the context of treatment for mental illness or personality disturbances. (The professional literature spent much more time addressing the understanding of sexual offenders.) Sutherland and Scherl outlined "three predictable sequential phases that represent a normal cycle of emotional responses by victims of sexual assault." The "acute reaction" involves the victim's feelings of

shock, disbelief, or dismay, followed by anxiety and fear . . . Outward adjustment: . . . as the victim deals with practical problems, various psychological mechanisms such as denial of affect, suppression, and rationalization are called into play . . . Integration: . . . the patient usually feels depressed and wants to talk . . . Two central issues must be worked out with the victim: her feelings about herself and her feelings about the assailant. (p. 503)

In 1974, Burgess and Holmstrom completed the first survey of a relatively large population of rape victims (146) who sought assistance at the Victim Counseling Program, Boston City Hospital, shortly after being assaulted. On the basis of the responses of victims to the rape events and their immediate sequelae, which they shared with the authors, this research stands as the most detailed documentation of rape victims' experiences to date. The authors developed a thorough, commonsense theoretical model explaining the "rape trauma syndrome" (Burgess and Holmstrom 1974:37).

Rape trauma syndrome is the acute or immediate phase of disorganization and the long-term process or reorganization that occurs as a result of attempted or actual forcible rape. The acute phase includes (1) the immediate impact reaction (either expressed or controlled emotions); (2) physical reactions; and (3) emotional reaction to a life-threatening situation. The long-term process includes (1) changes in life style; (2) dreams and nightmares; and (3) phobic reactions. (p. 49)

As the preceding examples from victim and researchers illustrate, the experience of being raped produces an acute crisis in a victim's

life. This crisis occurs not because the victim has experienced an unpleasant sexual encounter but because she has endured a terrorizing,
violent act. Rape is an externally imposed crisis—something that
happens to the woman, not something that she causes or for which
she is responsible.

Fear is the overwhelming response to such an act and is almost
universally experienced by rape victims. "The first and immediate
response of all individual to sudden, unexpected violence is shock
and disbelief. When realization sets in, the vast majority of victims
then experience fright which borders on panic" (Symonds 1976:29).

We did not find [shame and guilt] to be the primary reactions in the majority of victims we saw. To the contrary, the primary feeling expressed was
that of fear—fear of physical injury, mutilation, and death. It is this main
feeling of fear that explains why victims develop the range of symptoms we
call the rape trauma syndrome. Their symptoms are an acute stress reaction
to the threat of being killed. (Burgess and Holstrom 1974:39)

## Victims' Needs

Immediately following a sexual assault a woman needs a safe place to
go where the rapist cannot find her and where her fears can begin to
subside. She needs medical care, sensitively given, so that she can be
reassured about her physical health and unwanted pregnancy and
venereal disease can be prevented. She needs a person(s) with whom
she can talk—a person who is interested but never forces her to talk,
who clearly places all blame for the attack on the rapist (regardless of
the circumstances), and who validates and supports the expression of
anger at a time when the victim is ready to do so. It is also helpful to
explain to the victim that a crisis reaction is limited in duration, that
her emotions and reactions are common to many other victims, and
that a pattern of symptoms can be expected (i.e., the rape trauma
syndrome, including hypersensitivity, irritability, nightmares, haunt-
ing thoughts, reliving the assault). These preparations can give hope
and prevent a woman from later feeling that she is losing control of
her mind or emotions. When these symptoms occur the woman is
aware of the existence of resources to alleviate the problem. A victim
is also in need of practical information (e.g., how and where to ob-

tain good medical care, what is involved in reporting the crime to law enforcement authorities, resources for ongoing support and information for herself and her family as needed).

## Development of Services

Around 1970 there was a desperate need for the development of specialized services for victims of rape. Most women knew, or soon found out when they tried to report a rape, that procedures and personnel in legal, medical, and social institutions strongly tended to blame the victim for an assault. This was especially true for women who had been raped by assailants whom they knew prior to the rape. These official helping agencies, like the rest of society, reflected the beliefs that a woman who does not want to be raped cannot be raped, only "bad" women are raped, women who are raped "asked for it" through their attire or mannerisms, and women lie about or exaggerate rape.

The professions that supposedly exist to aid people experiencing physical and emotional trauma had not been able to recognize rape victims as legitimately in need of their services. Rush (1977:41), Herman and Hirschman (1977:737–738), and Peters (1976:401–402) have provided good examples and explanations for why the medical and mental health professions, with a strong heritage from Freudian and neo-Freudian theory, denied, minimized, or misinterpreted the effects of rape. If a woman was fortunate enough to find a doctor or counselor who did not blame her for the rape, then most likely the professional either discouraged any discussion of the rape or dealt with it only in the context of the woman's illness. The fact that a woman had been raped was often interpreted as a *symptom* of personality disturbance or mental illness, rather than an *event* that itself deeply affected the victim.

The helping professions and institutions, dominated by male thought, for the most part were incapable of understanding rape as a male crime of violence against women. The impetus for change in institutional attitudes and procedures had to come from the outside. In 1972 a half-dozen rape crisis centers were formed almost simultaneously in cities around the country (Brodyaga *et al.* 1975:123).

Today there are hundreds of organizations throughout the fifty states specifically dedicated to providing some combination of crisis counseling, legal advocacy, medical care, or evidence-gathering services for victims of sexual assault.

Initially almost all services for rape victims existed in rape crisis centers. These centers were, in effect, alternative social service agencies for women and were sometimes considered to be antiestablishment.

The initial purpose of rape crisis centers, staffed in part by victims themselves, was to provide empathetic support for rape victims by either hotline counseling or escort services. In hospitals, police stations, and courts the staffers served, in effect, as a buffer between the victim and the negative experiences she encountered there. The philosophy of the original crisis centers was "I do for you. You do for others." In addition to offering alternatives to women, centers sought to assist rape victims in regaining the self-determination denied them by their assailant and often by the very institutions which were supposed to aid them. (Largen 1976:69–70)

As the messages regarding rape victims' needs became more persistent and undeniable (through increasing numbers of women seeking rape services and the attendant media publicity), community institutions began "to rethink the desirability of their own existing procedures and training programs and to experiment with innovations" (p. 70). Hospitals and police departments were the first institutions to coordinate services with rape crisis centers and to adapt some of the knowledge and techniques gained by rape victim advocates. Both hospitals and police departments are places where some rape victims have traditionally sought front-line services; in those places where personnel were most sensitive, there already existed some awareness that services for rape victims were inadequate.

A number of hospitals, working with community women's groups, developed special units for the treatment of rape victims. At Harborview Medical Center (Seattle, Washington) the Sexual Assault Center was established in 1973. Emphasis was placed on the development and implementation of a written protocol (policy), to be used by all emergency room team members (physician, nurse, social worker, clerk), that emphasizes the particular needs of rape victims. The protocol covers all procedures necessary for medical care and gathering of medico-legal evidence (should the victims choose to prosecute); but it places more emphasis on attitudinal and behavioral interaction between emergency room staff and women seeking post-rape services.

At the Sexual Assault Center rape victims are given priority for treatment ahead of other patients in the emergency room; victims are not to be left alone at any time without support; staff are instructed on how to coordinate their roles so that the history of the assault is taken only once (and in a sensitive manner); and the standard of a nonjudgmental, nonaccusatory approach to the victim is required of all the medical, nursing, social work, and clerical personnel who may interact with the woman in the course of providing emergency services. In addition, when the Sexual Assault Center was established the hospital provided social work services on a 24-hour-a-day basis for the first time; hence, there is always someone available to offer the rape victim psychosocial services (Klingbeil et al. 1976).

Abarbanel (1976:479–480) has described a service model (in Santa Monica, California) that emphasizes the pivotal role a hospital emergency room department can play in overcoming victims' reluctance to seek post-rape services. In addition to medical care, the model includes information dissemination, staff training, and coordination with other agencies. McCombie et al. (1976:418–421) report on the development of a specialized hospital unit to serve rape victims, including the difficulties they encountered in getting rape accepted as a legitimate health issue. The objectives used in implementing this Boston model are as follows:

1. Providing both immediate and follow-up counseling that is aimed at resolving the psychological crisis.
2. Encouraging emergency room personnel to respond sensitively to the emotional needs of the victim.
3. Developing an understanding of the special needs of this patient population in order to provide expert consultation to community and professional groups.
4. Conducting research on the acute and long-term impact of rape on life adjustment. (p. 419)

Police departments in a few larger cities around the country also began the shift to a more humanistic interaction with rape victims in the mid-1970s. Stratton (1976:46), describing in a national police officers' magazine a new law enforcement approach to helping the victim, acknowledged the contributions of the women's movement in this arena as well. This particular Los Angeles-based program selected women officers for specialized training in crisis intervention counseling with rape victims and assigned them to support victims from the initial police report through prosecution stages.

The Law Enforcement Assistance Administration funded scores of "rape reduction" programs in the early and mid-1970s, all of which were designed, through one approach or another, to encourage and support women in reporting crimes of rape to local law enforcement agencies. (It is through this funding mechanism that many rape crisis centers obtained their first regular financial support.)

In 1973 New York City devoted a large amount of resources to a new approach in investigating sex crimes and became a model for other jurisdictions. Its success in meeting the dual goals of apprehending more rapists and relating positively to victims hinged on attitudinal and skill training programs for officers (Keefe 1976:162). The changes centered on encouraging and training officers to use specific investigative techniques that would win the confidence, gratitude, and cooperation of sexual assault victims.

In 1975 Congress passed legislation establishing the National Center for the Prevention and Control of Rape (administratively housed in the National Institute of Mental Health, Department of Health, Education, and Welfare). Currently, federally funded research is being conducted on the incidence of rape in the general community (including rapes not reported to police agencies), specific social and psychological effects of rape on victims and their families, special needs of elderly rape victims, the effects of incest on personality development, cross-cultural studies of rape, societal attitudes toward victims, rape prevention strategies, and (to a very small extent) strategies for rehabilitating rapists (National Center for Prevention and Control of Rape 1977).

## A New Perspective

The program examples described in the preceding section are only a few of the many specialized approaches to helping rape victims that have now become institutionalized, often working hand in hand with rape crisis centers (which fortunately still maintain much of their alternative character). There are also programs that have been developed in prosecuting attorneys' offices, mental health centers, and women's health collectives. Among the important dimensions of these new services, distinguishing them from what was previously available to rape victims in traditional agencies, are the following.

1. Respect for the content and extent of a rape victim's emotional reactions, or the *normalcy* dimension. All victims, regardless of their pre-rape functioning, will have strong feelings about being sexually assaulted. Even those women who are functioning optimally prior to a rape will experience disruptive rape trauma symptoms, at least temporarily. Women who have been raped are usually in an acute crisis state and deserve appropriate support, services, and understanding without being labeled hysterical, emotionally disturbed, or mentally ill.

2. A capacity for aggressively offering follow-up services to rape victims, or the *outreach* dimension. Many women still do not know that specialized services for rape victims are available. Some women may feel embarrassed about asking for rape services if they have no obvious physical trauma. Or they may be fearful of others' reactions to them following disclosure of a rape. There is also a feeling that "I ought to be able to handle this myself." Experience has shown that when follow-up counseling services are offered, rape victims readily utilize them. However, many women do not seek out ongoing services after an initial crisis contact.

3. A commitment to assisting the victim with the different systems she must negotiate if she is to fight back to the fullest—*advocacy*. There are still many medical, legal, and social agencies that take an unenlightened approach to rape victims. If there is no one available to serve as buffer between the victim and agency personnel, people and procedures that blame the victim can hurt her further at a time when she is most vulnerable. An advocate may accompany a victim to appointments (interviews, hearing, trial), interpret unfamiliar information (regarding legal procedures, for example), and provide education about victim reactions to the particular system involved.

4. A *political* dimension. Many women who are raped come to realize that their experiences were not isolated aberrations. Recognizing

and reacting to rape as a political crime against women can lead to a productive expression of anger for individual victims. This anger, shared by the victim and her loved ones, can contribute to her resolution of the rape trauma and can motivate actions to fight against rape in our society.

## Concluding Remarks

This chapter has highlighted our society's developing awareness of women as rape victims, focusing on institutional and professional helping roles. There are still many people and agencies who need to examine and change their sexist treatment of rape victims. Obvious prejudice against rape victims (such as rape jokes) has subsided in everyday vocabulary and routine agency procedures. Almost everyone knows that one is supposed to be sensitive to rape victims. The sexism that now exists is more subtle. Those of us who counsel victims are intensely aware of the need for more education.

Women regularly report to us that they have sought help for emotional problems, only to find that their therapists would not let them talk about their rape experiences. And we often encounter evaluations by professional counselors who conclude that certain children are lying or "fantasizing" about sexual abuse. For the sake of preserving the family unit, many children are being forced by respectable agencies to remain in homes where they live in constant fear of repeated sexual abuse.

Concentrating on refining and expanding victim services in itself is futile. The fight against rape must continue in other ways. As one product of rape victim services, training for women in rape prevention is also taking hold around the country. Women are learning everything from verbal assertiveness to karate skills. Rapists will not have as many easy targets as before. In many places groups of men (often known as Men Against Rape) are being organized that recognize that they have a role to play in stopping rape. Sensitized men educating other men (and boys) about the devastating effects of rape, and men making it clear to their fellow males that rape is no longer acceptable, may play a significant role in reducing the incidence of rape.

# Part Three

*Women in Particular Social Statuses*

# 6. Women as Single Parents: Alternative Services for a Neglected Population

DIANNE BURDEN

ONE OF the most important social trends in the United States in the past fifteen years has been the steady increase in female-headed households. Single women now account for almost one-quarter of all heads of households in the United States, and of these, over half are single mothers with children under 18 [U.S. Department of Labor (USDOL) 1975, 1978]. Recent data indicate that these trends have been rapidly accelerating in the mid-1970s (Ross and Sawhill 1975; USDOL 1978). Clearly, the myth of the typical American nuclear family (mother, father, two kids) is becoming increasingly illusive. Yet social services, programs, policies, and legislation continue to view the family as a two-parent family and have uniformly failed to keep pace with the urgent needs of the single-parent family in a period of rapid social change.

Single-parent families have traditionally been viewed by researchers and policy planners alike as a deviant, broken form of the family—a transitional, undesirable situation to be remedied by remarriage and a return to full nuclear family status. The reality of the situation today, however, is that rapidly increasing numbers of family heads are experiencing the single-parent life style (whether by choice

or otherwise); they are remaining single-parent families for long
periods; and increasingly they are choosing the single-parent form of
family as their permanent life style (Glick, 1978).

The most significant aspect of this change has been the tremendous increase in responsibility thrust upon women without a corresponding increase in income or provision of adequate support networks to ease the sometimes overwhelming pressure of the dual roles
of breadwinner and homemaker. From 1962 to 1972 there was a 46
percent increase in female heads of household (compared to a 17 percent increase for males). The same period saw a 33 percent increase
in female heads of families (children present), compared to a 13 percent increase for men (USDOL 1972). At present 90 percent of all
single-parent families in the United States are headed by women (Ross
and Sawhill 1975). Although it is becoming more common for men
to receive custody of their children following a divorce, single parenthood in this country is primarily a women's and children's issue. Indeed, the percent of female-headed families at any one census says
little about the actual numbers of women who pass through single
parenthood at one time or another. Although 75 percent of single
mothers eventually remarry (Bequaert 1976), the divorce rate for second marriages is even higher than for first marriages. It is not uncom-
mon for the single-mother experience to occur more than once in a
woman's life.

Although the single-parent experience is difficult for both women
and men, it is financially devastating for women to a degree that it is
not for men. Custodial single fathers generally continue their career
patterns as before and do not experience the rapid downward mobility
of women who become single parents. They do, however, experience
the same role conflicts as women in trying to keep up with the multiple demands of their situation. Men typically are not socialized to
care for children and consequently often report initial anxiety about
having to deal with the demands of being the primary caretaker
(Keshet and Rosenthal 1978).

Single mothers, on the other hand, are not financially rewarded
for their socialized skills of homemaking and child raising, and thus
must deal with the high-stress consequences of poverty.

## Poverty

Today the largest issues facing single mothers from all socioeconomic backgrounds are poverty and depression; and poverty is a major contributing factor to depression. Even though more than half of all single mothers are in the labor force, they are most commonly employed in low-paying sales, clerical, and domestic jobs. The median income of a female-headed family is *half* that of a male-headed family and *less than half* that of a family in which two parents work. Single parenthood works a financial hardship on men as well, but not nearly to the extent that it does on women (see table 1). Thirty-four percent of female-headed families fall below the poverty level, while only 7 percent of male-headed families are below the poverty level. The sex of the head of the household is the single most important variable in predicting poverty in this country (USDOL 1972, 1978). In 1972 there were more than 9 million children living in families headed by women. Among all families with income below the poverty level in 1977, 48 percent were headed by women; about 66 percent of low-income black families were headed by women (USDOL 1978). It has been estimated than one out of every five children in this country will at some time be living for a significant period in a one-parent family. In looking at the issue of poverty, then, as it relates to single-parent families, a sizable portion of the U.S. population is involved. The situation is even more acute for minority populations: 32 percent of black families, 14 percent of Mexican-

TABLE 1 *Comparison of Median Incomes of Family Groups*

| Type of Family | Median Income | |
|---|---|---|
| | White | Black |
| Husband–wife | | |
|   Wife in paid labor force | $13,098 | $10,274 |
|   Wife not in paid labor force | 9,976 | 6,503 |
| Male head, no wife | 9,208 | 6,826 |
| Female head | 5,842 | 3,645 |

SOURCE: USDOL Women's Bureau 1972.

American families, and 29 percent of Puerto Rican families are headed by women (USDOL 1972, 1978). The number of nonwhite families headed by women has grown twice as fast as that of white female-headed families since 1960 (Ross and Sawhill 1975:13).

For the single mother, however, the most significant predictor of the likelihood that she is in poverty is the number of children she has. There is a direct correlation between poverty and number of children (see table 2).

TABLE  2 *Comparison of Number of Children and Income Level in Female-Headed Families*

| Number of Children | Percent of Female-Headed Families Below Low-Income Level | |
|---|---|---|
| | White | Black |
| 1 | 27.4 | 49.2 |
| 2 | 32.8 | 51.3 |
| 3 | 45.7 | 72.1 |
| 4 | 55.6 | 71.3 |
| 5 | 75.7 | 76.2 |
| 6 or more | 81.4 | 75.2 |
| Without children | 11.5 | 21.7 |

SOURCE: USDOL Women's Bureau 1972.

The problem of poverty for single mothers is compounded when one considers the fact that even women who work full time all year round rarely earn more than the $10,041 that represents the Bureau of Labor Statistics' lowest standard of living for a U.S. family of four. Of those who earn $15,000 or more per year, 95 percent are men (USDOL, Women's Bureau 1975). Female-headed families in this country are essentially excluded from the middle class. Indeed, divorce commonly leads to poverty for women regardless of previous socioeconomic status. Studies have shown that incomes of ex-husbands of women receiving AFDC payments represent a cross-section of the society as a whole. Ex-wives of middle-class men are increasingly slipping into poverty (Winston and Forsher 1971). Since women are generally socialized into (a) marriage or (b) low-paying sex-role–stereotyped jobs, single parenthood presents a woman with two alternatives, both of which virtually guarantee continued poverty. A single mother can either work at a low-paying job or apply for welfare assistance. In any given year 60 percent of female-headed families receive welfare payments at some time during the year (U.S. Department of Health, Education and Welfare 1973). Most women in the richest country in the world are, in reality, one man away from welfare. "There is evidence that, currently, the most effective way for a female-headed family to get out of poverty and off welfare is to acquire a male head" (Ross and Sawhill 1975:113).

Once alone, the typical single mother faces a virtual absence of social supports. The United States is the only nation in the industrialized world (85 nations) that does not provide a series of family support systems as a basic right to all family members (such as day care, free medical and dental care, children's allowances, housekeeping services, family sick leave, and family vacation time). The primary governmental support system available to single mothers, AFDC, is at best a minimal system and at worst a punitive program reflecting the general stigmatization and negative social attitudes toward women and children who are not supported by a man. The single mother is left in the impossible double bind of being unable to earn an adequate living (owing to inadequate job training, multiple role responsibilities, and sex discrimination) and finding herself expected to carry the entire load of supporting and caring for her family. At the same time, noncustodial single fathers have been essentially released from the responsibilities of parenthood. One-third of such fathers are never ordered to make child support payments. Of those who are ordered to pay, 40 percent never or rarely pay and 11 percent pay irregularly. Four years after divorce 67 percent of fathers are not paying any child support at all (Citizens' Advisory Council on the Status of Women 1973). Although child support enforcement has recently begun to be strengthened, the fact remains that women are left in an inequitable state of financial stress due to divorce and single parenthood.

## Depression

Inadequate financial resources result in a multitude of distressing consequences for single mothers. Without enough money to provide a comfortable buffer between the family and economic hardship, the single mother must typically live from one crisis to another. When the extreme life stress of single parenthood is combined with the learned helplessness experienced by most women through their socialization, depression is the predictable result (Seligman 1974:82–126). Those at greatest risk for depression are low-income, nonwhite divorced women in the childbearing years (25–44) with a large number of children; they typically express job dissatisfaction (Guttentag and Salasin 1978). Single mothers, then, are the greatest at-risk group for depression.

The problem continues to increase as the divorce rate approaches 50 percent, and yet as Brandwein points out, few adequate studies on single mothers have been undertaken (1974b:498). Single parenthood has generally been viewed as a transitory state for which the solution is remarriage. The studies that do exist generally fall into the pattern of assumption of deviance. That is, they are focused on father absence rather than mother presence and conclude erroneously that a one-parent family is a broken family. Not enough attention has been paid to the situation of the mother who remains. The importance to single parents of adult emotional support has been demonstrated (Glasser and Navarre 1964:98–109). Children are not developmentally in a position to be able to give emotional support to their parents. To the contrary, the parent must be able to draw support from her or his environment in order to give adequate emotional support to the child. Probably the greatest advantage of a two-parent family is the built-in presence of another adult to lend emotional support in child rearing. This of course assumes a certain level of cooperation and lack of conflict. The one-parent family is at a disadvantage in that the parent needs to find her own emotional support elsewhere. Her success at finding adequate adult resources (friends, lovers, job, school, support groups, clubs) appears to be (along with financial stability) crucial for survival.

As Brandwein points out, the single-parent family is almost always viewed as a less-than-complete family. The advantages of single-parent families are rarely discussed. For instance, single parents often develop a special closeness with their children that is not found in two-parent families, because single parents and their children overcome stressful situations together. Lack of marital conflict appears to be a major advantage of single-parent families, along with consistency in parenting (only one set of rules and regulations to deal with). Numerous studies point out the desirability in terms of child development of a happy one-parent family versus an unhappy two-parent family (Brandwein 1974b:509). It is becoming increasingly evident that children thrive in a one-parent family as well as they do in a two-parent family (Burchinal 1964:44–51). The key seems to be in the situation of the mother. If she can overcome the barriers of making an adequate income and finding a supportive social network, then single parenthood can be a full, interesting, and enjoyable life whether it is a temporary situation (between marriages) or a permanent way of life. The major problem facing single mothers, however, is how to surmount those barriers, for the current social supports for single mothers are woefully inadequate.

## What Single Mothers Are Saying— Single Mothers' Support Groups

The results of questionnaires completed by single mothers in problem-solving and support groups facilitated by the author at the Women's Institute, a feminist counseling, research, and training center in Seattle, Washington, tend to reinforce on an individual scale what studies and statistics are indicating on a national scale.

The peer support group model developed by the author involves 6–10 weekly sessions of 2–3 hours each. Group size varies from 6 to 25, with an optimum size of 10–12. The focus of the group is fourfold: (1) to provide a warm, supportive group setting where single mothers can discuss their problems and concerns with other single mothers in similar situations; (2) to provide education about the situation of single parents, effects of the single-parent family style on children, ways to deal effectively with the ex-spouse, time management skills, stress management, financial management, legal issues, parenting skills, cooperative parenting strategies, available resources, career and vocational options, and a variety of other issues identified by the group in an initial needs assessment and ongoing monitoring; (3) to provide an individual problem-solving component in which each member discusses the issues of greatest concern in her life and picks one specific problem to work on (typical problems selected include deciding to go back to school, finding a better job, developing a better parent–child relationship, moving to more convenient housing, ending an unsatisfactory relationship, and having the children live more of the time with their father); (4) to train single mothers to run a peer support group so that when the formal sessions are over the group may opt to continue on its own with the professional facilitator available as an occasional consultant.

In the needs assessment stage single mothers list their job (or lack of one) as their main dissatisfaction. Their main concern seems to be how to find a way to make enough money to live a decent life. Most of these women grew up believing that a man would always take care of them. They are never career oriented and typically thought only in terms of the current "job." Many used the support group to begin making long-range educational and career plans for the first time in their lives.

The second area of major concern to the women in the groups was the need for intimacy—in terms of both close adult friendship ties and sexual companionship. The mothers typically felt lonely and isolated. They expressed feelings of being on a treadmill: Get up in the morning, feed the kids, go to the day care center, go to work, pick the kids up at the day care center, go home, fix dinner, put the kids to bed, clean house, fall into bed, and start again the next day. The mothers in the groups generally gave a low priority to their own needs. Time spent with children, job, school, housework, and shopping all came before time spent having fun. A large percentage of single mothers express little guilt at leaving their children to go to a job or to school because they see this as necessary for survival. They do express guilt, however, at leaving their children to do something enjoyable for themselves. Thus, the development of a strong social support system, which as we have seen is absolutely vital to the success of a single-parent family, is often the one thing that single mothers say they have no time for. Loneliness, isolation, and increased stress are the direct results.

Black women experienced a different pattern of socialization; they grew up expecting that they would have to work and take care of themselves. However, they too thought not in terms of long-term career development but rather in terms of the current job. The discontinuous nature of women's work patterns owing to childbearing and family responsibilities appears to be an important element in the difficulty of making long-term career plans. The crucial early career-building years (25–34) are precisely the period when the demands of small children at home are the greatest. Traditional employers (both public and private) expect the single-mother employee to deal with these multiple pressures on her own. They fail to offer innovative support systems that might lessen the strain on the single-parent employee and greatly increase her or his efficiency and productivity. Single fathers face the same difficulties in their work situation, with the difference that (1) their career is not interrupted by childbearing demands and (2) single fathers tend to be less stigmatized in general than single mothers.*

In a society where the primary form of social interaction seems to occur in couples or in traditional nuclear-family situations, the single parent often comes to feel very much outside of the mainstream. The problem again is compounded for women. They are not socialized to be as assertive as men, and even when they are assertive, negative consequences often result owing to their stepping out of the traditional feminine role.

It is important to note that divorced single mothers seeking service at the Women's Institute fall into two distinct categories: (1) those who have been divorced for two years or less and (2) those who have been divorced for more than two years. The first group (especially during the initial year following divorce) is undergoing an extremely stressful transition stage and is likely to exhibit much anxiety around rapid change and feelings of incompleteness while the family is adjusting to its new situation. Mothers who have been on their own for

* Information on single-father life styles is from interviews with single fathers participating in the Single Fathers' Program at the Metro Center YMCA, Seattle, Washington. The author is a member of the advisory board for this program.

more than two years, on the other hand, generally feel quite complete as a family and confident of their parenting skills. Their stress level is not nearly as high as that of the first group.* The concerns of the second group tend to center on job/career dissatisfaction and a need to expand their social support network. Mothers in this category often express feelings of being "stuck in a rut." The single-parent family changes over time, and the needs of the family members change as well.

Other issues of major concern to the mothers in the groups were single-parenting concerns, effects of divorce on children, coping with the multitude of daily management problems, how to deal with ex-husbands and ex–in-laws, how to fit new relationships into their lives, and what to do about sex as a single parent. The issue of sexuality for single mothers can be an especially perplexing one. In our culture sex is generally structured into the formal systems of marriage and living together. A single mother who is not involved in a regular relationship is often confused about how to integrate sex into her life, especially as it relates to the potential impact on her children.†

All these issues affect all single parents. However, it should be noted that different categories of single mothers have their own specific problems in addition to those that all have in common. Thus, the situation of never-married single mothers will differ from that of the divorced or separated single mother and the widowed single mother. Special services are needed for all these groups. In addition, the situation of lesbian single mothers in relation to a heterosexual majority also presents special issues of concern.

## Lesbian Single Mothers ‡

The problems and joys of lesbian parents are primarily those of any single mother. There are, however, some additional factors with which families headed by lesbian parents have to contend. The issue

---

* Brandwein (1974a:5) finds a similar grouping in her study of single parents.

† For a further discussion of this issue, see Adams (1978). See also Brandwein (1974a:14–16).

‡ The section on lesbian mothers was written by Cathryne Schmitz, a graduate student in social work at the University of Washington and coordinator of the Lesbian Parent Program at the Lesbian Resource Center, University YWCA, Seattle, Washington.

that is of greatest concern to many lesbian mothers is custody. While all single mothers can be sued for the custody of their children if they are considered "too" sexual, the lesbian mother, by virtue of her title, is commonly assumed to be "too" sexual. Though in recent years several lesbian mothers have won custody cases, more still lose their children not only to their ex-husbands but also to other family members, in-laws, and the state. Consequently, the fear of a custody suit produces much anxiety for lesbian mothers.

Because a lesbian mother may fear a custody suit if her identity becomes known, or because she may accept the heterosexual bias of society, which says that heterosexuality is better,* many lesbian parents hide their sexual identity from their children. As with other forms of deception in a family setting, tension is often a result (Clark 1977:133–39). The effects of the deception tend to be magnified if the children are adolescents or if the mother and her lover are sharing a home. These factors combined can result in a volatile situation.

An additional problem faced by many lesbian parents is that families headed by two parents of the same sex are not recognized as legitimate families. Several financial problems result, ranging from the difficulty of receiving welfare, insurance, and tax benefits to ineligibility for reduced travel rates, which are available to heterosexual families. This nonrecognition can also create friction between the lesbian mother, her partner, and/or the children. The partner is not seen as a "legitimate" parent by society, and even the couple may not recognize this role. This recognition, at least within the unit, is important for the creation of a viable working unit. The heterosexual single mother has similar problems if she is living with a man to whom she is not married. Fear of loss of custody can be aroused in her as well. However, she does have the option of marrying. In many respects the lesbian mother always remains a single parent unless she decides to marry a man.

Heterosexual bias can have a major effect on the family when the children of lesbian parents become 11–12 years of age. Once children reach the sixth or seventh grade, they receive a clear message that heterosexual is the only "right" way to be. The single heterosex-

---

* For further discussion on heterosexual bias, see Kalafus (1977).

ual mother must contend with a similar bias, as the "intact" nuclear family is always considered the ideal. The lesbian mother, however, with or without a lover, has no recognized status in the family style hierarchy. Consequently, the child has difficulty finding a category for her or his family.*

The positive side of being a member of a family headed by a lesbian parent is seldom discussed. Because lesbian families have no role models to follow, they are more often forced to examine their lives and the lives of their children, and the roles and relationships involved. Out of this examination can come a more egalitarian household in which the personality and needs of each individual are recognized. If handled well by the adults, exposure to alternative life styles can provide a valuable experience for the children.†

## Social Policy Issues

Although individual problem solving and peer support groups can be helpful to single mothers, the fact remains that the extreme hardship of the situation of single mothers is also a problem of the society at large in its failure to provide adequate support systems to all families in this country. It is typical for single mothers to internalize the blame for their situation and to feel that they are crazy—that their unhappiness is their own fault and that they should be able to do something about it. These feelings of self-blame are compounded by the tendency of society, and the social sciences in particular, to blame single mothers for everything from drug abuse to delinquency to the breakdown of the American family (Brandwein 1974:4).

The model of depression resulting from a combination of learned helplessness and life stress suggests that there are two major targets of intervention in working with single mothers. On both an individual and a group level, single mothers can learn ways of being less helpless and exerting more control over their lives. However, a large portion of the stress they experience is beyond their control and rests

* For a comparison of the plight of the children of gay people to that of the minority group child, see Clark (1977:35) and NGTF Packet (1973).

† For additional readings see Oberstone and Sukoneck (1976) and Friedman (1975:28–32).

with the society itself. The livelihood of a single mother, for instance, is absolutely dependent on the availability of reasonably priced, high-quality child care. The lack of child care programs in this country and the failure of both business and government to address the urgent needs of women in the area of employment and welfare reform are examples of the ways in which the social system works a direct hardship on female-headed families. Innovative social service delivery programs can be effective only when combined with increased efforts toward social policy change.

Such an effort occurred at the Washington State Women's Conference at Ellensburg, Washington in July 1977. A group of single mothers from all sections of the State of Washington met to discuss the specific problems of single mothers and to make recommendations for change to federal, state, and local governments as well as private enterprise. Similar conferences were held throughout the nation, culminating in the National Women's Conference at Houston in November 1977.

The recommendations made by the single mothers of Washington exemplify the changes that need to occur if single mothers in this country are to reverse their slide into a permanent impoverished underclass. All of the recommendations recognize the imperative need of American society to make a commitment to developing family support systems that will make life more tenable for the women and children who are being systematically relegated to poverty.

## Recommendations for Change

### 1. Increased Economic Opportunities for Women

It should be recognized that poverty is a women's and children's issue of increasing proportions in this country, and that if this trend is to be reversed, major programs need to be developed.

    a. *Pay rates in traditional female occupations should be upgraded* to levels comparable to those in traditional male occupations.

    b. Extensive *aid to education programs* should be developed for single parents.

c. *Alternative educational models* need to be developed that will prepare and encourage low-income single mothers to enter lucrative traditionally male occupations.

d. Social policy should be sensitive to the discontinuous nature of women's attachment to the work force owing to family responsibilities.

2. *Vigorous Enforcement of Child Support Legislation*

"As long as mothers bear major responsibility for the physical care and custody of children, fathers will need to bear major responsibility for their financial support" (Ross and Sawhill 1975:173).

3. *Quality Child Care Responsive to the Developmental Needs of Children*

Perhaps the greatest barrier to single mothers is the unfair and unrealistic expectation that they both support their children and take full responsibility for their care. A more equitable system of sharing this responsibility must be worked out.

a. Quality neighborhood-based child care should be available on a 24-hour basis on an ability-to-pay scale for children up to age 18.

b. The costs of private day care in home settings should be subsidized for parents who so choose.

c. Parents who choose to stay home to provide child care for their own children should receive a wage and job benefits similar to those received by all other workers.

4. *Welfare Reform*

Benefits should be increased and extended to include all low-income families and to provide a nationally uniform income maintenance program, with incentives to increase earnings through lower tax rates.

5. *Extensive Support Networks for Single-Parent Families*

It should be recognized that it is unreasonable to expect a single parent to manage the multiple demands that even two-parent families are finding increasingly difficult to handle. Support networks need to be developed that would enable single parents to function more efficiently and productively.

a. Neighborhood-based *family resource centers* should be established to provide such assistance as child care, counseling, support groups, referral services, education programs, and legal assistance, with special programs for single parents.

b. *Cooperative low-cost housing* should be made available to single parents.

c. Adequate *medical and dental care* should be available to all children and adults on an ability-to-pay basis.

d. Existing *sick leave* should be expanded to include family illness.

e. The *transportation* difficulties of many single parents should be recognized and addressed.

f. Existing *peer support programs* for single parents should be supported and expanded.

6. *Research Studies and Community Education Programs on the Special Situation and Problems of Single Parents*

It should be recognized that there is a dearth of adequate information on single-parent families and that extensive research efforts and public education programs need to be financed and encouraged in this area.*

In addition, the *status of homemakers should be upgraded* so that they receive a fair wage and become entitled to all of the benefits that workers outside the home receive. This recommendation is of paramount concern to single mothers if they are to have the right to be paid a decent wage for staying home and taking care of their children if they so desire.

## Services Currently Available to Single Mothers

Given the extent of the service needs of single parents, it is disconcerting that so few programs currently exist. Government and business at all levels have failed to provide adequate services to this large segment of the population. Social service agencies have also failed to provide much-needed special services to single mothers. Those services which are currently available fall into the following general categories.

---

* For a review of research in this area, see Brandwein (1974b), Ross and Sawhill (1975), and Schlesinger (1978).

## PEER-SUPPORT GROUPS

These groups are the most innovative of services for single mothers and can be most appropriately labeled alternative services. They are self-help groups that are feminist in orientation and are a direct result of the women's liberation movement of the past ten years. Most have come into existence in the past five years. These centers rely heavily on a large volunteer component and are notoriously underfunded. Many eventually fail because of lack of funding and lack of support from the community. The main advantage of this type of service is that single mothers can begin to counteract for each other the negative social attitudes toward one-parent families and can do much to end loneliness and isolation by creating a strong adult emotional support network. The major objection to self-help groups is that the burden of providing social support to families, which many feel is the obligation of society at large, falls entirely on the shoulders of those least able to afford it in terms of time, money, and energy, namely, single mothers themselves. Traditional social service agencies and government programs regularly refer clients to single-mother self-help centers, thus continuing to avoid their own responsibility to provide services for single mothers.

## MORE TRADITIONAL SOCIAL/SUPPORT ORGANIZATIONS

A variety of groups for single parents are becoming increasingly available through the sponsorship of more traditional organizations. Parents Without Partners is probably the best example of these groups. It has been in existence for twenty years and now has chapters throughout the country and in other countries as well. It is an all-volunteer organization for single parents and their children, and provides a multitude of opportunities for social interaction and recreation.

It is now becoming common for churches to sponsor single-parent activities. Singles groups, especially in large cities, have also been expanding to provide special services for single parents. All of these are valuable as referral sources for single mothers. They all share the disadvantage, however, of inadequate funding, and many must charge fees for their events. Again, single mothers, who are at the lowest end of the income scale, are caught in the bind of having the greatest need and the least ability to pay. For many single mothers, these groups provide excellent support systems. Others have less satisfactory experiences and feel that single-parent social groups tend to be "meat markets" where men go to "check out" the women.

## SOCIAL SERVICE AGENCIES

Community mental health centers and other counseling centers have traditionally seen a large number of single mothers in their caseloads. Until recently, however, single mothers were seen as regular out-patients, and few services existed for their particular needs. For example, child care and transportation, two major barriers to many single mothers receiving service, have been left to the mother to provide for herself. Mental health agencies, including community mental health centers, family and child service agencies, college and university counseling centers, and feminist counseling centers, now frequently offer specialized problem-solving and support groups for single mothers. The main drawback of these groups is that they tend to be short term and available only at certain times; and thus do not offer drop-in crisis support and/or a long-term social network. They can be instrumental, however, in teaching women the skills they need to develop an effective support network.

## INSTITUTIONAL AND GOVERNMENTAL SUPPORT

The most effective programs currently serving single mothers in an institutional setting are the educational women's programs and centers of community colleges. Many two-year colleges provide excellent career counseling, support groups, and job training programs for returning women students. This educational level is especially effective with single mothers, as it tends to be less threatening and less expensive than a traditional university setting, as well as more flexible in terms of course offerings, class times, and practical applicability of the material taught. The community college setting offers a potentially excellent alternative social service opportunity for many single mothers.

As we have seen, the primary federally funded support program for single mothers is AFDC. The support levels it provides are minimal and often punitive. Welfare reform that results in a more equitable situation for single mothers and their children is a necessity if single mothers are to rise above the lowest rungs of the economic ladder. Welfare reform is clearly a major women's issue in the United States.

### Alternative Services Currently Available to Single Mothers

The following are examples of services currently available to single mothers. Although increasing numbers of grassroots programs and organizations are springing up around the country, their services are rarely adequately funded or coordinated into a network of agencies providing services for single parents. The examples cited here are intended to give an indication of the types of programs that are beginning to be developed.

### SINGLE PARENT RESOURCE CENTER, SAN FRANCISCO

The Single Parent Resource Center in San Francisco was founded in 1973 by a group of single mothers in response to demands for such a center from single parents throughout the San Francisco Bay Area. It provides a variety of services to single parents (both women and men), including

a drop-in peer support group one evening a week
a choice of a weekly scheduled program or a weekly rap group
small ongoing groups for pregnant single mothers and single mothers with infants
an outreach program in the black community
consultation to people who want to start groups
coordination of seminars for leaders of single-parent groups throughout the Bay Area
information and referral
a shared-housing file

The Center is staffed by one full-time and two half-time CETA positions, along with a large contingent of volunteers. Lack of funding is a chronic problem, although a one-year federal grant from the Office of Child Development did facilitate the development of present programs and the publication of a *One-Parent Family* Magazine that is still much in demand. The Center is fortunate in that it is associated with the Child Care Switchboard in San Francisco, which received funding from a variety of federal, state, and local sources.

## SISTERHOOD OF BLACK SINGLE MOTHERS, BROOKLYN NEW YORK

The Sisterhood of Black Single Mothers is a self-help group for black women from a wide range of backgrounds in the New York Metropolitan area. The organization was founded four years ago with the objective of taking a positive approach toward single parenthood. Two hundred women belong to the group, which is minimally funded by occasional grants, both public and private, but staffed totally by volunteers. Additional funds are raised by $2.00 monthly dues, subscription rates to a newsletter published by the group, and an assortment of fund-raising events. The services provided include

a clothing cooperative
a baby-sitting cooperative in which hours are exchanged
special trips with children for group rates
information and referral (especially for housing)
speaking engagement on the situation of single mothers at colleges and other organizations

The principal purpose of the program is to provide a social network that enables mothers and children to socialize together in groups and to view the single-parent family as a viable and even preferable alternative to the traditional two-parent model.

## SINGLE PARENT FAMILY PROJECT, NEW YORK CITY

The Single Parent Family Project opened its storefront center in May 1976. It is funded by the Community Service Society of New York and is the first of its kind in the nation. The program is run by a director and three full-time staff members—a parents center coordinator, a group development coordinator, and a community organization assistant. The objectives and services of the program include

developing neighborhood-based single-parent support groups throughout the five boroughs of New York City
training single parents as group facilitators
gathering information about single parents
conducting weekly programs and discussion groups on topics of concern to single parents
publishing a monthly newsletter for single parents

The project also operates an Information and Resource Center at its main storefront location. The services offered there include

a drop-in gathering place
a library and information files on single parenthood
referral and guidance for parents in need
special interest programs

The Single Parent Family Project has received nationwide attention and as a result, according to its director, has been flooded with requests for information from all parts of the country.

The key to the extensive services that this program is able to provide is a stable funding base.

## WOMEN IN TRANSITION, PHILADELPHIA

Women in Transition is one of the oldest of the feminist self-help groups that provide alternative services for single mothers. It was formed in 1971 as a program of the Philadelphia Women's Center to respond to the needs of large numbers of women going through separation or divorce with nowhere to turn for social support. Enough funding was obtained from foundations to support a full-time staff of seven. The objective of the program is twofold: to provide emotional and legal support to women (primarily single mothers) in transition from marriage to singlehood. The services that WIT provides include

weekly support/discussion groups
therapy evaluation and referral
consultation to agencies
a divorce clinic for women who choose to do their own divorces
community workshops and outreach

Probably the greatest contribution of WIT (certainly on a national level) has been the publication of a 500-page *Women's Survival Manual: A Feminist Handbook on Separation and Divorce* (Women in Transition 1975). This book is one of the few resources available that deals in a positive, helpful way with the distinctive concerns of single mothers.

Like the vast majority of feminist self-help agencies, WIT suffers from a chronic shortage of funds. Its funding base is precarious at best, and its continued service to single mothers depends on the skill of other single mothers in finding money to continue the program.

## MOMMA,[*]

### PORTLAND, OREGON

An example of a self-help organization that was not able to withstand the pressures of trying to provide an urgently needed service with no funding base is the local chapter of MOMMA in Portland, Oregon. The Portland chapter was begun as an offshoot of the California-based single mothers' organization in 1974. At that time it had up to 100 members. Its goals were to serve as an extended family for single mothers, to plan activities together, and to invite speakers to appear on a variety of single-parent concerns. According to the former director of the group, the organization lasted exactly one year.

Portland MOMMA is an example of single mothers with little money, time, or resources attempting to set up an organization to serve other single mothers with even less money, time, or resources. The founders were simply overwhelmed by the extent of the response to the organization and by the urgency of the needs of the single mothers who looked to them for a support system. The majority of

* For further information about MOMMA see Hope and Young (1976).

the women involved were severely limited by their circumstances—low-income or welfare mothers. Their needs were so great they had no energy left to give back to the organization. The single mothers who started this group felt dragged down by the overwhelming responsibility of keeping the organization going, and finally could no longer continue. They received no funding from anyone and had no real idea of how to form themselves into an official organization. Self-help groups for single mothers typically have an extremely difficult time maintaining themselves, since the women who are attempting to keep them going have little time, money, or resources and are usually in great need of a strong support network themselves.

## MOTHER'S EMERGENCY STRESS SERVICE, SACRAMENTO, CALIFORNIA

The Mother's Emergency Stress Service in Sacramento, California, is an example of a 24-hour crisis line available to all mothers but especially useful for single mothers because of their special needs. This service is funded by revenue sharing and has a full-time staff of 19 (9 of which are CETA positions). The services provided include referral, counseling, rap sessions, a shelter for battered women, and a variety of child care programs such as referral to low-cost child care, exchange child care, and an emergency child care service (up to 23 hours). In spite of the large staff already available, the director emphasizes that the demand for services is much greater than the organization's capacity to provide them.

## THE FIVE CHURCH ASSOCIATION SUPPORT SYSTEM FOR SINGLE PARENTS AND AFDC MOTHERS, ST. LOUIS, MISSOURI

An excellent example of an innovative program sponsored by a more traditional organization is the program for single-parent families and AFDC mothers coordinated by a minister in St. Louis, Missouri. The program is funded by the Presbyterian Church Council on Women in the Church. It is a three-year pilot project that is being developed to help meet both the emergency and long-term needs of

AFDC mothers. The program will conduct regular small-group meetings of single mothers as well as provide an emergency housing network for battered women and children.

## WOMEN'S INSTITUTE, SEATTLE

The Women's Institute is a feminist counseling center near the University of Washington campus in Seattle that provides both individual and group counseling. Regular groups are scheduled that deal specifically with the concerns of single mothers. Others are offered that are especially useful in teaching single mothers new skills. Among the groups available are single mothers' support groups and parenting groups and groups focusing on financial assertiveness and money management, assertiveness training, problem solving, social skills for shyness, and abused women. However, the Institute receives no outside funding. Like other agencies, it must charge for its services. Even though fees are sometimes waived, the fact remains that the lowest-income single mothers are not assured of receiving many of the services available to single mothers.

## LESBIAN RESOURCE CENTER, UNIVERSITY YWCA, SEATTLE

The Lesbian Resource Center (LRC) at the University YWCA in Seattle has been conducting rap groups for lesbian mothers for several years and is trying to develop a model program. The staff has discovered that the concerns of parents with young children (under age 10) are very different from those with children over 10 years of age. They have also discovered that the concerns of lesbian mothers living in a couple relationship can be very different from those of lesbian mothers living alone or communally. When possible, they try to screen their groups into these categories in order to provide an atmosphere in which the women in the groups can discuss their particular experiences. The concerns, fears, and joys discussed by the women in the groups are similar to those discussed in any group of mothers. The basic difference is that the Lesbian Resource Center provides an atmosphere in which their lesbianism is not an overriding issue, so they can discuss their parenting without feeling different.

Unfortunately, the LRC does not reach a large population of lesbian mothers because many of them are afraid to be connected with the agency for fear of disclosure. Other social service agencies need to provide a relaxed atmosphere in which lesbian mothers can feel free to share their experiences.

## ADDITIONAL SERVICES NEEDED FOR LESBIAN MOTHERS

Therapists and agencies serving mothers need to examine their own as well as society's attitudes toward lesbian parents (NASW 1977). Too often when a family is in crisis and seeks help and the agency or counselor discovers that the mother chooses to have her primary affectional and sexual relationships with women, the therapist does not look any further for the source of the family's problem(s). For the most part, the problems of lesbian-headed families are the same as those of any other family. If *one* of the problems the family is facing is that the mother has not disclosed her sexual identity to the children, then the therapist should help her work this through if she can. If she cannot help the client through this because she does not know enough about the issue, then she should refer the client to another therapist or agency that can.

There are many agencies that now provide rap groups for gay people so that they can work out their own feelings about their homosexuality and discuss the adjustments they must often make to a hostile world. There are also rap groups for the parents of gays in large cities across the country, but as yet there are no rap groups for the adolescent children of gay people. These groups need to be developed in order to provide a peer group in which these children can discuss their concerns.

## SUMMARY OF RECOMMENDATIONS FOR CHANGE

The most pressing problems of single mothers are not personal problems: They are societal problems. The majority of female heads of families are laboring under a weight of responsibility that even the most successful two-parent families find difficult to cope with. Until the socialization of women is adapted to the changing family structure in this country, and until federal, state, and local governments recognize the reality of changing family patterns and the tremendous stress that results, and responds to this change with comprehensive family support systems, single mothers will continue to experience great difficulty.

In the meantime, however, cities can begin by developing local support systems for single parents analogous to those for other special groups. Social service professionals can be sensitized and trained to deal with the special problems of single parents, and can provide special programs for single parents that include the necessities of child care and transportation. Businesses can review their personnel policies and begin responding in a more flexible manner to the needs of the large numbers of single parents in their employ. Local funding agencies can lend their support to emerging self-help organizations that provide single mothers with the emotional support network so vital to raising healthy children. Society as a whole can begin to look at the single-parent family as a viable, healthy, whole family. The solution for single mothers does not lie in finding a husband; rather, it lies in finding employment that will provide a decent living, reasonable child care that will ensure a high-quality environment for their children, and a strong adult support network that will give them emotional sustenance.

The prevailing myth is that women will be taken care of by men all their lives. The reality is that most women will be alone for long periods, whether before marriage, between marriages, or as widows, and will work full time for most of their lives. Fewer women than men remarry after divorce, and the average woman stays single between marriages longer than the average man (Bernard 1972). Single mothers make up half of the women living alone in this country. Addressing their needs must be a high-priority item at all levels of society.

# 7. The Older Woman

## NAOMI GOTTLIEB

THE YEARS after age 45 can be problematic for women because the distinctive issues for the woman as she grows older begin to be evident when she is past the childbearing period. She loses one of the main purposes of her central role when her children are grown and leave home. Within a few years she is more and more likely to lose the other major focus of that role through widowhood. She loses the physical attributes associated with her central role when she can no longer meet the expectations of youthful beauty and sexuality. If she works, she is handicapped in her earning power by social conditions that discriminate against the woman worker, and upon divorce, widowhood, or retirement she suffers the consequences of long-term dependence on her husband's financial and work situation. Divorce or widowhood, of course, can occur at any age. However, when either occurs after age 45 (and widowhood is more likely after that time) a woman's problems are compounded because of other age-related factors. This chapter addresses the consequences of the changes peculiar to women that begin in the mid-40s and continue through the later years.

Prefaced by a demographic description of the older woman, this chapter addresses several issues of import to her condition: the impact of her socialization on her later years, the influence of social expectations concerning a woman's physical appearance and sexuality, and the effects of public attitudes and legal constraints on the older woman at work and in retirement.

The discussions of new services that follow will indicate that, by and large, few service programs address the older woman exclusively and separately. Though many older women are served in programs such as those for the widow and the displaced homemaker, older women are rarely treated as a distinct group but are included along with either men or younger women.

## Demographic Descriptions of the Older Woman

In 1970 there were 33.4 million American women over the age of 45 (Kreps and Clark 1975:28). Of that group, 21.8 million were between the ages of 45 and 64 (Sommers 1974:6), and 2 million of these women were in female-headed households. Of the group between the ages of 55 and 64, 25 percent were already widowed (Kutza 1975:9).

Of the 20 million people who were over the age of 65 in 1970, 11.6 million were women and 8.4 million men. Of the women, 6 million were widowed and 1.2 million were either divorced or single. Most women (62 percent) are alone at that age—widowed, single, or divorced (Preston 1975:2). Women live an average of seven years longer than men, and because of this and because they usually marry men older than themselves, they are very likely to be widowed, spending on the average the last two decades of their lives as widows (Payne and Whittington 1976:492; Preston 1975:52). Men not only die younger—in 1975 the U.S. life expectancy was 67.7 years for men and 74.6 years for women (U.S. Bureau of Census 1975)—but also have higher rates of remarriage, often to younger women (Payne and Whittington 1976:491). Men's shorter lifespan appears not to be related to their work history, for it does not seem to be the case "that when women enter the labor force in greater numbers, they too . . . have decreased longevity. . . . The available evidence indicates that women who work throughout their life still retain their average seven years of greater longevity" (Streib 1975:52). This is true despite the common observation that, though they live longer, women have more health problems, or at least report more illnesses. (See Part One for further discussion of women's health.) It remains to be seen whether the movement of women into nontraditional occupations and activities will be accompanied by a mortality rate similar to that of men.

Another way to look at this phenomenon is to note the ratio of elderly women to elderly men, a ratio that is increasing every decade. "In 1950 there were 112 [elderly] women per 100 men. In 1960 there were 121 women, and in 1970 there were 139 women per 100 men" (p. 51). The picture, then, is of considerably more elderly women than men, and most of those women lack marital partners in the last years of their lives.

A considerable portion of the younger cohort of the older-women group, those between the ages of 45 to 64, work mainly in the traditional female occupations—service, clerical, retail sales. The increase in labor force participation of this group of women has been dramatic—from 12 percent in 1890 to 47 percent in 1966, and now "it is not only the mother who works . . . but also the grandmother" (Neugarten and Moore 1968:11). By 1974, 53.4 percent of women between the ages of 45 and 54 and 44 percent of those aged 55–64 were at work (Kline 1975:488). These percentages are higher for unmarried women and for racial–ethnic minority women (Bart 1975:6). The percentage of women who work decreases dramatically after age 65, of course; but many women in the preceding 20-year age group are at work.

When women are aged, and widowed or single, they are very likely also to be poor. There are several ways of looking at this overrepresentation of women among the aged poor. Of the 4.3 million people over the age of 65 who live in poverty, two-thirds are women (Sommers 1975:269), and of all the elderly widows in the nation, two-thirds live below the poverty line (Kutza 1975:91). This condition is exacerbated among racial–ethnic minorities. For example, 80 percent of older black women (ages 55 to 64) have annual incomes of less than $4,000 (Lindsay 1975:91). The poorest individuals in the nation are women over 65 who are single or widowed, with an average annual income of $1,888 (Preston 1975:44).

It is encouraging that women are not necessarily physically alone during their later years. Fifty-nine percent of women 65 and over live in a family group, either with their husbands (33 percent), with relatives (16 percent), or as heads of households (10 percent). Only four percent live in institutions. The remaining 37 percent are in fact alone (Streib 1975:52). There is evidence that for all these groups, even those living alone, there is considerable contact between the elderly and other members of their families. This is particularly true of populations in metropolitan areas, where mobility and the resulting separation of families affect parents and children less than in rural areas. "With the massive movement from rural to urban areas that has been characteristic of American society for several generations . . . many older people are left in rural areas while their children move to the cities" (Cowgill 1972:255). In metropolitan areas there is extensive contact between the elderly and their children, one study reporting that "three-fourths of such older people are visited by their children at least once a month" (p. 255), and considerable mutual aid, including, as income allows, a flow from the parents to the children (p. 252). The general pattern, then, is that most elderly women live with their families; one-third are still with their husbands; and for the approximately two in five who live alone there is family contact.

In sum, the demographic data for women over 45 evidence the changes in women's roles and the fact of women's longevity. In the years after age 45, when her youngest child has left home (Neugarten and Moore 1968), the woman is more and more likely to be unmarried by virtue of either divorce or widowhood. In the early part of these later years, she is likely to be at work. After her retirement or the retirement or death of her husband, she is likely to be poor. The aging woman usually outlives her husband but in her later years usually maintains contact with other family members. However, from the middle 40s on, the woman is likely to lose more and more of the relationships and responsibilities that previously defined her existence.

## Women's Socialization and
### the Later Years

Many of the major aspects of female socialization have been discussed in earlier chapters, aspects that foster narrowly conceived roles for women, restricted competencies, and a propensity for negative evaluations and depression. Here, certain aspects are selected for emphasis because they bear directly on women's being poorly prepared for their later years.

The first of these is that women are raised not only to enact the central role of wife–mother but to develop a marked sense of psychological and practical dependence on their husbands. Not only will marriage fulfill the primary goal in life for the woman, but "women are still socialized to believe that acquiring a husband will provide everlasting security" (Trager 1975:ix). A study of individuals at four stages of life—high school seniors, newlyweds, the middle aged, and the elderly—indicated that the newlyweds and middle-aged women were "as dependent on their husbands as the high school girls apparently expected to be" (Lowenthal 1975:213). This practical dependence also means that the woman's emotional and material well-being is contingent on the continuation of her marriage. She therefore emphasizes the activities that will ensure continuation of the marriage. These include pleasing her husband, guarding her appearance, and playing the wifely role. None of these activities necessarily prepares her for her later years, particularly in widowhood. Lewis and Butler (1972) comment as follows:

> Thus, 65 percent of all older women are on their own, an ironic fact when one remembers that older women, more than any younger group, were raised from childhood to consider themselves dependent on men. Most of them married early, had little education or career preparation, functioned totally as housewives for 40 to 50 years, and then SHOCK! Their job descriptions, already diminished when their children grew up, vanished completely with the death of their husbands. They are left both unemployed and familyless at a point when they are least able to adjust. (p. 226)

Older women need to rely on their own efforts to take care of themselves in the years in which they may be widowed or divorced or, if married, lacking a useful substitute for the maternal role. From their socialization and experience in the traditional marriage, they acquire neither a clear sense of their own identity nor a set of competencies that would equip them for this task. Not only does the woman's identity derive essentially from her family roles, but as she enacts these roles, frequently caught in the middle between parents and children or husband and children, the focus is on meeting others' needs and continuing to hone primarily her nurturing and mediating skills. This matter of identity is stressed because independent and autonomous action, qualities one needs to take care of oneself, come from having a sense of separate identity, not from being tied in a dependent way to another individual.

Further, specific competencies, which are needed for independent living, are not developed during those years of family life. "Most wives in America never plan for a career, for single status or for competing roles" (Lopata 1973b:41). In addition, many women do not acquire even basic capabilities or knowledge about such mundane areas as car and home repairs, and the more essential matter of financial management. Widows, for example, report that they have no clear idea of their husband's exact earnings, the family worth, or estate planning (Caine 1974). Women have been excluded from both "formal and informal training in money management" (Payne and Whittington 1976:494) and do not approach the acquisition of other than home-related skills in an assertive manner. Lowenthal (1975:214) found that both middle-aged women and high school girls were uncertain about acknowledging self-confidence and self-directedness as valuable personal traits for themselves.

Women's lives are also characterized by discontinuities. Though there may be some movement toward a work career during the school years, this will be interrupted by marriage. There may be a job early in marriage, then childbirth and child rearing, then perhaps a return to employment—this cycle being repeated several times up to and after the departure of the children. Though the actual number of years at work may eventually be considerable, there has been no continuous career development. Most important, interruptions and discontinuities in roles and responsibilities do not necessarily leave the woman with a set of skills and a sense of competence to live and work as an independent individual as she grows older. This can be an issue for the older woman who is still married but needs substitutes for the maternal role. The effects of discontinuities can be devastating for the divorced or widowed woman who must suddenly take care of herself.

Positive aspects of both discontinuities and changing roles have been noted in the literature. Some writers assert that experience with discontinuities leads to an easier adjustment in old age and high morale at that period (Kline 1975; Dunkel 1972). In addition, women who are ambivalent about motherhood and the wifely role may very well be relieved when those responsibilities are over (Jacobs 1976:36). Other women, with a more positive experience in traditional roles, may experience a great sense of satisfaction at having successfully completed the job of child rearing and home maintenance. Even in such situations, however, there would still be the need to shift to other arenas in later years, and the ability to do so may be lacking.

There is accumulating evidence that psychological difficulties in later years are more prevalent in women than in men. As both men and women have been studied, certain similarities have been noted—as a whole, the "present cohort is a tough one, survivors of America's worst depression" (Trager 1975:xi), and by and large, both men and women become more egocentric and self-preoccupied as they age (Neugarten 1974)—but most investigators report that women encounter more areas of psychological stress and have fewer internal resources to cope with them. For example, Lowenthal and her associates (1975:152) found that older men under high stress were likely to feel challenged by such circumstances, whereas older women felt overwhelmed by similar stress. A parallel observation is that men cope with their environment in cognitive ways, women in affective and expressive ways (Neugarten 1974). Coupled with this is the apparent correlation between an older woman's sense of having little control over events and her hesitancy in trying to deal with those events. Lowenthal (1975) observed that "older women have fewer resources than men with which to counter relatively severe stress" (p. 152).

The Lowenthal study found a particular vulnerability in the group of middle-aged women, that is, women in the postparental stage.

These middle-aged women were also the least sure of themselves of all groups, and the uneasy and often conflicting characterization of themselves suggests identity confusion if not outright "crisis." The future in general looked bleak and empty to them, and the majority did not feel in control. They reported themselves to be unhappy; they reported more psychological symptoms than anyone else; and they were the most likely to say that they had at some time considered suicide. (p. 218)

The following discussions deal with some specific implications of the changes that take place in a woman's life as she ages. These include changing physical appearance and sexuality and a change in financial resources. These changes are related to societal expectations and the socialization issues discussed earlier. Each reflects the change from the youthful, family-oriented wife and mother to the older or aging woman, now with little or no immediate family to care for, experiencing the practical consequences of restrictive factors in work and retirement.

## The Double Jeopardy of Age and Sex: Physical Appearance and Sexuality

The emphasis on youth and beauty in women as contrasted with men can be seen clearly in the different social valuation of signs of the normal aging process in each. It has been said that "men mature, women obsolesce" (Preston 1975:42). This is borne out by the observation that signs of aging—lines on the face, gray hair, the maturity of years—are valued in men as signs of character and are abhorred in women. Faced by standards that glorify the young and beautiful woman, women may go to considerable lengths to try to meet these standards as they age.

After late adolescense, women become the caretakers of their bodies and faces, pursuing their essentially defensive strategy, a holding operation. A vast array of products and jars and tubes, a branch of surgery, and armies of hairdressers, masseuses, diet counselors and other professionals exist to stave off, or mask, developments that are entirely normal biologically. . . . In women, this perfectly natural process is regarded as a humiliating defeat, while nobody finds anything remarkably unattractive in the equivalent physical changes in men. Men are "allowed" to look older without sexual penalty. (Sontag 1972:35–36)

The amount of time and energy that women spend on their appearance seems almost ludicrous by comparison to the man's attention to how he looks. This frantic attention to looks is more common among middle-class than among lower-class women. The poor are "more fatalistic about aging; they can't afford to fight the cosmetic battle as long and as tenaciously" (p. 32), but they are as much a target of social disapproval as they age. Women are faced with the fact that they receive fewer rewards for aging than men and must try to retain those characteristics—youth and attractiveness—that do obtain approval. Ironically, though exceptional mental powers can increase with age and could be a source of positive valuation, "women are rarely encouraged to develop their minds above dilletante standards" (p. 31). A further irony is that though women are not permitted to become truly adult, in the sense of being autonomous, independent, and competent, they nevertheless become obsolescent earlier (p. 33). Moreover, the emphasis on physical appearance carries with it the implication of women as property—property that will be judged by the outside package. Compare another set of traits offered as a redefinition of the concept of beauty applicable to either sex: "character, intelligence, expressiveness, knowledge, achievement, disposition, tone of voice and speech patterns, posture and bearing, warmth, personal style, social skills" (Butler and Lewis 1976:6).

Closely related to the aging woman's physical appearance are the views both she and society hold about her sexuality. The recent findings about sexuality in aging men and women in the Kinsey (1953) and Masters and Johnson (1970) reports have been important to men as well as women in challenging myths and stereotypes. Sexuality among the aging has been ridiculed and not understood. These recent investigations, giving belated attention to the sexual needs of the elderly, have shown that, given good health, many women can be sexually active almost as long as they live. There are some inevitable and expected changes due to the aging process—vaginal lubrication takes longer, penile erection is more difficult to obtain and retain—but both men and women can continue to experience and enjoy sexual response well into old age (Butler and Lewis 1976).

Given a better general understanding of sexuality in the aged, there is still the need to address the special problems women face in remaining sexually active throughout their lives. First, the emphasis on youth and beauty relates directly to a woman's sexual desirability. Women

become sexually ineligible much earlier than men do. A man, even an ugly man, can remain eligible well into old age. He is an acceptable mate for a young, attractive woman. Women, even good looking women, become ineligible (except as partners of very old men) at a much younger age. Thus for most women, aging means a "humiliating process of gradual sexual disqualification." (Sontag 1972:31–32)

These observations illustrate two interrelated aspects of sexuality for the older woman. Not only does she soon become an undesirable sexual partner for a man of her own age group, but the age disparity accepted for the man who chooses a younger mate is not accessible to the older woman. The partnership of an older woman and a very young man, so poignantly portrayed in the film *Harold and Maude*, appears grotesque to most people. Pfeiffer (1969) notes that, given the disproportionate numbers of elderly women among the aged group, exhorting them "to an active sexual life would be a cruel hoax indeed" (p. 161). Payne and Whittington (1976) challenge the basis of that remark: "This interpretation assumes, however, that older women will continue to be culturally defined as inappropriate mates or sex partners for younger men" (p. 493).

Added to these restrictions on appropriate partners for the older woman is her lifelong socialization to sexual unassertiveness. In view of the reluctance of many women, even in the marital relationship, to assert their sexual needs, it would seem doubly difficult for the older woman to do so. She would have to withstand not only the general taboo against sexual activities among the elderly but the additional inappropriateness of a woman playing the assertive role. Given the ratio of older men to older women, and social disapproval of liaisons with younger men, considerable assertion might be required for the older woman to maintain sexual relationships. Butler and Lewis (1976:137–138) have listed among the values of sex in late life the "defiance of stereotypes" and "a means of self-assertion." Each of these would have special meaning for women, but their achievement is more difficult for women than for men.

## Work, Income, and the Elderly Woman

The work history of women throughout their adult years needs to be considered for several reasons: That history forms a prelude to later life and may explain the present condition of many older women;

greater longevity and the increased likelihood of the widowed or divorced state makes work for self-support and/or retirement an important factor; and, finally, an inquiry into women's work history may suggest why so many women are poor in their later years. Until recently studies of women as a separate work group were not reported in the manpower or retirement literature (Kline 1975:486). Studies conducted in recent years reveal some important and distinctive work patterns.

As the introductory data indicate, there has been a remarkable and steady increase in the labor force participation of older women. The following data describe more fully the work patterns of the married working woman. There are now more families in which both husband and wife work than there are households in which only the husband is employed (Bernstein 1974). In 1970, 38 percent of the work force consisted of women, for a total of 31 million. Sixty percent of those women were married, compared to 30 percent in 1940 (Sommers 1975:267; Kreps 1971b:4). Among all wives, 40 percent are at work, but that percentage increases dramatically (to 67 percent) among wives under 35 who do not have children (p. 5). Only 27 percent of all married women with preschool children work, but the figure is 44 percent for black married women with preschool children. The highest rate for married women who are in the work force occurs for women between the ages of 45 and 54—48 percent of married women in that age bracket are at work (p. 18). Ninety percent of all women work at some time in their adult lives (Sommers 1975:267).

The stereotype of the married woman who works just to provide pin money and extras for the family seems no longer valid (Kutza 1975:5). Kreps (1971b) comments:

Poverty families would . . . be more numerous, except for the contributions which wives make to family income, pushing many of the white and non-white families over the poverty threshhold. In the mid-sixties, 42 percent of all non-white husband-wife families would have been in poverty, but for wives' earnings. (p. 8)

In many other families the wife's work has financed the children's education and enabled the husband to retire earlier (Kreps and Clark 1975:57). These circumstances may explain why wives continue to enter the labor force despite their generally low earnings. Their work participation rates "more than doubled from 1900 to 1940 and then almost tripled between 1940 and 1970" (p. 8). The rates for single and divorced individuals have also risen during these years, and it is expected that the labor force of the future will contain more women and more nonmarried people of both sexes (p. 44).

By and large, the jobs women do are "public transcriptions of the servicing and nurturing roles that women have in family life" (Sontag 1972:31). In 1970 the vast majority of working women (76 percent) were in service-related jobs or work requiring little training—retail sales, unskilled or semiskilled factory work, private household or other service jobs, and clerical work (Allan 1975). Women have been socialized to expect to find work in certain areas, and they go where those jobs are (Kreps 1971b:3). Though some women can now be found in almost every officially listed occupation, the overwhelming majority remain in positions traditionally held by women (p. 99).

Some positions (e.g., airline cabin attendants, receptionists) are clearly restricted not only to women but to young, attractive women—an illustration of the compound effects of agism and sexism. A survey of employment advertisements showed that many specified physical attractiveness for positions like that of receptionist (Bell 1970:80). Even the use of the word *girl* rather than *woman* in such advertisements suggests that women's jobs are still considered by many to be "young girls' jobs, that is, the relatively unimportant work that a girl does before she gets married" (p. 80).

Women receive far less for their work than men—60 percent of the male rate in 1970 (Moser 1974:23). A key factor in this gap is, of course, the nature of the work that women do. As Moser indicates, "the issue of equal pay for equal work will not have its true impact until more men and women are actually doing the same work" (p. 24).

Another important difference between the work done by men and that done by women is in the work discontinuities experienced by women. Typically, a man will be in the labor force for "an unbroken block of some 40 years between leaving school and retirement " (Kutza 1975:6). Many women are in and out of employment, depending on circumstances at home. As women intermittently return to the labor force, they have to compete both with men and with younger women. The phenomenon of women's work discontinuities and the implications for employment training and other labor policies has not evoked much public interest (Kreps 1971b:viii). This is noteworthy, since women are not just brief visitors to the labor force scene. For example, on average, a 20-year-old wife with one child can expect to work for 25 years, and even a mother of four or more children will have a work life expectancy of 17 years (pp. 4–5). Furthermore, as families have fewer children, wives will be in the work force for longer periods.

The combination of restrictive jobs and the expectation of work discontinuities exerts a doubly damaging influence on women's work careers. Earlier in her married life a woman may opt not only for a woman's job but for one whose time pressures and work expectations do not interfere with family responsibilities. The woman thus becomes the "uncommitted worker whose work career is erratic and related primarily to the family welfare or economic necessity" (Payne and Whittington 1976:494).

As women reach middle age they face a different set of circumstances related to both work and income. If they are working, they will find that their salaries are still lower than those of men and lower than those of younger women as well. Only 20 percent of women are in top jobs such as manager or proprietor, although they earn 42 percent of all bachelor's and first professional degrees (Kreps 1971b:47). Many are likely to be classified as discouraged workers—people who have given up trying to find work. Their numbers do not appear in unemployment statistics, which include only people actually in the labor force, and though women over 45 have the lowest unemployment rate, the problem of their employment is hidden by their withdrawal from the roster of active job seekers (Moser 1974:19). Their discouragement is unfortunately well founded—in 1965 a Department of Labor report noted that half of the jobs in the private sector were closed to people over the age of 55 and one-fourth were unavailable to those past 45 (Bell 1970:78).

The continual increase in longevity, coupled with the unemployment and income picture for older women, leads to the observation that there will not only be "more and more surviving females" but also "more and more surviving poor females" (Trager 1975:ix). Women know both open and indirect bias, which limits their training opportunities and their access to a range of jobs and upward mobility. They suffer the effects of discontinuities and become discouraged workers, sometimes before they have even been workers at all. As they come to experience those systems that provide for the retirement years, they will find that biased inequities follow them there and further explain the dire straits of many elderly women.

## Women and Retirement

In a 1975 opinion Supreme Court Justice Brennan referred to "archaic" generalizations that "assume a man supports the family and women's earnings are not vital to its support" (Sommers 1975:268). In fact, the social security system as a whole is based on archaic assumptions about the work patterns of women and about family life. Essentially, the system rests on the expectation that a woman will marry, be dependent on her husband, and remain married to him until his retirement; that her attachment to the labor market will be a peripheral one; and that the work the woman does in the home is not real and valued work.

The operation of the social security system results in a number of clear inequities toward women. First, if a woman is married, her own contributions to the system during her work life (and this can be a considerable length of time) can count for little. Even if more than one person in the family works, the retirement benefits are based on only one income (the larger one).

A woman can receive benefits either based on her own work record, or, if married, upon a portion (50 percent) of her husband's benefits as his dependent, whichever is the highest. . . . Throughout their working life, these women are taxed individually upon their earned income just to find in retirement that they may be eligible for a higher benefit as a dependent of their husband. (Kutza 1975:6–7)

A woman who has worked a good part of her adult years may watch her never-employed female neighbor receive the same or more cash benefits from her husband's income without having made any contributions herself (Allan 1975:29). Sommers (1975:271) terms this "pay twice—collect once." There is, of course, no practical acknowledgment of the years of household work that the wife has provided. If (as is increasingly likely) the woman has divorced her husband before they have been married for 20 years, she receives no benefits at all. A woman might be married to one man for 10 years and another for 15 and collect nothing (Sommers 1974:8). If the woman's social security benefits derive solely from her own earnings, she will find that she continues to be penalized for the low-paid work into which the socialization process and society's biases have channeled her. "The average monthly cash benefits for retired workers, May 1974, were $204.45 for men and $163.52 for women" (Kutza 1975:10). This lower figure for women is of special significance, since more women (65 percent of all women who receive benefits) are receiving them in their own right rather than as wives of retired workers (p. 10). The very low average benefits serve to explain why so many elderly women are poor. In fact, social security income for elderly people keeps them close to the poverty line (Allan 1975:30).

There are additional inequities for the woman who is alone. If she is a widow, she will receive benefits only until her youngest child reaches 18, unless she is 60 by that time or completely disabled. These requirements affect especially the young, childless widow, often a person without previous employment and marketable skills. For the woman on her own in her later years, with an intermittent work history and faced with an age-biased employment market, there may be frantic and frustrating attempts to accumulate the necessary quarters of work (40 calendar quarters) to qualify for social security. Many other women, who are eligible for basic benefits, choose to retire before 65 because of the difficulty of finding continuing employment, even though any claim prior to age 65 results in lower monthly benefits for the remainder of their lives. As of 1970 half of women workers claimed benefits at age 62, and a total of 70 percent did not wait until they were 65 (Sommers 1975:270). The new liberal no-fault divorce laws may very well leave more and more women stranded after many years of either household work or an erratic, low-paid work career. Sommers (1974) comments on the irony that "while a massive child care bill was vetoed on the grounds that home care is essential to the fabric of American society, a homemaker receives not one penny in retirement benefits of her own" (p. 6).

Private pensions are not a recourse for most elderly women. First of all, pensions are in effect primarily in employment areas in which there is little female representation in the work force, so that few women can be directly covered by their own employment (Kutza 1975:11). Further, most private pension plans do not provide for widows—in 1974 only 2 percent of widows of husbands covered by such plans were receiving benefits (p. 13). Even if her husband was fully covered by a private pension plan and survivors' benefits were included, the widow receives no benefits should he die before the retirement age. The pension reform bill of 1974 did little to redress these inequities for women. Though survivors' benefits are now required in each plan, the employee can waive them, and death before retirement still leaves the widow without benefits (p. 13).

Much-needed changes have been proposed for the social security system. These include some form of work credit for the child-rearing years; excluding those years in averaging years of employment for purposes of establishing benefits; combination of the earnings of spouses so as to value both contributions in determining benefits; and alterations in the reduction in benefits prior to age 65 (Cohen 1975:97–98; Sommers 1975:275). Until such changes materialize, the social security system will do little to keep older women from poverty and will remain an extension of the marketplace that discriminates, overtly and covertly, against women.

## The Potentialities of Older Women

A major assumption of the preceding discussion has been that women experience their aging years differently than men. The understanding of these distinctions may suggest ways to provide more effective social intervention. The remainder of the discussion, as introduction to the presentation of specific programs, focuses on the potentialities of the older woman. Recent studies have highlighted the etiology of the difficulties of older women and have documented society's negative impact on them. Of equal importance are other studies that have suggested the potentialities of older women.

Research on the older woman is new. In fact, it is only somewhat younger than research on the elderly as a total group. It is in the past few decades, for example, that stereotypes about the intellectual capacities and sexuality of the aging as a group have been dispelled. Research on women as a separate group is just beginning, and even fairly recent reports on the aging as a whole ignore such research. For example, Butler, reporting in 1968, commented on "the predominant use of male subjects in the research literature on aging" (p. 236). Birren, in the same year, discussed principles of research in aging, delineating biological, social, and psychological ages but including no reference to sex differences. In specific areas such as retirement, emphasis has been placed on the man's retirement, with the suggestion in one commentary that because women's role remains unchanged through life, the transition is easier for them (Heyman 1970). Payne and Whittington (1976:488) refer to "the scientific indifference" to the separate study of males and females among the aging.

As recent attention has been addressed specifically to women, an interesting development has been the overrepresentation of women scholars in the field of social gerontology. It has been suggested that this may be because women identify with the devalued state of the elderly or that men, reflecting the rest of society may judge the study of the aging, particularly the aging woman, to be unimportant (Hochschild 1973b:144; Bart 1975:5). Scholars have begun to develop a literature on the older woman and have suggested further research approaches: the continued study of women "not just as a demographic category, or in relation to widowhood . . . [but in terms of] socialization for women and its consequences in aging" (Dunkel 1972:4); research into subgroups within the population of women (Payne and Whittington 1976:499); and use of sex as an independent variable to investigate "the complex of social differences between men and women" (p. 490). Even these early studies into the population of aging people and the older woman as a separate subgroup have developed important new understandings. These have included the elderly's intellectual capacity; the world of work for the elderly; possibilities of significant psychological changes, especially in older women; and the potential of social change, through naturally occurring demographic shifts as well as through the political activities of the elderly.

Research findings are accumulating that indicate that, barring ill health, aging does not inherently have an adverse effect on learning power (Comfort 1976:3; Eisdorfer 1969:237).

Studies made for the 1971 White House Conference on Aging found evidence that age has little to do with the ability to learn. Older persons can learn as well as young adults. Studies also showed that people tend to do better on tests measuring conceptual thinking as they grow older. A 1960 report by the Industrial Relations Division of the National Association of Manufacturers states that mature workers may learn differently, but they learn as well as younger persons, for through experience, the older worker has cultivated an ability to select, evaluate and grasp basic principles. (Allan 1975:27)

Further, older people have been found to be highly reliable in work situations, able to teach others well, and able to perform as good or even superior workers (Comfort 1975:27). In particular, older women have a greater sense of attachment to their job and are away less frequently because of illness than younger women (Allan 1975:27). Being at work in her later years appears to increase the older woman's general satisfaction with life (Maas and Kuypers 1974), a significant finding in light of the predicted continual increase in the number of women at work. "If present trends continue, by 1990, the number of working women in the United States will have increased 63 percent versus a male increase of 14 percent" (Trager 1975:xii). Much more needs to be done to facilitate the reentry of older women into the labor force, with a special sensitivity to the anxiety many older people feel about making the grade (Bilbin and Bilbin 1968:343). Kreps' (1971a) proposal for second-career training for everyone could be of special benefit to these women. The range of jobs open to women must be enlarged to increase their competencies, earning power, and retirement income. In sum, the world of work for older women will need continued expansion and cultivation in light of the increasing propensity for women to work throughout their adult lives; the thirty years the nonworking wife will live past the time her youngest child leaves home; the psychological value of work to all aging people, but especially to women who are normally restricted to the home; and their worth as workers in the marketplace.

There is accumulating evidence that women can change in significant psychological ways in their later years. At times, circumstances
in their current living situations foster this. As examples, older
women—Neugarten (1974:193) uses the term *young–old*, meaning
between the ages of 55 and 75—often have a living parent, which
contributes to their sense of youthfulness. Women who have had a
companionate marriage appear to have more personal resources to
adopt a new life style in widowhood than those who have experienced
a traditional marriage (Lopata 1973b:67). Many older women express
a desire for personal growth, to release themselves from family
boundaries (Lowenthal 1975:236), and as Livson (1976) suggests, it
may be that "parts of the personality that were suppressed because
they were not congruent with the roles of mother and young adult
may surface to add new dimensions to the person" (p. 108). Studies
indicate that women's behavior and outlook can alter significantly
after their 50s. Maas and Kuypers (1974:131) found that work-cen-
tered women expanded their interests in later years, becoming more
satisfied with their lives and exhibiting greater adaptation to changing
conditions than the men in their study groups. In fact, it is suggested
that expanding her role involvements—what Jacobson (1975) terms
having "multiple anchors"—enhances a woman's later years and encourages healthful psychological changes. Livson (1976) found that
women whose general health improved in their 50s were those who
were ambitious and unconventional and made a "dramatic rebound
in their intellectuality" (p. 112). Far from causing an inescapable
decline in later years, aging can "provide a second and better chance
at life," especially for women (Maas and Kuypers 1974:215).

As for social changes that may affect older women in a wider
arena, some writers suggest that the group of older people, living
longer and in more active ways, has great potential as social change
agents "to create an age-irrelevant society" (Neugarten 1974:187).
They are identified as the "assertive seniors" who are intent on fighting agism (Jacobs 1976:39). Bernard (1974) conjectures that the
middle-aged and aging groups of the 1990s are the ones who were
part of the protest against the Vietnam War as adults, were made

cynical by Watergate, and may be a force for change in their later years.

Clear nationwide shifts in the life styles of women may also portend social changes that will affect women in their later years. Women not only have more life style options available to them but appear to be acting on them. Predicted changes include greater emphasis on women's absorption in their own careers as they are no longer as dependent on the economic support of their husbands, elect not to have children, or choose not to marry at all (Kreps 1971b:104). It is clear that there is and will be a demand for greater options and life styles for women that will affect all their adult years, including their later ones.

In contrast to the picture drawn earlier in this chapter of the restrictive, stereotyped way in which most older women are viewed and act in our society, Sontag (1972) offers the possibility of a different older woman in the future. She suggests that women

can aspire to be wise, not merely nice; to be competent, not merely helpful; to be ambitious for themselves, not merely for themselves in relation to men and children. They can let themselves age naturally and without embarrassment, actively protesting and disobeying the conventions that stem from this society's double standard about aging. Instead of being girls, and girls as long as possible who then age humiliatingly into middle-aged women and then obscenely into old women, they can become women much earlier—and remain active adults. (p. 38)

## Services for the Older Woman

In the past decade a number of organizations have acted in behalf of older women within the political arena. Since the early 1970s, when more and more older women joined the National Organization for Women (NOW), that organization has had a special group for older women, first the Task Force on Older Women and now (1978) the Older Woman's Rights Committee. NOW has addressed such issues as the inequities of pensions and the social security system and various social manifestations of age discrimination, and as chapter 8 indicates, the work of the NOW did much to attract public attention to the needs of this group. The concern of the women's movement generally was reflected in the resolution on older women adopted at the International Women's Year convention in Houston in November 1977 (*Off Our Backs* 1978). That resolution stated in part

—that the federal and state governments, public and private women's organizations and social welfare groups should support efforts to provide sound
   health services
—innovative housing which creates as nearly as possible an environment
   that affords security and comfort
—home health and social services . . . that will offer older women alternatives to institutional care
—public transportation . . . for otherwise house-bound women
—continuing education
—elimination of the present inequities of Social Security benefits
—passage of the Displaced Homemakers' bill (p. 5)

Since 1970 the Gray Panthers has been an active political force for all the aging, and their "growing political effectiveness has been proved . . . with Congressional votes to raise the mandatory age to 70 for most Americans and to strengthen the Social Security System" (*New York Times* October 29, 1977).

In addition to benefiting from these political efforts, older women have been included in other programs and services. Colleges and universities have developed special sequences that foster the return of those students whose education has been interrupted. Although these programs serve students of all ages, many women past age 45 take advantage of these opportunities, and a few of these programs are focused specifically on women. Women have also been participants in the many senior centers throughout the country that serve the social and recreational needs of the elderly.

However, there appears to be a contrast, on the one hand, between the efforts of the women's movement and others to effect changes to benefit the older woman, as well as the many programs that include women, and on the other, the sparseness of services exclusively and specifically for the older woman developed from a nonsexist perspective. This observation is not meant to detract in any way from the importance of political efforts for the older woman or from any of the services that benefit older women, along with older men and younger women. It is meant to highlight the fact that comparatively few service programs address the distinctive issues faced by the older woman. To stress the need for that separate focus, two programs are described that emphasize the older woman's special concerns and do so from a feminist perspective. Women in Midstream is a program developed primarily around women's experience in menopause but expanded to include a range of issues that women face in their later years. The Widowed Information and Counseling Service serves mainly women and assumes a nonsexist stance in programs for them. To introduce the latter program, a discussion of some issues concerning widowhood is presented here.

## Widowhood

Widowhood is a common experience for the older woman, since women are far more likely than men to outlive their spouses. Given the average age of 56 at which the woman will be widowed, the typical married woman will face widowhood through the last twenty years of her life.

This discussion of older women as widows is based on two assumptions: (1) that widowhood is a major life stress for the older woman, though, as will be noted, there are compensations as well, and (2) that widowhood not only affects far more women than men but affects them in ways that reflect sex stereotypes.

Many widows are, of course, younger women in their twenties and thirties, though some of their concerns overlap those of their older counterparts. They share with older widows similar consequences of restrictive social roles that affect their capacity for self-support following the death of the spouse. Some issues, such as continuing child rearing alone, are unique to the younger group. The discussion of widows and the new services developed for them appears in this chapter on the older woman because the majority of widows are past 45 and their widowhood is compounded by the age-related factors considered earlier.

Holmes' scale (1967) of life stress places death of spouse at the top of the hierarchy of stressful events. This experience would seem to carry increased weight for the woman because of her psychological and material dependence on her husband, and because her family role has been the central one for her. When her husband dies, the wife suffers a number of losses that are distinctive for women. She loses the social status that her husband provided, and unless he had already retired, she experiences a drastic reduction in economic status as well. If she has not worked during the marriage, she is suddenly in the class of the unskilled and the unemployable (Jacobson 1975:3). If she has been in the work force, she will still suffer a marked decrease in family income. Further, she has lost the core of her life and can no longer enact a family-centered role, her major role (Maas and Kuypers 1974:206). Men may experience widowhood in a different and less devastating way than women because the marital role is only one of their life roles and not the primary one. From her study of widows Lopata (1972) comments on this status loss: "Few are able to use their own social roles to build a status equivalent to the one they carried by being married, by being married to that specific husband, and by belonging to various status groups through this social role" (p. 285).

The grieving process may in many ways be the same for men and women, and a large literature has developed offering important insights into the impact of death on an intimate (Parkes 1972). The new services for widows use this knowledge to be more sensitive to the stages of grief these women can be expected to experience. For the widow, the grief may be not only for the person of her husband but for the social milieu of their life together. The most important change is that she is now alone. Her childhood or adult life has not prepared her for this state, and little in this youth-, male-, and couple-oriented society will help her develop that state comfortably and creatively for herself. It has been suggested that widows suffer grief and require attention over a longer period because of these societal constraints (Barrett 1973).

Widowhood requires independence of action, while much traditional marriage relations call for a passive stance. Most widows report that loneliness is their most serious problem and appear hampered by lack of skills in assertively forming new relationships or developing new roles (Lopata 1973b:216). Though, in one study, black women stated that lack of finances was their most serious concern, they were, in fact, as socially isolated as other widows (Lopata 1973a). Widows may very well need both training in responsibilities previously assumed by their husbands and socialization for independent living (Lopata 1971).

Lopata has compiled a list of factors that constrain widows from full participation in modern society:

1. Widows are not married, in a society in which not having a mate is a handicap;
2. They feel they are second-class citizens in that "friends avoid them in an attempt to ignore the whole subject of death and grief";
3. They have been trained to be passive wives in a sexist society. They find it difficult to establish themselves independently and often suffer the effects of sexism in that attempt;
4. They know the bias and discrimination experienced by all older people, making it particularly difficult to find new employment and new social roles;
5. To compound agism and sexism, they are often members of ethnic minority groups and "must face, in addition, all the problems of their social race identity";
6. They are often poor, many becoming poor at the onset of widowhood. Their life must be restricted because of this and they must share the stigma of all the poor;
7. They are not knowledgeable about worldly affairs. (p. 75)

It is important to add that studies of widowhood also report compensations and positive occurrences in the lives of some widows. These women state that they do not necessarily wish to remarry. Many learn to live alone happily and report feeling freer and more independent than in marriage, experiencing "an independence denied . . . in earlier periods of . . . life" (Payne and Whittington 1976:494).

Given variations in ultimate adjustments, women who are widowed, usually older women, are affected not only by the loss of the marital relationship but also by the cluster of factors discussed earlier in this chapter. Newly developed services for widows recognize that widows face not only grieving but the effects of these factors.

## The Widowed Information and
## Consultation Service

In part, the Widowed Information and Consultation Service of Seattle has based its services on the pioneering work of Phyllis Silverman (1974) and the Boston Widowed to Widowed Program, in which the concept of services by the widowed to other widowed people was first developed. In another sense, the Seattle WICS is part of other grassroots movements that see the need for women to take control of their own lives. The WICS combines those two principles to provide widows with opportunities to resolve their grief and to develop new skills and options in their lives. The plan for having widowed people serve other widowed individuals, begun by the Boston group and developed in a few other centers such as the Widowed Services Program of Eugene, Oregon, is a creative use of one group of people for the benefit of others who share a common experience. The WICS of Seattle is described here because it not only has adopted this model of service as the format of its widowed program but also has stressed a nonstereotyped approach to women.

The program was begun in 1974 by two women, one a widow of the Vietnam conflict and the other a professional counselor. The program has served 1,400 widowed individuals since 1974, the great majority of whom were women between the ages of 45 and 65, 90 percent having been homemakers through most of their married life. The services are offered through group experiences, individual counseling, and referrals to other agencies and community groups, and include grief work, practical problem solving (legal, financial, vocational), new-life planning, and information and referral.

The program shares with other innovative programs the plan for services offered by other widows and widowers, and much of the program, particularly the grief work, is common to both men and women. However, this description emphasizes the services that are distinctive to women. The format for this discussion is a series of observations about the particular issues faced by women who are widows and the manner in which the services developed at WICS respond to each issue.

WICS encourages a nontraditional view of women within the

framework, shared by other new programs, of service by widowed people to other widows and widowers. Like these programs, WICS offers both group and individual services and uses widowed volunteers. Also like other programs, they canvass vital statistics records and write to newly widowed individiuals to inform them of the availability of WICS services. A pool of 300 volunteers is used, with matching done wherever possible, so that the volunteers and the person served have something in common, such as age, geographic area, or similar experiences. For example, if a widow is faced with a particular legal or financial difficulty WICS tries to refer her to a volunteer who has dealt with a similar predicament. A portion of each cohort of widows served wants to continue to be useful to the program and joins the roster of volunteers.

Among the issues that are of special concern to women is the fact that the widow usually is faced with the end of a marriage in which her life centered in her home and in which skills other than home-centered ones were not developed. Though there is much variability in the degree of the wife's passivity in the relationship, many widows report that their husbands were the dominant partners, were opposed to their wives' working outside the home, and controlled much of the important family planning. Many widows express frustration about their years of "knuckling under" and the lost time in which they did not pursue their own interests and abilities. The individual and group efforts in the program are attuned to the ambivalence women feel in this situation: loyalty to the husband who has died and a strong emotional tie to their years together, but also anger at the lives they, as wives, accepted in order to keep peace in the family. The individual and group experiences include attention to this ambivalence in the grieving process but are particularly sensitive to the consequences for women that result from the social expectations of a traditional marriage and the potential they now have to take more control of their own lives.

Possibilities for such control arise, as one example, in the frequent need for widows to deal with attorneys, banks, and other business organizations in settling their affairs and arranging for independent living. Many women have traditionally left these transactions to their husbands and, as a consequence, feel incompetent and even apprehensive at the prospect of such interactions. The program is responsive to these concerns in several ways. The staff may perform advocacy services through direct contact with the professionals involved—often a widow who has experienced and resolved the same dilemma and is now a volunteer for WICS will perform this function. More likely, the program will help the widow develop the skills to deal with the situation herself. She will be prepared for the encounter through behavioral rehearsal and by the staff's alerting her to what she might expect. She will be prepared with the materials and documents she might need for the interview and with the questions she needs to ask. Bank personnel and trust officers are often patronizing to the widow, reflecting the stereotyped view of women as limited in their ability to conduct financial or legal transactions. The widow will be helped not only to anticipate these attitudes but also, through the development of a confident, competent stance, to alter these stereotyped views. She will also be advised of free services that she might appropriately request from banks and trust divisions. WICS also tries to refer widows to attorneys who respect the widow's ability to take a more responsible role in estate planning, thereby reinforcing such behaviors. By these various means some widows learn about financial investments and assume responsibility for their own investment decisions rather than turning their money over to men to manage for them.

WICS has also found that people close to the widow, reflecting a more general view, assume that a woman cannot be seen as a competent adult if she is on her own. She has now become the son or daughter's responsibility or is just temporarily alone until the advent of a new marriage; she is not seen by others as an independent single adult. The view is manifested as her adult children, other relatives, and friends constantly give her advice—about where she should live, whether she whould work, how she should manage her money, whether she should remarry. In fact, many referrals to WICS come from people who have been active in advice-giving and assumption of responsibilities, but now want the widow "taken off their hands." The widow is particularly vulnerable to active intervention by various people. For example, widows frequently sell or give away material possessions such as residences and sources of income such as businesses to people who convince them that such items are no longer needed. The widow accedes because she as well as the others do not see her as capable of using these possessions or of making decisions about them. Other people may also reinforce the apprehensions she may have about living alone by urging her to change to some form of protected or group living.

In the face of all this advice-giving and the forces pulling her away from independence, WICS urges the widow to place emphasis on what she wants. It anticipates with her that others will urge courses of action upon her, but it encourages her to think of herself as an independent person. It suggests that she not discuss her finances even with her children, and that she resist the pressures to change her living situation until she is sure of what she wants to do with her life. Instead of succumbing to others' fears about her safety and agreeing with their suggestions that she alter her living arrangements because of this, WICS recommends other alternatives, such as an alert system in the neighborhood for mutual safety. Instead of hasty decisions, they recommend taking time to consider alternatives. Many widows state that they are unsure of who they are now that they are alone, and feel that they have few capabilities. The staff and the widowed volunteers assure them that they have abilities, that they can learn to make decisions, and that they need not respond passively to the urgings of others. Women begin to learn that they can assume responsibility for actions ranging from doing minor home repairs (or finding competent help to do them) to making vocational plans. Women also learn to give themselves permission to begin a social life in a world considerably different from the one they knew as younger women. They learn to look after their own needs, and they learn to assert themselves. During the time they are in contact with Widowed Information, there is an emphasis on developing self-confidence with no pressure to date or pair off, or to find a mate and remarry. There is gentle encouragement to the widow to develop her abilities and skills and to gain self-confidence.

A large part of WICS' efforts consists of suggesting options to widows and helping them increase their social skills in order to use these options. Instead of seeing another marriage or a life of dependence on relatives as the only possibilities, the widow is encouraged to see a single, independent life as a viable alternative. In the case of women who choose or need to work, the staff and volunteers help them value the skills they have developed as part of the homemaker role. Maturity and responsibility are presented as marketable assets in the business world, supplemented by training as needed. Referrals are made to community colleges and other resources for vocational counseling, career planning, and training, as well as for assertion training when needed. Widows also work with WICS to construct job resumes that tap the varied experiences they have had as homemakers and wives. These are often directly applicable to the world of paid employment, but most women have been taught to devalue their nonpaid work at home or in the volunteer sector. Since for a woman in her middle years the experience of not being hired can result in her feeling that she is unemployable and not worthy, the service tries to help her prepare planfully for job seeking. Referrals are also made to reputable groups serving the social needs of single people, and behavioral rehearsal for these encounters are provided when needed.

Assertion training has been found to be useful for interpersonal as well as vocational purposes. Since women have basically been encouraged to be passive, they often find it difficult to assert themselves to ask friends for assistance. They also find it difficult to accept favors from others when they are feeling vulnerable and unable to "pay people back." Women have been acculturated to believe it is all right for them to give to others but not all right for others to give to them. Assertiveness can be useful in helping women accept the appropriateness of asking for and receiving assistance from others, as well as setting limits on what they are able to do and learning to say no.

In several other ways WICS tries to break down the widow's stereotypic thinking about herself and others. In a mixed men's and women's group discussion series, widows and widowers are encouraged to relate to one another in other than the stereotyped ways. The widow can begin to see that she can interact with men in a nonsexist manner and can see that men share the commonality of the grieving process. The women are also encouraged to see that men have been stereotyped into certain behaviors as well, and that they share some of the same difficulties in making new social relationships. The group experience also helps women explore personal possibilities different from their traditional passive role in marriage; now they have an opportunity either to function as an independent single person or to take a more assertive stance in another relationship.

Another breakdown of stereotyped attitudes occurs as women learn to trust other women. Often this is the first time that they have formed friendships with women outside of marriage, and with women who are not part of a couple. Widowhood inevitably brings changes in friendship patterns. In groups and/or individual encounters with the widow volunteers, widows form friendships with women based on who they are as individuals, not on any competitive basis or reflective only of the men in their lives. Through contact with widows who have made healthy adjustments to their loss, women learn that they can be supportive of each other, rather than competitive. They describe these friendships as revelations to them, echoing what women of different ages and different circumstances have widely reported as a consequence of other activities of the women's movement.

Finally, women learn to counteract the stereotypic view that places the highest premium on the married state for women, and they begin to see compensations in widowhood. They find advantages in new freedoms. They do not have to minister to another person's needs— "I don't have to pick up after him any longer." They can return to interests they dropped when they married, or develop new ones. They find great satisfaction in learning to manage completely on their own, often for the first time in their lives. As they find satisfactions in taking responsibility for their own lives, they learn that it is all right to release old friends and to make new ones. Giving oneself permission to move on and grow personally is a large part of the grief process.

To many widows, the group discussion series is an important part of the service. Mixed-sex groups (though mostly women) meet for eight weeks in a loosely structured format. The participants may vary considerably in the recency of their widowhood (from a few months to several years), but work on the resolution of grief is part of each group experience. This grief work also attempts to teach the widow how to look to her own inner resources to survive, tapping the talents she has and obtaining the reinforcement that was formerly provided by one other person from her own inner strengths and from new relationships.

Much time is also spent in the group on practical problems facing the widow, on new alternatives for living, and on new personal relationships. Much reinforcement is given to the women participants for any successes, however small, in independent and autonomous actions.

The extent to which widows use the program varies according to the individual. Some just call to request answers to particular practical questions or referrals to community agencies; some accept a visit or series of visits from a volunteer; others attend the group discussion series and financial or vocational planning sessions; some use individual counseling. Some continue to drop in occasionally after they have used the service, and some become volunteers. Some widows contact the service to respond to a volunteer's call soon after their husband's death; others wait months or even years before responding.

Whatever the extent of the widow's interactions with the service, WICS builds its program around the combination of sensitivity to the grieving process and those implications of the widowed state common to both men and women, and the special circumstances of women who are widowed.

## Women in Midstream

JULIE CAMPBELL, IRMA LEVINE,
AND JANE PAGE

In 1972 several of the middle-aged women serving on the University of Washington (Seattle) YWCA's board of directors suggested that the organization consider investigating health problems related to older women. The YWCA already included a health clinic (Aradia) that served mainly young women.

It was agreed that the central health question for women in middle age was menopause, so the Ad Hoc Committee on Menopause was formed.

The committee decided first to gather information from women who had already experienced menopause. They compiled a questionnaire to be answered anonymously, and proceeded to distribute it to elderly women. The committee members approached groups of women in retirement homes and various senior citizen clubs, but these women were reluctant to answer such personal questions; most refused altogether.

Questionnaires were also sent at random to a number of women's groups. The response to this effort was meager; 70 out of 1,000 were returned.

Then the project received some unexpected newspaper publicity. A syndicated column, "Women Alone," appearing in newspapers across the country included a report about the Ad Hoc Committee's efforts to gather information on menopause. With that, the YWCA was inundated with requests for the questionnaire. Fortunately, the column did not appear in very large metropolitan newspapers because the YWCA had only a small volunteer staff to handle mail. Requests came in from places ranging from Binghamton, New York, to Hermosa Beach, California. But the majority were from the Seattle metropolitan area.

Many of the requests for questionnaires were accompanied by personal letters describing the physical and emotional difficulties women were experiencing. Two themes were repeated time after time: These women had felt patronized, if not ignored, by their doctors, and they felt isolated and embarrassed about discussing their difficulties.

The Ad Hoc Committee realized that it had hit a nerve, that hundreds of women throughout the country needed information about menopause. Of the 1,200 questionnaires sent out, over 700 were returned.

The first task for the committee was to gather as much information as possible. Two of the members interviewed doctors in the Seattle area. They found wide differences of opinion among them about both menopausal symptoms and their treatment.

All available books and pamphlets were also surveyed. These sources, too, revealed a wide range of opinion, especially about the desirability of hormonal treatments for menopausal symptoms.

By this time the Ad Hoc Committee on Menopause had decided to become a permanent group. It broadened its name to Women in Midstream, or WIM (combining the ideas of "mid-life" and "mainstream") because it had learned that during the physical transition of menopause women often confront other problems as well, with emotional, social, and economic causes.

## Programs

WIM's programs encompass two major functions: disemination of information and counseling/support for women.

### DISSEMINATION OF INFORMATION

#### Newsletter

WIM has tried to send out a regular newsletter (usually quarterly), but because the group has until recently depended entirely on volunteer help it has been unable to maintain that schedule. Now that WIM has acquired two part-time paid employees (with CETA funding), the quarterly mailing should again be possible. The mailing list has grown to 2,200 names, with the majority in the Seattle metropolitan area but also with a wide national range.

The newsletter has kept women informed about current information concerning both menopause and general health care. It has been especially useful as a means of reassuring women as controversies have arisen over the wisdom of using hormone therapy to treat menopausal symptoms. Though WIM never offers medical advice and always urges women to consult their doctors about specific problems, it has been able to describe other women's experiences.

For example, several correspondents have reported that they had difficulties with depression and nervous tension when they abruptly stopped taking estrogen, and recommended that others who wished to stop the therapy taper off gradually.

The newsletter is also used to report new books and magazine articles that are relevant to women's health, and occasionally includes a more complete review of a book that may be especially helpful.

And of course the newsletter is used to announce any new programs or discussion groups that WIM may be planning.

### Correspondence

The volume of mail received by WIM varies from one month to the next. Occasionally requests for information will flood the office after the group has received special publicity. Last year, for example, a doctor mentioned WIM in his syndicated newspaper column, which appeared in the Chicago and Sacramento areas. The office received several hundred requests for information at that time. The mail ranged from detailed descriptions of individuals' problems to a postcard with the scrawled message "Please help me."

In response to these requests WIM mailed a summary of the most recent information on the possible risks of estrogen replacement therapy for menopause and a list of readings on the subject.

### Speaking Engagements

Since WIM was founded, the group has received numerous requests for speakers. These have come mainly from professional groups and college classes. A staff person has taken the principal responsibility for these presentations. Each quarter she speaks to women's studies classes at the University of Washington and to several other classes at community colleges throughout the state. The presentations include descriptions of women's menopausal experiences and their physiological and emotional causes, as well as some of the things women can do to help themselves through these sometimes trying symptoms. It is encouraging to see the interest among young women, reflected in the questions they ask about themselves and the concerns they show for their mothers.

Besides the women's studies classes, WIM members have also spoken to women medical and nursing students. This audience was especially pleased with the additions WIM was able to make to their limited information about menopause. WIM members have also participated in older women's health care workshops and seminars, and have spoken to various women's clubs and groups throughout the state.

### Book Publication

After a few months' operation WIM decided that there were probably several thousand women throughout the country who would want a book about menopause that not only included medical information but also reflected the experiences of other women in this stage of life. The book, *The Other Awkward Age, Menopause* (Page 1977), includes a medical description of menopause, accounts of women's experiences with both menopause and other crises of middle age, summaries of a variety of doctors' opinions about the treatment of menopausal symptoms, and suggestions about things women can do themselves to deal with the experience. The book emphasizes the necessity for women to take responsibility for their own health care by understanding their own bodies and seeking solutions to their own problems.

## COUNSELING AND SUPPORT FOR WOMEN

### Individual Counseling

The WIM office receives several telephone calls every week from women seeking information. Until recently this service was strictly limited by its dependence on volunteer help and occasional work–study students. Too often a caller received no answer at all to her call, or, if a message were left, its response was often delayed. Now that WIM has regular staff members, this kind of service will be greatly enhanced.

The telephone inquiries range from the woman who is seeking a doctor referral because she is new in town to women in distress and in need of immediate counseling.

Questions pertaining to menopause generally arise because the woman has received inadequate information from her doctor. A

WIM staff member will talk over the symptoms the caller is experiencing, reassuring her that these are frequent and normal complaints. She is encouraged to join a group or read some material provided by WIM so that she will become better informed about her body and how it functions.

Anyone with serious medical or emotional problems is encouraged to see a physician or is referred to a therapist for more professional help. If she needs emotional support while visiting the doctor, WIM will provide an advocate to accompany her.

Occasionally a caller will want to come into the office to talk over her problems. In such a case she will meet with a sympathetic listener and peer counselor, but not a professional therapist. Once her situation is clarified she will be referred to appropriate community agencies for whatever help is necessary. These may include medical, legal, employment, and/or housing referrals.

*Support Groups*

From the beginning WIM has recognized the value of encouraging women to talk with each other about troublesome life situations. WIM has been fortunate in that one of its members has had a considerable amount of training and experience in guiding such groups.

So far WIM has conducted only daytime groups, but with its present additional staffing it hopes to organize an evening group as well.

WIM has offered awareness groups for the past three years, with varying success. During 1977 six to eight women met together in regular weekly sessions throughout most of the year. Occasionally others would join this nucleus for one or two sessions. In the spring and summer of 1976, five or six women formed a "walk and talk" group in which they would take a short hike, then stop for lunch and talk informally about their concerns.

So far this year (1978) there seems to be less interest among callers in participating in an ongoing group. A few women have met for one or two sessions but have not participated regularly.

Sometimes a woman will join a group for one meeting, express her feelings openly, and never return. WIM has come to feel that even such a brief experience may be valuable to these individuals. By expressing their feelings they have perhaps relieved the buildup of emotional pressure that could not be released in other ways.

WIM's groups are best described as "awareness" groups because their emphasis is on encouraging women to think about the image they have of themselves. Too many middle-aged women do not have a strong sense of self-worth. In fact, this may be one reason that the response to WIM's groups has been uneven—some women feel they should not spend time and money (a small fee is requested) "just on themselves."

Aside from specific physical menopausal symptoms, the problems women want to discuss with others arise from two main causes: dependency and suppressed anger. Although these emotions are not directly related to the physical aspects of menopause, they are occurring at a time when women are experiencing the physical instabilities of menopause and therefore are unusually susceptible to depression.

For example, one recent participant, who came to the group for nine months, had been widowed for one year and knew she was not handling her grief adequately. She told of her loneliness and depression over missing her husband. She had thought of herself as an independent individual and was angry that at almost 60 years of age she was not able to cope even with her finances. She suffered constant turmoil about her bank and its computers. Although she was fortunate in having adequate funds, she felt overwhelmed by the responsibility of managing them. After expressing such emotions for several months, she decided she should seek some new experiences and is now attending a special college program for the older student.

Another woman attending this group had been separated from her husband for five years. She had finally decided to initiate divorce proceedings but still saw herself as a failure. Her children disapproved of her decision, and she felt guilty that she was not living up to their expectations. The group members tried to encourage her to think about what was best for her, to decide that this time her interests came ahead of her family's.

Several women who had spent years as supermoms, always subordinating their desires to others' demands, have described the anger and emptiness they feel when their children leave. It is not so much that they miss their presence as that their purpose for living has disappeared. It is often more frightening than challenging to find new reasons for going on.

The routine followed by the groups is designed to encourage women to value themselves. At every session each participant is asked to brag about something she has done for herself during the week. If she cannot do that, she is asked to tell the group her good personal characteristics in a positive, unqualified way (i.e., "I'm an intelligent person," not "I'm a fairly intelligent person").

Those who want to talk about something are allotted time, with the amount determined by the time left in the session and the number who wish to speak. It is always understood that what is said is strictly confidential, and advice or criticism is not offered unless asked for. Other women may share their own similar experiences. The purpose of the group is to provide freedom for expression of feelings and ideas in an atmosphere of acceptance and support.

The group is not encouraged to be dependent on one leader who is a source of special wisdom. The facilitator always explains her methods, her reasons for using them, and the source from which she learned them. Thus, although it is important that the group be given some structure, there is no authority figure to lead the way.

*Future Plans*
Much of WIM's time in the near future will be spent on the distribution of the book *The Other Awkward Age*. Other plans include an evening group with a different format. It will be called "Read and Rap" and will use books that the women themselves will select for discussion. In the spring WIM will again offer an easy-hike and rap group for older women, which will involve walking in parks and byways in the vicinity of Seattle.

WIM is also working to develop a job referral support group whose members will update job leads and career resources into a working file.

WIM will continue to seek ways to help women in crisis by forming better communication links with agencies and programs dealing with housing, food, clothing, abuse, and divorce.

For years WIM has had other projects that it has intended to undertake but could not because of the lack of staff. Perhaps now some of those projects may be realized. They include a workshop on menopause for both nonprofessional women and health care deliverers; a slide show to assist in speaking engagements; and a traveling program that could be taken to other parts of the state and country to tell older women how they, too, could get something organized for women of their age in their communities.

## Concluding Remarks

In the introduction to this book it was noted that a matter of great concern is the exclusion of some programs because of lack of awareness about them. The area of the aging woman was particularly troubling in this regard. Though a number of inquiries were made, including some to national figures in the field of aging, the Women in Midstream program was the only one identified that extended its services to the older woman exclusive of any other status. As indicated earlier, services are available to older women because they are among the widowed or displaced homemakers or returning students, or part of a mixed-sex elderly group. Little was found in the way of programs for older women considered separately. There would seem to be some hindrance to responding to the needs of the older woman solely in the recognition that aging per se is problematic for the woman.

To the extent that such reluctance is there, and is not an artifact of information-gathering shortcomings, there may be an issue of concern to feminist service providers. It is possible, of course, that the older woman herself may not see the need for this exclusive treatment. If the problem for her is the death of her husband or the obsolescence of her homemaker role or the difficulties of resuming a long-interrupted education or the need for social companionship, inclusion in a group with men or younger women may not be an issue. Clearly, each of these avenues serves vital purposes. Many are provided from a feminist perspective, and the influence of the woman's aging on each of the other circumstances is considered. This summarizing point is not meant to deflect from current political activities with potential to alter crucial, practical aspects of the aging woman's condition.

A gnawing concern remains, however, that the distinctive effects on women of the aging process, in and of itself, is somehow not receiving needed attention. Such services may turn out to be vehicles for a more complete understanding of how women experience aging and a rich opportunity, within a feminist context, for the sharing of such experiences among older women.

# 8. The Displaced Homemaker

DONA LANSING BRACHT

THE RECOGNITION of displaced homemakers as a distinct group in need of social services grew out of the National Organization for Women's interest in the special problems of older women. Many women who devote 15 to 35 years to an unpaid career as a homemaker suddenly find themselves alone without enough money for self-sufficiency, and often encounter job discrimination because of their age or lack of past paid employment. The role change from homemaker to wage earner presents a unique combination of personal and economic problems. This chapter is concerned with the analysis of these problems and new service programs designed to meet the needs of this special population.

Although definitional criteria do vary from one state to another, a woman labeled "displaced homemaker" is likely to fit the following description:

1. She is between the ages of 35 and 65.
2. By virtue of divorce, widowhood, or unemployment of her spouse, she needs to find employment in order to survive.
3. Since she has spent most of her adult life in the role of homemaker, she is not entitled to unemployment insurance or social security. She may also lose health insurance benefits.
4. She has no recent paid work experience.

5. She often collects no alimony or child support.
6. Her children are usually over 18, and she does not qualify for AFDC.

It is estimated that there are between 3 and 7 million displaced homemakers in the United States today. An accurate statistical profile of this group is difficult to ascertain. This is partly because of the recent recognition of this population and partly because of the multiple variables that characterize the group.

While it may be difficult to give accurate data on the number of displaced homemakers on a national basis, selected sources render a statistical picture of "potential" numbers and further define the breadth of the problem. Prior to enactment of the California Displaced Homemaker Act (1976), testimony provided by the Los Angeles County Department of Social Services documented that one-third of all people on *general* relief in Los Angeles County were displaced homemakers. Of this number, 35% had been on the welfare rolls continuously for three years (Chen 1977). Census Bureau data (1975) indicate that 37% of American women over the age of 40 are without husbands. One-third of all women between the ages of 55 and 64 are on their own, and most do not qualify for social security. A total of 6.1 million women under the age of 60 are not in the labor force. Of the 7.2 million women who are heads of families, half have not obtained high school diplomas. Of additional interest in the fact that one out of three marriages is likely to end in divorce. Especially significant is the number of marriages that break up after 20 years.

Part of the dilemma faced by the displaced homemaker is best described as a unique combination of situational and institutional circumstances that come together to limit employment options. In addition to these variables, the transition to the world of paid employment is thwarted by the woman's values, attitudes, and established behaviors. As a background to describing current displaced homemaker services, this chapter discusses three major social and personal impediments to what may aptly be termed "a forced mid-life transition": First, from a sociological perspective the discriminatory aspects of the *legal system* are highlighted; second, the rapidly changing and technological *job market* is addressed; and third, the limitations and strengths of the *housewife role* are discussed in light of their socializing effects on the displaced homemaker.

A major assumption behind services directed at this population is that homemaking is a learned role and many of its tasks are transferable to a paid-employment setting. However, certain internalized values and behaviors associated with "housewifery" appear to be incompatible with the competitive demands of the "paycheck" world. The impact of each of these variables is further intensified by the emotional crisis resulting from divorce or the death of a spouse. There is little time for "grief work" when the immediate imperative is basic survival.

## The Displaced Homemaker and the Law

A review of the laws that directly affect married and divorced women reflects a legal system that is slow to respond to the changing nature of marriage and family in the United States today. Although several states are adopting more progressive laws with regard to divorce and the division of property, many statutes remain (even in progressive states) that perpetuate discrimination against married and divorced women. During the past century the courts in most states have consistently upheld the notion that it is a wife's duty to provide uncompensated services in the home and a husband's obligation to provide financial support for his family. The fact that women now constitute 40 percent of the labor force contradicts legal assumptions regarding the man as the sole supporter of his family (Weitzmann 1977). Contracts in which a man agrees to pay his wife for domestic services have not been upheld by the courts. The law states that "one of the implied terms of the contract of marriage is that the wife's services will be performed without compensation" (p. 292). If she decides to engage in paid employment, she is legally expected to do two jobs. Thus, the law plays a significant role in devaluing the importance of the wife's labor in the home. As Kay (1974) has noted, "When a woman's labor is seen as a service she owes her husband rather than a job deserving the dignity of economic return, the ultimate result is one of devaluation and underestimation of her contributions" (p. 142).

The implications of an antiquated legal system for the displaced homemaker are somewhat ironic. She is likely to feel that she is being punished for doing what the law insisted that she do. The provision of alimony by most states suggests that the law recognizes the economic and occupational barriers faced by a divorced middle-aged woman. As Weitzman (1977) notes, "Because the law encourages a woman to give up her independent earning potential in favor of marriage, the provision of alimony is based on the assumption that women have done just this and are, as a result, incapable of independent financial survival" (p. 291). However, alimony is awarded in only 15 percent of all divorce cases. The "legal" recognition of the husband as head of the household is used by creditors as justification for granting a married woman credit in her husband's name. The absence of a spouse through death or divorce means that the woman will have to establish financial credibility all over again. In the 42 states having separate property systems, the husband is declared the sole owner of property acquired in his name since the time of marriage.

The insidious effect of a legal system that diminishes the status of women can be understood from two standpoints. First of all, the discriminatory regulations that permeate American social institutions (i.e., marriage, family, and industry) are derived from the law's assumptions regarding the "oughts and shoulds" of male and female roles. The persistence of such assumptions thwarts the displaced homemaker's attempt at achieving personal security after years of service in a role whose boundaries are legally defined. Second, the displaced homemaker's diminished sense of personal worth is partly a result of the law's opinion of her contributions.

## The Displaced Homemaker
## and the Job Market

Several socioeconomic factors as well as a sexually segregated occupational system combine to produce what is to the displaced homemaker an impenetrable job market. While statistics show that middle-aged women are increasingly visible in the work force, women's overall economic position has deteriorated during the past fifteen years. Women continue to be segregated into low-status, low-paying jobs. Between 1960 and 1974 women's full-time medial earnings relative to men's dropped from 61 percent to 56 percent. The rates of female unemployment have been increasing relative to the rates for males. In 1960, female unemployment rates were 9 percent higher than males'. In 1974, unemployment rates for women were 31 percent higher than those for men (USDOL, Women's Bureau 1975:131).

Another factor that has shaped employment opportunities for women is the fact that they have historically constituted a reserve on the labor market. Their job market participation has been temporary and intermittent. If a displaced homemaker worked prior to her marriage or occasionally throughout it, she is likely to discover that prospective employers consider her lacking in technically *current* skills and theoretical knowledge (Gubbels 1977). The author's experience with this group supports the assumption that employers are more likely to hire a younger woman for jobs that entail a period of training.

For the homemaker, the occurrence of "displacement" involves much more than being fired or laid off from a job. Many homemakers believe that their jobs are expressions of affection for their husband and children (Feldberg and Kohen 1976). Research shows that homemakers separate the work from the role and that while they may find aspects of the former unpleasant, they prefer the latter to employment outside the home (Oakely 1974). However, this could be an expression of a preference based on the limitations and realities of the current job market; that is, there is a greater sense of personal freedom attributed to the role of homemaker than to that of telephone operator or waitress. Thus, many displaced homemakers find the idea of paid work distasteful; or, given the nature of the job market, the jobs they would like to have are not realistically possible for them.

## The Displaced Homemaker and
## the Homemaker Role

The emotional and interpersonal problems most often experienced by the displaced homemaker can best be understood as an intensification of those problems which are common to women as a group. They include low-esteem, depression, low frequency of assertive behaviors, and anxiety. Such problems and their concomitant behaviors are particularly dysfunctional for the displaced homemaker owing to the strenuous demands of her current circumstances, for example, job hunting and coping with feelings of loss and rejection due to divorce or death of the spouse. Bernard (1972) contends that traditional marriage makes women increasingly helpless, submissive, and conservative. The literature on depression, anxiety, and self-esteem is replete with data attesting to the high incidence of depressive illness among the homemaker population (Beck and Greenberg 1974). Glazer and Waehrer (1977) offer the following description of a "wife's" role that highlights the incompatibility of homemaking with independent achievement.

Marriage defines a woman's responsibilities and her appropriate social character. She does housework and cares for her children, while her husband leaves home to earn a living for the family. If she holds a job outside the home, she must not take it seriously. In her role as wife she is expected to be dependent and acquiescent; in her role as mother she is expected to be independent and assertive. She must be more concerned with meeting the emotional needs of her husband and children than with growing through an understanding of her own needs; this proves she has the so called "giving ability" of the mature woman. She must cope with a technical, bureaucratic society without having been encouraged, usually, to develop the necessary logic and assertiveness to do so. Furthermore, she must somehow manage to remain an interesting person in her own right, sexually and emotionally attractive to her husband and to other men (though disinterested in other men). (p. 228)

While certain personal and vocational aspects of the homemaker role may be incompatible with the structural demands of paid employment, it must be emphasized that the variety of skills that the homemaker acquires have much (albeit unrecognized) value. If she has been involved in community projects, she has probably developed certain organizational and managerial skills of which she is unaware. In addition, homemakers have developed hidden expertise in home decorating, gourmet cooking, sewing, the ability to stretch a dollar, child management (and/or psychology), and the ability to juggle several projects simultaneously. They might well be called the most expert of all generalists, though highly underpaid at that!

In assessing which personal and situational factors make it more or less difficult for the displaced homemaker to complete the necessary role changes, the following variables and observations (obtained from the author's research) are worth mentioning here:

1. The experience of displacement as described previously not only constitutes a mid-life crisis but provides a situation for significant new learning. For example, assertiveness training designed specifically for this population can bring about new behavior patterns that facilitate the task of seeking employment.

2. The idea of structured, paid employment is less distasteful to those women who grew up in homes in which their mother worked outside the home.

3. Emotional factors (e.g., sense of loss, rejection, low self-esteem) can interfere with the ability to utilize available job readiness training. Those who provide services to the displaced homemaker must be aware of the behavioral and emotional issues that preclude successful reentry into the job market.

4. According to the author's observations, peer support groups are most effective with structured outcome goals in addition to open-ended rap sessions. For example, behavioral role play and rehearsal of an actual job interview is more useful (in real job interview situations) than hearing about the anxiety and fears experienced by others during similar situations.

5. For some women, the idea of "performing" in a world of external evaluation is very frightening. This fear of a competitive situation represents itself in statements such as "I don't want to work—I never did." Such an attitude constitutes another aspect that must be assessed and dealt with as early as possible.

## Existing Services for
### Displaced Homemakers

The following section describes the thrust of current programs that provide vocational training and personal counseling specifically to the

displaced homemaker. As of this writing several states have implemented such programs, and a national displaced homemaker bill for
purposes of funding nationwide programs is under consideration. As
the plight of this population gains national attention, it is expected
that more states will enact legislation targeted toward helping the
displaced homemaker reenter the job market. Differences between
programs inhere in the amount and source of funding, characteristics
of the population served, as well as the extent and scope of available
services. However, three common threads run through the fabric of
most programs. The first is the recognition of the displaced homemaker as a *person* whose experiences and abilities are "translatable"
into marketable job skills. The second is the recognition of the displaced homemaker's personal crisis and related need for greater self-
confidence. A third common feature is found in each program's effort to utilize existing community agencies and form alliances with
state and private employment resources. Such accomplishments have
increased the network of job opportunities for the displaced homemaker and brought about recognition of her as a valuable member of
the work force. Staffing patterns within programs run the gamut from
professional to paraprofessional and include the use of displaced
homemakers as peer counselors as well as volunteers from vocational
and social service agencies.

## THE MILLS COLLEGE PROGRAM

The first Displaced Homemakers Act (SB825) was passed in California in 1975. It called for the funding of a multipurpose pilot center
that is located on the Mills College campus in Oakland. A total of
$180,000 was awarded for the two-year program through a contract
with the state health and welfare agency. The program opened its
doors on April 1, 1976. Overall program goals as specified in the act
were "to provide counseling, specified job training programs, assistance in finding employment, and programs to make the displaced
homemaker gainfully employed, healthy, and independent."

During its first year of operation the Mills College program assisted
over 1,000 displaced homemakers. Forty women received stipends of
up to $300 a month while going through a specialized concentrated

training program lasting six months. Perhaps the most outstanding achievement of the Mills College program has been the creation of new jobs for displaced homemakers through cooperative agreements with existing community organizations.

### The Homemaker Chore Program

In conjunction with a profit-making company, Comprehensive Health Care Services, a special program was designed to train displaced homemakers as chore workers. Entry-level jobs were made available to them by the company after on-the-job training and job readiness preparation by the displaced homemakers center. According to staff, any woman going through this program was guaranteed placement. The entry-level pay was higher than that offered by county health agencies, and the company was willing to develop job ladders for upward mobility in the area of health care.

### Paralegal Services for the Elderly

While the center provided job readiness training, it arranged to have the National Paralegal Institute conduct the specialized paralegal training, with costs assumed by the State Department on Aging. During an internship displaced homemakers provided legal services to the elderly through the Social Services Bureau of the East Bay Legal Assistance Project for the Elderly. This paralegal training program was then picked up by a local community college, which provides stipends for displaced homemakers as well as college credit and accreditation.

### The Kelly Services Program

This program combines job readiness training with an updating of clerical skills for women who may have had clerical experience at some time in their lives. The program is designed to provide gradual reentry into the business world on a part-time basis in accordance with the woman's level of proficiency. Additional skill training is also available.

### The Volunteer Contract Project

The volunteer contract was designed at the center as a way of legitimizing volunteer experience. A woman can acquire "recent job experience" by contracting with an agency as a volunteer. While on the job she receives supervision, evaluation of performed work, and necessary references when later applying for paid employment. This fundamental aspect of the center's program is becoming increasingly valuable to community agencies, churches, women's groups, and national organizations that have traditionally depended on volunteer help to extend their budgets.

The center currently operates on a "one-to-one" action plan that includes (1) individualized assessment of skills, past experience, and future goals and (2) referral to outside agencies or within the center for job readiness training. In addition to the training programs described earlier, several workshops are available to the displaced homemaker throughout the year. They cover the following subjects: skills assessment, assertiveness training, job focus, resume writing, money management, public assistance programs, health care and aging, widowhood, marital dissolution, self-employment, volunteerism as a career ladder, and stress in mid-life. A job resource file has been established and is available to any woman who enters the center.

## THE BELLEVUE COMMUNITY COLLEGE PROGRAM

The second displaced homemaker program in the United States was established through local revenue-sharing funds on the Bellevue Community College Campus in the State of Washington. Although the program's overall goals are similar to those of the Mills College program, the Bellevue program exemplifies the creative maximization of services despite limited funding. Funded for nine months in the amount of $7,000, the program operates under the auspices of the college's Women's Center. Owing to the small operating budget direct services to the displaced homemaker are rendered largely on a group basis (with a maximum of 20 per group). No stipends are available, and participants are encouraged to utilize existing community and college resources to supplement their vocational training and personal growth goals.

Basically, the program consists of two service components that are available to the displaced homemaker for a period of eleven weeks. Interim support groups are also provided for those waiting to enter the program. The support group component meets for two hours a week and is designed to deal specifically with issues of assertiveness, self-esteem, and transition to the role of single breadwinner. The vocational component includes career exploration and identification of marketable skills. Women are referred to other job training programs, and a week-long, state-sponsored vocational workshop is made available to them. A group of volunteer displaced homemakers is currently working to develop training programs in conjunction with community businesses. Since the State of Washington did not pass a proposed Displaced Homemakers Act, the Bellevue program will depend primarily on CETA funds to continue operating. The fact that 80 percent of all program participants found jobs within three months of program completion augurs well for continuing financial support.

Since several pilot projects have been shown to be effective in helping women through this transition, increased public funding support is fast becoming a mandate. For example, in both Oregon and Maryland state legislation has been responsible for the development of service programs designed specifically for displaced homemakers. Both programs are similar in services and staffing to the Mills College program and provide stipends to selected participants. Both are able to provide long-term vocational training within their centers and also to utilize displaced homemakers as part of their paid staff.

## Conclusion

The special problems and social service needs of displaced homemakers are gaining increased recognition by concerned citizens, professionals, and social policy makers alike. Several states have responded to this growing group of women through legislation aimed at supporting programs to assist them in gaining economic self-sufficiency and personal enhancement. Yet much remains to be done. Many communities ignore the very real concerns of displaced homemakers, thereby inviting long-term dependency on general welfare or, worse yet, complete pauperization. Antiquated legal precedents must be modified to take into account women's potential for equal and full participation in all social and economic arenas. Job opportunities must replace job discriminations. Humanitarian reasons aside, financial investment in multipurpose centers for displaced home-makers is a sound investment. Prevention of a downward spiral toward economic dependency not only helps the woman but also reduces the social cost to society. Displaced homemakers have on the average 10 to 25 years of productive, meaningful, paid work ahead of them. Better that those years be spent in a way that is both personally fulfilling and beneficial to the public.

# 9. The Ethnic Minority Woman

THROUGHOUT THIS book references to data about ethnic minority women and descriptions of services to them were intended to emphasize the fact that minority women have the special circumstances of sexism compounded by their minority status. This chapter presents two discussions in which those issues are given further attention.

The sections on the black woman and on the Hispanic woman are clearly not intended to be exhaustive of the subject of minority women and nonsexist services. Using just two examples, the aim of this chapter is to caution the providers of nonsexist services to women to be aware of the multiple effects of racism and sexism, and to understand the implications of the ethnicity of the individual minority woman for the social services she needs. Similar statements might be developed for the Asian and Native American woman. Such statements would also need to acknowledge and describe the variations among different Asian groups and different Native American tribes.

The issues raised in the discussions of black and Hispanic women are illustrative of the need to understand both sexism and racism, and the particular effects of their interrelationship on women of different ethnic groups. If alternative, nonsexist services to ethnic minority women are to be effective, such issues require careful consideration.

# Alternative Social Services and the Black Woman

## BARBARA SOLOMON

Black women are often overrepresented in the caseloads of social and mental health agencies. Yet their voices are rarely included in the rising sound of feminist protest against sexism in the delivery of services. This is consistent with the general uninvolvement of black women to any appreciable extent in the feminist movement of the past decade. A few, like the sociologist Jacquelyne Jackson (1972), have attempted to impress upon black women the need to participate in both racial and feminist liberation movements in order to avoid "being left out in'the kitchen and the nursery." However, more seem to agree with King (1975), who has suggested that sex role differences between black and white women make it inappropriate to apply the definition of the American woman's traditional status to black women and utilize it as a guide for action. This does not negate the idea that there is a black perspective on many issues raised by the feminists; it merely reflects alliance with white women as a means of achieving the goals of black women.

A black perspective can be identified in regard to three major feminist concerns: (1) sexism in the theoretical orientations that guide practice in the helping professions; (2) pressure on women to adjust to "traditional" family role expectations; and (3) social policies that institutionalize discrimination against women.

## Theoretical Orientations

There have been several scholarly reviews in the recent literature that have detailed the impact of sexist personality theory on the provision of services to women (Rauch 1978; Fabrikant 1974; Moskol 1976). The criticism has been directed primarily toward theoretical frameworks that have incorporated perceptions of women as sexually deficient and emotionally unstable or immature. This would include the view that passivity is a natural feminine personality trait or that "penis envy" is a normal part of the experience of growing up female. On the other hand, assertive or aggressive behavior is considered masculine and the assertive female may be labeled a "castrating female."

White feminists have emphasized the extent to which they have been disadvantaged by the expectation that they will be passive; for example, occupations that require assertiveness for effective performance have often been denied them. However, "equal time" has not been given to the similar disadvantage experienced by black women accused of being *too assertive*. Possession of this trait has not catapulted black women into the corporate heavens apparently envisioned by the white women who are anxious to develop it. At the same time, it has often poisoned their relationships with black males who have bought into the myth of the black woman as "castrating female." White feminists advocate personal assertiveness as behavior necessary for organizational advancement. However, the black woman's assertiveness has not helped her to such advancement. This differential outcome, depending on race rather than sex, serves to reinforce the idea that racism in our society is a more powerful force than sexism.

The characteristic passivity of many white women and the characteristic assertiveness of many black women may be influenced more by natural reinforcers in their respective social environments than by some sex-determined instinctual pattern. The notion that behavior is learned is hardly unique to any particular theory of human growth and development. On the other hand, the differentiating characteristics of most of these theories is the stipulation of *how* behavior is learned. The Freudian and neo-Freudian theorists have identified the major reinforcers within the supercharged emotional environment of the nuclear family, with little attention given to the wider social environment. Other, more socially focused theorists have tended to see the individual's behavior largely as a function of the social environment and whatever rewards or punishments it provides. Unfortunately, neither perspective presents a hopeful view of growth and change for *either* black men or black women; their families *and* their social environments have been characterized for the most part by the most influential theorists as problem-generating, that is, pathological (Clark 1954; Rainwater 1970; Moynihan 1965; Myrdal 1944).

## Family Role Expectations

Role theory has been an important source of concepts and principles that guide intervention in the helping professions. Feldman and Scherz (1967) have stated that "the healthy family carries out explicit and implicit roles appropriately . . . the disturbed family experiences serious difficulty in the management of roles." There is growing recognition, however, that (1) black families have developed "norms" for family role performance that are often quite different from "traditional" American family norms and (2) black women have had qualitatively different experiences in the traditional roles of wife, mother, and employee.

Beckett (1976) has analyzed a considerable number of research studies in which attitudes of black women and white women regarding work were compared. These studies suggest that black women expect to combine the role of wife, mother, and worker. Both black men and black women have more positive views of wives who work than of wives who do not work. In fact, the working wife is viewed as a good wife, a loving mother, and an efficient housekeeper. Beckett warns, however, of the risk inherent in accepting these findings without taking into consideration at least one intervening variable, that is, the primary reference group of the particular black family. If that reference group is constituted of other black families, there may indeed be less role conflict for the working wife. However, if the reference group is constituted of professional white families in which the wife is not permitted to work, then role conflict and marital disharmony may be a consequence for the black family.

In the past social scientists have contended that black males have been emasculated and that black women hold the power in most black families. Ladner (1971) suggests that this "emasculation theory" ignores more complex aspects of the intricate black-male–black-female relationship. What often appears to be female dominance to "outsiders" may not be dominance at all. Men can be very supportive and actually dominant in their relationships with women without being married and without being the chief provider.

Other researchers have drawn similar conclusions from their data. For example, Mack (1974) has observed that black women have tended to have higher education than black males and that this has led to the assumption (from a white perspective) that black women have more power in the relationship than their husbands. However, what is overlooked is the possibility that "power" in black marital relationships may be based on different criteria than in nonblack marriages. This is supported by the increasing number of studies that identify most black families as egalitarian (Hammond and Enoch 1976; TenHouten 1970; Mack 1970).

Family agencies hoping to serve black families in general and black women in particular must have practitioners who not only understand which myths are in fact myths (e.g., characteristic maternal domination) but also understand the reality of black family life. For example, Jackson (1972) has suggested that power in the black-male–black-female relationship is determined more by the scarcity of black males than by the economic or educational status of the black female. According to the 1970 census, there were 90.5 black males for every 100 black females as compared to 95.3 white males for every 100 white females. This relative scarcity places the black male at a distinct advantage in any power bargaining situation with black females. Moreover, there are additional factors that restrict the black female's access to black males even more (e.g., the strength of racially endogamous marital norms, the tendency for exogamous marriages to be between black males and white females rather than between white males and black females and social pressures to marry men with more education).

Given these fragments of reality, it is not surprising that there are relatively more single mothers and female-headed households in black communities. In developing alternative models of service delivery that are more appropriate to the needs of black women than traditional models, less emphasis on *marital* problems and *marital* counseling will certainly be required. There is still, however, a strong value placed on marriage among blacks, and the mental health implications for those black women who must remain unmarried owing to lack of opportunity have yet to be fully explored.

The relationship between black women and their children has received considerable attention in the social science literature. The fact that black women have the main responsibility for child rearing does not distinguish them from other American mothers. The fact that they have so often been identified as the source of problems presented by their children may be a matter of distinction. Black mothers have been accused of repressing aggressiveness in their sons and thereby emasculating them; of confusing their children with contradictory messages about the world outside the family; and of failing to provide adequate sensory stimulation, which provides the basis for development of the cognitive skills required to perform effectively in the educational system.

Services to black mothers and their children have often focused on the *relationship* as the key to change. However, in view of the lack of controlled studies that support this "mother blame" and the presence of many such studies that document the importance of the family's competence in dealing with systems as a major factor in building positive family relationships, it would appear to be more rational to develop services that focus on family interaction with external systems (e.g., schools, welfare department, probation department, etc.). In fact, service providers might experience much less "resistance" from mothers who are more vitally interested in learning how to deal more effectively with these systems than in exploring "feelings" about their children, which appear to them irrelevant given the presenting problem.

## Social Policy

Some major themes have emerged in the feminist movement that relate to the social policy changes needed in order to reduce discrimination against women and to facilitate their movement toward more equal status with men in the society. Most of these policy issues are relevant to black women. However, the motivations for black women to support those changes are frequently qualitatively different from those of white women. Consideration of the following policy issues will make this point clear.

## DAY CARE

Day care facilities are deemed necessary if women are to be able to work; the establishment of an extensive network of day care centers in every community has been a major plank in the feminist movement's platform. Since significantly more black children than white children have mothers who work, it is not surprising that this proposal would generate a great deal of support from black women. It is also true that many black women as well as white women utilize informal day care in the homes of neighbors, relatives, or friends. An issue, then, is to what extent this occurs by preference or because of lack of access to formal day care centers. Emlen et al. (1973) suggest that it is more often by preference, since the informal arrangement is convenient, flexible, and provides closer contact with and therefore greater psychological control over the caretaker. The strength of extended-family ties in black families would also tend to increase the probability that informal day care arrangements with a relative might be preferred, particularly if funds from governmental sources could be made available to the mother to be used as she wishes.

Since current proposals for the establishment of day care centers do not include provisions for informal day care located within the extended-family network, it is important that this also be considered. Although there is strong support for the centers, particularly in black communities, where the advantages of strong educational components and opportunities for skill learning seem quite attractive, it might be possible to effect a compromise. Such a compromise solution might be the development of small neighborhood centers, family sized, staffed by neighborhood residents who could be provided with consultation from specialists in early-childhood education regarding appropriate activities.

## EMPLOYMENT

The push by white women for equal opportunities in employment have brought some benefits but perhaps even greater risks to black women in the workplace. The feminist demand has been for access to previously male-dominated occupations and for equal pay for equal work. Although some semiskilled occupations have been sought (e.g., telephone linesperson), the main impetus has been in the skilled, managerial, and professional occupations. These are exactly the areas in which white women are much more likely to have qualifications than *either* black men or black women.

A study of employment information from 49 of the nation's 50 largest banks showed that from 1970 to 1975 the percentage of minority (racial) members employed as officers and managers almost doubled, from 5 percent to 9.3 percent. The percentage of female officers and managers nearly tripled during the same period, from 10 percent to 26 percent. However, the percentage of *black women officers and managers increased only slightly, from 0.7 percent to 2 percent* (Women in Banking 1979). Females generally did better than minorities; black females did not do better than white females despite the myth that black women have an advantage in the marketplace because they can be "counted twice"—as women and as a racial minority.

## WELFARE GRANTS

Many feminist organizations have included in their social policy proposals a demand that welfare grants for women in need of assistance to be made more adequate. The inclusion of this demand would appear to contradict the point of view that the orientation of the movement is solely middle class. However, the issue of adequacy of welfare grants is so complex that the simplistic form of the demand reinforces the limited perspective of its proponents. For example, from the black perspective perhaps the most damaging welfare requirement is the one that recipients with children over 6 years of age must seek work. The option *not to* work may be as important for some black women as the option *to* work is for some white women.

The matter of working or not working has high relevance for many low-income black women. Ladner (1971) has described the situation quite graphically:

There is a noticeable absence of formal and informal regulations in the community [housing project] which would help to counter the socially unapproved behavior. For example, an eight year old girl has a good chance of being exposed to rape and violence . . . and neither parent nor community leaders have the power to eliminate the anti-social behavior. (p. 62)

Yet the mother of an 8-year-old girl living in the housing project who would like to remain home to provide greater protection for her daughter cannot do so if work is available. The assumption underlying this requirement is that after age 6 children will be in school most of the day and therefore mothers are free to work. The low-status jobs for which these women are eligible are most likely to be unskilled and at some distance from the home. Therefore, the length of time between the children's arrival at home from school and the mother's arrival at home from work may be quite long. Not only would a change in welfare policy be helpful in order to make it possible for the mother who chooses to remain home and care for her children to do so; it is also important to develop more extensive social programs for children in low-income and black communities to reduce the problems identified by Ladner as endemic. Unfortunately, the tax reform legislation sweeping the country is likely to make such programs even more rare in the future than they are now.

## Conclusion

Black women have not participated extensively in the feminist push for a less sexist service delivery system. This does not mean that they have not often been victimized by service programs because of their sex. It does mean that more often their victimization is based on a complex interaction between sex and race and is therefore qualitatively different from the victimization experienced by white women.

# Social Services and the Hispanic Woman

RITA CEPEDA

In a recent effort conducted by the Women's Research Program Educational Equity Group under the National Institute for Community

Development, a coalition of Hispanic women met over a six-month period (June–December 1976) to determine and document the needs of Hispanic women in the United States.* One of the most important findings was realized only after a comprehensive composite picture was presented that reflected a problem of great magnitude. This concerned a very large population group that had been at best marginal in its inclusion into the mainstream of American society both as a participant and as a recipient of its social services. *Social services* here is used in the broadest sense of the term, including health, education, welfare, and social status in the United States.

The 20 million Hispanic women in the United States reflect a variety of races, religions, and historical and political experiences. We do share, however, a common language and a common colonization experience, and as such share in similar circumstances as members of U.S. society. The median age of Hispanic women is relatively low.

Women from Cuba; Central and South America have the highest median age—24.3 years. Mexican women have the lowest—19.7 years. Puerto Rican women's median age is 20.4 years. These statistics reveal that most of the Mexican and Puerto Rican women who comprise the majority of the Hispanic women are of college age. But a minuscule percentage of them are enrolled in college—only 4 percent of the total female population of Spanish origin.

Focusing on these two major groups, Chicanas and Puerto Rican women, we find the following.

## EMPLOYMENT CHARACTERISTICS

Close to one-third of all Chicanas are employed in low-skilled white-collar occupations. Over 40 percent of the total female population is employed in such positions.

About one-quarter (25 percent) of all employed Chicanas are in semiskilled blue-collar jobs, and another quarter (26 percent) are in low-skilled service jobs, compared to 14 percent and 20 percent, respectively, of women in the total U.S. population.

Among Puerto Ricans, the head of every fourth family is a young

---

* The term *Hispanic* is adopted here as the most inclusive of people with origins in Ibero-America and refers to a heterogeneous rather than homogeneous group.

woman who has the sole responsibility for supporting her children. Of all Puerto Rican female heads of household, 65 percent support their families on incomes under $4,000. (U.S. Department of Labor 1970.)

## EXISTING HISPANIC WOMEN'S ORGANIZATIONS

In spite of their long history and strength as a group, the documentation available on the needs of Hispanics is limited, and so are services exclusively geared to serve them. What is available as literature and documentation is termed "live literature," a literature in transition being developed actively through journals, newspaper articles, and position papers. This emerging, "live" nature is also true of Hispanic women's agencies. Organizations of this type have arisen as part and parcel of the whole *movimiento* focusing on the needs of the entire community, rather than as entities in their own right.

Hispanic women face a constant conflict between what has been seen as a need to choose between their needs and those of the entire community. As such, health centers, legal organizations, educational groups, and employment programs have engaged the energies of Hispanic women inasmuch as they have been the organizational backbone of the "movement." What has happened is that in some very special instances—such as child care, abortion, and birth control services, mental health and drug abuse and alcoholism treatment—the Hispanic woman must go beyond her ethnicity in securing adequate services and must come to the special needs of her sex.

As a general observation, the organizations with which Hispanic women tend to identify themselves most readily are those dealing with health, welfare, and bilingual education. Examples of these are MALDEF, a Chicana rights project in Los Angeles; the National Coalition of Hispanic Women (education oriented); and La Commission Femerial, also a Los Angeles-based organization.

## Necessary Characteristics of Agencies

### SERVING HISPANIC WOMEN

Some of the prerequisites for adequate, relevant services for Hispanic women are extremely basic in nature and by this very fact reflect some of the insurmountable barriers to the acquisition of such services.

### Bilingual Personnel

In every aspect of social service, whether it be financial, psychological, educational, or medical, there exists as a prerequisite for adequate services what has been variously termed empathy, ability to relate, establishing rapport, etc. This effort is not only impeded but defeated when the foremost means of communication, the language spoken by two parties, is different. In addition, in the "helper versus helpee" relationship it is expected that the helpee, who is in the one-down position, be the one to figure out a way of communicating. The accounts of inadequate service based solely on this factor are numerous and include veritable atrocities committed because of the lack of bilingual personnel. One vivid example is the account of a woman who, after having delivered a child in a public hospital in Los Angeles, was wheeled out and remained for sixteen hours on a guerney in the hallway of the emergency room, without seeing her child and, as she recounted, "dying of thirst" because she was unable to communicate her need to the "comings and goings" of nurses and doctors (Cepeda 1975).

### Communications/Public Relations

One of the frequent failures of agencies in making their services available is the lack of material available in Spanish, so that leaflets, brochures, and radio and television spots are virtually unavailable to women whose primary language is Spanish. The vehicles utilized for outreach are also important. Hispanic communities rely more heavily on the "oral tradition" for contact and information, and the grapevine (with some modifications) is a very legitimate and viable alternative.

Even when Hispanic women reach social agencies, misunderstandings due to the unavailability of bilingual service providers or bilingual written material can severely handicap effective service or even result in gross disservice. For example, MALDEF, a Chicana rights organization, documented instances in which sterilizations were performed on Hispanic women without their complete awareness. Because of lack of written material in Spanish, these women did not fully realize the consequences of the consent forms they signed (MALDEF 1976:2).

### Community Integration

"Chicanas must avoid polarization which isolates them from Chicanas and other women. They must carefully analyze each situation, as well as the means to reconcile differences. This is not easy—it requires a reservoir of understanding, patience and commitment. Yet unless it is done, success will not be ours" (Nieto 1974:42). The preceding quotation is included to illustrate the importance Chicanas and Hispanic women in general place on the integration of services sought and provided into the mainstream of the "movement" of Hispanics as a people. It is important, therefore, that the types of services and the means for providing those services be responsive to the pulse of the community in which they are based. For example, if the most important problem of a rural community is immigration laws and imminent deportation, it may be important for a group providing birth control education to address the issue of new legislation regarding naturalization and immigration laws. Perhaps information can be provided focusing on the health services available to migrants, immigrants, and undocumented workers.

### Cultural Integration

This aspect of service provision is one that should permeate all aspects of a social service agency. To illustrate, it does not suffice to provide mental health consultation in Spanish during a fifty-minute session that has merely translated psychoanalytic concepts from English to Spanish. Instead, it is necessary to integrate the concepts of body, mind, and spirit into the consultation and to deal with such day-to-day problems of living as food and shelter and the ways in which they affect the mental health of a person. It is important to know the culture and its orientation, which is not individualistic but group or family oriented. Providing a social service that by the very nature of its orientation offends a person's origin is simply adding to the conflict rather than resolving it. With specific regard to women, there is the concept of *Marianismo* "(veneration of the Virgin Mary). . . . Some Chicanas are . . . praised as they emulate the sanctified

example set by Mary. The woman par excellence is mother and wife.
. . . For a Chicana bent upon fulfillment of her personhood, this restricted perspective of her role as a woman is not only inadequate but crippling" (Nieto 1974:39). It is important nevertheless that the impact of such a cultural precept on the psyche of Hispanic women be recognized and placed in perspective. Social service providers need to know and respect the general cultural background of all Hispanic women but, as important, they need to understand the ways in which individual women may vary from the mainstream of that culture.

It is, then, these four basic aspects—personnel, communication, community, and cultural integration—that must be present at the outset in the development of social service agencies and organizations that expect to serve the needs of Hispanic women.

# Conclusion

NAOMI GOTTLIEB

This book has been based on a set of assumptions: some concerning the derivation and resolution of the interpersonal and social difficulties that women face; some related to the connection between knowledge and action in the ways in which social workers and other helping professionals address those issues. These concluding remarks briefly restate these rationales and give an overview of how the innovative programs discussed in preceding chapters build on the basic assumptions. Unfinished business is also noted. One of the most significant results of the search for new services for women has been identification of those problems and needs that are not being addressed and those clients who are not being reached. A description of apparent areas of neglect, including the need for a stronger knowledge base derived from empirical studies, is an important part of these concluding pages.

It is assumed that the problems women experience have long- and short-term solutions and that the issues women face will be resolved in various arenas. The attention paid in this book to the individual woman and her circumstances is not meant to deemphasize the fact that those circumstances are affected by a long political, economic, and social history. The condition of women and the reasons that they seek social services will be seriously influenced by the further development of that history.

As of this writing (early 1979), women are involved in a series of continuing battles—for the Equal Rights Amendment, for abortion and welfare reform, for day care programs, for equal pay for equal work, among others. New issues have also surfaced—for example, the displaced homemaker and the woman as a single parent. Many women's groups had been mobilized significantly in the efforts by the National Women's Conference of International Women's Year held at Houston in November 1977, but most politically active women are aware that this is an uphill fight. In all these efforts minority women face a double battle. Challenges are occurring in a series of public and private contexts, and any reasonable estimate would anticipate continued legal, political, and social struggles for many years.

For at least two reasons the progress and outcome of these struggles are crucial to the services and programs presented in this book. First, the clients of such services will be directly affected by political decisions. Federal funding for abortions, changes in social security procedures, increased welfare payments, and affirmative action monitoring are examples of political issues in which the clients and staff of innovative feminist services for women have a vital interest. Part of that interest derives from the recognition of social factors as causative in women's circumstances and of the impact of those factors in the daily functioning of the women they serve. The dicussion of the single parent illustrates the close tie between a series of political issues—such as upgrading of women's work and welfare reform—and any individual woman's circumstances. The other part is that both staff and clients are in the same political struggle for recognition and implementation of women's rights.

Second, the political scene directly influences the survival of these new programs, through shifts in funding from both government and private sources as well as through the general social and political climate in which feminist services must exist. Community acceptance and receptivity may very well fluctuate with national trends.

Notwithstanding the attention paid to the needs of individual women by the programs described here, there appears to be a strong conviction among program staff members that legal and political advances will affect the general population of women. However, it also seems to be the point of view of these service providers that women, suffering the effects of a damaging social environment, need individual attention in the present. Offering new ideas for this immediate attention has been the purpose of this book.

The first assumption, then, is that women's interpersonal and social problems are based in broader political and economic factors. Analogously, the particular individual approaches to these problems that this book has included have a broader base—the existence of a sexist society. There is considerable literature documenting the generally deleterious effects of women's social conditioning, and in each of the preceding chapters inferences have been drawn about the interrelationships between specific aspects of women's socialization and their particular problems. The other assumed effect of a sexist society may be found in the results of institutionalized sexism present in social service agencies and among their personnel. This is manifest in the diagnostic categories assigned to women's personal difficulties and in the choices of intervention techniques, as well as in the neglect of certain concerns of women. Here it is taken as given that traditional therapies and services have been affected by pervasive sexism. This book has addressed these circumstances, not through further documentation of the basic problem but through the presentation of specific, currently used alternative solutions.

The other major assumption that informs this book is the interplay between valid information about women and innovative services devised for them. The introduction to each chapter not only provides the background for each set of programs or services; each knowledge overview also restates the conviction that innovative services should be based on and feed into an accumulating set of empirically derived propositions about women's problems. Recent research reported in these chapters illustrates new understandings of the condition of women in varying circumstances. It is not clear, of course, to what extent individual service providers use research findings as they create new services. A value stance about nonsexist approaches and the strong motivation to fill unmet needs appear to be the likely and appropriate triggers. However, research and service will be mutually enhanced as the interplay between the two is more fully developed. The format of the book is an argument for this approach.

## Areas of Neglect

The separate chapters are intended to be a representative, but not exhaustive, reflection of innovative, nonsexist services for women. Constraints of time, resources, and space limited the number of areas covered and services described, and it is very possible that significant programs have been missed. Apologies are offered for whatever omissions have occurred. If these are considerable, it would be encouraging to learn that more services exist than these reports indicate.

It is likely, however, that service developments in entire areas have been neglected or given only rudimentary attention to date. These include programs for rural women, for adolescents, for minority women, for physically disabled women, for women in prison, for women receiving welfare. The latter may be a special case. During the 1960s, when welfare rights organizations were far more active than they are now, these groups served the needs of individual women by way of interpersonal support and individual services in addition to pursuing administrative and legal changes for welfare recipients generally. These efforts were not identified specifically as nonsexist, although they did deal with the consequences of sexism. As far as could be determined, these organizations, now diminished in number and level of activity, have only limited resources. As a consequence there is a lack of innovative services for the individual woman focusing on her welfare repiciency status.

Individuals and groups in various parts of the country may very well be concerned about these neglected aspects of services to women. The ability of women to initiate new programs, as documented in this book, may serve as a spur to others to do likewise. The specifics of new programs detailed in the foregoing chapters can provide practical models for these developments. The enthusiasm with which inquiries about new programs were met would indicate that the staffs of such programs would willingly offer both support and practical advice to encourage the efforts of others. The Feminist Women's Health Center is an illustration of a new service that explicitly states that such assistance is part of its responsibility.

## Future Research

This book argues for strong linkages between knowledge and action. One significant form that this will take is the evaluation of innovative programs. It was originally expected that evaluative studies would be well represented in the book. Few such critical analyses were found, and there appear to be good reasons for this. Most of the programs described here are bootstrap operations. They exist hesitantly on income from client fees alone, intermittent grant funding, individual donations, and the like. Resources for basic survival are often shaky; resources for program evaluations are virtually nonexistent. The descriptive materials from each program usually reflect the conviction that these new approaches are effective but, with few exceptions (e.g., see the report on Women Inc. in chapter 3), provide little empirical evidence to substantiate the claim. Women who serve other women in a nonsexist context have a strong commitment to the values of a feminist stance. In fact, these philosophical convictions have been the impetus for the creation of innovative services. Staff members will often testify, with much anecdotal support, to the positive responsiveness to this approach among the individual women they serve. However, enthusiasm and impressions are not sufficient. Systematic evaluation is required to determine whether, in fact, nonsexist services meet their objectives and are more effective than traditional programs. Resource limitations will make this task difficult, but service providers in both innovative and traditional services need verification of the practical worth of a different service stance toward women.

In this endeavor the imperatives for unbiased scrutiny, applicable to all researchers, are especially important. For this task the evaluators will most likely be feminist researchers and therefore most likely will have an investment in the positive outcomes of feminist services. Though no scientific enterprise is value-free and all research needs checks for bias, these researchers need to have a clear and simultaneous commitment to nonstereotyped attention to women and to the rules of scientific study. Concern for women's distinctive needs must include proof that new services are indeed better than old ones.

Along with the evaluation of services, scientifically substantiated knowledge is needed to understand fully the condition of women. Considerable literature testifies to the existence of differential socialization for men and women. However, it is not entirely clear how the conditioning of women is manifested in differing circumstances. The socialization process appears to show its main effects whatever the circumstances for women: compounding the problems of the minority woman, limiting the options of the single parent, constraining women's use of health care.

To date, much social science research about women has been handicapped by the same sexism that plagues much of social interaction. Seiden (1976) comments on several manifestations of this.

There has been a kind of (often unconscious) arrogance in the willingness of male professionals to tell women how to define their lives and, in parallel, a curious willingness of women to accept male definitions of women's needs. . . . [There has been] both the failure to detect important and interesting sex differences when they do exist and the failure to refute assumptions about sex differences when they do not exist. . . . Further, studies are frequently reported and summarized in such a way that findings from those studies conducted on men are generalized to everyone, while results from studies employing women are generalized only to other women. . . . Indeed, findings are likely to be explained in stereotyped ways even when support is available for alternative explanations. For example, one study ascribed female toddlers' staying closer to their mothers than did male toddlers to "timidity," just one page after noting that mothers reinforced proximity-seeking in girls while more frequently ignoring it in boys. . . . Women are said to be more manipulative, devious, inscrutable, and erratic; it has been accurately pointed out that these are characteristics to be expected from any group that has access to power and economic support only by means of pleasing another, dominant group. An accurate analysis of such stereotypy requires recognition of both true differences (reflecting different coping mechanisms) and perceived but untrue differences (arising from observer bias, lack of knowledge, and/or projective mechanisms). (pp. 1119–1120)

Nonstereotyped research calls for a whole other set of assumptions than those that have been commonly employed. The researcher's basic assumptions determine both the subject for inquiry and the methods of analysis. For example, single parenthood has been viewed as a problem, a temporary deviance to be resolved by remarriage. The disadvantage of the absence of the father has been viewed as inherent and studied for its effects. The advantages of the stable presence of the mother is ignored. The life cycle of the woman within traditional marriage and child rearing has not been considered problematic, and the difficulties that many women experience due to discontinuities have been presumed to be, and studied as, individual problems.

Findings based on questionable assumptions need revision: Whole new areas require investigation. Seiden is optimistic about the potential for this.

For the first time, we have a large number of well-trained investigators who are doing research on women and who are women themselves and have experienced a number of life events under study. The issue is similar to that regarding studies of other minority groups; while no one would be likely to make a convincing argument that *all* of the research about a particular minority group should be done by members of that group, there are compelling reasons why *much* of it should be. Researchers from a privileged group outside the group being studied are at risk of having shallow conceptualizations, lack of emphathic understanding of the salient variables, and perhaps a different axe to grind. Further, there has been a strong criticism that research done from the "outside" is not as likely to be conceived or later used in a way that benefits the people "inside" the group in question. . . . The infusion of numbers of investigators who belong to the group whose ox is being gored is probably the best remedy to this situation, and it can be expected to result in better research and quicker dissemination and application of findings. (pp. 1118–1119)

Seiden's additional observation about needed research activities in psychiatry is clearly applicable to social work and other helping professions as well.

It is even possible that the current increase in the number of women entering medicine and psychiatry, and the rapid expansion of women's studies as a related research field, may yet contribute to the hoped-for transformation of psychiatry into a more research-oriented field. This appears to have already occurred within the field of psychology, where the great discrepancies between what women have experienced for themselves and what psychological theories say about women have acted as a powerful stimulus to research curiosity. Women who are learning not to accept an argument from authority when it refers to women, who are learning to demand to see the evidence and review and gather it for themselves, may, it is hoped, continue to carry these healthy attitudes over other other areas of psychiatry. The result could only be stimulating and beneficial for our field and for all of us. (p. 1119)

As research inquiries continue, one of the more intriguing questions concerns the true differences between men and women that would be evident without the effects of stereotyped conditioning. It may be that those true differences become apparent only when sexism is no longer a social fact. That fortunate circumstance will also obviate the need for books such as this one.

# Bibliography

Abarbanel, Gail. 1976. "Helping Victims of Rape," *Social Work* 21:478–482.

Adams, Jane. 1978. *Sex and the Single Parent*. New York: Coward-McCann-Geoghegan.

Adler, F. 1975. "The Rise of the Female Crook," *Psychology Today* 42:42, 46, 48, 112–114.

Akiskal, Hagop, and William McKinney. 1973. "Depressive Disorders: Toward a Unified Hypothesis," *Science* 182:20–29.

——. 1975. "Overview of Recent Research in Depression," *Archives of General Psychiatry* 32:285–305.

Alberti, R. E. and M. L. Emmons. 1974. *Your Perfect Right*. San Luis Obispo, Calif.: Impact.

Allan, Virginia. 1975. "Economic and Legal Status of the Older Woman." In Natalie Trager, ed., *No Longer Young*, Occasional Papers in Gerontology, no. 11. Ann Arbor: University of Michigan, Institute of Gerontology.

American Medical Association. 1977. *Physician Distribution and Medical Licensure in 1977*. Center for Health Services Research and Development, Chicago.

Amundsen, Karen. 1971. *The Silenced Majority: Women and American Democracy*. Englewood Cliffs, N.J.: Prentice-Hall.

Anderson, Ronald, Joanne Lion, and Odin Anderson. 1976. *Two Decades of Health Services: Social Survey Trends in Uses and Expenditures*. Cambridge, Mass.: Ballinger.

Angrist, Shirley. 1969. "The Study of Sex Roles," *Journal of Social Issues* 25:215–232.

Aries, Elizabeth. 1974. "Interaction Patterns and Themes of Male, Female, and Mixed Groups." Paper presented at the American Psychological Association, New Orleans.

Arkowitz, H. 1975. "The Behavioral Assessment of Social Competence in Males," *Behavior Therapy* 6:3–13.

Astin, Helen. 1969. *The Woman Doctorate in America*. Hartford: Sage Foundation.

Back, T. M., F. La Binger, and P. How. 1976. "Attitudes Toward Abortion in the Pregnant Addict." Paper presented at Third National Conference on Drug Abuse, New York.

Backenheimer, Michael. 1975. "Use and Misuses of Tranquilizers." In *Drugs, Alcohol and Women*. Washington, D.C.: National Research and Communications Associates.

Bandura, A., and C. K. Whalen. 1966. "The Influence of Antecedent Reinforcement and Divergent Modeling Cues on Patterns of Self-Reward," *Journal of Personality and Social Psychology* 3:373–382.

Bard, Morton. 1970. *Training Police as Specialists in Family Crisis Intervention*. Washington, D.C.: Government Printing Office.

Bard, Morton, and Joseph Zacker. 1971. "The Prevention of Family Violence: Dilemmas of Community Intervention," *Journal of Marriage and the Family* 33:677–682.

——. 1974. "Assaultiveness and Alcohol Use in Family Disputes," *Criminology* 12:281.

Bardwick, Judith. 1972. "A Predictive Study of Psychological and Psychosomatic Responses to Oral Contraceptives." In Judith Bardwick, ed., *Readings on the Psychology of Women*. New York: Harper & Row.

Barrett, Carol. 1973. "A Comparison of Therapeutic Interventions for Widows." Paper presented at the 26th Annual Meeting of the Gerontological Society, Miami Beach.

Bart, Pauline. 1972. "Depression in Middle-Aged Women." In Judith Bardwick, ed., *Readings on the Psychology of Women*. New York: Harper & Row.

——. 1975. "Emotional and Social Status of the Older Woman." In Natalie Trager, ed., *No Longer Young*, Occasional Papers in Gerontology, no. 11. Ann Arbor: University of Michigan, Institute of Gerontology.

Bart, Pauline, and Marilyn Grossman. 1976. "Menopause," *Women and Health* 1:3–11.

Bateman, Nels, and David Peterson. 1972. "Factors Related to Outcome of Treatment of Hospitalized White Male and Female Alcoholics," *Journal of Drug Issues* 2:66–74.

Battelle Law and Justice Study Center (Seattle). 1977. *Forcible Rape: A National Survey of the Response by Police* (Police Volume I). Washington, D.C.: National Institute of Law Enforcement and Criminal Justice (U.S. Government Printing Office 027-000-00449-1).

Bazell, Robert. 1971. "Health Radicals: Crusade to Shift Medical Power to the People," *Science* 173:509.

Beck, Aaron T. 1967. *Depression: Clinical, Experimental and Theoretical Aspects.* New York: Harper & Row.

——. 1974. "The Development of Depression: A Cognitive Model." In R. J. Friedman and M. M. Katz, eds., *The Psychology of Depression: Contemporary Theory and Research.* New York: Wiley.

Beck, Aaron T., and Ruth L. Greenberg. 1974. "Cognitive Therapy with Depressed Women." In Violet Franks and Vasanti Burtle, eds., *Women in Therapy: New Psychotherapies for a Changing Society.* New York: Brunner/Mazel.

Becker, Howard. 1963. *Outsiders.* New York: Free Press.

——. 1967. "History, Culture and Subjective Experience: An Exploration of the Social Basis of Drug-Induced Experiences," *Journal of Health and Social Behavior* 8:163–176.

Beckett, Joyce O. 1976. "Working Wives: A Racial Comparison," *Social Work* 21:463–471.

Bell, Inge. 1970. "The Double Standard," *Transaction* 8:75–80.

Bequaert, Lucia H. 1976. *Single Women Alone and Together.* Boston: Beacon Press.

Berlin, Sharon. 1977. "Investigation of the Effect of Cognitive Behavior Modification with Problems of Self-Critical Behavior in Women." Unpublished paper, University of Washington, Seattle.

Berliner, Lucy. 1977. "Child Sexual Abuse: What Happens Next?" *Victimology: An International Journal* 2:327–331.

Bernard, Jesse. 1971. "The Paradox of the Happy Marriage." In Vivian Gornick and Barbara Moran, eds., *Woman in Sexist Society: Studies in Power and Powerlessness.* New York: Basic Books.

Bernard, Jesse. 1972. *The Future of Marriage*. New York: World.

——. 1974. "Age, Sex and Feminism," *Annals of the American Academy of Political and Social Sciences* 415:120–137.

Bernstein, Merton C. 1974. "Forecast of Women's Retirement Income: Cloudy and Colder, 25 Percent Chance of Poverty," *Industrial Gerontologist* 1:1–13.

Bilbin, Eunice, and R. M. Bilbin. 1968. "New Careers in Middle Life." In Bernice Neugarten, ed., *Middle Age and Aging*. Chicago: University of Chicago Press.

Binion, Victoria. 1976. "A Description of Selected Variables of Women Admitted to Demonstration Treatment Programs of the National Women's Drug Research Project from September 1975 through February 1976." Unpublished paper, Ann Arbor, Michigan.

Bird, Carolyn. 1968. *Born Female: The High Cost of Keeping Women Down*. New York: McKay.

Birren, James. 1968. "Principles of Research on Aging." In Bernice Neugarten, ed., *Middle Age and Aging*. Chicago: University of Chicago Press.

Block, Jack, Anna Von Der Lippe, and Jeanne Block. 1973. "Sex-Role and Socialization Patterns: Some Personality Concomitants and Environmental Antecedents," *Journal of Consulting and Clinical Psychology* 41:321–341.

Block, Jeanne H. 1973. "Conceptions of Sex Role: Some Cross-Cultural and Longitudinal Perspectives," *American Psychologist* 28:6.

Blum, R. 1972. *Horatio Alger's Children: The Role of the Family in the Origin and Prevention of Drug Risk*. San Francisco: Jossey-Bass.

Boston Women's Health Book Collective. 1976. *Our Bodies, Ourselves*. New York: Simon and Schuster.

Bower, S. A. 1976. "Assertiveness Training for Women." In J. P. Krumboltz and C. E. Thoresen, eds., *Counseling Methods*. New York: Holt, Rinehart and Winston.

Brandwein, Ruth A. 1974a. "The One-Parent Family as a Viable Life Style." Paper presented at the National Council of Family Relations, American Academy of Marriage Counselors, New York.

——. 1974b. "Women and Children Last: The Social Situation of Divorced Mothers and Their Families," *Journal of Marriage and the Family* 36:498–509.

Braucht, G. N., et al. 1973. "Deviant Drug Use in Adolescence: A Review of Psychosocial Correlates," Psychological Bulletin 79:92–106.

Brecher, Edward, et al. 1972. "What Kinds of People Use Opiates?" In Edward Brecher et al., eds., Licit and Illicit Drugs. Boston: Little, Brown.

Brodsky, Annette M. 1975. "Is There a Feminist Therapy?" Paper presented at the Southeastern Psychological Association Symposium, Atlanta.

Brodsky, Annette, et al. 1975. Report of the Task Force on Sex Bias and Sex Role Stereotyping in Therapeutic Practice. American Psychological Association, Chicago.

Brodyaga, Lisa, et al. 1975. A Prescriptive Package. Rape and Its Victims: A Report for Citizens, Health Facilities and Criminal Justice Agencies. Washington, D.C.: National Institute of Law Enforcement and Criminal Justice (U.S. Government Printing Office 1976-0-211-063/560).

Broverman, Inge K., et al. 1970. "Sex-Role Stereotypes and Clinical Judgments of Mental Health," Journal of Consulting Psychology 34:1–7.

Broverman, Inge K., et al. 1972. "Sex-Role Stereotypes—A Current Appraisal," Journal of Social Issues 28:59–77.

Brownmiller, Susan. 1975. Against Our Will: Men, Women, and Rape. New York: Simon and Schuster.

Burchinal, Lee. 1964. "Characteristics of Adolescents from Unbroken Homes and Reconstituted Families," Journal of Marriage and the Family 26:44–51.

Burgess, Ann, and Linda Lytle Holmstrom. 1974. Rape: Victims of Crisis. Bowie, Md.: Robert J. Brady.

Burgess, E. P. 1969. "The Modification of Depressive Disorders." In R. D. Rubin and C. M. Franks, eds., Advances in Behavior Therapy, 1968. New York: Academic Press.

Butler, Robert. 1968. "The Facade of Chronological Age." In Bernice Neugarten, ed., Middle Age and Aging. Chicago: University of Chicago Press.

Butler, Robert, and Myrna Lewis. 1976. Sex After Sixty. New York: Harper & Row.

Caine, Lynn. 1974. Widow. New York: William Morrow.

Cepeda, Rita. 1975. "Misassessment of Latin-American Women." Master's thesis. California State University, Long Beach.

Chafetz, Morris. 1974. *Alcohol and Health*. Washington, D.C.: U.S. Department of Health, Education, and Welfare.

Chambers, Carl, and Dodi Schultz. 1971. "Women and Drugs: The Drugs Women Use," *Ladies Home Journal* 88:130–131.

Chen, Lily Lee. 1977. "Experimental Job Project for Former Homemakers," *Los Angeles Times*, January 27, p. 1.

Chesler, Phyllis. 1971. "Patient and Patriarch: Women in the Psychotherapeutic Relationship." In Vivian Gornick and Barbara Moran, eds., *Woman in Sexist Society: Studies in Power and Powerlessness*. New York: Basic Books.

——. 1972. *Women and Madness*. Garden City, N.Y.: Doubleday.

Chodorow, Nancy. 1974. "Family Structure and Feminine Personality." In Michelle Z. Rosaldo and Louise Lamphere, eds., *Woman, Culture, and Society*. Stanford, Calif.: Stanford University Press.

Citizens' Advisory Council on the Status of Women. 1973. *The Equal Rights Amendment and Alimony and Child Support Laws* (Memorandum). Washington, D.C.

Clark, Don. 1977. *Loving Someone Gay*. Millbrae, Calif.: Celestial Arts.

Clark, Kenneth. 1954. *Dark Ghetto*. New York: Harper & Row.

Cohen, Wilbur. 1975. "Social Security: Next Steps." In Natalie Trager, ed., *No Longer Young*, Occasional Papers in Gerontology, no. 11. Ann Arbor: University of Michigan, Institute of Gerontology.

Cole, P. 1974. "Morbidity in the United States." In Carl Erhardt and Joyce Berlin, eds., *Mortality and Morbidity in the United States*. Cambridge, Mass.: Harvard University Press.

Coleman, R. E. 1975. "Manipulation of Self-Esteem as a Determinant of Mood of Elated and Depressed Women," *Journal of Abnormal Psychology* 84:693–700.

Comfort, Alexander. 1976. "Age Prejudice in America," *Social Policy* 7:3–8.

Coombs, R. H., L. J. Fry, and P. G. Lewis. 1976. *Socialization in Drug Abuse*. Cambridge, Mass.: Schenkman.

Cooperstock, Ruth. 1971. "Sex Differences in the Use of Mood Modifying Drugs: An Explanatory Model," *Journal of Health and Social Behavior* 12:238–244.

Cotler, Sherwin, and Julio Guerra. 1976. *Assertion Training: A Humanistic–Behavioral Guide to Self-Dignity.* Champaign, Ill.: Research Press.

Cowgill, Donald. 1972. "Aging in American Society." In Donald Cowgill and Lowell Holmes, eds., *Aging and Modernization.* New York: Appleton-Century-Crofts.

Curlee, Joan. 1969. "Alcoholism and the 'Empty Nest,' " *Bulletin of the Menninger Clinic* 33:165–171.

——. 1970. "A Comparison of Male and Female Patients at an Alcoholism Treatment Center," *Journal of Psychology* 74:239–247.

Curran, James. 1977. "Skills Training as an Approach to the Treatment of Heterosexual–Social Anxiety: A Review," *Psychological Bulletin* 84:140–157.

Curtis, B., D. D. Simpson, and G. W. Joe. 1974. "Description of Drug Users Entering Treatment in the DARP During 1969–1973." *Institute of Behavioral Research Report no. 74-8.* Fort Worth: Texas Christian University.

Cushman, P. 1972. "Methadone Maintenance Treatment of Narcotic Addiction—Analysis of Police Records of Arrests Before and During Treatment," *New York State Journal of Medicine* 72:1752–1755.

Cuskey, Walter, T. Premkumar, and Lois Sigel. 1972. "Survey of Opiate Addiction Among Females in the United States Between 1950 and 1970," *Public Health Review* 1:6–39.

Davis, C. 1975. "A Project in Sex-Role Socialization." Unpublished manuscript, University of Washington, School of Social Work, Seattle.

Decker, Albert. 1972. "Psychogenic Infertility: Fact or Fiction," *Medical Aspects of Human Sexuality* 6:168–171.

Delong, James V. 1972. "Treatment and Rehabilitation." *Dealing with Drug Abuse: A Report to the Ford Foundation.* New York: Praeger.

Denser-Gerber, J., M. Weiner, and R. Hochstedler. 1972. "Sexual Behavior, Abortion and Birth Control in Heroin Addicts: Legal and Psychiatric Considerations," *Contemporary Drug Problems: A Law Quarterly* 1:783–793.

Dewsbury, Anton R. 1975. "Battered Wives: Family Violence Seen in General Practice," *Royal Society of Health Journal* 6:290.

Doyle, Kathleen, et al. 1977. "Restructuring Rehabilitation for Women: Programs for the Female Drug Addict," American Journal of Psychiatry 134:1395–1399.

Drug Abuse Reporting Program, Institute of Behavioral Research. n.d. Fort Worth: Texas Christian University.

Dunkel, Ruth. 1972. "Life Experiences of Women in Old Age." Paper presented at the 25th Annual Meeting of the Gerontological Society, Puerto Rico.

Durbin, Karen. 1974. "Wife Beating," Ladies Home Journal 91:65.

Ehrenreich, Barbara, and Deirdre English. 1973. Complaints and Disorders. Old Westbury, N.Y.: Feminist Press.

Eisdorfer, Carl. 1969. "Intellectual and Cognitive Changes in the Aged." In Ewald Busse and Eric Pfeiffer, eds., Behavior and Adaptation in Later Life. Boston: Little, Brown.

Eisler, R. M., M. Hersen, and P. M. Miller. 1973a. "Components of Assertive Behavior," Journal of Clinical Psychology 29:295–299.

—. 1973b. "Effects of Modeling on Components of Assertive Behavior," Journal of Behavior Therapy and Experimental Psychiatry 4:1–6.

—. 1974. "Shaping Components of Assertive Behavior with Instructions and Feedback," American Journal of Psychiatry 131:1344–1347.

Eldred, Carolyn A., and Mabel N. Washington. 1975. "Female Heroin Addicts in a City Treatment Program: The Forgotten Minority," Psychiatry 38:75–85.

—. 1976. "Interpersonal Relationships in Heroin Use by Men and Women and Their Role in Treatment Outcome," International Journal of the Addictions 1:117–130.

Ellingwood, E. H., Jr., W. G. Smith, and G. E. Vaillant. 1966. "Narcotic Addiction in Males and Females: A Comparison," International Journal of Addictions 1:33–45.

Ellis, A. 1962. Reason and Emotion in Psychotherapy. New York: Stuart.

Emlen, Arthur C., Betty A. Donoghue, and Quentin D. Clarkson. 1973. The Stability of the Family Day Care Arrangement: A Longitudinal Study. Corvallis, Ore.: DCE Books.

Epstein, Cynthia. 1970. Woman's Place: Options and Limits in Professional Careers. Berkeley: University of California Press.

Erhardt, Carl, and Joyce Berlin. 1974. *Mortality and Morbidity in the United States*. Cambridge, Mass.: Harvard University Press.

Fabrikant, Benjamin. 1974. "The Psychotherapist and the Female Patient: Perceptions, Misconceptions and Change." In Violet Franks and Vasanti Burtle, eds., *Women in Therapy*. New York: Brunner/Mazel.

Faulk, M. 1974. "Men Who Assault Their Wives," *Medicine, Science and the Law* 14:180–183.

Feldberg, Rosyln, and Janet Kohen. 1976. "Family Life in an Anti-Family Setting: A Critique of Marriage and Divorce," *The Family Coordinator* 25:151–159.

Feldman, Frances Lomas, and Frances H. Scherz. 1967. *Family Social Welfare*. New York: Atherton.

Ferster, C. B. 1973. "A Functional Analysis of Depression," *American Psychologist* 28:857–870.

Fidell, Linda. 1973. "Put Her Down on Drugs: Prescribed Drug Usage in Women." Paper presented at the Western Psychological Association Meeting, Anaheim, California.

Field, G., and M. A. Test. 1975. "Group Assertive Training for Severely Disturbed Patients," *Journal of Behavior Therapy and Experimental Psychiatry* 6:129–134.

Field, Martha H., and Henry F. Field. 1973. "Marital Violence and the Criminal Process: Neither Justice Nor Peace," *Social Service Review* 47:230.

Fifield, Lillene. 1975. *On My Way to Nowhere: An Analysis of Gay Alcohol Abuse and an Evaluation of Alcoholism Rehabilitation Services of the Los Angeles Gay Community*. Los Angeles: County of Los Angeles.

Finkelstein, Norma, Brenda Weathers, and Bea Abruzese. 1977. "Testimony of the National Coalition of Women's Alcoholism Programs Before the Labor–HEW Subcommittee of the Committee on Appropriations," 95th Cong., 1st sess. (April). Washington, D.C.

Fojtik, Kathleen. 1976. *Wife Beating—How to Develop a Wife Assault Task Force and Project*. Ann Arbor: Ann Arbor–Washtenaw County National Organization for Women.

Fordyce, Wilbert. 1976. "Behavioral Concepts in Chronic Pain and Illness." In Park Davidson, ed., *The Behavioral Management of Anxiety, Depression and Pain*. New York: Brunner/Mazel.

Forrest, M. S., and J. E. Hokanson. 1975. "Depression and Autonomic Arousal Reduction Accompanying Self-Punitive Behavior," *Journal of Abnormal Psychology* 84:346–357.

Frankfort, Ellen. 1972. *Vaginal Politics*. New York: Quadrangle/The New York Times.

Fraser, Judy. 1973. "The Female Alcoholic," *Addictions* 20:64–80.

Freedman, T., H. Weiner, and L. Finegan. 1975. "The Family System of the Drug-Dependent Mother and Her Newborn." Paper presented at the Second National Drug Abuse Conference, New Orleans.

Freidson, Eliot. 1970. *Profession of Medicine*. New York: Donald Mead.

Friedan, Betty. 1963. *The Feminine Mystique*. New York: Dell.

Friedman, Mark. 1975. "Homosexuals May Be Healthier Than Straights," *Psychology Today* 8:28–32.

Friedman, Raymond J., and Martin M. Katz. 1974. *The Psychology of Depression*. New York: Wiley.

Fuchs, C., and L. P. Rehm. 1975. "A Self-Control Behavior Therapy Program for Depression." Unpublished manuscript, Department of Psychology, University of Pittsburgh.

Galassi, J., M. Galassi, and M. C. Litz. 1974. "Assertive Training in Groups Using Video Feedback," *Journal of Counseling Psychology* 21:390–394.

Gambrill, Eileen D. 1973. "A Behavioral Program for Increasing Social Interaction." Paper presented at the Seventh Annual Convention of the Association for the Advancement of Behavior Therapy, Chicago.

——. 1977. *Behavior Modification: Handbook of Assessment, Intervention, and Evaluation*. San Francisco: Jossey-Bass.

Gambrill, Eileen D., and Cheryl A. Richey. 1975. "An Assertion Inventory for Use in Assessment and Research," *Behavior Therapy* 6:550–561.

——. 1976. *It's Up to You: Developing Assertive Social Skills*. Millbrae, Calif.: Les Femmes.

Gay, M. L., J. G. Hollandsworth, and J. P. Galassi. 1975. "An Assertiveness Inventory for Adults," *Journal of Counseling Psychology* 4:340–344.

Gayford, J. J. 1975a. "Wife Battering: A Preliminary Survey of 100 Cases," *British Medical Journal* 25:194–197.

———. 1975b. "Battered Wives: Research on Battered Wives," *Royal Society of Health Journal* 6:289.

Geis, Gilbert. 1978. "Rape-in-Marriage: Law and Law Reform in England, the United States, and Sweden," *Adelaide Law Review* 6:2, 285–303.

Geis, H. J. 1971. "Rational Emotive Therapy with a Culturally Deprived Teenager." In A. Ellis, ed., *Growth Through Reason*. Palo Alto, Calif.: Science and Behavior Books.

Gelles, Richard J. 1974. *The Violent Home: A Study of Physical Aggression Between Husbands and Wives*. Beverly Hills, Calif.: Sage.

———. 1975. "Violence and Pregnancy: A Note on the Extent of the Problem and Needed Services," *Family Coordinator* 24:81–87.

———. 1976. "Abused Wives: Why Do They Stay?" *Journal of Marriage and the Family* 38:659–668.

Geracimos, Ann. 1976. "How I Stopped Beating My Wife," *Ms.* 5:53.

Gingold, Judith. 1976. "One of These Days—Pow—Right in the Kisser," *Ms.* 5:51.

Glaser, Frederick B. 1966. "Narcotic Addiction in the Pain-Prone Female Patient. I. A Comparison with Addict Controls," *The International Journal of the Addictions* 1:47–59.

———. 1968. "Narcotic Addiction in the Pain-Prone Female Patient. II. Some Factors in the Doctor–Patient Relationship," *The International Journal of the Addictions* 1:149–161.

Glasser, Paul, and Elizabeth Navarre. 1964. "Structural Problems of the One-Parent Family," *Journal of Social Issues* 21:98–109.

Glazer, Nona, and Helen Waehrer. 1977. *Woman in a Man-Made World*. Chicago: Rand McNally.

Glick, Paul C. 1978. "Demographic Changes and the Family." Paper presented at the National Conference on Work and Family, New York.

Goldberg, Susan, and Michael Lewis. 1972. "Play Behavior in the Year-Old Infant: Early Sex Differences." In Judith Bardwick, ed., *Readings on the Psychology of Women*. New York: Harper & Row.

Goldfried, M. R., E. T. Decenteceo, and L. Weinberg. 1974. "Systematic Rational Restructuring as a Self-Control Technique," *Behavior Therapy* 5:247–254.

Goldman, Noreen, and Renee Ravid. 1979. "Community Surveys: Sex Differences in Mental Illness." In Marcia Guttentag and Susan Salasin, eds., *Lives in Stress: A Context for Depression*. Cambridge, Mass.: Harvard University School of Education.

Greenwood, Ernest. 1957. "Attributes of a Profession," *Social Work* 2:45–55.

Gubbels, Robert. 1977. "The Supply and Demand for Women Workers." In Nona Glazer and Helen Waehrer, eds., *Woman in a Man-Made World*. Chicago: Rand McNally.

Guthrie, Lee. 1976. "Wife Beating," *Seattle Times*, October 10–11.

Guttentag, Marcia, and Susan Salasin. 1979. *Lives in Stress: A Context for Depression*. Cambridge, Mass.: Harvard University School of Education.

Halas, Celia. 1973. "All-Woman Groups: A View from Inside," *Personnel and Guidance Journal* 52:91.

Hammen, C., and D. R. Glass. 1975. "Depression, Activity, and Evaluation of Reinforcement," *Journal of Abnormal Psychology* 84:718–721.

Hammond, Judith, and J. Rex Enoch. 1976. "Conjugal Power Relations Among Black Working Class Families," *Journal of Black Studies* 7:107–128.

Hardin, Garrett. 1968. "Abortion—Or Compulsory Pregnancy," *Journal of Marriage and the Family* 30:246–251.

Havens, Elizabeth. 1973. "Women, Work and Wedlock: A Note on Female Marital Patterns in the United States." In Joan Huber, ed., *Changing Women in a Changing Society*. Chicago: University of Chicago Press.

Hays, V., and K. J. Waddell. 1976. "A Self-Reinforcing Procedure for Thought Stopping," *Behavior Therapy* 7:559.

Hedquist, F. J., and B. K. Weinhold. 1970. "Behavioral Group Counseling with Socially Anxious and Unassertive College Students," *Journal of Counseling Psychology* 17:237–242.

Hennig, Margaret, and Anne Jardin. 1977. *The Managerial Woman*. Garden City, N.Y.: Doubleday.

Herman, Judith, and Lisa Hirschman. 1977. "Father–Daughter Incest," *Signs: Journal of Women in Culture and Society* 2:735–756.

Hersen, M., *et al.* 1973. "Effects of Practice, Instructions and Modeling on Components of Assertive Behavior," *Behavior Research and Therapy* 11:443–451.

Heyman, Dorothy. 1970. "Does a Wife Retire?" *The Gerontologist* 10:54–56.

Hochschild, Arlie. 1973a. "A Review of Sex Role Research." In Joan Huber, ed., *Changing Woman in a Changing Society*. Chicago: University of Chicago Press.

——. 1973b. *The Unexpected Community*. Englewood Cliffs, N.J.: Prentice-Hall.

Hodnett, S. 1977. "The Use of Graded Tasks with a Depressed Woman Client." Unpublished manuscript, University of Washington, School of Social Work, Seattle.

Hoffman, Lois. 1972. "Early Childhood Experiences and Women's Achievement Motives," *Journal of Social Issues* 28:129–155.

Holmes, T. H., and R. H. Rahe. 1967. "The Social Readjustment Rating Scale," *Journal of Psychosomatic Research* 11:213–218.

Homme, L. E. 1965. "Perspectives in Psychology. Part 24, Control of Coverants, the Operants of the Mind," *Psychological Record* 15:501–511.

Hooker, Carol. 1976. "Learned Helplessness," *Social Work* 21:194–198.

Hope, Karol, and Nancy Young. 1976. *MOMMA: The Sourcebook for Single Mothers*. New York: New American Library.

Jackson, B. 1972. "Treaatment of Depression by Self-Reinforcement," *Behavior Therapy* 3:298–307.

Jackson, Jacquelyne. 1972. "Black Women in a Racist Society." In Charles Willie, Bernard M. Kramer, and Bertram Brown, eds., *Racism and Mental Health*. Pittsburgh: University of Pittsburgh Press.

Jacobs, Ruth, 1976. "A Typology of Older American Women," *Social Policy* 73:34–39.

Jacobson, Solomon. 1975. "The Woman Alone." In Natalie Trager, ed., *No Longer Young*, Occasional Papers in Gerontology, no. 11. Ann Arbor: University of Michigan, Institute of Gerontology.

Jakubowski-Spector, P. 1973. "Facilitating the Growth of Women Through Assertive Training," *The Counseling Psychologist* 4:75–86.

James, J. 1974. "Female Addict Research." Unpublished paper, University of Washington, Seattle.

James, Jane. 1975. "Symptoms of Alcoholism in Women: A Preliminary Survey of AA Members," *Journal of Studies on Alcohol* 36:1564–1569.

Jeffcoate, Thomas. 1967. *Principles of Gynecology*. London: Butterworth.

Johnson, W. G. 1971. "Some Applications of Homme's Coverant Control Therapy: Two Case Reports," *Behavior Therapy* 2:240–248.

Kalafus, Pat. 1977. "Heterosexual Bias and a New Model of Sexual Orientation Among Women." Unpublished paper, University of Washington, School of Social Work, Seattle.

Kanfer, F. H., and J. S. Phillips. 1970. *Learning Foundations of Behavior Therapy*. New York: Wiley.

Katz, Sidney. 1975. "Battered Wives Seek Refuge," *Toronto Star*, August 23.

Katz, S. J., J. M. Long, and D. Churchman. 1975. "A Formative Evaluation of a Residential Drug Treatment Center," *International Journal of the Addictions* 10:643–657.

Kay, Herma H. 1974. *Sex-Based Discrimination in Family Law*. St. Paul, Minn.: West.

Kazdin, A. E. 1975. "Covert Modeling, Imagery Assessment and Assertive Behavior," *Journal of Consulting and Clinical Psychology* 43:716–724.

Keefe, Mary L., and Henry R. O'Reilly. 1976. "Changing Perspectives in Sex Crimes Investigations." In Marcia Walker and Stanley L. Brodsky, eds., *Sexual Assault*. Lexington, Mass.: Lexington Books.

Keller, Suzanne. 1974. "The Female Role: Constants and Change." In Violet Franks and Vasanti Burtle, eds., *Women in Therapy: New Psychotherapies for a Changing Society*. New York: Brunner/Mazel.

Keshet, Harry F., and Kristine M. Rosenthal. 1978. "Fathering After Marital Separation," *Social Work* 23:11–18.

King, Mae C. 1975. "Oppression and Power: The Unique Status of the Black Woman in the American Political System," *Social Science Quarterly* 56:116–128.

Kinsey, Alfred, et al. 1953. *Sexual Behavior in the Human Female*. New York: Simon and Schuster.

Kirsh, Barbara. 1974. "Consciousness-Raising Groups as Therapy for Women." In Violet Franks and Vasanti Burtle, eds., *Women in Therapy: New Psychotherapies for a Changing Society*. New York: Brunner/Mazel.

Klein, D. C., E. Fencel-Morse, and M. Seligman. 1976. "Learned Helplessness, Depression and the Attribution of Failure," *Journal of Personality and Social Psychology* 33:508–516.

Klein, D. C., and M. Seligman. 1976. "Reversal of Performance Deficits and Perceptual Deficits in Learned Helplessness and Depression," *Journal of Abnormal Psychology* 85:11–26.

Klerman, Gerald, and Myrna Weissman. 1979. "Depressions Among Woman: Their Nature and Causes." In Marcia Guttentag and Susan Salasin, eds., *Lives in Stress: A Context for Depression*. Cambridge, Mass.: Harvard University School of Medicine.

Kline, Chrysee. 1975. "The Socialization Process of Women," *The Gerontologist* 15:486–492.

Klingbeil, Karil S., Shirley Cooke Anderson, and Louis Vontver. 1976. "Multidisciplinary Care for Sexual Assault Victims," *Nurse Practitioner* 1:21–25.

Kremen, Eleanor. 1976. "The 'Discovery' of Battered Wives: Considerations for the Development of a Social Service Network." Manuscript presented to the roundtable, working session on marital violence at the Conference of the American Sociological Association, New York.

Kreps, Juanita. 1971a. "Career Options After Fifty: Suggested Research," *The Gerontologist* 11:4–8.

——. 1971b. *Sex in the Marketplace: American Women at Work*. Baltimore: Johns Hopkins Press.

Kreps, Juanita, and Robert Clark. 1975. *Sex, Age and Work*. Baltimore: Johns Hopkins Press.

Krolik, Cynthia. 1975. "Study Says No Legal Protection From Husband Assault," *Michigan Free Press*, April 4.

Kutza, Elizabeth. 1975. *Policy Lag: Its Impact on Income Security for Older Women*, Occasional Paper 6, University of Chicago, School of Social Service Administration.

Ladner, Joyce. 1971. *Tomorrow's Tomorrow: The Black Woman*. New York: Anchor Books.

Lange, Arthur, and Patricia Jakubowski. 1976. *Responsible Assertive Behavior: Cognitive/Behavioral Procedures for Trainers*. Champaign, Ill.: Research Press.

Largen, Mary Ann. 1976. "History of Women's Movement in Changing Attitudes, Laws, and Treatment Toward Rape Victims." In Marcia Walker and Stanley L. Brodsky, eds., *Sexual Assault*. Lexington, Mass.: Lexington Books.

Law and Justice Planning Division, Office of Policy Planning. 1978. *City of Seattle Criminal Justice Plan—1978.* Seattle.

Lazarus, A. A. 1968. "Learning Theory and the Treatment of Depression," *Behaviour Research and Therapy* 6:83–89.

———. 1971. *Behavior Therapy and Beyond.* New York: McGraw-Hill.

Lennane, K. Jean, and R. John Lennane. 1973. "Alleged Psychogenic Disorders in Women—A Possible Manifestation of Sexual Prejudice," *The New England Journal of Medicine* 288:288–292.

Lester, David. 1973. "How Gynecologists Can Fulfill the Intimate Needs of Today's Woman," *Today's World* 51:17–21, 65–66.

Levy, Stephan, and Kathleen Doyle. 1974. "Attitudes Toward Women in a Drug Abuse Treatment Program." Paper presented at the National Drug Abuse Conference, Chicago.

Lewinsohn, Peter M. 1974. "Clinical and Theoretical Aspects of Depression." In K. S. Calhoun, H. E. Adams, and K. M. Mitchell, eds., *Innovative Treatment Methods in Psychopathology.* New York: Wiley.

———. 1975a. "The Behavioral Study and Treatment of Depression." In M. Hersen, R. M. Eisler, and P. M. Miller, eds., *Progress in Behavior Modification.* New York: Academic Press.

———. 1975b. "Engagement in Pleasant Activities and Depression Level," *Journal of Abnormal Psychology* 84:729–731.

Lewinsohn, Peter, Anthony Biglan, and Antonette Zeiss. 1976. "Behavioral Treatment of Depression." In Park Davidson, ed., *The Behavioral Management of Anxiety, Depression and Pain.* New York: Brunner/Mazel.

Lewinsohn, P., M. Weinstein, and D. Shaw. 1969. "Depression: A Clinical-Research Approach." In R. Rubin and C. Franks, eds., *Advances in Behavior Therapy, 1968.* New York: Academic Press.

Lewis, Myrna, and Robert Butler. 1972. "Why Is Women's Lib Ignoring Old Women?" *Aging and Human Development* 3:223–231.

Lindsay, Isabel B. 1975. "Coping Capacities of the Black Aged." In Natalie Trager, ed., *No Longer Young,* Occasional Papers in Gerontology, no. 11. Ann Arbor: University of Michigan, Isntitute of Gerontology.

Livson, Florence. 1976. "Patterns of Personality Development in Middle-Aged Women: A Longitudinal Study," *International Journal of Aging and Human Development* 7:107–116.

Lomont, J. F., et al. 1969. "Group Assertive Training and Group Insight Therapies," Psychological Reports 25:463–470.

Lopata, Helen. 1971. "Widows as a Minority Group," The Gerontologist 11:67–77.

——. 1972. "Role Changes in Widowhood: A World Perspective." In Donald Cowgill and Lowell Holmes, eds., Aging and Modernization. New York: Appleton-Century-Crofts.

——. 1973a. "Social Relations of Black and White Widows in a Northern Metropolis." In Joan Huber, ed., Changing Women in a Changing Society. Chicago: University of Chicago Press.

——. 1973b. Widowhood in an American City. Cambridge, Mass.: Schenkman.

Lowenthal, Marjorie F., et al. 1975. Four Stages of Life. San Francisco: Jossey-Bass.

Lubin, B. 1965. "Adjective Checklists for the Measurement of Depression," Archives of General Psychiatry 12:57–62.

Maas, Henry. 1973. "Early Adult Antecedents of Aging Mother 'Life Styles': Some Berkeley Longitudinal Study Findings." Paper presented at the 26th Annual Meeting of the Gerontological Society, Miami Beach.

Maas, Henry, and Joseph Kuypers. 1974. From Thirty to Seventy. San Francisco: Jossey-Bass.

Maccoby, Eleanor. 1971. "Sex Differences and Their Implications for Sex Roles." Paper presented at the American Psychological Association, Washington, D.C.

——. 1972. "Sex Differences in Intellectual Functioning." In Judith Bardwick, ed., Readings on the Psychology of Women. New York: Harper & Row.

Maccoby, Eleanor, and Carol N. Jacklin. 1974. The Psychology of Sex Differences. Stanford, Calif.: Stanford University Press.

MacDonald, M. 1974. "A Behavioral Assessment Methodology as Applied to the Measurement of Assertion." Unpublished Ph.D. diss., University of Illinois, Urbana.

Mack, Delores. 1970. "The Husband and Wife Power Relationship in Black Families and White Families." Unpublished Ph.D. diss., Stanford University, Stanford, Calif.

Mack, Delores. 1974. "The Power Relationship in Black Families and White Families," *Journal of Personality and Social Psychology* 30:409–413.

MacPhillamy, D. J., and P. M. Lewinsohn. 1975. *Manual for the Pleasant Events Schedule.* University of Oregon, Eugene.

Mahoney, M. J. 1971. "The Self-Management of Covert Behavior: A Case Study," *Behavior Therapy* 2:575–578.

MALDEF, Chicana Rights Project. 1976. Review of "Informed Consent" Project prepared for Chicana Rights Project Task Force Meeting, San Francisco.

Marieskind, Helen. 1975. "The Women's Health Movement," *International Journal of Health Services* 5:217–223.

Marsden, Dennis, and David Owens. 1975. "The Jekyll and Hyde Marriages," *New Society* 32:334.

Martin, Dell. 1976. *Battered Wives.* San Francisco: Glide Publications.

Masters, William, and Virginia Johnson. 1970. *Human Sexual Inadequacy.* Boston: Little, Brown.

Mayer, Joseph, and Rebecca Black. 1976. "Child Abuse and Neglect in Families with an Alcoholic or Opiate Addicted Parent." Paper presented at the Third National Conference on Drug Abuse, New York.

Mayo, M., M. Bloom, and J. Pearlman. 1975. "Effectiveness of Assertive Training for Women." Unpublished manuscript, cited in L. Z. Bloom, K. Coburn, and J. Pearlman, eds., *The New Assertive Woman.* New York: Delacorte Press.

McCombie, Sharon L, et al. 1976. "Development of a Medical Center Rape Crisis Intervention Program," *American Journal of Psychiatry* 133:4, 418–421.

McFall, R. M., and A. R. Marston. 1970. "An Experimental Investigation of Behavioral Rehearsal in Assertive Training," *Journal of Abnormal Psychology* 76:295–303.

McFall, R. M., and D. B. Lillesand. 1971. "Behavioral Rehearsal with Modeling and Coaching in Assertive Training," *Journal of Abnormal Psychology* 77:313–323.

McFall, R. M., and C. T. Twentyman. 1973. "Four Experiments on the Relative Contributions of Rehearsal, Modeling, and Coaching to Assertion Training," *Journal of Abnormal Psychology* 81:199–218.

McLean, Peter. 1976. "Therapeutic Decision-Making in the Behavioral Treatment of Depression." In Park Davidson, ed., *The Behavioral Management of Anxiety, Depression and Pain*. New York: Brunner/Mazel.

McMains, M., and R. Liebert. 1968. "Influence of Discrepancies Between Successively Modeled Self-Reward Criteria on the Adoption of a Self-Imposed Standard," *Journal of Personality and Social Psychology* 8:166–171.

Meador, Betty, Evelyn Solomon, and Marcia Bowen. 1972. "Encounter Groups for Women Only." In Lawrence N. Solomon and Betty Belzon, eds., *New Perspectives on Encounter Groups*. New York: Jossey-Bass.

Mechanic, David. 1962. "The Concept of Illness Behavior," *Journal of Chronic Diseases* 15:189–194.

——. 1966. "Response Factors in Illness: The Study of Illness Behavior," *Social Psychiatry* 1:11–20.

Meichenbaum, D. H. 1975. "Self-Instructional Methods." In F. H. Kanfer and A. P. Goldstein, eds., *Helping People Change: A Textbook of Methods*. New York: Pergamon Press.

Mellinger, Glen, Mitchell Balter, and Dean Manheimer. 1971. "Patterns of Psychotherapeutic Drug Use Among Adults in San Francisco," *Archives of General Psychiatry* 25:385–394.

Micklow, Pat, and Sue Eisenberg. 1974. "The Assaulted Wife: Catch 22 Revisited." Unpublished manuscript, University of Michigan Law School, Ann Arbor.

Miller, J. S., *et al.* 1973. "Value Patterns of Drug Addicts as a Function of Race and Sex," *The International Journal of the Addictions* 8:589–598.

Miller, Jean Baker. 1973. *Psychoanalysis and Women*. Baltimore: Penguin.

——. 1976. *Toward a New Psychology of Women*. Boston: Beacon Press.

Miller, Michael. 1973. "Who Receives Optimal Medical Care?" *Journal of Health and Social Behavior* 14:176–182.

Miller, W. R., and Martin Seligman. 1975. "Depression and Learned Helplessness in Man," *Journal of Abnormal Psychology* 84:228–238.

Mitchell, K. R., R. J. Kirkby, and D. M. Mitchell. 1970. "Note on Sex Differences in Student Drug Use," *Psychological Reports* 27:116.

Morrissey, Elizabeth, and Marc Schuckit. 1977. "Stressful Life Events and Alcoholism in Women Seen at a Detoxification Center." Unpublished paper, University of Washington, Seattle.

Moser, Collette. 1974. "Mature Women: The New Labor Force," *Industrial Gerontologist* 1:14–25.

Moskol, Marjorie. 1976. "Feminist Theory and Casework Practice." In Bernard Ross and S. K. Khinduka, eds., *Social Work in Practice*. New York: National Association of Social Workers.

Moss, Howard. 1972. "Sex, Age, and State as Determinants of Mother–Infant Interaction." In Judith Bardwick, ed., *Readings on the Psychology of Women*. New York: Harper & Row.

Mostow, E., and P. Newberry. 1975. "Work Role and Depression in Women," *American Journal of Orthopsychiatry* 45:538–548.

Moynihan, Daniel Patrick. 1965. *The Negro Family: A Case For National Action*. Washington, D.C.: U.S. Department of Labor.

*Ms.* 1976. "Battered Wives: Help for the Victim Next Door," *Ms.* 5:95.

Mybans, Seth. 1975. "Wife Beating," *Ann Arbor News*, July 29.

Myers, Jane. 1975. "The Beaten Wife," *Ann Arbor News*, September 18.

Myrdal, Gunnar. 1944. *An American Dilemma*. New York: Harper & Row.

Nathanson, D. 1975. "Illness and the Feminine Role: A Theoretical Review," *Social Science and Medicine* 9:57–62.

National Association of Social Workers. (NASW). 1977. "Policy Statement on Gay Issues." 1977 Delegate Assembly.

National Center for the Prevention and Control of Rape. 1977. *Research Grants Awarded*. Rockville, Md.: U.S. Department of Health, Education and Welfare, National Institute of Mental Health.

Navarro, Vicente. 1972. "Women in Health Care," *The New England Journal of Medicine* 292:398–402.

Neugarten, Bernice. 1974. "Age Groups in American Society and the Rise of the Young–Old," *Annals of the American Academy of Political and Social Science* 415:187–198.

Neugarten, Bernice, and Joan Moore. 1968. "The Changing Age-Status System." In Bernice Neugarten, ed., *Middle Age and Aging*. Chicago: University of Chicago Press.

*New Woman's Survival Sourcebook, The*. 1975. New York: Knopf.

*New York Times*. 1977. "Gray Panthers Fighting Society's Treatment of the Elderly," October 29.

Newman, Jill. 1976. "How Battered Wives Are Fighting Back," *Parade*, April 11.

*Newsweek*. 1973. "Lesbian a Mother," September 24, pp. 75–76.

*Newsweek*. 1979. "Was It Rape?" January 1, p. 55.

*Newsweek*. 1979. "As the World Turns," January 22, p. 26.

Newton, Esther, and Shirley Walton. 1971. "The Personal Is Political: Consciousness-Raising and Personal Change in the Women's Liberation Movement." In B. Schoepf, ed., *Anthropologists Look at the Study of Women*. Symposium presented at the American Psychological Association, Washington, D.C.

"NGTF Gay Parent Support Packet." 1973. Educational material supplied by the National Gay Task Force. New York.

Nichols, Beverly B. 1976. "The Abused Wife Problem," *Social Casework* 57:29.

Nieto, Consuelo. 1974. "The Chicana and the Women's Rights Movement." *Civil Rights Digest: A Quarterly* (U.S. Commission on Civil Rights) 6:3.

Novak, Emil, and Edmund Novak. 1952. *Textbook of Gynecology*. Baltimore: Williams & Wilkins.

Oakely, Ann. 1974. *The Sociology of Housework*. New York: Pantheon Books.

Oberstone, Andrea Kincses, and Harriet Sukoneck. 1976. "Psychological Adjustment and Life Style of Single Lesbians and Single Heterosexual Women," *Psychology of Women Quarterly* 1:172–189.

O'Brien, John E. 1971. "Violence in Divorce Prone Families," *Journal of Marriage and the Family* 33:692–697.

Osborn, Susan, and Gloria Harris. 1975. *Assertive Training for Women*. Springfield, Ill.: Charles C Thomas.

Osofsky, Howard, and Robert Seidenberg. 1970. "Is Female Menopausal Depression Inevitable?" *Obstetrics and Gynecology* 36:611–615.

Page, Jane. 1977. *The Other Awkward Age—Menopause*. Berkeley, Calif.: The Ten Speed Press.

Pancoast, Ruth, *et al*. 1974. "Feminist Psychotherapy: A Method for Fighting the Social Control of Women." Paper presented before the American Orthopsychiatric Association, San Francisco.

Parker, Frederick. 1972. "Sex-Role Adjustment of Women Alcoholics," *Quarterly Journal of Studies in Alcohol* 33:647–657.

——. 1975. "Sex-Role Adjustment and Drinking Disposition of Women College Students," *Journal of Studies in Alcohol* 36:1570–1573.

Parkes, Colen. 1972. *Bereavement: Studies of Grief in Adult Life.* New York: International University Press.

Parsons, Talcott. 1951. *The Social System.* New York: Free Press.

Payne, Barbara, and Frank Whittington. 1976. "Older Women: An Examination of Popular Stereotypes and Research Evidence," *Social Problems* 23:488–504.

Peters, Joseph F. 1976. "Children Who Are Victims of Sexual Assault and the Psychology of Offenders," *American Journal of Psychotherapy* 3:398–421.

Pfeiffer, Eric. 1969. "Sexual Behavior in Old Age." In Ewald Busse and Eric Pfeiffer, eds., *Behavior and Adaptation in Later Life.* Boston: Little, Brown.

Phillips, Derek L., and Bernard F. Segal. 1969. "Sexual Status and Psychiatric Symptoms," *American Sociological Review* 34:58–72.

Polster, Miriam. 1974. "Women in Therapy—A Gestalt Therapist's View." In Violet Franks and Vasanti Burtle, eds., *Women in Therapy: New Psychotherapies for a Changing Society.* New York: Brunner/Mazel.

Ponse, Barbara. 1976. "Secrecy in the Lesbian World," *Urban Life* 5:313–337.

Prather, Jane, and Linda Fidell. 1972. "Put Her Down and Drug Her Up." Paper presented at the American Sociological Association meeting, New Orleans.

——. 1975. "Sex Differences in the Context and Style of Medical Advertisement," *Social Science and Medicine* 9:23–26.

Premack, D. 1965. "Reinforcement Theory." In D. Levine, ed., *Nebraska Symposium on Motivation: 1965.* Lincoln: University of Nebraska Press.

Preston, Caroline. 1975. "An Old Bag: The Stereotype of the Older Woman." In Natalie Trager, ed., *No Longer Young,* Occasional Papers in Gerontology, no. 11. Ann Arbor: University of Michigan, Institute of Gerontology.

Proceedings of the Washington State Women's Conference. 1977. Ellensburg, Washington.

Radloff, Lenore. 1975. "Sex Differences in Depression—The Effects of Occupation and Marital Status," *Sex Roles* 1:249–265.

——. In press. "Sex Differences in Helplessness—With Implications for Depression." In L. S. Hansen and R. S. Rapoza, eds., *Career Development and Counselling of Women*. Springfield, Ill.: Charles C Thomas.

Rahe, R. H. 1968. "Life Change Measurement as a Predictor of Illness," *Proceedings of Royal Society of Medicine* 61:1124–1126.

Rainwater, Lee. 1970. *Behind Ghetto Walls*. Chicago: Aldine.

Rape Relief. 1979. Personal communication. Seattle, Washington.

Rathus, S. 1972. "An Experimental Investigation of Assertive Training in a Group Setting," *Journal of Behavior Therapy and Experimental Psychiatry* 3:81–86.

Rauch, Julia B. 1978. "Gender as a Factor in Practice," *Social Work* 23:388–395.

Reed, Beth, and Judith Herr. 1977. "Deviant Social Careers and Heroin-Addicted Women: Issues in Treatment." Unpublished paper, Women's Drug Research Coordinating Project, Ann Arbor, Michigan.

Rehm, L. P., and A. P. Marston. 1968. "Reduction of Social Anxiety Through Modification of Self-Reinforcement: An Instigation Therapy Technique," *Journal of Consulting and Clinical Psychology* 32:565–574.

Resnick, Mindy. n.d. *Wife Beating—Counselor Training Manual No. 1*. Ann Arbor, Mich.: Ann Arbor–Washtenaw County National Organization for Women.

Richey, Cheryl A. 1974. "Increased Female Assertiveness Through Self-Reinforcement." Unpublished Ph.D. diss., University of California at Berkeley.

——. 1975. "Utilizing Self-Reinforcement in Group Assertion Training for Women: A Follow-Up Report." Paper presented at the Ninth Annual Convention of the Association for Advancement of Behavior Therapy, San Francisco.

——. In press. "Assertion Training for Women." In S. Schinke, ed., *Community Applications of Behavioral Methods: A Sourcebook for Social Workers*. Chicago: Aldine.

Rimm, D. C., and J. C. Masters. 1974. *Behavior Therapy: Techniques and Empirical Findings*. New York: Wiley.

Rippere, V. 1977. "What's the Thing to Do When You're Feeling Depressed?: A Pilot Study," *Behaviour Research and Therapy* 15:185–191.

Rivkin, M. O. 1972. "Contextual Effects of Families on Female Response to Illness." Unpublished doctoral dissertation, Johns Hopkins University.

Robinson, J. C., and P. M. Lewinsohn. 1973. "Experimental Analysis of a Technique Based on the Premack Principle for Changing Verbal Behavior of Depressed Individuals," *Psychological Reports* 32:199–210.

Rosaldo, Michelle Z. 1974. "Woman, Culture, and Society: A Theoretical Overview." In Michelle Z. Rosaldo and Louise Lamphere, eds., *Woman, Culture, and Society*. Stanford, Calif.: Stanford University Press.

Rose, S. 1975. "In Pursuit of Social Competence," *Social Work* 20:33–37.

Rosenbaum, Marsha. 1973. "The World and Career of Women Heroin Addicts." Unpublished paper.

Ross, Heather L., and Isabel V. Sawhill. 1975. *Time of Transition: The Growth of Families Headed By Women*. Washington, D.C.: Urban Institute.

Rossi, Alice. 1964. "The Equality of Women: An Immodest Proposal," *Daedalus* 93:607–652.

——. 1968. "Transition to Parenthood," *Journal of Marriage and the Family* 30:26–39.

——. 1972. "The Roots of Ambivalence in American Women." In Judith Bardwick, ed., *Readings on the Psychology of Women*. New York: Harper & Row.

Roth, J. A. 1962. "The Treatment of the Sick." In J. Kosa *et al.*, eds., *Poverty and Health: A Sociological Analysis*. Cambridge, Mass.: Harvard University Press.

Rubin, I. C., and Josef Novak. 1956. *Integrated Gynecology: Principles and Practice*. New York: McGraw-Hill.

Rubington, E. 1967. "Drug Addiction as a Deviant Career," *International Journal of the Addictions* 2:3–20.

Ruczek, Sheryl. 1975. *Women and Health Care*. Evanston, Ill.: Northwestern University, Program on Women.

Rush, Augustus J., *et al.* 1977. "Comparative Efficacy of Cognitive Therapy and Pharmacotherapy in the Treatment of Depressed Outpatients." Unpublished paper.

Rush, Florence J. 1977. "The Freudian Cover-Up," *Chrysalis*, 31–45.

Russell, Diana E. H. 1975. *The Politics of Rape: The Victim's Perspective.* New York: Stein and Day.

Sandmaier, Marian. 1977. "Women Helping Women: Opening the Door to Treatment," *Alcohol Health and Research World* 2:17–23.

Sarbin, Theodore. 1954. "Role Theory." In G. Lindzey, ed., *Handbook of Social Psychology*, vol. I. Cambridge, Mass.: Addison-Wesley.

Schlesinger, Benjamin. 1978. *The One-Parent Family: Perspectives and Annotated Bibliography.* Toronto: University of Toronto Press.

Schuckit, Marc, and George Winokur. 1972. "A Short-Term Follow Up of Women Alcoholics," *Diseases of the Nervous System* 33:672–676.

Schultz, Ardelle. 1974. "Radical Feminism: A Treatment Modality for Addicted Women." Unpublished paper.

Schwartz, D. A. 1964. "The Paranoid–Depressive Existential Continuum," *Psychiatric Quarterly* 38:690–706.

Scott, P. D. 1974. "Battered Wives," *British Journal of Psychiatry* 125:438.

Scully, Diane, and Pauline Bart. 1973. "A Funny Thing Happened on the Way to the Orifice: Women in Gynecology Textbooks," *American Journal of Sociology* 78:1045–1050.

Seiden, Anne. 1976. "Overview: Research on the Psychology of Women. II. Women in Families, Work, and Psychotherapy," *American Journal of Psychiatry* 133:1111–1123.

Seligman, Martin E. P. 1974. "Depression and Learned Helplessness." In R. J. Friedman and M. M. Katz, eds., *The Psychology of Depression: Contemporary Theory and Research*. Washington, D.C.: Winston and Sons.

——. 1975. *Helplessness: On Depression, Development and Death*. San Francisco: W. E. Freeman.

Senseman, Lawrence. 1966. "The Housewife's Secret Illness—How to Recognize the Female Alcoholic," *Rhode Island Medical Journal* 49:40–42.

Sexual Assault Center. 1979. Personal communication. Seattle, Washington.

Shainess, Natalie. 1970. "Abortion and Womankind." In Robert Hall, ed., *Abortion in a Changing World*. New York: Columbia University Press.

Shipley, C. R., and A. F. Fazio. 1973. "Pilot Study of a Treatment for Psychological Depression," *Journal of Abnormal Psychology* 82:372–376.

Shoemaker, M. E., and T. L. Paulson. 1976. "Group Assertion Training for Mothers: A Family Intervention Strategy." In E. J. Mash, L. C. Handy, and L. A. Hamerlynck, eds., *Behavior Modification Approaches to Parenting.* New York: Brunner/Mazel.

Silverman, Charlotte. 1968. *The Epidemiology of Depression.* Baltimore: Johns Hopkins Press.

Silverman, Phyllis, *et al.* 1974. *Helping Each Other in Widowhood.* New York: Health Sciences Publishing Group.

Smith, Alma D. 1975. "Consciousness Raising Groups: A Viable Alternative to Therapy for Women." Paper presented at the Southeastern Psychological Association, Atlanta.

Soler, Esta, Laura Ponsor, and Jennifer Abod. 1974. "The A-B-C's of Drug Treatment for Women." Paper presented at the North American Congress on Alcoholism and Drug Abuse, San Francisco.

Sommers, Tish. 1974. "The Compounding Impact of Age and Sex," *Civil Rights Digest* 7:2–9.

——. 1975. "Social Security: A Woman's Viewpoint," *The Gerontologist* 2:266–279.

Sontag, Susan. 1972. "The Double Standard of Aging," *Saturday Review of the Society,* September 23, pp. 29–38.

Spiegelman, Mortimer, and Carl Erhardt. 1974. "Mortality and Longevity in the United States." In Carl Erhardt and Joyce Berlin, eds., *Mortality and Morbidity in the United States.* Cambridge, Mass.: Harvard University Press.

Stark, Rodney, and James McEvoy. 1970. "Middle Class Violence," *Psychology Today* 4:54–56, 110–112.

Stern, R. 1966. "The Pregnant Addict: A Study of 66 Case Histories, 1950–1959," *American Journal of Obstetrics and Gynecology* 94:253–257.

Stone, M. L., *et al.* 1971. "Narcotic Addiction in Pregnancy," *American Journal of Obstetrics and Gynecology* 5:716–723.

Stratton, John. 1976. "Law Enforcement's Participation in Crisis Counseling for Rape Victims," *The Police Chief* 43:3, 46–49.

Straus, Murray A. 1974. "Leveling, Civility and Violence in the Family," *Journal of Marriage and the Family* 36:13–29.

Streib, Gordon. 1975. "Mechanisms for Change—Viewed in a Sociological Context." In Natalie Trager, ed., *No Longer Young*, Occasional Papers in Gerontology, no. 11. Ann Arbor: University of Michigan, Institute of Gerontology.

Sutherland, Sandra and Donald J. Scherl. 1970. "Patterns of Response Among Victims of Rape," *American Journal of Orthopsychiatry* 40:3, 503–511.

Symonds, Martin. 1976. "The Rape Victim: Psychological Patterns of Response," *The American Journal of Psychoanalysis* 36:27–34.

Taulbee, E. and A. Wright. 1971. "A Psychosocial–Behavioral Model for Therapeutic Intervention." In C. D. Spielberger, ed., *Current Topics in Clinical and Community Psychology*. New York: Academic Press.

Taylor, F. G., and W. L. Marshall. 1977. "Experimental Analysis of a Cognitive–Behavioral Therapy for Depression," *Cognitive Therapy and Research* 1:59–72.

TenHouten, Warren. 1970. "The Black Family: Myth and Reality," *Psychiatry* 33:145–173.

Thomlinson, Ralph. 1965. *Population Dynamics*. New York: Random House.

Thure, Karin L., and Bettye A. Moore. 1977. "Woman in the Age of Aquarius." Paper presented at the Fourth National Conference on Drug Abuse, San Francisco.

*Time*. 1964. "Fewer Drugs for Happier Mothers," September 25, p. 82.

Todd, F. J. 1972. "Coverant Control of Self-Evaluative Responses in the Treatment of Depression: A New Use for an Old Principle," *Behavior Therapy* 3:91–94.

Trager, Natalie. 1975. *No Longer Young: The Older Woman in America*. Ann Arbor, Michigan: University of Michigan Institute of Gerontology.

Tripp, C. E. 1975. *The Homosexual Matrix*. New York: McGraw-Hill.

*Uniform Crime Reports for the United States*. 1977. Washington, D.C.: Federal Bureau of Investigation.

U.S. Bureau of the Census. 1975. *Census Reports*. Washington, D.C.

U.S. Department of Health, Education, and Welfare. n.d. *Client Oriented Data Acquisition Process.* Washington, D.C.

———. 1973. *Public Assistance Statistics.* No. SRS 73-03100, NCSS Report A2. Washington, D.C.

U.S. Department of Labor. 1971. A *Study of Selected Socio-Economic Characteristics of Ethnic Minorities Based on the 1970 Census,* vol. I, *Americans of Spanish Origin.* Washington, D.C.

U.S. Department of Labor, Women's Bureau. 1972. *Facts About Women Heads of Households and Heads of Families.* Washington, D.C.

———. 1975. "Current Population Report," *Handbook on Women Workers. Population Characteristics Series P-20.* Washington, D.C.

———. 1978. *Twenty Facts on Women Workers.* Washington, D.C.

Vann, D. 1974. "Help-Seeking and Self-Praise in Pre-School Children." Unpublished manuscript, University of Washington, School of Social Work.

Velten, E. 1968. "A Laboratory Task for Induction of Mood States," *Behavior Research and Therapy* 6:473–482.

Verbrugge, Lois. 1976. "Females and Illness: Recent Trends in Sex Differences in the United States," *Journal of Health and Social Behavior* 17:387–403.

Waldorf, Dan. 1970. "Family Disorganization of Women Heroin Addicts." Unpublished manuscript, Columbia University, Bureau of Applied Research.

Warrior, Betsy. 1976. *Working on Wife Abuse.* Cambridge, Mass.: November.

———. n.d. *Battered Lives.* Pittsburgh: KNOW.

Washington State Law. 1974. Chapter 9.79 Revised Code of Washington (.090, 140-220, 9A.64.020, 9A.88.020, 9A.88.100). Olympia, Washington.

Watson, D., and R. Friend. 1969. "Measurement of Social Evaluative Anxiety," *Journal of Consulting and Clinical Psychology* 33:448–457.

Wax, Murray. 1962. "On Public Dissatisfaction with the Medical Profession: Personal Observations," *Journal of Health and Human Behavior* 3:152–156.

Weaver, Jerry. 1976. "Government Response to Contraceptive and Cosmetic Health Risks," *Women and Health* 1:5–11.

Weiss, Kay. 1976. "Cancer and Estrogens—A Review," *Women and Health* 1:3–4.

Weissman, J. C., and K. N. File. n.d. "Criminal Behavior Patterns of Female Addicts: A Comparison of Findings in Two Cities." Unpublished paper, Denver.

Weissman, Myrna, and E. Paykel. 1974. *The Depressed Woman: A Study of Social Relationships*. Chicago: University of Chicago Press.

Weissman, Myrna, *et al*. 1971. "The Social Role Performance of Depressed Women: Comparisons with a Normal Group," *American Journal of Orthopsychiatry* 41:390–405.

Weisstein, Naomi. 1969. "Kinder, Kuche, Kirche as Scientific Law: Psychology Constructs the Female," *Motive* 29:6.

Weitzman, Lenore J. 1977. "Legal Equality in Marriage." In Nona Glazer and Helen Waehrer, eds., *Woman in a Man-Made World*. Chicago: Rand McNally.

Whiteley, Rita M. 1973. "Women in Groups," *The Counseling Psychologist* 4:27.

Whitlock, F. A. 1970. "The Syndrome of Barbiturate Dependence," *Medical Journal of Australia* 2:391–396.

Wilcoxon, L. A., S. L. Schrader, and R. E. Nelson. 1976. "Behavioral Formulations of Depression." In W. E. Craighead, A. E. Kazdin, and M. J. Mahoney, eds., *Behavior Modification: Principles, Issues, and Applications*. Boston: Houghton Mifflin.

Willson, James, Clayton Beecham, and Elsie Carrington. 1971. *Obstetrics and Gynecology*. St. Louis: Mosley.

Wilsnack, Sharon. 1976. "The Impact of Sex Roles and Women's Alcohol Use and Abuse." In Milton Greenblatt and Marc Schuckit, eds., *Alcoholism Problems in Women and Children*. New York: Greene and Stratton.

Wilson, E. 1975. "A Social Worker's Viewpoint," *Royal Society of Health Journal* 6:294–297.

Winick, C. 1962. "Maturing Out of Narcotic Addiction," *United Nations Bulletin on Narcotics* 14:1–7.

Winston, Marian P. and Trude Forsher. 1971. *Nonsupport of Legitimate Children by Affluent Fathers as a Cause of Poverty and Welfare Dependence*. Santa Monica, Calif.: Rand Corporation.

Wolfgang, Marvin E., and Franco Ferracuti. 1967. *The Sub-Culture of Violence*. London: Tavistock.

Wolpe, J., and A. Lazarus. 1966. *Behavior Therapy Techniques*. New York: Pergamon.

*Women and Drugs: An Annotated Bibliography*. 1975. National Institute on Drug Abuse, Ruckville, Maryland.

"Women in Banking." 1979. *Essence*, January, p. 10.

*Women in Transition: A Feminist Handbook on Separation and Divorce*. 1975. New York: Scribner's.

Wynn, Karen, and Patrick Clement. 1977. "The Junkie Treatment," *Human Behavior* 6:16–21.

Yankowitz, R., and J. Randell. 1976. "Ex-Addicts Get the Job Done," *Psychology Today* 10:20.

Zimbardo, P. G. 1977. *Shyness: What It Is and What to Do About It*. Reading, Mass.: Addison-Wesley.

Zintl, Terry. 1975. "Ann Arbor NOW Shelters Battered Wives," *Detroit Free Press*, August 29.

Zola, Irving. 1972. "Medicine as an Institution of Social Control," *Sociological Review* 20:487–503.

# Index